Palgrave Shakespeare Studies

Series Editors
Michael Dobson, The Shakespeare Institute, University of Birmingham,
Stratford-upon-Avon, UK
Dympna Callaghan, Syracuse University, Syracuse, NY, USA

Palgrave Shakespeare Studies takes Shakespeare as its focus but strives to understand the significance of his oeuvre in relation to his contemporaries, to subsequent writers and to historical and political contexts. By extending the scope of Shakespeare and English Renaissance Studies, the series aims to open up the field to examinations of previously neglected aspects or sources in the period's art and thought. Titles in the *Palgrave Shakespeare Studies* series seek to understand anew both where the literary achievements of the English Renaissance came from and where they have brought us, and provide the reader with a combination of cutting-edge critical thought and archival scholarly rigour.

More information about this series at
https://link.springer.com/bookseries/14658

William E. Engel · Grant Williams
Editors

The Shakespearean Death Arts

Hamlet Among the Tombs

palgrave
macmillan

Editors
William E. Engel
Sewanee, TN, USA

Grant Williams
Quebec, ON, Canada

ISSN 2731-3204 ISSN 2731-3212 (electronic)
Palgrave Shakespeare Studies
ISBN 978-3-030-88489-5 ISBN 978-3-030-88490-1 (eBook)
https://doi.org/10.1007/978-3-030-88490-1

© The Editor(s) (if applicable) and The Author(s), under exclusive license to Springer Nature Switzerland AG 2022
This work is subject to copyright. All rights are solely and exclusively licensed by the Publisher, whether the whole or part of the material is concerned, specifically the rights of translation, reprinting, reuse of illustrations, recitation, broadcasting, reproduction on microfilms or in any other physical way, and transmission or information storage and retrieval, electronic adaptation, computer software, or by similar or dissimilar methodology now known or hereafter developed.
The use of general descriptive names, registered names, trademarks, service marks, etc. in this publication does not imply, even in the absence of a specific statement, that such names are exempt from the relevant protective laws and regulations and therefore free for general use.
The publisher, the authors and the editors are safe to assume that the advice and information in this book are believed to be true and accurate at the date of publication. Neither the publisher nor the authors or the editors give a warranty, expressed or implied, with respect to the material contained herein or for any errors or omissions that may have been made. The publisher remains neutral with regard to jurisdictional claims in published maps and institutional affiliations.

Cover illustration: Pedro Américo—Hamlet's Vision—Google Art Project

This Palgrave Macmillan imprint is published by the registered company Springer Nature Switzerland AG
The registered company address is: Gewerbestrasse 11, 6330 Cham, Switzerland

This is the first book to view Shakespeare's plays from the prospect of the premodern death arts, not only the *ars moriendi* tradition but also the plurality of cultural expressions of *memento mori*, funeral rituals, commemorative activities, and rhetorical techniques and strategies fundamental to the performance of the work of dying, death, and the dead. The volume is divided into two parts: first, critically nuanced examinations of Shakespeare's corpus and then, second, of *Hamlet* exclusively as the ultimate proving ground of the death arts in practice. This book revitalizes discussion around key and enduring themes of mortality by reframing Shakespeare's plays within a newly conceptualized historical category that posits a cultural divide—at once epistemological and phenomenological—between premodernity and the Enlightenment.

Acknowledgments

Like Tennyson's "Flower in the crannied wall," this collection of essays has deep roots "all in all"—and a backstory. *The Shakespearean Death Arts* stems from a seminar (of the same name) that did not convene as originally planned at the Forty-Eighth Annual Shakespeare Association of America meeting in Denver, April 17, 2020, owing to the global pandemic. Our first thanks therefore need to go to the 2020 SAA Program Planning Committee for accepting our proposed seminar (Gina Bloom, Davis Dennis Britton, Laura A. Estill, Timothy Francisco, Susan Frye, Wendy Beth Hyman, and Rory Loughnane); and to SAA Executive Director, Karen Raber, and her staff, for their dedication and resourcefulness leading up to the decision to cancel the meeting but also to accommodate the ongoing work of those seminars, such as ours, still actively engaged with their specialized topic. Anyone familiar with the SAA seminar format knows that participants work throughout the year in advance of the conference to prepare, share, and team-edit essays which then are discussed at the annual meeting in the presence of auditors. Since the seminarians had worked so diligently for so long, we thought it worth everyone's while to continue the dialogue but now with an eye toward publishing the contributions in a coherently organized volume. We are extremely grateful that Eileen Srebernik at Palgrave-Macmillan contacted us and encouraged us to pursue this project in earnest. We also gratefully acknowledge the editors of the Palgrave Shakespeare series, Michael Dobson and Dympna Callaghan, who offered much-needed critical insights early and late. While we regret a few of the original seminarians were unable to take part in the volume, we are indebted to several experts in the field who graciously came on board in May 2020 and whose contributions truly add luster to the project.

Engel would like to thank the Office of the Dean at The University of the South, for allowing a year of research leave, 2020–2021; the successive chairs of Sewanee's English Department, Jennifer Michael and Matthew Irvine, for their unflagging support; and long-time collaborator, Grant Williams, as patient as he is wise. Grant would like to acknowledge his supportive family during the challenge of working at home throughout multiple lockdowns and will miss the stimulating Zoom sessions with Bill Engel from and about whom, even after all these years, he still learns unexpected things.

Contents

1	Introduction William E. Engel and Grant Williams	1

Part I Staging the Death Arts

2	Shakespeare's *Ars Moriendi* Andrew D. McCarthy	33
3	Deciphering the Dead: Speaking for Corpses in Early Modern Drama Brian J. Harries	49
4	"As Thou Art, I Once Was": Death and the Bodies in *2 Henry IV* Eileen Sperry	67
5	The *Exemplum*, Posterity, and Dramatic Irony in *Antony and Cleopatra* Grant Williams	85
6	Ash, Rust, and Ooze: Funereal Rituals and Tombs in *Pericles* Dorothy Todd	113

7   Empathetic Reflections on Love, Life, and Death Art
    in *Othello*   133
    Jessica Tooker

8   *Othello's* Speaking Corpses and the Performance
    of *Memento Mori*   153
    Maggie Vinter

Part II   *Hamlet* and the Death Arts

9   "Must I Remember?": The Burden of the Past Tense
    in *Hamlet*   179
    Jonathan Baldo

10 The Theater of Hamlet's Judgments   203
    Zackariah Long

11 Death, Loss, and Description in Early Modern
    Rhetoric and Drama   223
    Amanda K. Ruud

12 "Native and Indued / Unto that Element":
    Dissolution, Permeability, and the Death of Ophelia   241
    Pamela Royston Macfie

13 The Soul of Agrippina: Gender, Suicide,
    and Reproductive Rights in *Hamlet*   261
    Lina Perkins Wilder

14 Artless Deaths in *Hamlet*: The Play as *Danse Macabre*   281
    Isabel Karremann

15 "A Consummation Devoutly to Be Wished"? Middles
    and Ends in *Hamlet*   307
    Michael Neill

Afterword: Shakespeare and the Duties of the Living   327
Rory Loughnane

Index   335

Notes on Contributors

Jonathan Baldo is Professor of English in the Eastman School of Music, the University of Rochester. He is the author of *Memory in Shakespeare's Histories: Stages of Forgetting in Early Modern England* (Routledge, 2012) and co-editor, with Isabel Karremann, of *Forms of Faith: Literary Form and Religious Conflict in Shakespeare's England* (Manchester University Press, 2017).

William E. Engel is the Nick B. Williams Professor of Literature at The University of the South, in Sewanee, Tennessee, United States. He has published eight books on literary history and applied emblematics including, with Rory Loughnane and Grant Williams, *The Memory Arts in Renaissance England* (Cambridge University Press, 2016) and *The Death Arts in Renaissance England* (Cambridge University Press, 2022).

Brian J. Harries is an Associate Professor and Chair of English at Concordia University Wisconsin, specializing in medieval and Renaissance literature. He has published several articles and essays, including "Sacral Objects and the Measure of Kingship in Shakespeare's *Henry VI*," in Mardock and McPherson, eds., *Stages of Engagement: Drama and Religion in Post-reformation England* (2015) and "The Fall of Mediterranean Rome in *Titus Andronicus*" in *Mediterranean Studies* (2018). As a Dramaturge and Assistant Director, he regularly collaborates on theater productions at his university.

Isabel Karremann is Professor for Early Modern Literature at the University of Zurich. She has published widely on early modern drama, memory studies, and religious conflict, and is the author of *The Drama of Memory in Shakespeare's History Plays* (CUP, 2015) as well as general editor of Shakespeare-Jahrbuch. She is currently co-editing a volume on *Memory and Affect in Shakespeare's England*. Her new project explores the spatial, cognitive, affective, and perceptual ecologies of early modern drama.

Zackariah Long (Ohio Wesleyan University) is an Associate Professor of English who publishes on early modern memory and early modern trauma. His book project is entitled *This Distracted Globe: Hamlet and the Renaissance Memory Theatre*. His most recent publication is "Shakespeare, Memory, and the Early Modern Theatre" in *The Routledge Handbook of Shakespeare and Memory* (2018).

Rory Loughnane is Reader in Early Modern Studies at the University of Kent. He is the author and editor of many books and play editions, including, for Cambridge University Press, *Late Shakespeare, 1608–1613* (2012), *The Memory Arts in Renaissance England: A Critical Anthology* (2016), and *Early Shakespeare, 1588–1594* (2020). He is a general editor of The Revels Plays series (Manchester University Press) and a series editor of *Elements in Shakespeare and Text* (Cambridge University Press).

Pamela Royston Macfie is the Samuel R. Williamson Distinguished University Professor at Sewanee (The University of the South), where she teaches Shakespeare, Dante, and Early Modern English Literature. Her publications have addressed Ovid's influence on Dante, Marlowe, and Shakespeare; Shakespeare in performance and film; and the poetics of allusion. A member of the American Shakespeare Center Board, she has also published work on their initiative, Shakespeare's New Contemporaries, which will debut 38 new plays that engage Shakespeare's 38 plays in conversation.

Andrew D. McCarthy is the UC Foundation Associate Professor and Head of the Department of English at University of Tennessee, Chattanooga, where he teaches courses on Shakespeare and early modern literature. He is finishing a book on masculine performances of grief on the early modern English stage and has co-edited *Staging the Superstitions of Early Modern Europe* (Ashgate). His work has recently appeared in *Marlowe Studies*.

Michael Neill is Emeritus Professor of English at the University of Auckland. He is the author of *Issues of Death* (1997) and *Putting History to the Question* (2000). His numerous editions of Renaissance plays include *Anthony and Cleopatra* (1994) and *Othello* (2006) for the Oxford Shakespeare. More recently, he co-edited *The Oxford Handbook of Shakespearean Tragedy* (2016).

Amanda K. Ruud is a Lecturer of English at the University of Southern California. Her interdisciplinary research draws on rhetorical poetics, art history, and performance studies to examine how early modern English poets and playwrights address the philosophical and aesthetic challenge of representing grief and mourning. Her essay on ekphrasis in *Lucrece* appears in the summer 2020 edition of *Philological Quarterly*, and currently, she is completing a book, *Shakespeare's Speaking Pictures: Rhetoric, Visual Art, and the Poetics of Mourning in Early Modern England*.

Eileen Sperry does research that centers on Shakespeare, poetics, and early modern cultures of embodiment. Her work has appeared in *Sixteenth Century Journal*, *Cambridge Quarterly*, *Shakespeare Bulletin*, and *Studies in English Literature*. Her forthcoming book explores the relationship between form and mortality in the early modern English lyric. She also serves as an editor for *Nursing Clio*.

Dorothy Todd teaches English at Texas A&M University (College Station) and is an Associate Editor of the World Shakespeare Bibliography, a searchable electronic database consisting of the most comprehensive record of Shakespeare-related scholarship and theatrical productions published or produced worldwide from 1960 to the present. Her work "'Oh This Learning, What a Thing It Is!': Service Learning Shakespeare and Community Partnerships" has appeared in *This Rough Magic*—a peer-reviewed, academic, online journal dedicated to the teaching of Medieval and Renaissance Literature.

Jessica Tooker received her Ph.D. in English from Indiana University, Bloomington, with a dissertation titled, "To See It Feelingly: Towards a Theory of Theatrical Empathy in Shakespeare's Plays." Her research interests include critical and psychoanalytic theory as well as empathy theory, Chaucer, Spenser, and Shakespeare.

Maggie Vinter is an Associate Professor in the English Department at Case Western Reserve, where she teaches courses in Shakespeare and other early modern dramatists. *Last Acts: the Art of Dying on the Early Modern Stage* (Fordham University Press, 2019) argues that the Elizabethan and Jacobean theater offered playwrights, actors, and audiences important opportunities to practice arts of dying.

Lina Perkins Wilder is Professor of English at Connecticut College. She is the author of *Shakespeare's Memory Theatre* (Cambridge, 2010) and, with Andrew Hiscock, co-editor of *The Routledge Handbook of Shakespeare and Memory* (2018). Her current book project is on science as literary theory in seventeenth-century England.

Grant Williams is an Associate Professor of English Literature at Carleton University, in Ottawa, Canada and has co-edited three books, *Forgetting in Early Modern English Literature and Culture* (2004), *Ars reminiscendi* (2009), and *Taking Exception to the Law* (2015), and co-authored *The Memory Arts in Renaissance England* (Cambridge University Press, 2016) and *The Death Arts in Renaissance England* (Cambridge University Press, 2022).

List of Figures

Fig. 1.1	Skeleton contemplating skull (Andrea Vesalius, *De Humani Corporis Fabrica*)	5
Fig. 1.2	Hamlet with Skull (David Tennent as Hamlet)	10
Fig. 4.1	Deathbed scene (Christopher Sutton, *Disce Mori*)	68
Fig. 4.2	Death Triumphant (Christopher Sutton, *Disce Mori*)	73
Fig. 5.1	John Day's printer's mark (final leaf in John Foxe's *Acts and Monuments*)	98
Fig. 14.1	Hans Holbein, death abducts a queen	286
Fig. 14.2	Death stalks a couple (Albrecht Dürer, *The Promenade*)	296

CHAPTER 1

Introduction

William E. Engel and Grant Williams

What ceremony else? (*Ham.* 5.1.185)[1]

This volume takes as its point of departure the assumption that "the death arts" designates a historical category vital for understanding early modern social interaction and cultural production. By the "death arts" we do not refer to necromancy or occult practices, although, technically speaking, what we mean by the term would not rule out altogether such strands as being among the many possible "arts" to investigate under this rubric in future studies along these lines. Rather, our engagement with the death arts seeks principally to acknowledge the enduring legacy of the medieval *ars moriendi*, which instructed the dying person (the *moriens*) and their

W. E. Engel (✉)
The University of the South, Sewanee, TN, USA
e-mail: wengel@sewanee.edu

G. Williams
Carleton University, Ottawa, ON, Canada
e-mail: grant.williams@carleton.ca

© The Author(s), under exclusive license to Springer Nature Switzerland AG 2022
W. E. Engel and G. Williams (eds.), *The Shakespearean Death Arts*, Palgrave Shakespeare Studies,
https://doi.org/10.1007/978-3-030-88490-1_1

family in how to prepare for a religiously auspicious passing—that is, a "good death."[2]

As Amy Appleford's recent work demonstrates, however, the medieval *ars moriendi*'s influence was not confined to a private, ecclesiastically controlled death-bed scene but entered the civic sphere through the process of laicization, bearing an imprint upon the management of households and the administration of the city.[3] After the Reformation, the English *ars moriendi* did not die out with the prohibition of Catholic rituals,[4] for in the words of Robert Hill, the puritan-minded clergyman who devotes to it a quarter of his popular catechism, *The Pathway to Prayer and Piety* (1609), "it is the art of all arts, science of all sciences, to learn how to die."[5] Hill's claim, notwithstanding its zeal-fueled hyperbole, conveys a sense of the continuing relevance of the *ars moriendi* for seventeenth-century Protestant society.

While not diminishing this traditional art's contributions to cultural work, the phrase "the death arts" also widens the scope of scholarly inquiry by recognizing the pluralization of knowledge and practice around dying, death, and the dead in the period. They include varied and sundry activities: funeral and burial rituals; mourning the dead; constructing monuments, tombs, and epitaphs; Protestant and Catholic speculation on the apocalypse and the after-life; *memento mori* habits; meditative techniques; sermonizing and homiletics; the making of emblems and woodcuts; remembering martyrs, fallen military heroes, and the executed; writing wills and other legal documents around inheritance; the practice of anatomy and barber-surgery; and many more besides.

The difference between the single art and the multiple arts of mortality may be discerned most clearly in the early modern print industry. "The art" was primarily transmitted by translated versions and home-grown variants of the *Tractatus artis bene moriendi*, starting with William Caxton's *Arte and Crafte to Know Well to Dye* (1490),[6] while the death arts reveal themselves throughout assorted types of book production: elegiac and commemorative verse; collections of sermons; theological, meditational, and devotional works; psalters, primers, and prayer books; conduct books; moral philosophy treatises; commonplace and emblem books; anatomical, medical, and surgical treatises; narrative poetry, romance, histories, and popular literature, such as ballads and repentance pamphlets—and the list goes on.

The death arts reach beyond the traditional *ars moriendi* to encompass the secular implications of mortality stimulated by humanism's revival of interest in ancient philosophy. William Baldwin's *A Treatise of Morall Philosophie Contayning the Sayings of the Wise*, a popular commonplace book that went through twenty-four editions between 1547 and 1651, not only circulated adages on why one should not fear death but also recounted the exemplary suicides of Socrates and Seneca. Clearly stoicism, epitomized by the Roman way of death, proposed alternative ways to think about how to die outside the Catholic and Protestant traditions. In *Antony and Cleopatra*, Eros chooses suicide as a means to avoid dispatching his master Antony, prompting the latter to exclaim: "But I will be / A bridegroom in my death, and run into't / As to a lover's bed. Come then, and Eros, / Thy master dies thy scholar. To do thus / I learned of thee" (*Ant.* 4.15.98–102). He thanks his brave lieutenant for giving him timely instruction in the noble art of death. Implicit in this declaration is the role of stoicism in teaching one how to die well.[7] Choosing honorable death over the abrogation of one's moral duty was a theme that resonated powerfully during the period, recapitulated in Horatio's proclamation to his dying friend, Hamlet, "I am more an antique Roman than a Dane" (*Ham.* 5.2.299).[8]

Tudor court culture provides another source for the worldly death arts. In the collection of lyric verse, commonly known as *Tottel's Miscellany*, whose multiple editions over the decades left a lasting impact on Elizabethan love poetry and drama, both Thomas Wyatt and Henry Howard, Earl of Surrey, serve as ambassadors to European Petrarchanism and in doing so import the conceit of the paramour's melancholic suffering darkened by death's long shadow. The choice "[t]hat death or mercy end my woeful smart," in the stark words of Wyatt's speaker, operates according to an uncompromising logic that escalates the *ars amatoria* to a secular kind of *ars moriendi*.[9] However much the poetic language of "ending it all" signifies an idle or figurative threat in the period's literature, Shakespeare intriguingly gravitates toward lovers whose circumstances and responses to those circumstances literalize this hysterical courtly discourse, in effect transforming Petrarchan rhetoric into spectacular scenes of dying. The sequential suicides of Romeo and Juliet enact the grave logic driving Petrarchanism and Ovidianism,[10] whereas the melodramatic deaths represented by *Venus and Adonis* and *The Rape of Lucrece*, two narrative poems written, perhaps not incidentally, during plague times, explore the emotional gulf separating the indifferent beloved from a manic if not psychotic suitor.

The various and sundry death arts prove significant for studying the period's artifacts in that they entrench further the deep cultural divide between premodernity and the Enlightenment. With respect to this divide, our thinking is indebted to the argument originally formulated by Phillipe Ariès[11], whose work traces the evolving Western attitudes toward dying: the Renaissance marks a liminal period when the acceptance of mortality as an integral part of communal life started to give way to Protestant and capitalist notions of dying and burial as a personal act; as individual relationships and the concomitant sentiments around those relationships gained increasing social value, modernity excluded the corpse along with its funeral rituals from public purview, fostering defensive emotional reactions to death: denial, horror, and aesthetic fascination. Where we differ from Ariès's argument is in our methodological focus. Not only do the death arts posit a historical firewall between premodernity and the Enlightenment rather than a long duration through the ages, but their scope also moves beyond the confines of *l'histoire des mentalités*. Death is not just an attitude; it is an art. More precisely, it recruits many premodern arts.

One might suppose that, given the extensive scholarship, death as a Shakespearean topic would have expired years ago. It is our contention that the death arts reinvigorate an old, tired theme. The broad hermeneutic framework of the death arts recasts the uniqueness of premodern cultural production, accentuating the distance between Shakespeare and contemporary readers and inviting new ways of assessing the significance of his individual plays and plots where dying, death, and the dead are regularly staged and verbally represented.[12] We propose three interrelated positions on how the death arts can shift our perspective on premodern death and thereby reframe our approach to Shakespeare's plays. These arts convey death's epistemological difference, its cultural difference, and its phenomenological difference—in other words, its relationships to knowledge, civilization, and the perceived world.

Generally speaking, the Renaissance arts operated according to Aristotelian epistemology, an inheritance from medieval and classical times. Unlike an empirical science, an art does not quantify and measure objects in an attempt to master the material world but shapes a human enterprise to the lessons and limits of nature. Whereas modern medicine develops therapies and technologies to steal from death's audit book as many precious moments as possible, premodern knowledge accepted death as something you could not cheat. Consider the *memento mori* messages in

Fig. 1.1 Skeleton contemplating skull (Andrea Vesalius, *De Humani Corporis Fabrica*)

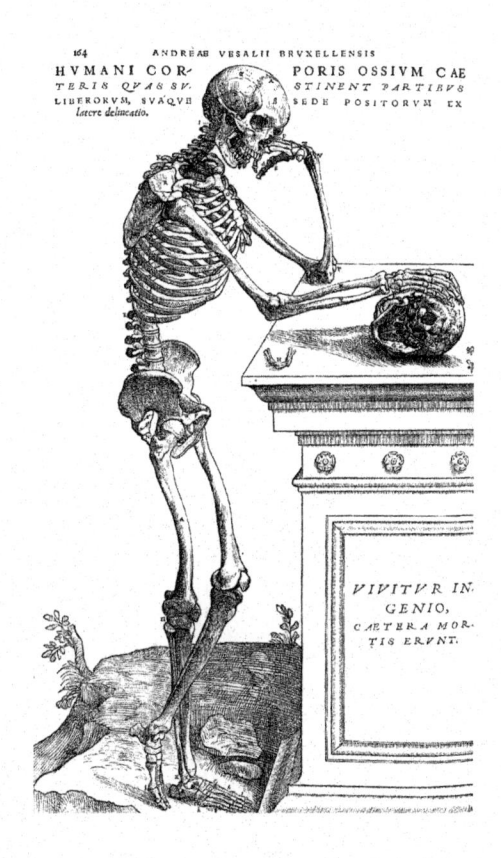

Vesalius's anatomical plates (see Fig. 1.1), in which, for example, a skeletal figure poses over a tomb, resting its hand contemplatively on a skull.[13]

Here death is not a pathological state to be negated at all costs but, instead, represents a part of the natural order, which the anatomist must duly recognize even as he divulges the body's secrets. Such knowledge looks for the human not the object in the cadaver, for Aristotelian epistemology conceived of the art as the all-important means by which human subjects could actualize their potential.[14] An individual existing in a natural state could not obtain the virtue necessary for achieving the good life without exercising intellectual judgment to supplement the deficiencies one was born with. Thus for Cicero, the art of rhetoric raised humans from a savage and bestial condition by equipping them with the oratorical technique and discipline through which they could establish civic order.[15] This epistemological reasoning behind the arts applied equally to death insofar as a natural death stripped of funeral and burial rites presupposed an uncivilized, even an animal state—it may, by the way, contextualize the long-held fear of death by drowning at sea.[16] Knowing about and preparing for death belonged to the goal of fulfilling one's humanity.

Premodern death's positive epistemological value fed into and was fed by its ubiquitous cultural presence—our second position on the critical difference of the death arts. The death arts do not take their cues from an individual's mournful sentiment, which, notwithstanding its overwhelming power and therapeutic significance, often fixates on loss, privation, and absence and fosters by extension denial, paralysis, and inactivity. The death arts shift our perspective from the claustrophobic sphere of inwardly experienced feeling to the materiality of public expression and production, where mourning, for example, may manifest itself in elegies, commemorations, and monuments. For the death arts, then, the deterioration and expiration of life do not spell civilization's decay; rather, dying, death, and the dead spark the energy that built up early modern London culture, injecting vigor and animation into everyday existence. With its affiliations to artifice and techne, the premodern conception of art also highlights the artisanal dimension of this robust cultural activity. For Shakespeare's age, death was not just a knowing, but a doing and a making. One could trade and traffic in it. Priests who prepared their parishioners for passing on—and also collected fees from the deceased—were by no means the only death-mongers.[17] Think of playwrights, especially those of revenge tragedies, whose craft exploited the theatricality of agonizing death throes and saintly sleep-like passing away, while strewing the stage with make-believe cadavers. Bosola, that death-mongering factotum in Webster's *Duchess of Malfi*, parodically arrogates to himself a number of such occupations.

The death arts reveal a thanatological plenitude in mainstream early modern culture—not sequestered to media and genre silos as it is today in goth and metal music, crime television, and horror film and literature. From ballads to sermons, one witnesses the presence of death in life. Death listens, it speaks, it dances, and it plays among the living. George Herbert and John Donne address conversational poems to death as though they were sitting in its company.[18] Indeed, thanatological plenitude and proliferation manifest themselves in a kind of generative, copious discourse. Capulet laments to Paris,

O son, the night before thy wedding day
Hath death lain with thy wife. See there she lies,
Flower as she was, deflowerèd by him.
Death is my son-in-law, death is my heir.
My daughter he hath wedded. I will die.
And leave him all. Life, living, all is death's. (*Rom.* 4.4.63–68)

Romeo speaks of death as an adulterous rival as well: "Shall I believe / That unsubstantial death is amorous, / And that the lean abhorrèd monster keeps / Thee here in dark to be his paramour?" (*Rom.* 5.3.102–105). Shakespeare depicts death as though it has the same urges and desire as the living[19], almost promoting it to a character in the play and most certainly marshaling the topos to copiously dilate Capulet's and Romeo's speeches with lively wit and irony mixed with pathos.

The thanatological plenitude found throughout premodern cultural activity suggests a phenomenological or existential ground alien from what we have in contemporary society. Death's prominence made the world appear quite differently to premodern individuals so much so that contemporaries may mistake its prominence for a fascination with the macabre.[20] In post-Enlightenment society, we regard death through the lens of a living world, the experiences of which induce us to deem it a threatening, unhealthy negation. Death, properly understood nowadays, holds a subordinate place as a culminating stage or boundary in an entire life cycle, a concept that, for example, informs the method of early modern social history conducted by David Cressy's thorough study *Birth, Marriage, and Death*. But early modern documents and artifacts do not restrict death to a final event terminating existence. When Robert Greene reflects upon his reprobate behavior of languishing in the sinful moment, he exclaims, "neither did I care for death, but held it only as the end of life."[21] For Protestants, a good life was considered the best preparation for a good death.[22] And so when we look at life through the prism of the death arts—as Hamlet does when he gazes at Yorick's skull—our world becomes bathed in shades, tints, and hues hitherto unseen. The prismatic light of mortality casts colorful shadows on persons, places, and things, as well as actions, habits, and thoughts. In other words, every activity, every gesture, and every expenditure of energy potentially direct themselves toward mortifying ends—"mortifying," etymologically speaking, as "making death." The initial conceit of "A Valediction Forbidding Mourning" may sound farfetched in comparing the lovers' temporary parting to the gentle passing of a good death which makes "no noise" (l. 5),[23] until Donne's later homiletic observation illuminates the larger early modern perspective behind the comparison: "In all our periods and transitions in this life, are so many passages from death to death."[24] Enobarbus depicts Cleopatra's emotional fragility at Antony's departure in mortifying terms that could well be read as parodying Donne's valediction: "Cleopatra catching but the least noise of this dies instantly. I have seen her die twenty times upon far poorer moment. I do think there is mettle in death, which commits some loving act upon her, she hath such a celerity in dying" (*Ant.* 1.2.121–123). Enobarbus, ever the cynic, capitalizes on another death conceit that Donne employs in his love poetry[25]: dying as a synonym for experiencing orgasm exposes the motivation underlying Cleopatra's readiness to abandon herself to stereotypical feminine histrionics. Much like Donne, Shakespeare makes us see the many deaths punctuating life's intense experiences.

No phrase, mantra, or algorithm captures better this making of death in everyday existence than *memento mori*, the elegiac habit of thought in which the mortality of creatures revealed their ongoing decay and decrepitude. To contemplate one's death arises from taking to heart the doctrine of the fall and its legacy of dank pessimism. The meditative act of *memento mori* is a strange remembering because one does not look toward the past but toward what will come. When meditating, one imagines the finitude of the future in the present as though one's entire history were now already finished. Remembering one's death orients the self to the teleological concept of time promulgated by Christianity—one labors toward the inevitable end times. Through the prism of *memento mori*, not only every perception and sensation but also every feeling and thought come saturated in mortification. *Memento mori* is a watchword that trains the mind to understand death as an ever-present condition of existence. In its capacity to prepare the individual mentally for the end, this incantation exerts tremendous cognitive pressure: death becomes a continuous event that weighs heavily on the here and now.

One of the ways in which *memento mori* was put into practice was through ruminating upon any number of germane verses from holy scripture: for example, "Whatsoever thou takest in hand, remember the end, and thou shalt never do amiss" (Ecclesiasticus 7:36) and "O that they were wise, that they understood this, that they would consider their latter end" (Deuteronomy 32:29).[26] In his catechism, Robert Hill provides mental fodder for his catechumens by listing Old Testament quotations that figure forth the fragility and misery of life: a pilgrimage, a flower, smoke, a clay house, a weaver's shuttle, a shepherd's tent, a wave-tossed ship, a mariner, a shadow, a thought, a dream, vanity, and nothing.[27] But *memento mori* could spiral off in secular directions too. Shakespeare's Sonnet 64 teaches the reader to ruminate on ruins as an elegiac experience of earthly love and, as such, exemplifies a death art woven throughout his sonneteering. The moribund is already present in plenitude. It is plenitude's hidden freight, its invisible potential.

Contemplating death during the sixteenth century, far from signaling a morbid fascination with mortality, was considered a sensible and mature response to the vagaries of everyday life and the moral choices that arise as a result. Erasmus sums up this commonplace Renaissance attitude well, at once typically and proverbially, in his popular treatment of the theme[28]:

> Nothing is so much before our eyes as death—then why is nothing further from our minds? Even our name—mortals—is taken from "mortality," so that we cannot hear our name pronounced even in a casual manner without our own ears reminding us of death. […] In our own times as well we observe that death spares no class of man. […]. If we kept in mind the uncertain promise of our treacherous age, if we kept death, which threatens us at all times, in mind at all times, we would pour into our ears the words spoken by the famous prophet to the ailing king: Set your house in order, for you will die [2 Kings 20:1].[29]

Accordingly, Roland Frye has said of Hamlet's holding Yorick's skull (*Ham.* 5.1.151ff.), perhaps the most iconic image now associated with confronting mortality in the West,[30] that "Shakespeare's audience in the Globe Theatre can be presumed to have seen Hamlet here as being at once most realistic and most rational […] thinking through the ultimate realities of death to arrive at what becomes, for him as it had been for others, a new sanity and even serenity."[31] The same applies to Pericles, another of Shakespeare's young princes (though less often discussed) who, like Hamlet, seeks to navigate his way in a world beset by treachery and court intrigue.[32] When confronted by the heads of those who failed to answer the riddle to win the Princess—thereby, as with the graveyard scene in *Hamlet*, bringing center stage the quintessential *memento mori* symbol (see Fig. 1.2)—Pericles shows himself to be pragmatically schooled in the fundamentals of the death arts.

Fig. 1.2 Hamlet with Skull (David Tennent as Hamlet)

> ANTIOCHUS Yon sometimes famous princes, like thyself,
> Drawn by report, adventurous by desire,
> Tell thee with speechless tongues and semblance pale
> That without covering save yon field of stars
> Here they stand, martyrs slain in Cupid's wars,
> And with dead cheeks advise thee to desist
> For going on death's net, whom none resist.
>
> PERICLES   Antiochus, I thank thee, who hath taught
> My frail mortality to know itself,
> And by those fearful objects to prepare
> This body, like to them, to what I must;
> For death remembered should be like a mirror
> Who tells us life's but breath, to trust it error.
> I'll make my will then, and, as sick men do,
> Who know the world, see heaven, but feeling woe
> Grip not at earthly joys as erst they did,
> So I bequeath a happy peace to you
> And all good men, as every prince should do;
> My riches to the earth from whence they came;
> [*To the Daughter*] But my unspotted fire of love to you.
> [*To Antiochus*] Thus ready for the way of life or death,
> I wait the sharpest blow, Antiochus. (*Per.* 1.1.35–56)

This long quotation from *Pericles* sums up well the range of commonplace understandings of the period about lessons the living stand to learn from the dead, especially when confronted symbolically by the face of death in the form a skull, which came to be known simply as "a death's head." A dried human skull thus became a popular *memento mori* ornament in the Renaissance that adorned desks of the circumspect and pious—as well as those, of course, who might want to be perceived as being so: high-minded, contemplative, and stoic in the face of one's mortality. It was the gift of just such a "token" from the Queen Mother, Lady Margaret Beaufort (mother of the future king Henry VIII), to John Skelton, that ostensibly inspired him to write a "ghostly meditation [...] in sentence commendable, lamentable, lachrymable, profitable for the soul."[33] With such precedents in mind, Frye was at pains to argue in his survey of likely responses to *Hamlet* in 1600, and consonant with our position throughout this volume, that recovering and understanding Shakespeare's plays in their original terms gives them new depth of meaning and renewed affective power for our own time. Principal elements of the death arts therefore are developed more particularly with respect to *Hamlet* in the second half of this volume, while the first, through other plays, explores and discloses the cultural, intellectual, social, and religious contexts for understanding *in situ* the dynamics of their reception.[34]

Shakespeare draws on and significantly contributes to the Renaissance death arts in important and far-reaching ways. The fundamental question that first needs to be considered, though, is in what ways does Shakespeare put his stamp on the death arts through his ongoing and intense engagement with them, ranging from episodes like the scene just mentioned in *Pericles*, to the grisly literalization of the maxim that "death's a great disguiser" with the severed head of a notorious pirate to stand in for that of Claudio (*MM* 4.2.150)[35]; from Falstaff's comic description of Bardolph's red nose as "a death's head, or a memento mori" because it makes him "think upon hell-fire" (*1H4* 3.3.23–24), to his admonition to Doll Tearsheet not to "speak like a death's head, do not bid me remember mine end" (*2H4* 2.4.201–202).[36] And there are of course dozens of even more well-known passages such as the "contempt for the world" monologue spoken by deposed Richard II beginning "Let's talk of graves, of worms, and epitaphs" (*R2* 3.2.141ff.); the famous conflation of the tomb and marriage bed in *Romeo and Juliet* with "worms that are thy chambermaids" (*Rom.* 5.3.109); and the grandiose expression of Cleopatra's "immortal longings," with her monumental staging of her own death to fix and memorialize a lasting image of her grandeur—in hopes of preempting in Rome "[s]ome squeaking Cleopatra boy my greatness / I'th' posture of a whore" (*Ant.* 5.2.216–217):

> Show me, my women, like a queen. Go fetch
> My best attires. I am again for Cydnus
> To meet Mark Antony. Sirrah Iras, go.
> Now, noble Charmian, we'll dispatch indeed,
> And when thou hast done this chore I'll give thee leave
> To play till doomsday—Bring our crown and all. (*Ant.* 5.2.223–228)

With scenes such as this one in mind (and many more besides), there are very good reasons why the death arts figure so significantly in Shakespeare's plays: paramount among them, the inherent theatricality of death and dying. There is something unmistakably spectacular—harkening to earlier religious rituals—about the on-stage revelation of recessed spaces covered by curtains for the presentation of corpses and solemn ceremonies involving (and sometimes denying) last rites.[37] And the obverse is true as well: there is something that smells of death in the mocking shadows of actors playing out the lives of characters for others to see and to marvel at the cunning counterfeit. This is taken into account—at once tongue-in-cheek and with evident metatheatrical resonance—with Falstaff's playing dead only to rise and mock one who is dead (within, of course, the fiction of the play) and then claim as booty the lifeless body of Hotspur:

> 'Sblood, 'twas time to counterfeit,
> or that hot termagant Scot had paid me, scot and lot too. Counterfeit? I lie. I am no counterfeit. To die is to be a counterfeit, for he is but the counterfeit of a man who hath not the life of a man. But to counterfeit dying when a man thereby liveth is to be no counterfeit, but the true and perfect image of life indeed. The better part of valour is discretion, in the which better part I have saved my life. 'Swounds, I am afraid of this gunpowder Percy, though he be dead. How if he should counterfeit too, and rise? By my faith, I am afraid he would prove the better counterfeit. Therefore I'll make him sure, yea, and I'll swear I killed him. Why may not he rise as well as I? Nothing confutes me but eyes, and nobody sees me. Therefore, sirrah, [stabbing Hotspur] with a new wound in your thigh, come you along with me. (*1H4* 5.4.111–123)

The self-conscious sporting with conventions relating to actors repeatedly impersonating characters throughout the run of play, even and especially those who die on stage, is given its due in many Elizabethan plays, exemplarily Thomas Kyd's *Spanish Tragedy*. This play long has been seen as sharing "many elements" with Shakespeare's consummate revenge play, *Hamlet*.[38] Immediately prior to the on-stage breaking of the theatrical spectacle's fourth wall with the play within a play, the person responsible for the deadly court entertainment, Hieronimo, admonishes the audience (both on stage and off) as to the performative nature of theatrical impersonation involved with viewing fatal spectacles—comparable to Hamlet's asides to Ophelia as we watch them watching the command performance of "The Murder of Gonzago" (*Ham.* 3.2.117–240). Hieronimo's speech literally reframes the spectacle, calling attention to and putting into perspective the operative conventions of mimetic illusion—especially as regards deaths on stage:

> Haply you think—but bootless are your thoughts—
> That this is fabulously counterfeit,
> And that we do as all tragedians do:
> To die today, for fashioning our scene—
> The death of Ajax, or some Roman peer—
> And, in a minute starting up again,
> Revive to please tomorrow's audience. (*The Spanish Tragedy* 4.4.77–82)[39]

The same aesthetic affinity between theater (where the lives and deaths of characters are counterfeited by flesh and blood actors) and death (where people newly dead are ceremonially staged for one final scene by the living) shows up in comedy as well as tragedy, thereby attesting to the sometimes unexpected—and, at times, even mad-cap—ways that the death arts can be seen to inform and animate Renaissance dramas. In *Midsummer Night's Dream*, for example, the "mechanicals" strive to present the tragic deaths of Pyramus and Thisbe as their contribution to the Athenian court's nuptial celebration, about a "lover, that kills himself most gallant for love" (*MND* 1.2.18). Apart from "Pyramus and Thisbe" being an absurdly indecorous choice for the occasion, the mechanicals' earnestness reveals, indeed highlights, the cracks in the seams of mimetic illusionism.[40] The comedic miscalculation of the power of their performance to embody, portray, and bring to life the thing itself is hilariously presented in their rehearsals—and even is written into their play:

> [SNUG] [as Lion] You, ladies, you whose gentle hearts do fear
> The smallest monstrous mouse that creeps on floor,

> May now perchance both quake and tremble here
>   When lion rough in wildest rage doth roar.
> Then know that I as Snug the joiner am
> A lion fell, nor else no lion's dam.
> For if I should as Lion come in strife
> Into this place, 'twere pity on my life. (*MND* 5.1.212–219)

Their raucous enactment of a play involving the death arts, in effect, turns tragedy into farce. They bungle their way through a story in which the lovers, owing to parental disapproval, arrange to meet at an out-of-the-way place, among the tombs—specifically "Ninny's tomb," by which Bottom means "Ninus' tomb" (*MND* 2.2.241, 5.1.198)—and end up both dying because of a mistake about whether the beloved actually is dead. This motif, characterizing the fatal end of Pyramus and Thisbe, and likewise set among the tombs, essentially describes the denouement of *The Most Excellent and Lamentable Tragedy of Romeo and Juliet* (to give the full title according to the 1599 quarto). The easily discerned parallel between the mechanicals' theatrical travesty of the demise of Pyramus and Thisbe and the abject pathos of *Romeo and Juliet* attests to the ubiquity of the death arts in the period, and also indicates something about how it can show up in seemingly unexpected places. For just as the tragic deaths of Pyramus and Thisbe can be played as farce in a comedy like *Midsummer Night's Dream*, so too the constitutive elements of the death arts can be parodied—creating a kind of affective comic frisson—for a moment of grim levity in this otherwise relentless tragedy of young love gone awry, as is the case with *Romeo and Juliet*. With the prospect of being united at last with her beloved, but only after a drug-induced death-like sleep that will cause her kinsmen to inter her in the family vault, Juliet's free-wheeling imagination spins out an associative checklist of youthful fears about being entombed alive.

> How if, when I am laid into the tomb,
> I wake before the time that Romeo
> Come to redeem me? There's a fearful point.
> Shall I not then be stifled in the vault,
> To whose foul mouth no healthsome air breathes in,
> And there die strangled ere my Romeo comes?
> Or, if I live, is it not very like
> The horrible conceit of death and night,
> Together with the terror of the place—

> As in a vault, an ancient rèceptacle,
> Where for this many hundred years the bones
> Of all my buried ancestors are packed;
> Where bloody Tybalt, yet but green in earth,
> Lies fest'ring in his shroud; where, as they say,
> At some hours in the night spirits resort—
> Alack, alack, is it not like that I,
> So early waking—what with loathsome smells,
> And shrieks like mandrakes torn out of the earth,
> That living mortals, hearing them, run mad—
> O, if I wake, shall I not be distraught,
> Environèd with all these hideous fears,
> And madly play with my forefathers' joints,
> And pluck the mangled Tybalt from his shroud,
> And, in this rage, with some great kinsman's bone
> As with a club, dash out my desp'rate brains? (*Rom.* 4.3.28–53)

In both instances, whether expressed farcically in the play within a play of "Pyramus and Thisbe" in *Midsummer Night's Dream*, or as lugubrious fancy reduced to manic humor in Juliet's bedroom soliloquy in *Romeo and Juliet*, the death arts flow unchecked. Moreover, the death arts tend to stand out more prominently, freighted as they are with a special kind of affective poignance, when self-reflective elements within the work hint at or explicitly reveal the imbrication of mortal transience in the construction and delivery of the representation. Hence Macbeth's hollow reflection on his wife's death reverberates with a deeper resonance owing to the metatheatrical allusion that guides his grief:

> Tomorrow, and tomorrow, and tomorrow
> Creeps in this petty pace from day to day
> To the last syllable of recorded time;
> And all our yesterdays have lighted fools
> The way to dusty death. Out, out, brief candle!
> Life's but a walking shadow, a poor player
> That struts and frets his hour upon the stage
> And then is heard no more. It is a tale
> Told by an idiot, full of sound and fury,
> Signifying nothing. (*Mac.* 5.5.18–27)

This much having been observed, we are in a position now to circle back to the perennial case in point already mentioned. The situational context of Hamlet's reflection on Yorick's skull embodies even as it breathes new life into the conventions associated with Renaissance death arts. Furthermore, the sly mixture of the clown's quibbles and low comedy with Hamlet's grand words and Yorick's silence succeeds in elevating and expanding upon an unmistakable *memento mori* moment by tapping into the rudimentary performative mechanisms activated by theatrical spectacularity.[41] And so, in assessing Shakespeare's considerable contribution to the death arts, we do well to keep in mind the manifold and various references to mortality, including death scenes both on stage and reported, good and bad deaths discussed and moralized, funerals, elegies, and "dead march" exits. There is a special way that stage plays in general, and Shakespeare's works in particular (and not just his tragedies but also, as has been shown in this brief Introduction, all genres as well) tend to develop, push the boundaries of, and to some extent revivify the Renaissance death arts.

In this respect, *Hamlet* historically has become a privileged text for studying this topic and, as such, understandably receives the lion's share of critical attention.[42] This is the case in part because of the sheer superabundance of tropes and themes relating to the death arts—not the least being the soldier's reply to Hamlet about the lives of "two thousand souls" impawned for a battle: "We go to gain a little patch of ground / That hath in it no profit but the name" (*Ham.* 4.1.15–16). Furthermore, this play everywhere and persistently is concerned with peculiar ways to die (counterfeit death warrants, an eavesdropper stabbed behind an arras, drowning in a shallow brook, a poisoned pearl dropped into a carousing cup, and—as a repeated theme—pouring poison into a sleeper's ear). It is likewise a play much concerned with preparations for funerals and the desire for ever more pomp and ceremony, as in Laertes' demanding question, which we use as our epigraph (*Ham.* 5.1.185). And, above all else, it is a play conditioned by dynastic stakes—hovering over *Hamlet* like an avenging angel—involving as it does king-on-king mortal combat principally between Old Hamlet and Old Fortinbras. And this is just to scratch the surface; hence, each of the essays in Section Two probes and examines how, in what ways, and to what end *Hamlet* is the play *par excellence* for investigating the death arts.

While something of the same can be claimed for all of Shakespeare's tragedies, as well as indeed those by his contemporaries, for whatever the reason *Hamlet* has long held pride of place when it comes to locating the right text for teasing out, exposing, and trying to make sense of the Renaissance death arts. One of the main reasons why this play persists in asserting its predominance in the cultural consciousness of the West can be attributed in large measure to the graveyard scene (*Ham.* 5.1). As already indicated, this *memento mori* moment is a histrionic *tour de force*, with the skull of the court jester, Yorick, serving as a loadstone activating and augmenting the magnetic pull of traditional death symbols made manifest in this episode (including tombs, grave-digging implements, skulls, and scattered bones). Additionally, other key aspects of the death arts swarm about in this play making for, as it were, a persistent and ineluctable hum betokening the omnipresence of death in life and life in death,[43] not the least of which includes Claudius's cold-comfort commonplace "your father lost a father, / That father lost, lost his" (*Ham.* 1.2.89–90). Hence, our underlying argument in this collection is that *Hamlet* can be considered a performative pinnacle of death art expression in the period. In the dynamics of its transmission, this play calls forth and thereby bespeaks its own unique, overdetermined expression of the death arts broadly conceived. In this regard, it is both *sui generis* and yet, at the same time, wholly representative of revenge tragedies of the period with respect to how it ends up refracting and expressing what can be recognized as the constitutive elements of the death arts. We acknowledge as much in the decision to devote half of this volume to *Hamlet* which, we contend, in the long run conduces to a more enriched understanding overall of the death arts in the period, and thus paves the way for new directions in Shakespeare studies. This is what we mean to imply by the adjectivally inflected "Shakespearean" death arts.

At the same time, *Hamlet*—again, in the dynamics of its transmission—makes visible and attests to the plurality and multi-dimensionality of the death arts. In *Hamlet* we can discern and isolate terms and tropes that enable the beginning of a new kind of dialogue about the importance of the death arts in Shakespeare's canon.[44] Our aim ultimately is to revitalize discussion around traditional and enduring themes of mortality, dying, and the dead in the drama of the period. In doing so we highlight the crucial phenomenological discontinuity between Shakespeare's time and our own, a discontinuity that has been noted and developed more thoroughly by social and cultural historians.[45] We are not so much interested in making any claims, though, about when exactly such a break occurs, as we are in reconstructing and analyzing the constituent elements of what makes the Shakespearean death arts such an instructive way to think about and discuss the plays. And so the contributions make use of a variety of critical methodologies and approaches to literary historiography, including anthropology, the social sciences, cognitive theory, gender studies, and philology, while keeping foremost in mind the shifting sands of variously predominating and receding Reformation practices, as well as the telling and troubled emergence of dynastic national identity in early modern England.

The pedagogical payoff of our having a dedicated group of leading and emerging scholars attend to Shakespeare's plays vis-à-vis the death arts is that, through a range of diverse voices and approaches represented, we have opened up a rich vein for further investigations along comparable lines no matter what one's critical orientation to literary studies or performance practices. Established here is a solid and sensible scholarly foundation upon which future investigations can be undertaken. Specifically, in the first half of the book, we look head on at what amounts to Shakespeare's *ars moriendi*; consider how and to what end "speaking for corpses" takes place in early modern drama; explore the unstable binary constructs associated with death and dying in Renaissance England; take into account the vicissitudes of monumentalization through a close reading of *Antony and Cleopatra*; account for the ready references and polysemic implications of tombs, ooze, and ashes with reference to *Pericles*; single out "empathetic reflections" on love, life, and death in *Othello*; and, coming full circle to reconsider a crucial issue in the Shakespearean death arts, the first half of the volume concludes by resituating the cultural performance of *memento mori* with reference to *Othello*.

The remaining essays, as already mentioned, are devoted to *Hamlet*, by way of setting up an exemplary case study for gauging and appreciating the value of reclaiming and critically reassessing the early modern death arts so as to read afresh and get more out of Shakespeare's plays. What readers will find here about *Hamlet* has remarkable resonance for a wide array of cultural expressions and lived practices. Specifically, the second half of the volume concerns the ludic interplay of riddles, death, and burial; patterns of judgment in "Hamlet's Memory Theatre"; understanding the art of loss in early modern rhetoric; issues of dissolution and permeability in the death of Ophelia; women's agency and foreshortened classical allusions in *Hamlet*; the remnant religious strands of the Dance of Death woven into *Hamlet*; and silenced tales and frustratingly deferred endings as a recurring and telling death motif in the play.

By virtue of our identifying and putting into context fundamental aspects of what we are calling the Shakespearean death arts, future scholars, students, and general readers alike will have a ready way to approach and understand in their original terms Shakespeare's plays and, by extension, those by his contemporaries. It is our hope that future researchers will take up where this volume leaves off and press on, mindful of the Shakespearean death arts, to find new inroads into the plays—especially those we have not been able to include in this first pass at the canon.[46] And, according to the *New Oxford Shakespeare*, there are fifty works in whole or in part attributable to Shakespeare; works we are convinced will yield some exciting new readings and expository studies when approached with an eye toward the Shakespearean death arts.

Notes

1. Quotations from Shakespeare in this Introduction follow *The New Oxford Shakespeare* (*NOS*) hereafter cited parenthetically with play abbreviations as given in *The MLA Handbook* (2016). Consistent with the overarching aims of this volume to acknowledge, recognize, and pay tribute to the plurality of Shakespearean texts, in subsequent chapters contributors will indicate which edition they have elected to use.
2. Beier, "Good Death in Seventeenth-Century England," pp. 43–61.
3. Appleford, *Learning to Die in London*, pp. 11–13.
4. Cummings, "Remembering the Dead in *Hamlet*," p. 114.
5. Hill, *Path-Way to Prayer and Pietie*, p. 197.
6. O'Connor, *The Art of Dying Well*, p. 7; on Caxton's place in the tradition, see entry I.1 in Engel, Loughnane, and Williams, *The Death Arts in Renaissance England*.
7. On this "most Roman of acts, heroic suicide" and Eros's role in "Antony's botched suicide," see Smith, *This is Shakespeare*, pp. 259–60.
8. On Seneca's suicide in its early modern English context, see entry III.8 in Engel, Loughnane, and Williams, *The Death Arts in Renaissance England*.
9. "The lover sendeth sighs to moan his suit," in *Songes and Sonettes*, sig. k2^r.
10. See Newstok, *Quoting Death in Early Modern England*, p. 160, on the "enactment of the lie / lie pun" which "reaches an almost parodic excess in the final scenes of *Romeo and Juliet*."
11. Ariès, *The Hour of Our Death*; originally published as *L'Homme devant la mort* (Paris: Éditions du Seuil, 1977).
12. For an engaging treatment of the physiology of death in premodern times, see Harkup, *Death by Shakespeare*.

13. Geminus, *Compendiosa totius anatomie delineation*, sig. B4-B6, directly reproduced images from Andreas Vesalius's *Epitome* and *De humani corporis fabrica* for his English audience.
14. Tayler, *Nature and Art in Renaissance Literature*, pp. 46–48.
15. Thomas Wilson Christianizes the Ciceronian trope in *Arte of Rhetorique*, sig. A3r-A4r.
16. Daniell, *Death and Burial in Medieval England*, p. 65.
17. The "mortuary" was the customary gift—really a fee—owed to a parish minister from the estate of a dead parishioner (*OED*).
18. George Herbert's "Death" in *The Temple* and John Donne's holy sonnet "Death, be not proud."
19. On death being figured as a rival or lover, see Guthke, *The Gender of Death*, p. 96.
20. Huizinga, *The Waning of the Middle Ages*, p. 145, characterizes the "whole vision" of late medieval death as *macabre*; and, for an anthropological interpretation of the extent to which an interest in death in contemporary times is viewed as morose if not sick, see Barley, *Dancing on the Grave*, p. 11.
21. Greene, *[R]epentance*, sig. B2r.
22. Beier, pp. 48–49.
23. "A Valediction Forbidding Mourning" in *John Donne's Poetry*, pp. 71–72.
24. Donne, *Deaths duel*, sig. B3r.
25. See, for example, "The Canonization" in *John Donne's Poetry*, pp. 77–78.
26. Insofar as The Geneva Bible, printed in English, was circulating widely in London during the time of Shakespeare's plays, references to scripture follow this version cited hereafter parenthetically.
27. Hill, *Path-Way*, pp. 199–200.
28. Erasmus's *Contempt for the World*, originally written in Latin in the 1480s, was first translated into English by Thomas Paynell in 1533.
29. Erasmus, *De Contemptus Mundi*, pp. 147–49.
30. Cf. Harkup, *Death by Shakespeare*, p. 61.
31. Frye, pp. 219–20.
32. Although we refer here to Shakespeare alone, it is "now widely accepted that the first eleven scenes are written primarily by George Wilkins" (*NOS*, p. 2662).
33. Engel, Loughnane, and Williams, *The Memory Arts in Renaissance England*, pp. 279–83.
34. We are mindful of and indebted to a range of relevant monographs along these lines, especially Watson, *The Rest Is Silence*; Greenblatt, *Hamlet in Purgatory*; Chalk, *Monuments and Literary Posterity*; Lewis, *Hamlet and the Vision of Darkness*; Garrison, *Shakespeare and the Afterlife*; and Griffin, *Untimely Deaths in Renaissance Drama*.

35. Leggatt, "Substitution in *Measure for Measure*," p. 350; see also Crunelle-Vanrigh, "Coming to a head," pp. 83ff.
36. Death's head rings appear to have been standard issue for bawds during period, perhaps identifying them as being "in the trade," at least insofar as this item of jewelry served as a visual cue of the character type for the stage (a further link between *thanatos* and *eros* in the popular imagination); see, for example, John Marston, *The Dutch Courtesan* (1.2.50–56); and Thomas Middleton, William Rowley, and Philip Massinger, *The Old Law* (4.1.151–55).
37. Kernodle, *From Art to Theatre*, pp. 10–12, 214–215; Zimmerman, *The Early Modern Corpse*, pp. 24–89; Lin, *Shakespeare and the Materiality of Performance*, pp. 107ff.
38. Dobson and Wells (eds.), *Oxford Companion to Shakespeare*, p. 248. Shakespeare is a likely contender for having written new episodes expanding the part of Hieronimo about 1599 (*NOS*, p. 1678), around the same time he was working on *Hamlet*.
39. Kyd, *The Spanish Tragedy*, pp. 106–107. See also Knapp, *Shakespeare Only*, p. 108. It is worth noting that Shakespeare's *Macbeth* borrows from this passage: "Why should I play the Roman fool, and die / On my own sword?" (5.10.1–2).
40. Egan, "Platonism and bathos in Shakespeare," pp. 59–78.
41. See Engel, *Death and Drama*, pp. 63–77.
42. Garrison, p. 77: "discussion of the afterlife inevitably returns us to *Hamlet*."
43. So too, both the catalog of flowers in Ophelia's mad scene (4.2) and Gertrude's report of her "fantastic garlands" and watery death, including a reference to "long purples" as "dead men's fingers" (4.4.162–165), are consistent with the flowers seen in *memento mori* artworks of the period.
44. *Hamlet* likewise has served as a focal case study in early modern book history, especially as regards variations between the quartos and folios: Stallybrass et al., "Hamlet's Tables," pp. 379–419; Lesser and Stallybrass, "The First Literary *Hamlet*," pp. 371–420; Menzer, *The Hamlets*; Kirk Melnikoff, "Nicholas Ling's Republican *Hamlet*," pp. 95–111; Chartier, *The Author's Hand*; Bourus, *Young Shakespeare's Young Hamlet*; Lesser, "*Hamlet*" after Q1; and Bruster, "Quoting *Hamlet*."
45. Pollmann and Kuijpers, pp. 1–23.
46. We envision and encourage new studies in the years to come that accommodate and interrogate issues pertaining to race, the performance of gender, cognitive studies, and the growing field of speculative fiction on Shakespeare, such as Kenneth Branagh's recent film *All is True* (2019) and Maggie O'Farrell's historical novel, *Hamnet* (2020). While we see our book as connecting meaningfully to these and other contiguous fields of research, our principal aim has been to historize and theorize the death

arts in Shakespeare's time. We anticipate therefore that our book will serve as a complementary companion work to bolster future studies relating to global Shakespeare and performance studies used alongside, for example, Litvin, *Hamlet's Arab Journey*; *The Hamlet Zone: Reworking "Hamlet" for European Cultures*, ed. by Ruth J. Owen; Carlson, *Shattering Hamlet's Mirror*; *Shakespeare's "Hamlet" in an Era of Textual Exhaustion*, ed. by Sonya Freeman Loftis et al.; Dromgoole, *Hamlet Globe to Globe*; Croall, *Performing "Hamlet"*; and Burnett, *"Hamlet" and World Cinema*.

References

Appleford, Amy. *Learning to Die in London, 1380–1540*. Philadelphia, PA: University of Pennsylvania Press, 2014.

Ariès, Phillipe. *The Hour of Our Death: The Cassic History of Western Attitudes Toward Death Over the Last One Thousand Years*. Translated by Helen Weaver. 2nd edition. New York: Vintage Books, 2008.

Baldwin, William. *A Treatise of Morall Phylosophie Contaynyng the Sayinges of the Wyse*. London: Edwarde Whitchurche, 1547.

Barley, Nigel. *Dancing on the Grave: Encounters with Death*. London: John Murray, 1995.

Beier, Lucinda McCray. "Good Death in Seventeenth-Century England." In *Death, Ritual, and Bereavement*. Edited by Ralph Houlbrooke. London and New York: Routledge, 1989. pp. 43–61.

Bourus, Terri. *Young Shakespeare's Young Hamlet*. London: Palgrave Macmillan, 2014.

Bruster, Douglas. "Quoting *Hamlet*." In *Shakespeare and Quotation*. Edited by Julie Maxwell and Kate Rumbold. Cambridge: Cambridge University Press, 2018. pp. 72–86.

Burnett, Mark Thornton. *"Hamlet" and World Cinema*. Cambridge: Cambridge University Press, 2019.

Carlson, Marvin. *Shattering Hamlet's Mirror*. Ann Arbor, MI: University of Michigan Press, 2016.

Croall, Jonathan. *Performing "Hamlet": Actors in the Modern Age*. London: Arden Shakespeare, 2018.

Chalk, Brian. *Monuments and Literary Posterity in Early Modern Drama*. Cambridge: Cambridge University Press, 2015.

Chartier, Roger. *The Author's Hand and the Printer's Mind*. Cambridge: Polity Press, 2013.

Cressy, David. *Birth, Marriage, and Death: Ritual, Religion, and the Life-Cycle in Tudor and Stuart England*. Oxford: Oxford University Press, 1997.

Crunelle-Vanrigh, Anny. "Coming to a Head: Ragozine as Pirate Money in Act 4 Scene 3 of Shakespeare's *Measure for Measure*." *Cahiers Élisabéthains* 89.1 (2016): 83–90.

Cummings, Brian. "Remembering the Dead in *Hamlet*." In *The Cambridge Companion to Shakespeare and Religion*. Edited by Hannibal Hamlin. Cambridge: Cambridge University Press, 2019. pp. 100–117.

Daniell, Christopher. *Death and Burial in Medieval England, 1066–1550*. New York: Routledge, 1977.

Dobson, Michael and Stanley Wells (eds.). *The Oxford Companion to Shakespeare*. Oxford: Oxford University Press, 2011.

Donne, John. *Deaths Duell, or, A Consolation to the Soule, Against the Dying Life*. London: Thomas Harper, 1632.

———. *John Donne's Poetry*. Edited by Donald R. Dickson. New York: W. W. Norton, 2007.

Dromgoole, Dominic. *Hamlet Globe to Globe*. New York: Grove Press, 2017.

Egan, Gabriel. "Platonism and Bathos in Shakespeare and Other Early Modern Drama." In *Refiguring Mimesis: Representation in Early Modern Literature*. Edited by Jonathan Holmes and Adrian Streete. Hatfield, UK: University of Hertfordshire Press, 2005.

Engel, William E. *Death and Drama in Renaissance England: Shades of Memory*. Oxford: Oxford University Press, 2002; rpt. 2005.

Engel, William E., Rory Loughnane, and Grant Williams. *The Death Arts in Renaissance England: A Critical Anthology*. Cambridge: Cambridge University Press, 2022.

———. *The Memory Death Arts in Renaissance England: A Critical Anthology*. Cambridge: Cambridge University Press, 2016.

Erasmus, Desiderius. *De Contemptus Mundi*. Translated by Erika Rummel. In *Collected Works of Erasmus. Volume 66 Spiritualia*. Edited by John W. O'Malley. Toronto: University of Toronto Press, 1988.

Frye, Roland Mushat. *The Renaissance Hamlet: Issues and Responses in 1600*. Princeton, NJ: Princeton University Press, 1984.

Garrison, John S. *Shakespeare and the Afterlife*. Oxford: Oxford University Press, 2018.

Geminus, Thomas. *Compendiosa totius anatomie delineatio, ære exarate*. London: John Herford, 1545.

Greenblatt, Stephen. *Hamlet in Purgatory*. Princeton, NJ: Princeton University Press, 2001.

Greene, Robert. *The repentance of Robert Greene Maister of Artes*. London: John Danter, 1592.

Griffin, Andrew. *Untimely Deaths in Renaissance Drama*. Toronto: University of Toronto Press, 2019.

Guthke, Karl. *The Gender of Death: A Cultural History in Art and Literature*. Cambridge: Cambridge University Press, 1999.
Harkup, Kathryn. *Death by Shakespeare: Snake-bites, Stabbings and Broken Hearts*. London: Bloomsbury, 2020.
Hill, Robert. *The Path-Way to Prayer and Pietie*. London: F.K. for William Cotton, 1609.
Huizinga, Johan. *The Waning of the Middle Ages*. Translated by Frederik Jan Hopman. Harmondsworth: Penguin, 1922.
Kernodle, George R. *From Art to Theatre: Form and Convention in the Renaissance*. Chicago, IL: University of Chicago Press, 1947.
Knapp, Jeffrey. *Shakespeare Only*. Chicago, IL: University of Chicago Press, 2009.
Kyd, Thomas. *The Spanish Tragedy*. Edited by Michael Neill. New York: W.W. Norton & Co, 2013.
Leggatt, Alexander. "Substitution in *Measure for Measure*." *Shakespeare Quarterly* 39.3 (1988): 342–359.
Lesser, Zachary. *"Hamlet" after Q1: An Uncanny History of the Shakespearean Text*. Philadelphia, PA: University of Pennsylvania Press, 2015.
Lesser, Zachary and Peter Stallybrass. "The First Literary *Hamlet* and the Commonplacing of Professional Plays." *Shakespeare Quarterly* 59.4 (Winter, 2008): 371–420.
Lewis, Rhodri. *Hamlet and the Vision of Darkness*. Princeton, NJ: Princeton University Press, 2017.
Lin, Erika T. *Shakespeare and the Materiality of Performance*. Houndmills, UK: Palgrave, 2012.
Litvin, Margaret. *Hamlet's Arab Journey*. Princeton, NJ: Princeton University Press, 2011.
Loftis, Sonya Freeman, Allison Kellar, and Lisa Ulevich (eds.). *Shakespeare's "Hamlet" in an Era of Textual Exhaustion*. London: Routledge, 2017.
Marston, John. *The Dutch Courtesan*. Edited by Karen Britland. London: Bloomsbury, 2018.
Melnikoff, Kirk. "Nicholas Ling's Republican *Hamlet* (1603)." In *Shakespeare's Stationers: Studies in Cultural Bibliography*. Edited by Marta Straznicky. Philadelphia, PA: University of Pennsylvania Press, 2012. pp. 95–111.
Menzer, Paul. *The Hamlets: Cues, Qs, and Remembered Texts*. Newark, DE: University of Delaware Press, 2008.
Middleton, Thomas, William Rowley, and Philip Massinger. *The Old Law*. Edited by Catherine M. Shaw. New York and London: Garland Publishing, 1982.
Newstok, Scott. *Quoting Death in Early Modern England: The Poetics of Epitaphs Beyond the Tomb*. Houndmills, UK: Palgrave, 2009.
O'Connor, Mary Catharine. *The Art of Dying Well: the Development of the Ars Moriendi*. New York: Columbia University Press, 1942.

Owen, Ruth J. (ed.) *The Hamlet Zone: Reworking "Hamlet" for European Cultures*. Newcastle upon Tyne, UK: Cambridge Scholars, 2012.

Pollmann, Judith and Erika Kuijpers. "Introduction: On the Early Modernity of Modern Memory." In *Memory Before Modernity: Practices of Memory in Early Modern Europe*. Edited by Erika Kuijpers, Judith Pollmann, Johannes Müller, and Jasper van der Steen. Leiden: Brill, 2013. pp. 1–23.

Shakespeare, William. *The New Oxford Shakespeare, The Complete Works*. General edited by Gary Taylor, John Jowett, Terri Bourus, and Gabriel Egan. Oxford: Oxford University Press, 2017.

Smith, Emma. *This is Shakespeare*. New York: Pantheon Books, 2019.

Songes and Sonettes, Written by the Right Honorable Lorde Henry Haward Late Earle of Surrey, and Other. London: Richard Tottel, 1557.

Stallybrass, Peter, Roger Chartier, J. Franklin Mowery and Heather Wolfe. "Hamlet's Tables and the Technologies of Writing in Renaissance England." *Shakespeare Quarterly* 55.4 (Winter, 2004): 379–419.

Tayler, Edward W. *Nature and Art in Renaissance Literature*. New York: Columbia UniversityPress: 1964.

Watson, Robert N. *The Rest Is Silence: Death as Annihilation in the English Renaissance*. Berkeley, CA: University of California Press, 1995.

Wilson, Thomas. *The Arte of Rhetorique*. London: Richard Grafton, 1553.

Zimmerman, Susan. *The Early Modern Corpse and Shakespeare's Theatre*. Edinburgh: Edinburgh University Press, 2007.

PART I

Staging the Death Arts

Preface to Part I

So shalt thou feed on death, that feeds on men,
And, death once dead, there's no more dying then.[1]

One of the last poems in Shakespeare's sonnet cycle, the one beginning "Poor soul, the centre of my sinful earth," figures the "fading mansion" of the body as the "excess" to be inherited—and fed on—by worms (sonnet 146, 1.7). Its closing couplet provides an apt epigraph for this Preface, primarily because it showcases the apparent ease with which Shakespeare traded in the tropes and poetic conceits of mortal temporality—but always with a purpose beyond what one finds at first glance. For, as when Biron toward the end of *Love's Labour's Lost* is tasked with a year of visiting the "speechless sick" and to use "all the fierce endeavour of your wit / To enforce the painèd impotent to smile" (5.2.811, 5.2.814–5.2.815), Shakespeare's lovelorn character gives voice to the profound realization that clever language can only take one so far when actually in the presence of someone about to die: "To move wild laughter in the throat of death? / It cannot be, it is impossible. / Mirth cannot move a soul in agony" (5.2.815–5.2.817). Assessing Shakespeare's treatment of mortality, loss, and mourning solely in terms of conventional tropes and cultural norms, therefore, tends to occlude the more subtle ways his oeuvre both reflects and productively complicates the early modern death arts.[2] As was pointed out in the Introduction, the English Renaissance death arts, as a hermeneutic category, recasts the uniqueness of premodern cultural production, accentuating the distance between Shakespeare and contemporary readers and inviting new ways of assessing the significance of his individual plays and plots where dying, death, and the dead are regularly staged and verbally represented.

The first part of this volume accordingly is devoted to some of the specific ways that Shakespeare puts his stamp on the death arts through his ongoing and intense engagement with them, recognizing that the death arts serve to shift our perspective from the claustrophobic sphere of inwardly experienced feeling alone to the materiality of public expression and production. Well aware of the mourning rituals and customs of his day, Shakespeare was just as prone to revive antique Roman expressions of patient stoicism in on-stage depictions of fatal adversity as he was to represent rebellious resistance to unwelcomed death. The desire for futurity, securing a reputation and even fame, and striving to assure that one's deeds and identity are not forgotten, all figure significantly in his plays early and late. The various stagings of mortal temporality in Shakespeare's plays suggest in fact a willful if not self-conscious protest against matter-of-factly falling into and merely replicated standard responses to and typical conventions associated with early modern death and dying.[3] The first seven chapters collectively present the underlying contexts—religious, political, social, and cultural—requisite for assessing the death arts as a basis to explore and interpret Shakespeare's drawing on and at times turning inside-out period specific expressions of living in the long shadow of death. While the second part will disclose ways in which the principal elements and perennial tropes of the death arts are developed more particularly with respect to *Hamlet*, the first ranges throughout his other plays, teasing out the intellectual and doctrinal contexts that bring into focus the dynamics of their reception. Our goal in arranging the collection this way has been to set up a rational and heuristic foundation upon which future inquiry can be undertaken.

More specifically, the first part begins with Shakespeare's grounding in the *ars moriendi* tradition. Andrew C. McCarthy carefully surveys the early modern lineaments of this quintessentially medieval tradition to take the full measure of predominating Elizabethan perceptions of death and dying with reference to religious treatises and consolation tracts (most notably Thomas Becon's *Sicke Mans Salve*) as well as the elegiac admonition to bear up serenely under illness and patiently to receive instruction in how to die well. Along the way, references are made to plays that variously exemplify and sometimes contest the commonplaces associated with this aspect of the early modern death arts, including *Measure for Measure*, *Titus Andronicus*, *Henry V*, *King Lear*, and also Marlowe's *Doctor Faustus*.

From here, Brian Harries goes on to consider how and to what end "speaking for corpses" takes place in early modern drama, especially as pertains to that broader aspect of the death arts involving acts of commemoration as they take part in, or even precede, funerary rites. His analysis zeroes in on three exemplary test cases—Hamlet, Brutus, and Locrine in the eponymous play that still holds a special place in the so-called Shakespeare apocrypha.[4] All three of these characters encounter the deceased whom they have eulogized shortly after death but in the absence of the formal burial rituals for the dead. Each speaking corpse functions as a chilling *memento mori*, arresting the action of the play in that given moment and calling for contemplation; each thus represents a verbal vignette of a lived life that is wholly and unsettlingly open for interpretation at the moment a person passes from being a living member of society to being a remembered, memorialized name in the past.

Eileen Sperry continues with the exploration of Shakespeare's repurposing of earlier traditions by focusing on a familiar, conventional expression of the early modern death arts, namely the Latin *"tu fui, ego eris"* (in English summed up in the motto: "As you are, so once was I / As I am, so shall you be"), the dying person's message. She points out how, like many other *memento mori*, the *tu fui* form relies on a set of internal binaries and thus involves two people: a soon-to-be dead speaker, and a healthy, young listener who is asked to think about the relationships between both past and present and also present and future. With reference to the images and text of Christopher Sutton's much reprinted *Disce Mori* [*Learn to Die*] Sperry analyzes the implication of these binaries coming together to create a central Simple Paradox that pervades the history plays, exemplarily in *2 Henry IV*.

This notion of futurity is resumed, albeit from a different critical, dramaturgical, and historiographical set of theoretical coordinates, by Grant Williams. His contribution to the collection takes into account the vicissitudes of monumentalization in an analysis of *Antony and Cleopatra*, especially as regards the fantasy of becoming a living monument so as to capture the immortal longings articulated by Antony and Cleopatra in various ways throughout the play. For both—and each in her or his own way—care desperately about how they will be remembered when they are gone, making all the more poignant the ultimate dramatic irony implicit in Shakespeare's treatment of their being buried together (at least per Octavius Caesar's ostensible order to his Romanentourage), namely that their actualmemorial site remains unknown. With his consideration of imaginative exempla, Williams identifies their final resting place as "somewhere in our mass-produced fantasies." Tombs, and the idea of marking the place of the dead,[5] are then taken up by Dorothy Todd in her account of the ready references and polysemic implications of tombs, ooze, and ashesin *Pericles*. Her essay thus considers the movement between the putative stability of the monument and the absolute instability of the waterygrave.

Similar uncertainties constitutive of the death arts in the Renaissance are taken up finally in two essays dealing with *Othello* as the common touchstone of critical concern. Jessica Tooker's "emphatic reflections" address the fragile web of love, life, and death as expressed within the play. The tragedy of "The Moor of Venice," as the subtitle is given in early printingsof *Othello*,[6] contains multitudes and is, in the words of one of its most cerebral and wise critics, a tragedy of probability "constructed upon a series of SimpleParadoxes."[7] Maggie Vinter, by resituating the cultural performanceof*memento mori* with reference to *Othello*, rounds out this first part of the collection with a return to the larger question of what Shakespeare accomplishes by means of alluding to voices from beyond the grave. Like Sperry (in Chapter 3), Vinter examines theSimpleParadox of *tu fui* and goes on to reassess its place in the early modern death arts as continually threatening to collapse into either pure difference or pure identity, each of which evades "the full scandal of life's proximity to death." Vinter analyzes what exactly audiences are hearing when Desdemona sings Barbary's Willow Song, by reconstructing the pretexts and subtexts of prior voices—of those now dead—which come through to show how they are subtly filtered and amplified by means of Shakespeare's dramaturgical concerns with the death arts on stage. For, while Desdemona seemingly tells Barbary's story to disavow the Willow Song and distinguish herself from her mother's maid, she still finds herself repeating snatches of it, not only recounting to Emilia the occasion when she first heard it, but also performing it—which has the on-stage effect of virtually reviving the voice of the dead woman to whom it was attributed.

Our overarching goal in this first part is to identify and put into context key aspects of the Shakespearean death arts. The plays considered here provide a viable sampling of works to approach and understand in their original terms how the death arts figure into and are set to work in Shakespeare's dramatic output. At all events, these seven essays covering a dozen plays offer ample grounding for the second part on *Hamlet*. As indicated in the Introduction, we are mindful, of course, that this is something of a first pass at the canon with respect to the Shakespearean death arts, and it is our earnest hope that others will pick up where we have left off. Such is our hope for futurity.

William E. Engel

Notes

1. Shakespeare, Sonnet 146 (ll.13–14), p. 2879; *The New Oxford Shakespeare, The Complete Works*, gen. ed. Gary Taylor, John Jowett, Terri Bourus, and Gabriel Egan. All quotations from Shakespeare in this Preface follow this edition.
2. For a more detailed discussion of how this approach moves away from seeing death merely as theme in early modern dramatic and cultural studies, see William E. Engel, Rory Loughnane, and Grant Williams, *The Death Arts in Renaissance England*, Introduction.
3. The same, of course, can be said of the sonnets (especially 30, 39, 55, 66, 71, and 146) and is the subject of several excellent studies of Shakespeare's craft in the light of the death arts broadly conceived; see, for example, Garrison, "Recollection and Preemptive Resurrection in Shakespeare's Sonnets," in *Memory and Mortality in Renaissance England*, ch. 3.
4. Even though George Peele and Robert Greene are more likely candidates for the authorship of *Locrine*, it was one of seven new attributions in Philip Chetwinde's publication of the Third Folio of Shakespeare's plays (1664) on the basis of an advertisement printed on the 1595 quarto title-page, "Newly set foorth, overseene and corrected, by W.S."; see Kirwan, *Shakespeare and the Idea of Apocrypha: Negotiating the Boundaries of the Dramatic Canon*, pp. 129–135.
5. Cf. Belsey, "In Defiance of Death: Shakespeare and Tomb Sculpture," p. 15: "But popular culture must move more slowly than orthodoxy, or lay people would hardly need constant exhortation. A variety of meanings for death is thus available to Shakespeare."
6. *New Oxford Shakespeare*, p. 2115.
7. Altman, *The Improbability of Othello: Rhetorical Anthropology and Shakespearean Selfhood*, p. 12; further, Altman astutely argues, "Shakespeare

was playing a double game in *Othello*[...] exposing his audience's potentially tragic dependency on probable discourse even as he exploited their predisposition to probabilize the anomalies they experienced" (pp. 13–14).

REFERENCES

Altman, Joel. B. *The Improbability of Othello: Rhetorical Anthropology and Shakespearean Selfhood*. Chicago, IL: University of Chicago Press, 2010.

Belsey, Catherine. "In Defiance of Death: Shakespeare and Tomb Sculpture." *Memoria di Shakespeare: A Journal of Shakespeare Studies* 6 (2019): 1–20.

Belsey, Catherine. "In Defiance of Death: Shakespeare and Tomb Sculpture." *Memoria di Shakespeare: A Journal of Shakespeare Studies* 6 (2019): 1–20.

Engel, William E., Rory Loughnane, and Grant Williams (eds.). *Memory and Mortality in Renaissance England*. Cambridge: Cambridge University Press, 2022.

Engel, William E., Rory Loughnane, and Grant Williams. *The Death Arts in Renaissance England: A Critical Anthology*. Cambridge: Cambridge University Press, 2022.

Garrison, John. "Recollection and Preemptive Resurrection in Shakespeare's Sonnets." In *Memory and Mortality in Renaissance England*. Edited by William E. Engel, Rory Loughnane, and Grant Williams. Cambridge: Cambridge University Press, 2022.

Kirwan, Peter. *Shakespeare and the Idea of Apocrypha: Negotiating the Boundaries of the Dramatic Canon*. Cambridge: Cambridge University Press, 2015.

Shakespeare, William. *The New Oxford Shakespeare, the Complete Works*. General edited by Gary Taylor, John Jowett, Terri Bourus, and Gabriel Egan. Oxford: Oxford University Press, 2017.

CHAPTER 2

Shakespeare's *Ars Moriendi*

Andrew D. McCarthy

> Were I a composer of books
> I would keep a register
> Commented of the diverse deaths which
> In teaching men to die
> Should after teach them to live.—Michel de Montaigne[1]

In 2016, the Catholic Church brought the late medieval *ars moriendi* into the bright lights of the digital age, launching a website hosted by St. Mary's University (www.artofdyingwell.org). Replacing the fifteenth-century woodcuts with animations and interviews with the terminally ill, the website "offers practical and spiritual support to those faced with the prospect of death and dying. It is a site for everyone."[2] Even with attempts at establishing an ecumenical ethos, the website repeatedly draws upon and highlights the rich Catholic traditions surrounding death and dying, "After centuries of ministering to the dying, the Catholic Church

---

A. D. McCarthy (✉)
Department of English, University of Tennessee, Chattanooga, TN, USA
e-mail: andrew-mccarthy@utc.edu

© The Author(s), under exclusive license to Springer Nature Switzerland AG 2022
W. E. Engel and G. Williams (eds.), *The Shakespearean Death Arts*, Palgrave Shakespeare Studies,
https://doi.org/10.1007/978-3-030-88490-1_2

has a fund of experience to share in what was traditionally called the art of dying well, or in Latin, Ars Moriendi."[3] The website has an aesthetically fresh look with welcoming fonts and calming colors, not to mention a notable lack of deathbed demons, but the content remains the same. The drama of the original guidebooks is still intact with clear step-by-step rituals to guide a loved one's final moments. Considering this continued fascination with and investment in the art of dying well over the span of six centuries, it is not much of a surprise that early modern playwrights writing in the immediate wake of these texts recognized their potential for the London stage. Though the relationship between these guidebooks and early modern dramatists has not been the subject of extensive study, Shakespeare and his contemporaries repeatedly drew on the tradition, infusing their plays with reflections on the art and drama of dying. Shakespeare in particular returned to the ars moriendi throughout his career, ultimately offering a rich and complex picture of the variety of ways the art of dying informed early modern thinking about one's final earthly moments.

Appearing in English manuscript translations of the Latin *Tractatus de arte bene moriendi* in the mid-fifteenth century, the *Ars Moriendi* or Craft of Dying texts were incredibly popular, with versions appearing in every European language. William Caxton's abridged *The Arte and Crafte to Know Well to Dye* (1490), a translation from French, is the earliest English print version. Essentially a "do-it-yourself handbook," the ars moriendi texts meant to provide step-by-step guidance for one's final moments as a way to assuage the terror that often surrounded death and dying.[4] Divided into six sections or chapters, the tract begins by emphasizing the importance of learning to die well and then proceeds to detail the temptations the dying typically experience (loss of faith, despair, impatience, spiritual pride, and greed), presents questions that should be asked of the dying (along with the appropriate answer), prayers for the dying to recite, instructions to assist the dying, and finally, prayers for those witnessing the death. This structure forms the foundation for the art of dying tradition, a tradition that extends all the way into seventeenth century and beyond.[5]

Given the ubiquitous nature of these texts and their long-standing place in the literature surrounding death and dying, the popular impulse of the early texts is not surprising; *The Arte or Crafte to Lyve Well and to Dye Well* (1505) contains numerous block-prints depicting the various temptations, allowing all who encountered them to understand their meaning, literate and illiterate alike.[6] As Paul Binski has argued: "The

Ars moriendi represents a lay appropriation both of a body of knowledge and of a body of procedure; its pastoral character reminds us of those widespread efforts by the Church from the thirteenth century to educate laypeople in the basic tenets of sin, its character and remedies."[7] Considering the social aspect of death and dying in late medieval and early modern society—that people typically died in bed, surrounded by family and community members—the ars moriendi filled an important space in instructing all those present at the sick-bed, healthy and unhealthy alike, to participate constructively in the art of dying. This participation required clearly articulated roles and, as Eamon Duffy has shown, "it is clear that there was a well-defined set of attitudes and gestures which dying Christians were expected to manifest at this, the most solemn and important moment of their lives. The deathbed was a communal event, not a private one."[8]

All of this gestures toward the dramatic nature that was part and parcel of the art of dying. Historians of the period have been quick to point out the inherent performance that emerges from the ars moriendi texts, calling the sickroom "the arena of a drama" and "the centre of a moral theatre."[9] The scripted questions and answers along with the printed prayers emphasize the integral role speaking played—for both the living and the dying—in the final moments, doing much to aid the impression that these are theatrical moments. The block-prints, replete with various devils lying in wait in hopes to tempt the dying Christian vie for space with angels just as members of the community, lay and clergy alike, surround the bed. The dying Christian then becomes the "focal point for a powerfully communal vision of the world, in which every individual is surrounded by a host of helpers and opposers, every lonely step in the drama of dying in reality a participation in a communal effort."[10] Those composing ars moriendi texts similarly understood their works as participating in this theatrical vein, their words stage directions to be superimposed on the drama of dying. In the preface to *A Preparation to Deathe*, Erasmus makes this connection explicit, "For this is of mans lyfe the last part (as it were) of the playe, wherof hangeth eyther euerlastynge blysse of man, of euerlastynge damnation."[11] Death is the final act in the play that is life, an act upon which hangs the dying's soul.

Thomas Becon, theologian and clergyman in the Church of England, was similarly aware of the dramatic potential of the ars moriendi and exploits it to significant effect in *The Sicke Mans Salve* (1561). One of the period's most popular devotional books and an important contribution to the English ars moriendi tradition, *Sicke Mans Salve* went through eleven editions between its initial publication and 1600, with an additional seven in the first third of the seventeenth century.[12] While the tract is often noted for its significant length and its role as a Protestant contribution to the ars moriendi tradition, it also draws explicit attention to the inherent drama of the art of dying, both in form and content.[13]

Described as an "explicit closet drama" and a "curious blend of Job, the classical dialogue, and perhaps genuine drama as well," the text develops a lengthy conversation between Philemon (Becon's literary stand-in) and three friends who pay a visit to the suddenly ill Epaphroditus.[14] While Caxton's *Arte & Crafte* contains printed questions and responses, Becon's *Salve* is a full-blown theatrical performance. Establishing the purpose of the visit, not to mention the larger goals of the tract, Philemon remarks, "Let vs therefore go and visite our sicke neighbour, Epaphroditus, and comfort him with the heauenly consolation of the holy scriptures *that* he may beare this hys sicknesse both the more paciently and thankfully. For to this end did I send for you that we should go together vnto him, and so comfort him."[15] When they encounter their dying neighbor, the group discovers a grim scene, with Epaphroditus crying out in pain, longing for the end. What follows is a prolonged lesson in the art of dying. The four friends begin by offering Epaphroditus religious instruction, helping him calm down from the initial outburst. They take turns quoting from the Bible and noting biblical precedents meant to comfort the dying man by situating sickness and death in a larger redemptive narrative.

Having weathered the initial storm, the four neighbors proceed to guide him through a confession of his sins and then provide Epaphroditus with a pen, ink, and paper so he may compose his will. This is not an anomalous addition. Given the communal nature of dying, the deathbed was often the place wherein will-making took place and "the dying property-owner was likely to be surrounded by family, business associates, and executors, concerned with the disposal of property."[16] Having completed his will, the dying man asks for his wife, children, and servants to join them. Though these characters do not speak, Becon goes to great lengths to ensure that his readers envision a crowded stage, a full sickroom not unlike those seen in the popular block-prints. Epaphroditus addresses his wife and children, offering them final words of guidance and religious instruction that trend, in some ways, toward Polonius's advice for Laertes.

With his affairs settled, the real drama of the tract begins. Philemon asks that his dying friend make a profession of faith "that we may be able to testify hereafter that you departed in the fayth of Christ."[17] In other words, he's hoping to see an artful death, one that can be shared as an example for others. After doing so, Epaphroditus is nevertheless besieged by the standard deathbed temptations of greed and despair. It begins with the sick man's observations that "Death is terrible and fearfull" and "Death is painfull."[18] These lines call to mind those of the condemned Claudio in *Measure for Measure* who, after insisting that his sister will not give up her chastity in exchange for his life, finds his initial resolution crumbling under the weight of eternity, confessing, "Death is a fearful thing" (3.1.115).[19] Initially concerned with all of the worldly delights he is about to lose, Epaphroditus complains, "Death taketh me away from my gorgious and pleasaunte houses, and from all the temporall things that I haue" and "Death taketh me away from my deare frends in whose company I greatly delyght."[20] In response, Philemon offers extensive correctives, citing the biblical passages that emphasize the transitory nature of both human existence and earthly things and encourages a focus on the promise of heaven.

The initial concerns about material loss give way to full-blown despair, as Epaphroditus cries out, "now I am so troubled in my conscience that I begin almost to dispaire of Gods mercy towards me, yea and wishe that there were no God, nor no life after this." Like Marlowe's Faustus, the dying man's despair is palpable, "O my conscience is greuously vexed, troubled, and disquieted while I behold the fierce wrath of God against sinne, and consider how wicked a life I haue lead, and how often I haue broken Gods holy commaundementes."[21] Sensing his opportunity to enter the battlefield, the devil promptly makes his appearance, much in the same way as the mute family members who previously gathered around the deathbed. Satan's presence is made known through Epaphroditus's dialogue with Philemon, the former describing the sensations, "I feele a very hell within my breast" and the latter offering assurance that this is to be expected, that such a feeling is Satan's "olde propertie."[22] In the end, it isn't much of a battle—nothing like the block-prints—as Philemon successfully guides his friend out of danger and into a series of prayers, culminating in a final confession and Epaphroditus's peaceful passing.

Despite the final temptations and Satan's appearance, the ministering neighbors are in agreement that the death has been a good one. One remarks, "A Christen and godly end made hee. God geue vs all grace to make the like" and Philemon adds, "Of a good life commeth a good death, if the departure of the godly may be called a death, and not rather a passage vnto a better life."[23] *The Sicke Mans Salve* is very clearly a didactic text where extensive instruction in the form of dialogue is punctuated with moments of drama. But all of the elements of the shorter, more utilitarian ars moriendi texts are present.[24] The temptations, the instructions, and the various prayers structure the text. Most noteworthy is the dramatic impulse to recognize the inherent theatricality both of these materials and the process of dying and cast the tract as an explicit drama.

Given the ars moriendi's wide-spread popularity, especially the important role it played as a lay text to navigate one's final moments in life, it is unsurprising that early modern writers thought deeply about the artful death. Dying well is at the heart of Montaigne's essay, "That to Philosophize Is to Learn How to Die": "It is uncertain where death looks for us; let us expect her everywhere: the premeditation of death is a fore-thinking of liberty. He who hath learned to die, hath unlearned to serve. [...] To know how to die doth free us from all subjections and constraint."[25] For the essayist, the studied artful death is a path to freedom. While Montaigne's understanding of the studied, artful death is more abstract, Ben Jonson's poem "An Elegy on the Lady Jane Pawlet, Marchioness of Winton" reveals a practical conversance with the ars moriendi tradition. Jonson describes Pawlet's death in detail as a means of praise:

> How did she leave the world? With what contempt?
> Just as she in it lived! And so exempt
> From all affliction! When they urged the cure
> Of her disease, how did her soul assure
> Her sufferings, as the body had been away!
> And to the torturers (her doctors) say,
> Stick on your cupping-glasses, fear not, put
> Your hottest caustics to burn, lance, or cut:
> 'Tis but a body which you can torment,
> And I, into the world, all soul, was sent!
> Then comforted her lord! And blessed her son!
> Cheered her fair sisters in her race to run!
> With gladness tempered her sad parents' tears!
> Made her friends joys, to get above their fears!
> And, in her last act, taught the standers-by,
> With admiration, and applause to die! (ll. 47–64)[26]

Unlike Epaphroditus's drama, Lady Jane is heroic in managing her final moments. Her eyes are focused on heaven and she comforts the various family members who have gathered around her, teaching them how to die. I have argued elsewhere that Christopher Marlowe re-worked the ars moriendi for his dramatic purposes.[27] Specifically, Marlowe shifts the focus from dying well in *2 Tamburlaine* to the pleasure derived from crafting the deaths of others in *The Jew of Malta*. In a subversive recasting of the tradition, the playwright deploys Barabas, a character obsessed with the artful death, who gleefully constructs increasingly elaborate plots to execute his revenge until he is finally caught up in his own trap. Shakespeare appears to have attempted something similar early in his career with the villainous Aaron in *Titus Andronicus*, a play roughly contemporary with Marlowe's. Late in the play, Lucius questions the captured Aaron, asking if he feels remorse for all of the cruelty he has just confessed to stage-managing. He responds,

> Ay, that I had not done a thousand more.
> Even now I curse the day—and yet I think
> Few come within the compass of my curse—
> Wherein I did not some notorious ill
> As kill a man, or else devise his death [....] (5.1.124–28)

Aaron then proceeds to boast about a disturbing list of crimes he's perpetrated, many of which involve artfully manipulating death—from fostering mortal animosity between two friends to digging up the recently deceased only to place them in front of a loved one's door. And just as Barabas casts himself as "an engineer" of death, so too does Aaron, claiming to be Chiron and Demetrius's "tutor to instruct them" and "That bloody mind I think they learned of me" (5.1.98, 100).

While it is difficult to determine the extent to which he was subversively engaging with the ars moriendi tradition in *Titus* à la Marlowe and how much of it was simply echoing a popular villain from a contemporary's play, Shakespeare is explicit in his use of the materials by mid-career. In the mid-twentieth century, Kathrine Koller suggested that Shakespeare satirizes the ars moriendi in the Hostess's account of Falstaff's death in *Henry V*.[28] While this may be the case, the disguised Henry offers an abbreviated lesson on the art of dying well on the eve of the battle at Agincourt. As the king tries to justify his position, insisting that he is both happy to be on the fields of France with his men and that his cause is just, his pessimistic soldiers question who is ultimately responsible in the morally ambiguous world of war. Williams remarks, "I am afeard there are few die well that die in a battle, from how can they charitably dispose of anything, when blood is the argument? Now, if these men do not die well, it will be a black matter for the King that led them to it—who to disobey were against all proportion of subjection" (4.1.126–130). Williams's concern is both for the unpleasant physical death that occurs in the cut and thrust warfare of the medieval battlefield, but his emphasis on the "black matter" reveals an alertness to the spiritual element that accompanies dying well. In response, Henry offers a pre-battle lesson in the art of dying,

> Therefore should every soldier in the wars do as every sick man in his bed: wash every mote out of his conscience. And dying so, death is to him advantage; or, not dying, the time was blessedly lost wherein such preparation was gained. And in him that escapes, it were not sin to think that, making God so free an offer, he let him outlive that day to see his greatness and to teach others how they should prepare. (4.1.154–160)

Henry envisions a situation where the soldiers artfully prepare for death as preparation for battle. The English encampment becomes, by extension, the sickroom. In the event they survive the conflict, rising miraculously from their beds, the soldiers are then in the fortunate and blessed position to share the craft with others. Just as Philemon speaks with admiration of Epaphroditus's end in Becon's *Sicke Mans Salve*, noting that his passing serves as an example of a good death as well as a life well lived, Henry attempts to cast this pre-battle moment as an opportunity for his soldiers to become divinely sanctioned exemplars of the art and craft of dying. Williams's response, "'Tis certain, every man that dies ill, the ill upon his own head, the King is not to answer to it" (4.1.161–62), recognizes the king's point that each soldier, like the dying man, must make account of his own life. Henry's camp-fire lesson in the art of dying is significant, marking the only moment in the exchange that doesn't prompt an adversarial rebuttal from one of his men. Instead, there is general agreement in the disguised king's point regarding the importance in adequately preparing for death. The ars moriendi then becomes a bridge, a sort of fleeting common cultural ground between the king and his men, thus emphasizing the power these materials had in the late medieval and early modern imagination.

If lessons in the art of dying are the solution to the terror of impending death in *Henry V*, its complete failure in *Measure for Measure*, a play set in Catholic Vienna, is telling. Initially, it appears as though Claudio is going to be offered a course in the ars moriendi, as the disguised Duke tells Juliet, "Your partner, as I hear, must die tomorrow / And I am going with instruction to him" (2.3.39–40). When the Duke and Claudio appear on stage together, they are presented mid-conversation, and when asked if he hopes to be pardoned by Angelo, Claudio responds, "The miserable have no other medicine / But only hope. I've hope to live, and am prepared to die" (3.1.3). There is no evidence of this preparation and the disguised Duke's lengthy speech, one that emphasizes life's many vanities, does little to offer Claudio any guidance in the art of dying. This is perhaps to be expected from a Duke disguised as a Friar, though Claudio insists that he is ready, "To sue to live, I find I seek to die, /And seeking death, find life. Let it come on" (3.1.41–42). Significantly, Claudio still hopes that Isabella's intercession on his behalf will work on Angelo, but as the scene progresses, it is clear he is not adequately prepared or that the "instruction" provided has taken hold. Fortunately, when Isabella finally arrives, it is a ready-made moment for a lesson in the ars moriendi. There is no Shakespearean character better equipped to offer that instruction than Isabella and she appears ready to do so, encouraging her brother, "Be ready, Claudio, for your death tomorrow" (3.1.105). But as the reality of his impending death sets in, Claudio launches into a lengthy speech that indicates a blend of despair, impatience, and loss of faith, three temptations common to the dying Christian:[29]

> Ay, but to die, and go we know not where;
> To lie in cold obstruction, and to rot;
> This sensible warm motion to become
> A kneaded clod, and the dilated spirit
> To bathe in fiery floods, or to reside
> In thrilling region of thick-ribbèd ice;
> To be imprisoned in the viewless winds,
> And blown with restless violence round about
> The pendant world; or to be worse than worst
> Of those lawless and incertain thought
> Imagine howling—'tis too horrible!
> The weariest and most loathèd worldly life
> That age, ache, penury, and imprisonment

Can lay on nature is a paradise
To what we fear of death. (3.1.117–131)

Claudio does not know what comes after death and is terrified by this uncertainty in one of Shakespeare's most unrelentingly bleak passages. Echoing and expanding upon the sentiments expressed by Hamlet in his famous soliloquy, Claudio claims that even the worst human existence is better than the fear that accompanies death. The religious cast of *Measure for Measure* and its heroine primes this moment for a lesson in the art of dying even more detailed than the one offered by the disguised Henry to his soldiers. Instead, Isabella responds with "Alas, alas!" (3.1.132), an ineffectual and deeply inadequate expression of pity that opens up the space into which Claudio pleads that she accept Angelo's terms to save his life. There is no instruction in the art of dying and while Isabella does say "I'll pray a thousand prayers for thy death" (3.1.146), these words are not spoken in the spirit of the ars moriendi. She is no Philemon, praying repeatedly with the dying and hoping to bring comfort and hope to the final moments. Instead, her final words to Claudio are "'Tis best that thou diest quickly" (3.1.152). As the earlier discussion of *Henry V* shows, Shakespeare incorporated elements of the ars moriendi into his plays for dramatic effect and here he chooses to let it falter jarringly, its absence forcing Claudio and, by extension, the audience to contemplate impending mortality without the rituals meant to offer solace.

In *King Lear*, Shakespeare draws once again on the art of dying as the king explains his decision to divide the kingdom, "'tis our first intent / To shake all cares and business off our state, / Confirming them on younger years" (1.1.32–34). Ostensibly nearing the end of his life, the king looks to redistribute the affairs of state before death makes such a transition impossible. The crowded throne room, filled with family, members of the court, and servants is essentially the sick room presented in tracts like Becon's *Sicke Mans Salve* and depicted in block-prints meant to offer instruction in the art of dying. Lear's instinct is toward will-writing in preparation for death. The Folio is even more explicit in this impulse, "'tis fast our intent / To shake all cares and business from our age, / Conferring them on younger strengths while we / *Unburdened crawl toward death*" (1.1.36–39, emphasis added).[30] Though the Reformation sought to establish the composition of wills as something to be undertaken in good health, will-making traditionally occurred on the deathbed, as a "majority of testators were sick or close to death when they made their last wills. A number of them did so on the day of death, or within a few hours of it."[31] Lear's eldest daughters understand the king's sudden outburst as symptomatic of age and ill health, with Regan noting, "'Tis the infirmity of his age" and Goneril recognizing the "unruly waywardness that infirm and choleric years bring with them" (1.1.273, 277–78). From the play's outset, Shakespeare draws attention to Lear's age and proximity to death. In beginning with a scene that can be easily understood as a dramatic representation of the events and dramatis personae common to the deathbed, Shakespeare situates his play within the ars moriendi tradition.

Shakespeare's use of the ars moriendi to structure *King Lear* becomes explicit as Lear's behavior—and much of the language that describes it—draws repeated attention to the sin of impatience, one of the final sins the dying Christian is cautioned against. Caxton's *The Arte & Crafte to Know Well to Dye* (1490) describes impatience in this way—though not as immediately straightforward as the other four vices: "Now is it thus that to them that deye cometh right gret sorowe & payne of hert & of body, be it that the deth come naturelly, or that it come by ony other euyll accident, for by payne & sorowe many ther be that ben impacyent & grutchynge, and deyen in suche wyse as they semen madde or oute of theyr wytte."[32] A mixture of grief and terror at the prospect of death, impatience causes an intense emotional reaction that throws into doubt the love between man and God, potentially causing the dying to lose their mind to madness, to "semen madde or oute of theyr wytte." The tract then cautions against the sin, instructing, "therefore it is necessary to eueri man *that* wyll deye that in what seknes, be it short or long, that he murmure ne grutche not, but suffer it paciently, for we suffer by good right all theuylles that comen to vs."[33] In order to die well, the Christian is encouraged to "murmure ne grutche not" regardless of the pain the sickness causes or the length of his or her ailment. The dying should behave as Lady Jane Pawlett in Jonson's elegy, calmly bearing the illness and thereby offering instruction on how to die. The constant repetition of "patience" and "impatience" throughout the play, coupled with Lear's initial impulse toward will-writing, reveals the play's indebtedness to and continuation of the art of dying.

The connection between Lear and the sin of impatience becomes explicit as the king uses this language to make sense of his tormented mental state once he begins to understand the error of his ways. Just prior to heading out into the storm, the frazzled king begs, "You heavens, give me that *patience; patience* I need. / You see me here, you gods, a poor old fellow, / As full of grief as age, wretched in both!" (2.2.417–19, emphasis added). Even as he rages, Lear expresses a desire (or recognizes the need) to recalibrate his emotional response. While he and his fool attempt to brave the weather, his thoughts are clearly focused on achieving a calmness, "No, I will be the pattern of all patience" (3.2.34). Since Lear begins the play noting that he is at the end of his life and that his motivation for dividing the kingdom is in preparation for his death, these attempts at patience are significant.

Despite Lear's awareness that he ought to achieve and maintain patience, especially as he approaches the end, Kent tells Gloucester, "All the power of his wits have given way to impatience" (3.6.4). Lear's behavior is most certainly "madde or oute of theyr wytte." In fact, it is through the character of Gloucester and the way Shakespeare contrasts him with the mad Lear that we get the clearest sense of the playwright working with the art of dying. In preparation for his own death, Gloucester similarly engages with the deathbed tradition of dealing with matters of inheritance, though the degree to which he is doing so isn't at all clear to him. Paying Poor Tom for his services, Gloucester instructs, "Here, friend's another purse, in it a jewel / Well worth a poor man's taking" (4.6.28–29). A moment of significant dramatic irony, Gloucester has, in fact, properly bestowed his remaining wealth on his true son Edgar. The blind and broken man then calls out to the gods in what he believes to be his final act, defiantly proclaiming, "O you mighty gods! / This world I do renounce, and in your sights / Shake *patiently* my great affliction off" (4.6.34–36, emphasis added). Gloucester is certainly the opposite of Lear in the manner in which he attempts to artfully navigate the final moments before his death. While the king rants and rages, tearing at his hair in the storm, Gloucester calmly plans to take his own life, to exit this world on his own terms. Yet despite the characterization of his behavior as patient, this movement toward suicide is the ultimate manifestation of impatience and despair. As he continues to speak, this becomes even more clear:

> If I could bear it longer, and not fall
> To quarrel with your great opposeless wills,
> My snuff and loathèd part of nature should
> Burn itself out. (4.6.37–40)

Gloucester confesses that he can no longer bear the trials of his tormented existence. If he could, he'd allow nature to run its course. While his behavior isn't as extravagant as the king's, Gloucester reveals all the hallmarks of the sin—he is "impacyent & grutchynge" and full of grief. Remarkably, after he survives his fall and is greeted by a newly disguised Edgar who cheerfully explains the miraculous occurrence that has prolonged the blind man's life, Gloucester commits himself to patience, "Henceforth I'll bear / Affliction till it do cry out itself / 'Enough, enough' and die" (4.6.75–77). While he was predisposed to impatience prior to his attempt to take his life, Gloucester will now become the model of patience in his suffering, encouraged by the disguised Edgar to "Bear free and patient thoughts" (4.6.80). It is an instance of savage irony when the two men are brought together not long after this that Lear lectures Gloucester, "Thou must be patient. We came crying hither. / Thou knowest the first time that we smell the air / We wail and cry. I will preach to thee" (4.6.158–60). In a moment of insight and clarity that belies all we've seen from him since the play's outset, Lear suggests humankind spend their lives in a constant struggle with their eventual end. The solution, of course, is something neither he nor Gloucester can ever quite possess despite all of their effort.

While Shakespeare's treatment of the ars moriendi varies between plays, artful deaths make up a thread that runs throughout his most popular works. Whether a subversive recasting, adherence to tradition, a deliberate omission, or a fixation on the final temptations, the playwright holds up and examines, not only death as a final result, but also the processes of dying. Death may be the outcome of many plots, but Shakespeare is fascinated with the complexities of dying as an art to learn, practice, and master. In *Macbeth*, even the traitorous Thane of Cawdor's artful death is the subject of praise, "He died" reports Malcolm, "As one that had been studied in his death" (1.4.8–9). Not unlike the late medieval tracts upon which he drew, Shakespeare's plays provide his audiences with a popular ars moriendi, live-action guidebooks that offer hope even in the midst of tragedy. To return to where this essay began, if we consider the ars moriendi's move to the digital world coupled with Shakespeare's continued cultural relevance, perhaps the playwright's greatest achievement is that he taught—and continues to teach—his audiences how to die.

Notes

1. "That to Philosophize is to Learn How to Die" in *Shakespeare's Montaigne*, p. 24.
2. "The Art of Dying Well," *Art of Dying Well*, https://www.artofdyingwell.org/about-this-site/why-we-created-the-art-of-dying-well/ (accessed July 28, 2021).
3. Ibid.
4. Ashton, "Death," p. 208.
5. As Amy Appleford points out in *Learning to Die in London*, "The ideal of the "good death," central to the ars moriendi, has become a controversial issue in contemporary hospice care. If anything, the ars moriendi is a sign of cultural continuity across the centuries, not disjuncture" (p. 10).
6. See Ariès, *The Hour of Our Death*, p. 107; and Duffy, *The Stripping of the Altars*, pp. 316–17.
7. See Binski, *Medieval Death: Ritual and Representation*, p. 4; and Duffy, *The Stripping of the Altars*, p. 316.
8. Duffy, *The Stripping of the Altars*, p. 322; Beier, "The Good Death," p. 44; and Morgan, "Of Worms and War," p. 127.
9. See Ariès, *The Hour of Our Death*, p. 108; and Cressy, *Birth, Marriage, and Death*, p. 392. Indeed, the sickroom as the stage for the theater of dying appears in nearly all writing about the ars moriendi.
10. Duffy, *The Stripping of the Altars*, p. 318.
11. Erasmus, *Preparation to Deathe* (1538), STC 10,505.
12. Beaty, *The Craft of Dying*, p. 110.
13. *The Sicke Mans Salve*'s length is much longer than many of the other ars moriendi tracts prompting O'Connor's acerbic assessment, "Actually a man at the peak of good health would be overcome by exhaustion before the four were half through, but the hardy Epaphroditus has a seemingly endless flow of language, very good language, too" (p. 195).
14. Beaty, *The Craft of Dying*, pp. 112–13.
15. Becon, *The Sicke Mans Salve*, p. 89.
16. Duffy, *The Stripping of the Altars*, p. 322.
17. Becon, *The Sicke Mans Salve*, p. 109.
18. Ibid., p. 113.
19. Quotations from Shakespeare, unless otherwise noted, are taken from *The New Oxford Shakespeare* and are cited parenthetically within the text.
20. Becon, *The Sicke Mans Salve*, p. 114.
21. Ibid., p. 115. For more on Marlowe's *Doctor Faustus* and the art of dying, see Langston, "Marlowe's *Faustus* and the *Ars Moriendi* Tradition," pp. 152–54.
22. Becon, *The Sicke Mans Salve*, p. 116.
23. Ibid., p. 126.

24. As O'Connor points out in *The Art of Dying Well*: "As a method for the deathbed the *Ars Moriendi* is essentially practical" (p. 195).
25. "That to Philosophize is to Learn How to Die" in *Shakespeare's Montaigne*, p. 20.
26. "An Elegy on the Lady Jane Pawlet, Marchion[ess] of Winton" in *Ben Jonson: The Complete Poems*, pp. 232–34.
27. McCarthy, "Marlowe's *Ars Moriendi*," pp. 56–70.
28. Koller, "Falstaff and the Art of Dying," pp. 383–386.
29. Spinrad, *The Summons of Death*, pp. 165–71.
30. These lines from the Folio version of *The Tragedy of King Lear* are taken from *The Norton Shakespeare*.
31. Houlbrooke, *Death, Religion and the Family*, p. 98.
32. Caxton, *The Arte & Crafte to Know Well to Dye*, p. 24.
33. Ibid., p. 24.

References

Appleford, Amy. *Learning to Die in London, 1380–1540*. Philadelphia, PA: University of Pennsylvania Press, 2014.

Ariès, Phillip. *The Hour of Our Death*. Translated by Helen Weaver. New York and Oxford: Oxford University Press, 1981.

Ashton, Margaret. "Death." In *Fifteenth-Century Attitudes: Perceptions of Society in Late Medieval England*. Edited by Rosemary Horrox. Cambridge: Cambridge University Press, 1996. pp. 202–228.

Beaty, Nancy Lee. *The Craft of Dying: A Study in the Literary Tradition of the Ars Moriendi in England*. New Haven and London: Yale University Press, 1970.

Becon, Thomas. "The Sicke Mans Salve." In *The English Ars Moriendi*. Edited by David William Atkinson. New York: Peter Lang, 1992. pp. 87–126.

Beier, Lucinda McCray. "Good Death in Seventeenth-Century England." In *Death, Ritual, and Bereavement*. Edited by Ralph Houlbrooke. London and New York: Routledge, 1989. pp. 43–61.

Binski, Paul. *Medieval Death: Ritual and Representation*. Ithaca, NY: Cornell University Press, 1996.

Caxton, William. "The Arte & Crafte to Know Well to Dye." In *The English ars moriendi*. Edited by David William Atkinson. New York: Peter Lang, 1992. pp. 21–36.

Cressy, David. *Birth, Marriage, and Death: Ritual, Religion, and the Life-Cycle in Tudor and Stuart England*. Oxford: Oxford University Press, 1999.

Duffy, Eamon. *The Stripping of the Altars: Traditional Religion in England 1400–1580*. New Haven, CT and London: Yale University Press, 1992.

Erasmus, Desiderius. *Preparation to Deathe A Booke as Deuout as Eloquent.* London, 1538. STC 10505.

Houlbrooke, Ralph. *Death, Religion and the Family in England 1480–1750.* Oxford: Oxford University Press, 2000.

Jonson, Ben. *The Complete Poems.* Edited by George Parfitt. New York: Penguin, 1996.

Koller, Katherine. "Falstaff and the Art of Dying." *Modern Language Notes* 60 (1945): 383–86.

Langston, Beach. "Marlowe's Faustus and the *Ars Moriendi* Tradition." *A Tribute to George Coffin Taylor.* Edited by A. Williams. Chapel Hill, NC: University of North Carolina Press, 1952. pp. 148–167.

McCarthy, Andrew. "Marlowe's *Ars Moriendi.*" *Marlowe Studies: An Annual* 2 (2012): 57–70.

Montaigne, Michel de. *Shakespeare's Montaigne: The Florio Translation of the Essays, A Selection.* Edited by Stephen Greenblatt and Peter G. Platt. New York: New York Review Books, 2014.

Morgan, Philip. "Of Worms and War: 1380–1558." In *Death in England: An Illustrated History.* Edited by Peter C. Jupp and Clare Gittings. New Brunswick, NJ: Rutgers University Press, 2000. pp. 119–146.

O'Connor, Mary Catharine. *The Art of Dying Well: the Development of the Ars Moriendi.* New York: Columbia University Press, 1942.

Shakespeare, William. *The New Oxford Shakespeare, The Complete Works.* General edited by Gary Taylor, John Jowett, Terri Bourus, and Gabriel Egan. Oxford: Oxford University Press, 2016.

———. *The Norton Shakespeare.* Edited by Stephen Greenblatt, Walter Cohen, Suzanne Gossett, Jean E. Howard, Katharine Eisaman Maus, and Gordon McMullan. New York: W.W. Norton, 2016.

Spinrad, Phoebe S. *The Summons of Death on the Medieval and Renaissance English Stage.* Columbus, OH: Ohio State University Press, 1987.

The Art of Dying Well. The Center for the Art of Dying Well at St. Mary's University, https://artofdyingwell.org. Accessed July 28, 2021.

CHAPTER 3

Deciphering the Dead: Speaking for Corpses in Early Modern Drama

Brian J. Harries

When Richard III's body was discovered in 2012 underneath the parking lot of a government building in Leicester, the details of his burial proved anything but kingly. Archaeologists said that the body had suffered "humiliation injuries" (probably *post mortem*), meant to defile the corpse of the defeated ruler. The last of the Plantagenet line appeared still to have his wrists bound when he was placed, without coffin or shroud, into a hastily dug grave. This grave itself was shallow and insufficient in length to lay the body straight, forcing the neck and legs to be bent at awkward angles to fit. The chronicle sources tell us that Richard's body had been exhibited for as much as five days as proof of his overthrow prior to burial, so the order of Greyfriars entrusted with his interment may have been acting hurriedly as decay set in. These unpleasant details paint a picture of the most ignominious ending a king could receive; his earthly remains

B. J. Harries (✉)
Concordia University Wisconsin, Mequon, WI, USA
e-mail: brian.harries@cuw.edu

© The Author(s), under exclusive license to Springer Nature Switzerland AG 2022
W. E. Engel and G. Williams (eds.), *The Shakespearean Death Arts*, Palgrave Shakespeare Studies,
https://doi.org/10.1007/978-3-030-88490-1_3

endured as much dishonor as possible while still technically giving him a Christian burial.

Given the circumstances of his death at Bosworth Field, this gravesite fits our imaginative expectations of what happens when one faction ultimately triumphs over another in a contentious and bloody civil war. Having defeated Richard on the battlefield, Henry Tudor stripped him of his title, his legacy, and his honor, leaving him in a near-anonymous grave at an unnotable abbey. Yet, three years after the initial modern exhumation, Richard's bones were re-interred in 2015 next to the altar in Leicester Cathedral, with the full rites of an English royal funeral. The Archbishop of Canterbury presided over the ceremony, and Cardinal Vincent Nichols, the highest-ranking prelate of the Catholic Church in England, blessed the body on its procession to the church.

It's easy to credit this change of circumstance to the healing nature of time. In the more than 500 years that Richard spent in the ground, the Wars of the Roses have become a subject of distant history rather than a raw wound of political division. Modern historians and groups like The Richard III Society have challenged the Tudor narrative that cast Richard as a monster of moral and physical deformity. Cooler heads, we tell ourselves, separated from the events by many generations and several centuries of hindsight, can better understand the situation and provide a more fitting resting place for one of England's most (in)famous kings.

And yet, this process of reconciliation that took 500 years to move Richard from the grave of a usurper to that of a king often takes place in a matter of hours, or even minutes, in Elizabethan plays. In the anonymous play *Locrine*, and in Shakespeare's *Julius Caesar* and *Hamlet*, surviving enemies of deceased figures frequently use a moment of remembrance not to denigrate a *quondam* adversary, but rather to recast them in a positive light. I argue that dead bodies in these moments on stage are unstable signifiers of the lives they lived, allowing the living to complete and revise the deceased's narrative for their own purposes.

In order to provide a model of how we might think about this, I would like to turn to one more example outside the realm of English drama for a moment. Near the end of his book detailing the theological disputes between Desiderius Erasmus and Philip Melanchthon, Timothy J. Wengert describes the change in Melanchthon's attitude toward Erasmus after the latter's death in 1536. Almost immediately, Melanchthon stopped referring to Erasmus as a man of misguided ideas and corrupt doctrine and, instead, started praising him for the good ideas he held and the ways he helped the German Reformers. Wengert clarifies that this change had less to do with a change of heart than it did with constructing a coherent narrative of the Reformation:

> To take these statements as reflections of changes in Melanchthon's theology would completely misconstrue the role they played in Melanchthon's thought. They were *exempla* within Melanchthon's developing history of the church's return to the gospel and human beings' return to the sources. Erasmus's death transformed him into a cipher that Melanchthon could then decipher for his own historical and theological purposes.[1]

In Wengert's analysis, Erasmus's death fundamentally changes his identity for Melanchthon, in a way that goes beyond an ethos of "speak no ill of the dead." While alive, Erasmus was an adversary and an active participant in an ongoing argument about Catholic orthodoxy and Protestant reform. Once dead, he becomes passive, and his life allows, even requires, interpretation. His name becomes a fluid, if not open, signifier that someone like Melanchthon can step in to define. Moreover, it means the survivor gains a certain amount of control over the deceased's ideas. With the argument over and Erasmus safely in the ground, Melanchthon can focus on places where the two men agreed and recast his former adversary as a profound, if contentious, ally.

Wengert's description of a deceased person as a "cipher" that needs to be "deciphered," while modern, certainly fits with early modern sensibilities we see displayed in English drama. One of the most familiar usages of the term comes at the beginning of Shakespeare's *Henry V*, where the Prologue implores the audience to indulge the actors' efforts:

> O Pardon! Since a crooked figure may
> Attest in little place a million;
> And let us, ciphers to this great account,
> On your imaginary forces work. (Pro. 15–18).[2]

The chorus figure uses the language of accounting here to instruct the audience: just as small marks on a page may indicate vast wealth or multitudes of people, so each man on the stage will indicate thousands in the warring armies. While this speech makes a fascinating discursion on the nature of theater, we might focus here on the rhetorical move of employing bodies as ciphers. In this case, the living bodies of the actors point to larger stories outside of themselves that the audience must expand and elaborate, if the scene in front of them is to make any sense.

Within the fictive worlds of the plays, the final moments of *Hamlet* contain a similar situation. For the characters, however, it is not the living bodies of actors that need interpretation, but the dead bodies of the Danish court. When Fortinbras enters the stage immediately after Hamlet's death, what he sees forces him into an interrogative mode:

> Where is this sight? [...]
> [...] O proud Death,
> What feast is toward in thine eternal cell
> That thou so many princes at a shot
> So bloodily hast struck? (19.320, 323–326).[3]

The audience remains somewhat unsure of Fortinbras's purpose for coming to Elsinore at this point. Act Four established his campaign into Poland to reclaim Norwegian territory there, so he may be returning to pay tribute to Claudius/Hamlet for allowing his troops passage through Denmark. However, the opening tension of the play arises from Fortinbras's desire to attack Denmark to reclaim lands lost in war by his father. While he earlier promised "never more / to give assay of arms against" Denmark (7.70–71), he arrives at the palace accompanied by marching drums at the head of his army. Whatever he expected, he finds the Danish throne vacant, and so he claims it immediately through "some rights of memory in this kingdom / which now to claim [his] vantage doth invite [him]" (19.348–349). He conquers Denmark without literally or proverbially firing a shot, and he installs himself easily and clearly on the throne he has long desired.

The dead bodies strewn across the stage, however, remain a troubling problem. As ciphers, they point to tragedy and struggle, and they require an interpreter to decipher them. Horatio offers his services in this role, since he may be the only survivor privy to the palace intrigue that ended in such carnage. Faced with a likely new (and foreign) king, he constructs the "bloody question" of the scene around him into a sort of *memento mori*,[4] with a *Mirror for Magistrates* overlay:

> [L]et me speak to the yet unknowing world
> How these things came about. So shall you hear
> Of carnal, bloody, and unnatural acts,
> Of accidental judgements, casual slaughters,

> Of deaths put on by cunning and forced cause,
> And, in this upshot, purposes mistook
> Fall'n on the inventors' heads. All this can I
> Truly deliver. (19.338–345)

Asked by Hamlet to tell his story, Horatio delivers a sort of *eris quod sum* to Fortinbras on the deceased prince's behalf.[5] Not only is death inevitable, he suggests, but unwise government and political machinations hasten it on. Should Denmark's new ruler (or those assembled, or the audience) doubt this, the proof lies dead and bleeding on the floor.

In his final moments, Hamlet shows acute awareness of the need for intersession by the living on behalf of the dead. He tells Horatio: "I am dead; / Thou liv'st. Report me and my cause aright / To the unsatisfied" (19.296–298). He worries "what a wounded name / Things standing thus unknown" he will leave behind, so he essentially echoes the ghost's command "remember me" (5.110). Yet, it is worth noting that the nature of Hamlet's request for remembrance differs fundamentally from his father's. Old Hamlet speaks as a soul from purgatory, needing the memory and prayers of the living for his spiritual relief. Brian Cummings details the ways Shakespeare's audience would have retained these practices from Catholicism as important communal acts, even after the English Reformation.[6] He points out that Old Hamlet represents an extreme case, because as a ghost he embodies a "malfunction of religion," where the usual rites and intercessions have failed to put him to rest.[7] In this case, memory urges prayer as an intercession with the divine, much like Hamlet asks of Ophelia when he requests, "in thy orisons be all my sins remembered" (8.90–91). At the end of the play, by contrast, Hamlet does not need Horatio's intervention with God, but rather with the state of his living memory. He realizes that the legacy of his life as prince and near-ruler of Denmark is at stake, and he seeks to craft the final understanding of his actions through Horatio.

At this point, however, Fortinbras takes subtle control of the narrative through control of the corpses. Horatio starts his narrative introduction by saying "give order that these bodies / High on a stage be placed to view" (19.336–337). He seems to intend that the volume of death displayed in these four bodies (along with the remembered bodies of Polonius, Ophelia, Rosencrantz, and Guildenstern) will give weight to his story and reinforce his moral purpose. Fortinbras readily agrees to hear Horatio's account, but he refocuses the instructions about the bodies solely on Hamlet:

> Let four captains
> Bear Hamlet like a soldier to the stage,
> For he was likely, had he been put on,
> To have proved most royal; and for his passage
> The soldiers' music and the rite of war
> Speak loudly for him. (19.354–359).

Rather than a display of tragic consequences, Fortinbras repurposes the moment to give Hamlet a military funeral. He singles the Danish prince out as a noble, courageous, and worthy rival, whose lived life and princely promise deserve celebrating.

This likely strikes the audience as odd, since we've seen nothing martial to Hamlet's character in the preceding play, other than the sporting duel that claimed his life. Indeed, the Danish prince has repeatedly defined himself as a scholar and lamented his lack of action or options for action. In this moment, however, the story of Hamlet as presented in the previous hours on the stage is less important than how Hamlet fits into Fortinbras's own narrative. Hamlet saw Fortinbras as a foil for himself in Act Four when he observed the Norwegian prince, a man of his own age and condition, leading an army to defend and regain his honor. The audience can only assume that Fortinbras has similarly seen Hamlet as a sort of counterpart, possibly imagining him as a future adversary as the two rehearse the battles fought by their fathers. Thus, by lauding Hamlet's potential military prowess and royal greatness, Fortinbras claims some of these qualities for himself. Hamlet's story is part of his story; by shaping the public narrative of the Danish prince, he augments his own reputation and mythology. Moreover, by giving the body such prominent display and respect as a fallen hero (Claudius is, at best, afforded mention as one of "the bodies" to be removed a few lines later), he provides a visual representation of these events as he and Horatio will commence narrating the transition of power in Denmark.

This concern with the honorable disposition of an enemy's body (and his story) crowns the end of numerous other plays, as well—especially those about the virtues of leadership. At the very end of *Julius Caesar*, Antony and Octavius enter the scene with their soldiers and discover that Brutus has died with a little help from his friends. They finally encounter the man they've been fighting for months in a civil war, and he has acknowledged their victory by taking his own life. The logic of the scene, as well as the final stage direction ("*Exeunt with Brutus' body*"), indicates that their following conversation takes place with Brutus's corpse visually present and as the central object of interest. Rather than exult over Brutus's end, their words express lament at the loss of his nobility. On hearing the method of his death, Marc Antony says:

> This was the noblest Roman of them all.
> All the conspirators save only he
> Did that they did in envy of great Caesar.
> He only in general honest thought
> And common good to all made one of them.
> His life was gentle, and the elements
> So mixed in him that nature might stand up
> And say to all the world, "This was a man." (5.5.67–74).

These last words, in particular, seem a far cry from Antony's repeated and deeply ironic statement earlier in the play that "Brutus is an honorable man."

We might consider the possibility that the intervening time has proven to Antony how right Brutus and his cause were, but as he's standing alongside Octavius, that conclusion seems unlikely. Rather, the more probable answer here is that, Brutus being dead, Antony gains nothing by fighting him. Brutus is no longer an active participant in any quarrel— only his memory and the bloody corpse in the center of the stage remain of him. Certainly, Antony may continue his fight with Brutus' memory and the ideas he stood for, but only a few short scenes earlier, the play showed us that this was Brutus's downfall. When he recognizes the coming end to the war, he says, "Caesar, thou art mighty yet. / Thy spirit walks abroad and turns our swords / In our own proper entrails" (5.3.94–96). Having killed Caesar himself, Brutus must fight against Caesar's legacy. This presents an unwinnable situation for him, since fighting a dead and absent enemy becomes a kind of dangerous shadow boxing where only Brutus can be hurt.

Brutus having been conquered, then, Antony can acknowledge his good qualities. What he did may have been treasonous, but he did it according to the most Roman of virtues. Standing over the body, Antony repurposes his story from that of regicide to one of a man guilty only of immoderate devotion to the state. Octavius picks up this thread and takes it a step farther, simultaneously letting this narrative dictate the treatment of Brutus's body and letting that treatment reinforce the narrative:

> According to his virtue let us use him,
> With all respect and rites of burial.
> Within my tent his bones shall lie,
> Most like a soldier, ordered honorably. (5.5.75–8).

In proclaiming this, Octavius establishes himself as a fair ruler who can recognize and reward virtue, even in his enemies. Moreover, he takes ownership of Brutus's story in a very real way as he takes ownership of the body, folding both into his own national narrative of Rome on the cusp of empire.

The possession of the physical body seems to hold great importance in these plays. Fortinbras and Octavius do not simply appeal to the names of their deceased, *quondam* adversaries; they valorize Hamlet and Brutus's bodies through display in a military funeral and a place of honor in the general's tent, respectively. These are very tangible objects that point to something larger outside themselves, namely the spirits of two men and the associated lives they lived. We may think here of Augustine's definition of a sign as "a thing which of itself makes some other thing come to mind, beside the impression it presents to the senses,"[8] which allows the corpses to function as signs for the lives they lived. By laying ahold of a physical sign for something ephemeral, these victors obtain the ability to shape the nature of the "signified" in the Augustinian sense. Lisa Frienkel suggests that this "theology of figure," specifically that "the *flesh* is the *figure* (typos in Greek; *figura* in Latin) of the *spirit*," was crucially important for Shakespeare's audience, since it lies at the heart of numerous issues of Protestant theology.[9] She demonstrates that the linking of body and soul, one pointing to the condition of the other as complementary parts of one entity, dominated the imaginative conception of humanity from the time of Augustine until the early sixteenth century. At that point, Martin Luther's idea that flesh and spirit work in opposition to one another, only ever united in moments of grace offered by the sacraments, redefined the relationship of the spiritual to the physical.[10] To reduce the soul to something expressed and represented by the body is to oversimplify the nature of man. Brutus is far more than the body he leaves behind, or even a legacy of the actions that his body performed.

Thomas Cranmer discusses the idea of physical signs and figures as a foundational tenet of the English church, as a way to help English readers struggling with the relationship of the corporeal and the spiritual. In the preface to his *Answer to a Crafty and Sophisticated Cavillation Devised by Stephen Gardiner* (1551), he proposes a way that his reader should understand these concepts:

> First, this word "sacrament" I do sometimes use (as it is many times taken among writers and holy doctors) for the sacramental bread, water, or wine; as when they say, that *sacramentum est sacrae rei signum*, "a sacrament is the sign of an holy thing."[11]

As he progresses in the book, he devotes a significant amount of space to understanding what it means for a physical object to be a "sign of an holy thing." Ultimately, he explains that such sacramental things allow access to deeper understanding. About the Lord's Supper, he says, "the bread is a figure and a sacrament of Christ's body. And yet, as he giveth the bread to be eaten with our mouths, so he giveth his very body to be eaten with our faith."[12] So, too, in baptism, "the washing outwardly in water is not a vain token, but teacheth such a washing as God worketh inwardly."[13] I have elsewhere described Cranmer's definition of sacraments as "figures, but more than figures," and "analogies that do not negate their initial terms but employ them and their immediate effects to provide understanding" of something abstract.[14] This potentially provides a useful way to understand the role of the corpses discussed so far. The body that Fortinbras has brought to the stage is Hamlet, but it is not Hamlet. It is only the remaining physical element of the person that was Hamlet, but much like Cranmer's description of the sacramental bread or water, it points to the fullness of the prince's life and identity in which it took part. The conceptual difference it holds from the sacraments is that they engage a divinely ordained meaning that is reinforced by the institutional Church. The significance of Hamlet's body becomes unstable at the moment of his death. In the fraught political situations of these and similar plays, a leader's death—and specifically the resulting corpse—leaves open the possibility of negotiation of its final significance. In *Hamlet*, Fortinbras firmly settles the question of what Hamlet's body means, and Octavius does likewise in *Julius Caesar*, establishing some element of stability that works to their respective advantages in the final moments of both plays.

By contrast, Henry V's funeral at the beginning of Shakespeare's *1 Henry VI* shows us a royal body as cipher or figure still under debate. While Fortinbras and Octavius both step into the interpretive rupture to decisively shape the narrative of the deceased and assert their authority through an ownership of that narrative, the nobles here disagree on how to interpret the corpse of the dead king. Henry's body is a figure for the life he lived as king, but also a cipher for the loss the country has suffered with his death. His brother, the Duke of Gloucester, begins with common and expected funerary rhetoric for a heroic king:

> Virtue he had, deserving to command.
> His brandished sword did blind men with his beams.
> His arms spread wider than a dragon's wings.
> His sparkling eyes, replete with wrathful fire,
> More dazzled and drove back his enemies
> Than the midday sun, fierce bent against their faces. (1.1.9–14)

Gloucester here attempts to cast Henry as a conquering hero and his legacy as one of victory, valor, and nobility. The rest of the scene, however, seems to undermine, or at least question, the legitimacy of this story for the English. Exeter immediately responds to this paean by asking "We mourn in black; why mourn we not in blood?" lamenting their obsequious attention to a "wooden coffin," when they should be getting on with business of waging war on France (1.1.17). This reference simultaneously draws attention to Henry's corpse while also dismissing it. It has become an object to him without relevance, if not without meaning, in the present moment.

Winchester, by contrast, attempts to build on Gloucester's original rhetoric, while also claiming the story of the deceased king in their presence for the benefit of his own institution, the Church:

> He was a king blessed of the King of Kings.
> Unto the French, the dreadful judgment day
> So dreadful will not be as was his sight.
> The battles of the Lord of Hosts he fought.
> The church's prayers made him so prosperous. (1.1.28–32).

Here, the audience becomes aware of the underlying conflict. Gloucester's angry rejoinder that "Had not churchmen prayed / His thread of life had not so soon decayed" (1.1.33–34) indicates that the institutional Church had been an obstacle, rather than a contributing factor, to Henry's great deeds. Much like the examples discussed above, Winchester uses his proximity to a former enemy's corpse to recast their relationship as one of alliance. He hopes to claim a role in the king's victories and, in doing so, solidify his position of power. In this case, however, his narrative faces opposition. In the context of the nobles gathered, Henry's body is distinctly less open as a signifier. Each of these men, in fact, has a very closed, even totalizing, view of Henry that conflicts with the others. Significantly, this reflects the very real power dynamic at work among the nobles themselves—none of them possesses the clear authority to decipher what this dead body means, and their attempts to do so represent multiple attempts to specifically claim that authority.

The disposition of the body itself presents an interesting problem in this scene. The opening stage direction includes the coffin: "*Dead march. Enter the funeral procession of Henry the Fifth*," attended on by the various nobles (1.1.1). Most modern editions dismiss the casket mid-argument after Bedford's line "Let's to the altar. Heralds, wait on us" (1.1.45), specifying that the heralds remove the body accompanied by the Duke of Somerset and the Earl of Warwick.[15] Problematically, however, the characters make clear reference to the corpse's presence some 20 lines later. When the messenger arrives from France and recites a litany of the French towns that the English have lost, Bedford chides him, saying:

> What sayest thou, man, before dead Henry's corpse?
> Speak softly, or the loss of those great towns
> Will make him burst his lead and rise from death. (1.1.62–64)

This hardly seems to suggest that the dead king, in some nearby chapel, might overhear; rather it implies that he still lies close at hand, physically in the middle of their argument. A look at the folio text reveals that it has no stage direction about removing the body at this moment of the action. In fact, it never denotes a specific place where the heralds and the casket leave the stage. Likewise, the scene lacks any direction about when the various messengers should exit. The modern stage directions, understandably, aim to provide this information at moments that seem to make sense according to the dialogue.[16] Yet, the conflict between what they indicate and what the dialogue indicates with regard to Henry's body suggests that we might see something very different happening in this scene. A staging scenario at the opposite end of the spectrum, where no indicated exits means the characters stay and accumulate on stage until the end, produces a different effect entirely. In this case, rather than the fairly orderly scenario provided to us by the modern text, where the arguing nobles are left alone onstage to depart one by one, we have something increasingly chaotic, disorganized, and uncentered. Gloucester, Exeter, Bedford, and Winchester don't carve out a private space to air their grievances with one another; they become increasingly angry and distracted in the midst of an ongoing royal funeral, each storming out to pursue his own stated plot. Moreover, the messengers arriving on stage are forgotten as soon as their words are delivered, and they are never officially dismissed by those they serve. The competing priorities, the interrupted and broken ceremony, and the lack of clear leadership show us an England truly in disarray. In short, it is hard to imagine a more apt image to presage the rest of *1 Henry VI* than Henry V's unburied corpse forgotten by those with other agendas and surrounded by bit players without a clear sense of whom to follow.

As such, Henry's reign lacks a sense of completion and definitive finality. We see a funeral started, but never completed. The competing perspectives of the nobles first find literalization in the mobs armed with sticks and rocks, and eventually play into the bloody civil war that will propel England through the entire first tetralogy. It's almost easy to forget the funeral that opens the action, and it may be more central to the plot than we often acknowledge. Henry's legacy, like his body, remains unfinished business—unsettled, unresolved, and waiting to be put to rest.

In a historical context, we can see the impact a royal burial can have in the way James I treated the body of his predecessor Elizabeth only a few years later. Julia M. Walker has detailed how James sought to realign the legacy of Elizabeth's reign by repositioning where and how her body could be read among the English monarchs.[17] In the first few years after coming to the English throne, he had Elizabeth removed from her tomb near Henry VII in Henry's chapel in Westminster, reserving that spot for his own later burial. Instead, he had her coffin re-interred in the same sarcophagus with her half-sister Mary I in an adjoining aisle. At the same time, he ordered the body of his mother, Mary Queen of Scots, moved to Westminster and placed in a sumptuous tomb among the forebears of great English monarchs. Fundamentally, "James was placing his own mother in a line of fruitful dynasty, while Elizabeth and her equally childless sister were isolated from the line of inherited power."[18] He does this specifically by recontextualizing their bodies. He has Elizabeth physically removed from association with her grandfather's authority and relegated to the literal position of a dynastic dead end. Moreover, by reserving her former resting spot for himself, he erases (or at least occludes) some element of his Scottishness and claims a position in the continuing English descent and power of Henry VII.

The anonymous play, *Locrine* (1595), near the end of Elizabeth's reign provides one final example to indicate how significant such a burial location could be in the long-term deciphering of a leader's body. The play depicts the legendary history of Brutus's three sons, Locrine, Camber, and Albanect, as they divide the kingdom of Britain after their father's death and, ultimately, war bitterly with one another. In the final scene of the play, Guendoline, the one-time queen and wife of the title character, very pointedly shapes the national narrative of the Britons[19] through her instructions about burying her estranged husband:

> And as for Locrine, our deceased spouse,
> Because he was the sonne of mightie Brute,
> To whom we owe our country, lives, and goods,
> He shall be buried in a stately tombe,
> Close by his aged father Brutus bones,
> With such great pomp and great solemnitie,
> As well beseames so brave a prince as he was.
> Let Estrild lie without the shallow vauts,
> Without the honour due unto the dead,
> Because she was the author of the warre. (2255–64).[20]

Unlike the previous examples, Locrine has done little in this play worthy of reverence or celebration. He broke his pledge to his father that he would maintain alliances with his brothers. He abandoned his wife for the foreign queen, Estrild, and then waged war on all parties involved. When his eventual defeat seemed inevitable, he and Estrild both committed suicide. Yet, within her speech here, Guendoline makes clear that Locrine will be remembered as a heroic king. If his own actions did him no favors, the people can commemorate him as a son of Brutus. Although he abandoned his duties and fought against his own people while alive, Guendoline will put things to rights using his dead corpse. By giving him a public royal burial, interred next to his father and separated from Estrild, she establishes this as the official history. In the end, the placement of his body in Brutus's tomb overrides and overwrites everything he did.

This may bring us back full circle to Richard III's body and the fraught question of his burial. In her official statement on the occasion, Queen Elizabeth II (herself not in attendance that day) said, "The reinterment of King Richard III is an event of great national and international significance. Today we recognize a king who lived through turbulent times and whose Christian faith sustained him in life and death." Likewise, John F. Burns reported in the *New York Times*, "Some saw the message encoded in the public acclaim less as one of embracing the idea of Richard as a 'good king,' [...] than one of redemption beyond the grave, a theme that has compelling force, across all ages and religions."[21] As with the early modern dramatic examples, there seems to be an effort in this modern instance to correct the actions of the past by acknowledging their part in the larger historical narrative. More than 500 years after his death, Richard's body received a new official interpretation, reframing his place in English monarchy.

Notes

1. Timothy J. Wengert, *Human Freedom, Christian Righteousness: Philip Melanchthon's Exegetical Dispute with Erasmus of Rotterdam*, p. 153.
2. All references to Shakespeare's plays come from *The New Oxford Shakespeare*, gen. ed. Gary Taylor, John Jowett, Terri Bourus, and Gabriel Egan (Oxford: Oxford University Press, 2016).
3. It should be noted that, for editorial reasons explained in the introduction to the *New Oxford Shakespeare*, the scenes of this play text are numbered continuously throughout.
4. Harry Morris provides a survey of the *memento mori* lyric trope in early modern English poetry in the appendix to his book *Last Things in Shakespare*.
5. The Latin phrase *Eram quod es, eris quod sum* ("I was what you are, you will be what I am") was a common motto associated with the *memento mori* tradition, spoken by the dead as a reminder to the living. Specifically, these words often accompanied the artistic trope of the *danse macabre*, which depicted Death leading away people of all classes and social positions. Shakespeare's audience may have been most familiar with Han Holbein's *The Dance of Death* (1538), where the seventh image shows death removing the

crown from a seated monarch. See Hans Holbein, *The Dance of Death*.
6. Cummings, "Remembering the Dead in *Hamlet*," pp. 200–217. He echoes and builds on Stephen Greenblatt's idea that one central aspect of *Hamlet* is a protestant character haunted by a Catholic past in *Hamlet in Purgatory*. On this idea, see also Freeman, "This Side of Purgatory: Ghostly Fathers and the Recusant Legacy in *Hamlet*," pp. 222–259.
7. Cummings, p. 209.
8. Augustine, *On Christian Learning* (Book II), p. 158.
9. Freinkel, *Reading Shakespeare's Will: The Theology of Figure from Augustine to the Sonnets*. Freinkel argues that the telling of any person's story must begin at its end, capped and represented by the figure of the name. Part of what I'm hoping to show here is that, in many of these scenes, the physical body of the deceased becomes the literal manifestation of that figural name and the story to which it points.
10. See, in particular, Freinkel, Chapter 3, "Luther Disfiguring the Word".
11. Cranmer, *Writings and Disputations of Thomas Cranmer, Archbishop of Canterbury, Martyr, 1556, Relative to the Lord's Supper*, p. 3.
12. Ibid., p. 15.
13. Ibid., p. 16.
14. Harries, "Sacral Objects and the Measure of Kingship in Shakespeare's *Henry VI*," pp. 148–149.
15. Among other editions of this play, the Pelican, the Norton, and the New Oxford Shakespeare all contain a version of this stage direction following line 45.
16. The Norton edition also contains a footnote justifying the editor's choice, saying that the heralds need to leave the stage at this moment to change costumes for the next scene where they undoubtedly play French soldiers.
17. Walker, "Reading the Tombs of Elizabeth I," pp. 510–530.
18. Ibid., p. 524.
19. The modern concept of a "nation" would, of course, be anachronistic in the mythic past involving Brutus and his sons. For an Elizabethan audience, especially given Ate's speech that ends the play, such a notion is in fact very central to this story.

20. *The Lamentable Tragedy of Locrine*, ed. Robert B. McKerrow.
21. Burns, "Richard III Gets a Royal Burial, on Second Try".

References

Augustine. "On Christian Learning (Book II)." In *The Norton Anthology of Theory and Criticism*. 2nd edition. Edited by Vincent B. Leitch et al. New York: Norton, 2010.

Burns, John F. "Richard III Gets a Royal Burial, on Second Try." *The New York Times* (March 26, 2015).

Cranmer, Thomas. *Writings and Disputations of Thomas Cranmer, Archbishop of Canterbury, Martyr, 1556, Relative to the Lord's Supper*. Edited by John Edmund Cox. Cambridge: Cambridge University Press, 1844; rpt. 1968.

Cummings, Brian. "Remembering the Dead in *Hamlet*." In *The Cambridge Companion to Shakespeare and Religion*. Edited by Hannibal Hamlin. Cambridge: Cambridge University Press, 2019. pp. 200–217.

Freeman, John. "This Side of Purgatory: Ghostly Fathers and the Recusant Legacy in *Hamlet*." In *Shakespeare and the Culture of Christianity in Early Modern England*. Edited by Dennis Taylor and David N. Beauregard. New York: Fordham University Press, 2003. pp. 222–259.

Freinkel, Lisa. *Reading Shakespeare's Will: The Theology of Figure from Augustine to the Sonnets*. New York: Columbia University Press, 2002.

Greenblatt, Stephen. *Hamlet in Purgatory*. Princeton, NJ: Princeton University Press, 2001.

Harries, Brian J. "Sacral Objects and the Measure of Kingship in Shakespeare's *Henry VI*." In *Stages of Engagement: Drama and Religion in Post-Reformation England*. Edited by James D. Mardock and Katherine R. McPherson. Pittsburgh, PA: Duquesne University Press, 2014. pp. 135–154.

Holbein, Hans. *The Dance of Death*. Edited and with commentary by Ulinka Rublack. New York: Penguin, 2016.

Morris, Harry. *Last Things in Shakespeare*. Tallahassee, FL: Florida State University Press, 1985.

Shakespeare, William. *The New Oxford Shakespeare: The Complete Works*. General Edited by Gary Taylor, John Jowett, Terri Bourus, and Gabriel Egan. Oxford: Oxford University Press, 2016.

The Lamentable Tragedy of Locrine. Edited by Robert B. McKerrow. Malone Society Reprints. Oxford: Oxford University Press, 1908.

Walker, Julia M. "Reading the Tombs of Elizabeth I." *English Literary Renaissance* 26.3 (1996): 510–530.

Wengert, Timothy J. *Human Freedom, Christian Righteousness: Philip Melanchthon's Exegetical Dispute with Erasmus of Rotterdam*. Oxford: Oxford University Press, 1998.

CHAPTER 4

"As Thou Art, I Once Was": Death and the Bodies in *2 Henry IV*

Eileen Sperry

One of the first images of Christopher Sutton's *Disce Mori*, a popular seventeenth-century English *ars moriendi*, depicts a stereotypical early modern deathbed scene (see Fig. 4.1).

An older man lies in bed, pointing admonishingly at the young man standing by his side. The dying man's warning is spelled out across the top of the frame: "As thou art, I once was," he says, "As I am, thou shalt be." His primary audience is a young soldier, dressed in full armor and holding a lance. This young man stands next to the bed, but his body

---

Many thanks to Andrew Bozio, David Morrow, Ineke Murakami, Christi Spain-Savage, Maggie Vinter, and Pattie Wareh for their generous and constructive feedback on this chapter. Additional thanks to the Folger Shakespeare Library for their support in this research.

E. Sperry (✉)
Skidmore College, Saratoga Springs, New York, USA

© The Author(s), under exclusive license to Springer Nature Switzerland AG 2022
W. E. Engel and G. Williams (eds.), *The Shakespearean Death Arts*, Palgrave Shakespeare Studies,
https://doi.org/10.1007/978-3-030-88490-1_4

67

Fig. 4.1 Deathbed scene (Christopher Sutton, *Disce Mori*)

is angled away; with one hand on his hip, he looks backward over his shoulder in a clear sign of disdain.

Sometimes rendered in its original Latin—*tu fui, ego eris*—the dying man's message is a conventional one, a familiar trope of the early modern death arts. Like many other *memento mori*, the *tu fui* form relies on a set of internal binaries. First, it necessarily involves two people: a dead—or, in this case, dying—speaker, and a young, healthy listener. These provide the "I" and "thou" of the statement, the self/other. In addition, the motif requires several temporal binaries, asking the listener to think about the relationships between past/present and present/future. These binaries come together to create a central paradox. In each pair, the objects must be utterly identical, totally the same: "I" and "thou" are subject to the same conditions of humanity, the same fragile materiality and will suffer the same eventual fate of death. The things that happened in the past are happening in the present and will happen again in future. The form

4 "AS THOU ART, I ONCE WAS": DEATH AND THE BODIES IN *2 HENRY IV* 69

makes the claim that every living body is also a corpse in waiting, and that any apparent difference between the two is superficial; all bodies are identical, and all bodies must die. At the same time, the *tu fui* also insists on total difference. The living and the dead, the present and the future, these are represented—grammatically, dramatically, visually, logically—as distinct from one another. There is the speaker who knows death, and the listener who refuses to recognize it; a present where death is only a vague threat, and a future where it is an unavoidable certainty.

In what follows, I explore how the many paradoxes of the *tu fui* intersect with and often run counter to the conventions of linear narratives and, in doing so, force us to think about the relationship between literary form and our understanding of mortality. I first look to Sutton's treatise, considering how this *tu fui* image functions as a paratextual landmark that shapes and guides his readers' experience of *Disce Mori*. Following that, I turn to *2 Henry IV* and Hal's misrecognition of his father's death in Act 4. In this moment, Shakespeare uses both the *tu fui* and the related language of the sovereign's two bodies to engage the play's concerns with lineage and continuity in the face of certain death. In both texts, readers and audience members can feel the friction between the two forms at work. Both explore the model of mortality afforded by the *tu fui*'s dialectic structures, a framework that imagines death as both present and absent, inevitable and indefinitely delayed. Ultimately, however, both works revert to narrative, resolving the *tu fui*'s dialectics and reestablishing a linear approach to mortality. These moments of collision and resolution, I argue, reveal the complexity of early modern attitudes about death and the integral role of form in shaping those beliefs.

Disce Mori was first published in England in 1600. This text, like its many *ars moriendi* predecessors, focused on helping its readers prepare for a good death. For Sutton, clergy of the Church of England and devoted Protestant, this meant a lifetime of spiritual discipline: studying scripture, living righteously, and praying regularly. As D.W. Atkinson has noted, while the genre was grounded in medieval Catholic traditions, "Protestants [...] retained what was valuable of the established tradition and adapted it to a theological framework" more suited to new orthodoxy.[1] *Disce Mori*, in particular, is an excellent illustration of the genre's adaptability to a wide range of Reform doctrines. Sutton, Atkinson argues elsewhere, demonstrates a strategically ecumenical approach to dying; "In *Disce Mori*," he writes, "the major elements of the *ars moriendi*," including both Calvinist emphasis on election and traditional Catholic interest in the specific sufferings of damnation, "are modified to signal Sutton's wish for a unified Christianity."[2] *Disce Mori* shows its readers "howe behoovefull it is for everie Christian man, soberly to meditate of his end" and "That we need not feare Death, much lesse to meditate thereof."[3] Sutton directs "the manner of commending the sicke into the hands of God, at the houre of Death," and gives prayers for "those that undertake any dangerous attempt, either by sea or land, wherein they are in perill of Death," so that these may "make themselves readie for God."[4]

Perhaps because of its ecumenical bent, *Disce Mori* immediately proved popular with English readers. The text, a squat duodecimo of twenty-two gatherings, was printed first in 1600 by John Windet, who also produced subsequent editions in 1601, 1602, 1604, 1607, and 1609. After that, *Disce Mori* was reprinted by Ambrose Garband in 1613, by George Purslowe twice in 1616 and once in 1618, and finally by Ame Hunt in 1662. The treatise then appeared alongside Sutton's subsequent work, *Disce Vivere*, in combined editions printed in 1626 by I. Dawson, 1629 by I. Beal, and 1634 by Richard Badger. All told, *Disce Mori* appeared in at least eleven stand-alone editions and three dual editions. Such popularity was not entirely unusual for an *ars moriendi* treatise. Thomas Becon's *Sick Mans Salve*, for instance, first appearing in 1558, went through "between twenty-nine and thirty-one known editions (more if one counts those contained in the larger collections of Becon's works) and remained in demand for six decades after his death."[5] Still, Sutton's lengthy run puts *Disce Mori* among the most widely read texts of the early seventeenth century, making it an important artifact of England's early modern death arts.

The illustration of the deathbed scene is present from the text's first edition and remains a stable fixture of the treatise's opening paratexts throughout its long print run. In the 1600 edition, it appears at the end of the first gathering, positioned between Sutton's letter to the reader and a letter from an Oxford reader, R.K., testifying to the treatise's value. While R.K.'s letter disappears from the next edition, the deathbed scene remains in place as the image closest to the beginning of the treatise. This position suggests that a reader's experience of *Disce Mori* would be contextualized by and grounded in the model of mortality afforded by the *tu fui* form. This death art, like many of its fellow *memento mori*, invites the viewer into what Rose Marie San Juan describes as a deep sense of identification. *Memento mori* present viewers with the growth, death, and decay of another's body as a way of making them recognize the inevitability of such changes to their own bodies. Looking at another commonplace of the *memento mori* tradition, the de-fleshed skull, San Juan notes how that particular image creates a kind of empathy between viewer and object. Viewers impose a face and thus a persona, on the bones, creating in effect a mirror of ourselves. But, like the *tu fui*, this exchange relies on an internal paradox:

> But the problems of faciality are further compounded when the face is projected within the skull. There is a longstanding link between the materiality of the skull and the allegorical tradition of the *memento mori*, not surprising given that bones, due to their enduring properties, not only remain after death but also convey a sense of wholeness and containment that gives them the semblance of presence [....] Yet the skull's undeniable ability to forge a connection between the dead and the living is highly ambiguous, charged as it is by its transitory status in which presence and absence, visibility and invisibility, can never be fully extricated from each other. The skull thus becomes a key transit point in life and death, both the furthest point before complete material disappearance and oblivion, and the closest point from which one might imagine being looked at from the other side.[6]

The skull, while inviting the viewer to project onto it a face (and thus an identity), also resists that projection; it is both a reminder of personhood and a denial of that same quality. The viewer thus sees in it both a version of themselves—the future of their own face—and something utterly foreign.

Such is the paradox of Sutton's deathbed image. The dying man's gesture emphasizes similarity and identification; he tries to impress on the young man that they are fundamentally the same. But, as is evident from the young man's response, this claim fails to take hold. The young man's refusal to acknowledge the inevitability of death is emblematic of the societal problems Sutton's treatise is intended to address. Individual sinfulness, he argues, is a result of the failure to recognize one's own mortality. Sutton dedicates a chapter early on in *Disce Mori* to "the causes why men so seldome enter into a serious remembrance of their end."[7] The neglect of our own deaths, he continues, is an extension of Satan's Edenic deception. "To induce the sons of men lightly and loosely to pass over a religious remembrance of this their end," he writes, "is the sleight of him, whose business was, and is, at, and since the fall of Adam, to slay souls, *Nequaqum morienmini;* Tush, saith he, you shall not die at all."[8]

And while the evidence of the fallen world should lay bare that deception, Sutton notes, humanity seems to cling desperately to the temptation of exceptionalism.

> It is a marvel above marvels that in a battle where so many before our eyes go to the ground, paying the debt to nature daily, our remiss hearts can take no warning to enter into some remembrance of our state. The neighbours fire cannot but give warning of approaching flames. *Mihi heri, tibi hodie*: Yesterday to me, today to thee, saith the wise man: whose turn is next, God only knows [....][9]

Even when death is clearly visible, he notes, our human tendency is toward denial: they may die, but not I. Entering into *Disce Mori* through this deathbed woodcut, therefore, allows readers to remain in this state of plausible denial. The two competing claims of the image—the older man's insistence that the young man will become the same as him, and the young man's insistence that he is different and will suffer a different fate—form a dialectic that is in effect sustained over the entirety of Sutton's treatise. While the textual argument confirms, over and over again, that the young man is wrong, the very existence of the book belies the psychological and rhetorical hold of that denial on the readers' thinking. Even if the reader can easily acknowledge that *of course* the young man will die, they may be much less likely to embrace that truth about themselves.

It isn't until the appearance of a subsequent woodcut, added to the 1601 edition, that the young man's error is fully confirmed. Several hundred pages later, after the end of the body of the text but before a series of allegoric dialogues, appears a second image—the other half of the pair (see Fig. 4.2).[10] The young man is now dead on the battlefield, broken lance in one hand. Standing above him is a skeleton, wearing a sash and waving a flag victoriously. The skeleton has one foot planted squarely on the fallen soldier's chest, demonstrating his conquest. The paradox of the initial *tu fui*—the notion that while the soldier, like the dying man, is subject to the inevitability of death, perhaps he (like the reader) might also somehow be different—collapses in this second image. Death the great leveler wins out.

What this second image does, in effect, is shift the treatise's prevailing formal framing device from *tu fui* to narrative. The deathbed scene relies on the absence of time in order to facilitate its characteristic dialectic. That is, as a static visual medium, the *tu fui* contains no movement forward or

4 "AS THOU ART, I ONCE WAS": DEATH AND THE BODIES IN *2 HENRY IV* 73

Fig. 4.2 Death Triumphant (Christopher Sutton, *Disce Mori*)

backward; it allows only for a perpetual present, a single moment captured outside the flow of time. This is what allows a message like the dying man's to stand; in a mode comprised only of present, a claim that one's past is another's future—as I am, thou shalt be—cannot be proven or unproven, because nothing can change. The *tu fui*, in this way, is as much an escape from mortality as it is a reflection on it. At the very same time the form insists on the inevitability of death, it also takes the reader out of the entropic flow of time responsible for that inevitability. However, the addition of the second woodcut at the other end of Sutton's treatise imposes a narrative structure on these two moments. The soldier now exists within time, rather than outside it. With the deathbed image now past, the victory woodcut becomes his future, a future that ends (as it must) in death. These two images, viewed retrospectively, ground the narrative arc of Sutton's treatise, emblematizing the reader's passage from denial to acceptance, from youthful resistance to inevitable defeat.

In Sutton's text, therefore, we can begin to see and feel the intersection of these two forms—narrative and *tu fui*. On the one hand, the *tu fui* sentiment of the deathbed image calls us to approach mortality as a paradox: our death is always present, always imminent, and yet never actually realized. And on the other hand, the appearance of the second image at the close of the text suggests the foreclosure of those possibilities, the movement of time finally catching up with us. Rather than an accident of the paratextual shuffling of Sutton's many printers, this kind of collision is occasioned by the unique affordances of the *tu fui* itself. To further explore the ways this death art intersects with other literary forms, I turn now to Shakespeare's *2 Henry IV*, a play explicitly concerned with the rituals and forms of dying.

Here, in many ways, King Henry and Hal are the ideal candidates for an onstage *tu fui*. As both father and son and king and heir, their relationship is one of overdetermined continuity, of lineage and repetition. Henry, hearing of Hal's ongoing association with Poins and company, wryly refers to his son as "the noble image of my youth" (4.3.55).[11] Rather than just describing a sense of physical resemblance, Henry's choice of term here—"image"—signifies a far more substantial connection. The term occurs in only one other place in the play, in the Lord Chief Justice's speech to Hal after his father's death. There, explaining why he acted toward Hal as he had, the Lord Chief Justice justifies himself by noting that he was acting as the "image" of the late king:

> I then did use the person of your father;
> The image of his power lay then in me;
> And in th' administration of his law,
> Whiles I was busy for the commonwealth,
> Your Highness pleased to forget my place,
> The majesty and power of law and justice,
> The image of the King whom I presented,
> And struck me in my very seat of judgment [....]
>   If the deed were ill,
> Be you contented, wearing now the garland,
> To have a son set your decrees at nought,
> To pluck down justice from your awful bench,
> To trip the course of law, and blunt the sword
> That guards the peace and safety of your person;
> Nay, more, to spurn at your most royal image,
> And mock your workings in a second body. (5.2.72–79, 82–89)

Here, the Lord Chief Justice challenges Hal to imagine himself in his father's shoes, wondering how he would feel if he also had a son who "spurn[ed] at your most royal image" and "mock[ed] your workings in a second body." This imagistic relationship goes beyond filial connection; the Lord Chief Justice also notes that, in exercising royal power, he too became "the image of the King," acting as an extension of his person in enforcing the law. To be the "image" of another, therefore, means acting as a social and political proxy—to be both oneself and another.

Such a transference of personhood is made possible partly by Henry's special status as monarch. Following the work of Ernst Kantorowicz, we know that early modern audiences would have been familiar with the political theology of the king's two bodies. Indeed, Kantorowicz argues, Shakespeare's work was integral in making this notion commonplace: "The legal concept of the King's Two Bodies cannot [...] be separated from Shakespeare. For if that curious image, which from modern constitutional thought has vanished all but completely, still has a very real and human meaning today, this is largely due to Shakespeare. It is he who has eternalized that metaphor."[12] The theory of the two bodies—the idea that the sovereign's personal body is both unique and mortal, but the body politic somehow both transferable and immortal—is, I'd like to suggest, itself a subspecies of the *tu fui* form. It is at its core a death art concerned with articulating the paradox of simultaneous identity (the everlasting body of the state) and difference (the multiple mortal bodies of subsequent monarchs). And while Kantorowicz proposes that, above all others, *Richard II* is "the tragedy of the King's Two Bodies," *2 Henry IV* has as much—perhaps more—to say about the possibilities and limitations of this political theology.

When the ailing Henry appears onstage at the beginning of Act 4, therefore, Shakespeare's audience is perhaps already calling to mind the peculiar affordances of royal death and their own expectations concerning the king's two bodies. Hal's subsequent entrance in Scene 3, coupled with Henry's position in his literal deathbed, reinforces the influence of the *tu fui* form on this interaction.[13]

With the actors on stage taking up positions not unlike the two individuals of Sutton's deathbed image—itself an echo of the long tradition of deathbed tableaus stretching back through medieval *ars moriendi*—there can be no question that audience members were primed to think about

Henry's death through the lens of the *tu fui*, as a moment of both separation and continuity. And so when Hal speaks to his supposedly dead father, the influence of the *tu fui* form on his thoughts is clear.

> Thy due from me
> Is tears and heavy sorrows of the blood,
> Which nature, love, and filial tenderness
> Shall, O dear father, pay thee plenteously.
> My due from thee is this imperial crown,
> Which, as immediate from thy place and blood,
> Derives itself to me.
> *[He puts the crown on his head].*
>   Lo, where it sits,
> Which God shall guard; and put the world's whole strength
> Into one giant arm, it shall not force
> This lineal honour from me. This from thee
> Will I to mine leave, as 'tis left to me. (4.3.167–173)

Hal sees his father's death as a moment both of transition and transaction; he imagines stepping seamlessly into his father's role as patriarch and monarch. With Henry's natural body presumed dead, Hal sees the English body politic flowing ceaselessly into himself. Henry has already articulated the resemblance between past and present; an old man on his deathbed, he has already told the audience that he once too was a youth like Hal—"as he is," we hear, "I once was." And likewise, Hal's reaction to his father's apparent death blends present and future. He notes that he too will rise to the role of king, a ruler who someday will likewise find himself on his deathbed, passing his crown to his own children. "As you are," Hal seems to say to his father's corpse, "I will be."

But Hal's assumptions are incorrect; Henry is, in fact, still very much alive, a fact that transforms this moment from an exemplum of the death arts into an illustration of how they might transform under pressure. Hal's error is, in part, fostered by the medium of performance. Like Juliet and Imogen, Henry's sleep is indistinguishable (at least to other characters) from his death. As Maggie Vinter has noted, this is because sleep and death are, from a performance standpoint, virtually indistinguishable. "The resemblance between sleep and death is compounded onstage," she writes, "since the postures of inactivity actors use to represent sleepers and bloodless bodies are identical."[14] This porous relationship between sleep and death is then compounded by Henry's special status as king.

As Benjamin Parris has argued, Shakespeare regularly exploits the trope of the sleeping monarch in order to explore the tenuous relationship between the king's two bodies. "Sleep creates an image of human imperfection in the sovereign body natural," he notes; "bodily life in sleep resembles death, and so the king's mortality resurfaces, even though his body natural's flaws are supposedly taken up and wiped away by the presence of the body politic."[15] Specifically, Parris argues, such scenes trouble the transition of power, making the anticipated seamless transition of body politic from sovereign to heir transparent and uncertain. Drawing attention to the materiality of the actor's body—and the king's natural body—such sleeping "deaths" in Shakespeare remind us that death itself falls beyond the limits of performance, phenomenologically resistant to replication.

But Hal's error here is not only a result of the nuances of embodied performance. Rather, as Henry points out when he confronts his son, the core error here is one of timing. Henry has *not* died, making this act of succession an act of sedition. When Henry rebukes Hal for his mistake, his criticism centers on Hal's overeager approach:

> I stay too long for thee, I weary thee.
> Dost thou so hunger for mine empty chair
> That thou wilt needs invest thee with my honours
> Before thy hour be ripe? [...]
> Thou hast stol'n that which, after some few hours,
> Were thine without offense; and at my death
> Thou hast seal'd up my expectation.
> Thy life did manifest thou loved'st me not,
> And thou wilt have me die assured of it.
> Thou hid'st a thousand daggers in thy thoughts,
> Whom thou hast whetted on thy stony heart
> To stab at half an hour of my life.
> What, canst thou not forbear me half an hour?
> Then get thee gone and dig my grave thyself [....] (4.3.221–224, 229–238)

Hal has jumped the gun, creating a fractured timeline. As Henry's response stresses, Hal has missed the mark only by mere minutes—"canst thou not forbear me half an hour?" Henry asks, indicating both his awareness that his death is imminent and the fact that the actions of these few moments are crucial. In Hal's eagerness to create an unbroken dynastic line, he has in fact ruptured political temporality to create a new reality in which his self-crowning precedes the king's death, echoing (to his father's horror) Henry's own act of usurpation.

The emphasis on time in Henry's response lays bare the conflict between *tu fui* and the narratives in which it is often embedded. Shakespeare creates the briefest of moments on stage in which Hal—and perhaps even the audience—is suspended in the paradoxes of the *tu fui*. Hal can be both himself and his father, the prince and the monarch; the sovereign can be both dead *and* alive. But this can be true for only moments before Henry and the audience realize its impossibility. And just as *Disce Mori* suspends the dialectic over the course of the treatise, separating the *tu fui* image and its resolution by hundreds of pages, Shakespeare creates a similar moment of suspension in those moments of misapprehension before time reasserts itself. For the political concerns of the play, narrative—lineage—is everything. As Henry points out, an uninterrupted line of succession is the difference between national wellbeing and a deadly power vacuum. And in order for that to happen, the dialectic of the *tu fui* must be resolved. Time must march on, and Hal must become not his father, but himself.

The *tu fui* form thus creates in its audience a set of paradoxical expectations: that all individuals are simultaneously the same and distinct, that time is both linear and utterly flat. And, when those expectations intersect with the conventions of narrative mortality, the result is a sense of increasing formal pressure: the *tu fui*'s dialectic structure is, ultimately, replaced by narrative linearity. In *2 Henry IV*, as shown above, Hal's drive for similarity and simultaneity—that he might, according to the conventions of the *tu fui* and the political theology of the king's two bodies, occupy that elusive moment in which the king is both dead *and* alive—runs counter to the need for the progression of dynastic time. In *Disce Mori*, the friction between forms is so strong that it appears to have shaped even the print history of the treatise itself. As I noted earlier, the 1601 edition of Sutton's text positions the pair of woodcuts on either end of the text of the treatise itself, creating a separation—and thus a kind of narrative suspension—of several hundred pages. While these paratexts remain stable for a few decades, in the final two editions (1634 and 1662), the victory woodcut is moved from its place following the treatise to the page just following the deathbed woodcut. The initial space of several hundred pages is reduced now to a single page turn. Rather than sustaining the claims of the deathbed scene over the entire treatise, readers would now encounter both the dialectic and its resolution in virtually the same moment, prior to reading Sutton's treatise. These late editions of *Disce Mori* begin not on a note of denial and resistance—a refusal to die—but with a stark reminder of death's inevitability. The *tu fui* is over almost before it has even begun to take hold.

Why is it, then, that these two disparate works—Sutton's *ars moriendi* treatise and Shakespeare's *2 Henry IV*—both illustrate this same effect? That is, why do both demonstrate the collapse of the *tu fui*'s internal paradoxes? The reason, I'd like to suggest, is formal: specifically, the conjunction of the *tu fui*'s form with the affordances of narrative. And while both *tu fui* and narrative call to mind the static use of form—of form as literary object—both, more importantly, participate in what recent work in formalist theory has described as the activity of form—of *forming*, shaping, of the ability of esthetic conventions to mold the political, social, phenomenological possibilities of the world. Following Ellen Rooney's call for critics to read for "the work that form does,"[16] Ben Burton and Elizabeth Scott-Baumann have noted that "form is as useful as a verb as a noun, and indeed [...] many of the problems of defining form as an object come into clearer focus when we think of it as an action or series of actions."[17] A literary or aesthetic form, the scholars of the Group Phi collective argue, "provides a way to make and remake the world through performing and intervening in an everyday imaginary."[18] "Forms matter," Caroline Levine has most recently noted, "because they shape what it is possible to think, say, and do in a given context."[19]

This critical framework is appropriate, perhaps even obligatory, when thinking about the early modern death arts. As William Engel and Grant Williams note in the introduction to this volume, early modern death was defined in and by its many formal manifestations: *ars moriendi, memento mori* motifs, the rich tradition of devotional literature surrounding death and dying, to name only a few. And in so many instances, mortality has been shaped by narrative. Take, for instance, Sutton's counsel to his readers. "Like the flower," he writes, "we have a time of growing, and a time of withering away againe."[20] Because of this, he urges his readers to practice "thriving husbandry, sowing the seed of godly actions in the field of a repentant heart that so at the Autumne or end of our age, we may reap the fruits of everlasting comfort."[21] Mortality, Sutton reminds us, is an effect of time; it is because we exist in and through time that our bodies fail and our lives end. To help make meaning out of this gradual decay, authors and artists thus frequently turned to narrative. Death is an ending, Sutton observes, the last part of the story; the flower withers, the year ends. The persistent grasp of this framework is apparent even when Sutton takes a more resurrectionist tone. "That which we count death is in the sequel a very birth day of life," Sutton later argues, "for that indeed makes us to live."[22] Even if death is transformed from an ending to a beginning, as Sutton does here, it still remains part of a linear, narrative structure.

While such narrative frameworks are incredibly useful for Sutton's purposes, helping to draw meaning out of the chaos of existence, they also introduce specific mimetic limitations when taken to their logical extremes. D. Vance Smith has recently noted that, particularly in medieval literature, narrative models of death created for Scholastic thinkers a kind of representational impossibility. "The state of death cannot be signified," he writes; "the naked souls we see in art and literature are either living a life after death or still in the process of losing being."[23] That is, if death is a moment in a narrative, that point must always be an absent one; it is the moment when experience, and therefore representation, cease. Death is therefore an impossible presence. To these medieval writers, according to Smith,

> death can never be a predicate of the human; it is false to say that a man "*is* dead" (*est mortuus*), false to say that being can be a predicate of nonbeing. We can talk only about the duration of dying itself: *homo moritur, homo moriebatur*.... Death takes us out of time and beyond language. Only dying can be linguistically analyzed, because it is still a movement toward something, an aspect of the unfolding of time [original emphasis].[24]

While death is a condition of time, its very timeliness makes it impossible to represent. Death, because of its unique phenomenological nature, can never actually be present. It must always be somewhere—or rather, sometime—else.

However, as a non-narrative form, the *tu fui* offers alternate possibilities for contemplating death. This form invites viewers and readers to step outside the flow of narrative into a more fluid relationship with temporality and mortality. This is encapsulated by the Schrodinger's box-like paradox of the sovereign death ritual Hal imagines onstage: the king is both dead and alive, the conditions of mortality both present and absent. In *Disce Mori*'s deathbed woodcut, the young soldier's death lies far before him, but the old man's is imminent; the future of the young man folds in upon the present of the old man, itself a past future recalled to mind. What this allows for is a shift like the one Smith describes from death to dying, from death as a fixed point in time to mortality as a constant, ongoing experience. In some ways, as I've noted earlier, that transition represents an escape from death. If we are forever dying, that is, we are never dead; the *tu fui* allows us as audience members to sustain a state of indefinite denial. But consequently, this emphasis on dying (rather than death) transforms mortality into something that directly affects the viewer themselves. They aren't dead—but they *are* dying. This is an inherent feature of *memento mori* in general, the affordance that imbues them with so much didactic power. San Juan describes the effect: "Although one might fill up the desiccated face" of the disembodied skull "with narrative potential," she writes, imagining there the death of another, these transformative "effects are only visited upon the beholder. In the exchange with the face of the skull, it is not the skull that is affected but the beholder whose very look becomes infected with fear, as if death itself is a virus one might catch."[25] While the *tu fui* allows an escape from the inevitable conclusion of death, it insists upon the viewer's constant state of mortality.

The intersections of *tu fui* with narrative, in the examples explored here, provide a prime example of what Levine has referred to as the "collision" of forms. When two forms collide, Levine asks, "Which will organize the other? It is not always predictable. New encounters may activate latent affordances or foreclose otherwise dominant ones. Forms will often fail to impose their order when they run up against other forms that disrupt their logic and frustrate their organizing ends, producing aleatory and sometimes contradictory effects."[26] The death arts with which this volume is concerned might just as readily be considered forms of death: cultural models through which mortality is given shape and meaning. To contemplate death in this period necessarily meant to think formally, to consider the possible models made available for making sense of one's own mortality—and, perhaps more importantly, to consider the intersections and collisions among these many models. It is at these nexus points where the complexity of mortality is most salient and the forming effects of the early modern death arts become most legible.

Notes

1. Atkinson, "The English *ars moriendi*: its Protestant Transformation," p. 1.
2. Atkinson, "The Devotionalism of Christopher Sutton," p. 208.
3. Sutton, *Disce Mori*, sig. A9^r. All citations from *Disce Mori* are from the 1662 edition unless otherwise indicated.
4. Ibid., sig. A10^r.
5. Patterson, *Domesticating the Reformation*, p. 24.
6. San Juan, "The Turn of the Skull," p. 961.
7. Sig. B12^v.
8. Sig. B12^v–C1^r.
9. Sig. C2^r.
10. This arrangement is true of all editions in which both images appear. Having examined either physical copies or digitized facsimiles of all fourteen editions, there are a few instances where the victory woodcut is either missing or not printed. In the original 1600 Windet, the victory woodcut seems not yet to have been added; in its place is an image of a single skeleton holding a shovel, incongruous with the style and layout of the deathbed illustration. There are several subsequent editions—the Folger's copy of the 1604 Windet edition, for instance—with missing gatherings where the images would likely have appeared.
11. All quotations from *2 Henry IV* come from *The Norton Shakespeare* 2nd edition, ed. Stephen Greenblatt et al.
12. Kantorowicz, *The King's Two Bodies*, p. 26.
13. There is some disagreement about when, precisely, Henry gets into bed. The Folio does not include any initial stage directions about how Henry is to come onstage. *The Norton Shakespeare* includes a stage direction indicating that Henry is to be carried onstage already in bed. James C. Bulan, in his edition of the play for Arden, notes that while "The King's illness has seemed to many editors to require that he be carried in on a chair or even a bed," that ultimately "There is no compelling reason [...] that the King should not enter under his own power. It makes theatrical sense for him to sit at the point he mentions feeling unwell and calls those in attendance to come near him" (p. 358 n. 4.3). Regardless of how the scene begins, editors agree that by its close, Henry is confined to bed.

14. Vinter, *Last Acts*, p. 112.
15. Parris, "'The Body Is with the King, But the King Is Not with the Body,'" p. 102.
16. Rooney, "Form and Contentment," p. 36.
17. Burton and Scott-Baumann, *The Work of Form*, p. 5.
18. Group Phi, "Doing Genre," p. 58.
19. Levine, *Forms*, p. 5.
20. Sutton, *Disce Mori*, sig. B8^r.
21. Ibid., sig. B11^r.
22. Ibid., sig. F4^{r-v}.
23. Smith, *Arts of Dying*, p. 1.
24. Ibid., p. 22.
25. San Juan, p. 960.
26. Levine, p. 7.

References

Atkinson, D.W. "The Devotionalism of Christopher Sutton." *Historical Magazine of the Protestant Episcopal Church* 54.3 (1985): 207–217.
———. "The English *ars moriendi*: its Protestant Transformation." *Renaissance and Reformation* (1982): 1–10.
Burton, Ben, and Elizabeth Scott-Baumann. *The Work of Form—Poetics and Materiality in Early Modern Culture*. Oxford: Oxford University Press, 2014.
Group Phi. "Doing Genre." In *New Formalisms and Literary Theory*. Edited by Verena Theile and Linda Tredennick. Houndmills, Basingstoke: Palgrave Macmillan, 2013. pp. 54–68.
Kantorowicz, Ernst. *The King's Two Bodies—A Study in Medieval Political Theology*. Princeton, NJ: Princeton University Press, 2016.
Levine, Caroline. *Forms*. Princeton, NJ: Princeton University Press, 2015.
Parris, Benjamin. "'The Body Is with the King, but the King Is Not with the Body': Sovereign Sleep in *Hamlet* and *Macbeth*." *Shakespeare Studies* 40 (2012): 101–42.
Patterson, Mary Hampson. *Domesticating the Reformation: Protestant Best Sellers, Private Devotion, and the Revolution of English Piety*. Madison, NJ: Farleigh Dickinson University Press, 2007.
Rooney, Ellen. "Form and Contentment." *Modern Language Quarterly* 61.1 (March 2000): 17–40.

San Juan, Rose Marie. "The Turn of the Skull: Andreas Vesalius and the Early Modern Memento Mori." *Art History: Journal of the Association of Art Historians* 35.5 (2012): 958–975.

Shakespeare, William. *2 Henry IV.* In *The Norton Shakespeare* 2nd edition. Edited by Stephen Greenblatt et al. New York: W.W. Norton & Co., 1997.

———. *King Henry IV Part 2*. Edited by James C. Bulan. The Arden Shakespeare Series. London: Bloomsbury, 2016.

Smith, D. Vance. *Arts of Dying—Literature and Finitude in Medieval England*. Chicago: University of Chicago Press, 2020.

Sutton, Christopher. *Disce Mori Learn to Dye: A Religious Discourse Moving Every Christian Man to Enter into a Serious Remembrance of His End*. London: 1662.

Vinter, Maggie. *Last Acts—The Art of Dying on the Early Modern Stage*. New York: Fordham University Press, 2019.

CHAPTER 5

The *Exemplum*, Posterity, and Dramatic Irony in *Antony and Cleopatra*

Grant Williams

Upon first meeting Dolabella after Antony's suicide, Cleopatra tells him of her wondrous dream, in which Antony, demi-god like, illuminates the earth with his heavenly face, spreads his copious bounty throughout the empire, and shakes the world with his terrifying might (5.2.78–91).[1] The audience would have heard in her eulogistic blazon an allusion to the Colossus of Rhodes, whose "legs bestrid the ocean" (5.2.81) echoed, by the way, in Shakespeare's companion play *Julius Caesar*.[2] Cleopatra's afterlife image of Antony suggests that he has been transfigured into the Colossus, that is, the statue of the sun god Helios. He miraculously incarnates—brings to life—one of the seven wonders of the ancient world.[3] This fantasy of becoming a "living monument"[4] captures the immortal longings articulated by Antony and Cleopatra in various ways throughout the play.[5] They care desperately about how they will be remembered when

G. Williams (✉)
Carleton University, Ottawa, ON, Canada
e-mail: grant.williams@carleton.ca

© The Author(s), under exclusive license to Springer Nature Switzerland AG 2022
W. E. Engel and G. Williams (eds.), *The Shakespearean Death Arts*, Palgrave Shakespeare Studies,
https://doi.org/10.1007/978-3-030-88490-1_5

they are gone. Commentators have accordingly discerned and scrutinized the play's abiding concern with memorialization.[6]

The audience, however, would have also heard Cleopatra's oneiric blazon strike a discordant note with another allusion: Nebuchadnezzar II's dream of a gigantic statue with a head of gold.[7] Echoes of the biblical *exemplum* in which a stone obliterates the statue make it difficult for the spectator to sustain Cleopatra's fantasy of an everlasting legacy, since the dream, interpreted by Daniel, warned of the divine punishment later visited upon this Babylonian king for, among other things, building and worshiping the graven image that haunted him. As Henry Smith moralizes in one of his popular religious pamphlets on the king's rise and fall, "what hath [Nebuchadnezzar] done [...] that [he] should erect such monuments, to be praised after death, which were not worthy to be praised in [his] life?"[8] Antony as Colossus is just one example of how the monument for Shakespeare conveys not so much the power of memory to preserve one's image as a *memento-mori* lesson on the vanity of seeking everlasting fame. Indeed, the play's last scene deflates the significance of the magisterial tomb even further. Much of the action takes place under the shadow of Egypt's pyramids and within the precinct of an actual monument, where each eventually dies. But, in his final speech, Caesar commands his men to remove Cleopatra's bed and women from the monument and bury her by Antony (5.2.345–347), while never mentioning the details of Suetonius's specific account: "This honor he did unto them both, namely to bury them in one sepulcher, and the tomb by them begun, he commanded to be finished."[9] Shakespeare's vague and reductive language about their burial is one of a few omissions made at the expense of physical memorials, including Plutarch's reference to strange omens around Antony's statuary before the civil wars with Octavius and his reference to Caesar ordering Antony's statues, images, and metals to be overthrown after his death.[10] In the play's world, the mausoleum performs no decisive role in memorializing the dead lovers: a curious fact given that Plutarch, Antony's oft-cited biographer, claims, "Cleopatra had long before made many sumptuous tombs and monuments, as well for excellency of workmanship, as for height and greatness of building, joining hard to the temple of Isis."[11]

My chapter argues that Shakespeare is interested less in physical memorials than in rhetorical ones, such as Cleopatra's blazonic eulogy. After all, his *Sonnets*, which were published around the same time as *Antony and Cleopatra*, scorns the transient enshrinement of heraldry and tombs, preferring instead the relative perdurability of praise and verse.[12] Since the early modern word "monument" signifies an array of structures and artifacts, for Shakespeare, who interrogates the efficacy of poetic memorials, not all monuments are created equally.[13] If Antony and Cleopatra's images have survived down through the ages, it is not because of any grandiose architecture but on account of the device of the *exemplum*, another kind of Roman monument, well known to Shakespeare and his audience members schooled in humanist rhetorical practices. Humanism had revived Cicero's use of *exempla* to commemorate and model the honorable behavior of civic leaders for pupils aspiring to follow in their footsteps. The student's treasure house of memory thus becomes the resting place of the posthumous image. Shakespeare's implementation of exemplarity throughout the play, however, generates dramatic irony at the expense of Antony and Cleopatra, who do not know that they are already dead—that they are actively being conjured by posterity. Apprehending the discrepancy between their immortal longings and their posthumous images, the spectator realizes that the protagonists reside less in the audience's memory than in its imagination—a cognitive state brought about by the vulgarization of the *exemplum* through the commercialization of the stage and press.

When expounding upon the utility of education, the Plymouth grammar school teacher William Kempe states, "Do not we see their presence [that is, the presence of noteworthy figures] most lively, and bear their voice most plainly in their examples, in their sayings and doings, which are left unto us as noble monuments for our instruction."[14] Kempe is not indulging here in a fanciful or farfetched metaphor, for during the period "example"—English for "*exemplum*" in Latin and divided by Cicero into historical, fictional, or plausible narratives[15]—functioned monumentally. The two words, known to appear contiguously, could thus supplement one another as in Geoffrey Fenton's *The Golden Epistles*: "much less may we refer to the conquest of fortune the virtue of Regulus, who being led to the gibbet was made there a monument of faith and an example of patience."[16] Kempe continues, "Let us therefore diligently look upon their deeds, and hearken unto their words, expressing withal the same in our lives and conversation, seeing we can follow no examples that may advance us to so great honor, or bring unto us so great profit."[17] *Exempla* aimed to commemorate the great deeds of past figures so as to edify the student,[18] who would emulate the modeled behavior with the ambition that he would himself be preserved some day in similarly honorable anecdotes.

What rhetorically mediates, in good part, the images of Antony and Cleopatra is Roman *exempla*, which Shakespeare predominantly extracts from Plutarch's *Life of Mark Antony*, the play's primary classical source. I do not want to linger upon their elemental yet prosaic function as building blocks for elocutionary discourse and thus for theatrical monologues. Along with ethopoeia, description, proverb, encomium, and other exercises in the *progymnasmata*, *exempla* provided the material out of which playwrights fabricated the speech of their historical personages.[19] More significantly for my purposes, this form of persuasive evidence, one of two described by Aristotle,[20] was the means by which a person could leave his image to posterity, for its Greek term, *paradeigma*, connotes a sense of light, showing, and seeing, which Renaissance practice confirms by associating it with "painting, inlaid pavement, and rhetorical imago."[21] To craft one's posthumous image within Shakespeare's Roman world, one must thus conform to the constraints of exemplarity, illustrative conduct worthy enough for remembrance. Pompey, Enobarbus, and Caesar know this principle well. They realize that they are accountable to the future, and history can be unforgiving. When the pirate Menas proposes to Pompey that they seize control of the empire by slaughtering the Triumvirate who are currently guests on their ship, Pompey reprimands his henchman for disclosing the plan and not seizing the initiative: "In me 'tis villainy, / In thee't had been good service. Thou must know / 'Tis not my profit that does lead mine honour; / Mine honour, it" (2.7.69–72). Pompey may as well have been summarizing the *De Officiis*, where Cicero labors to insulate the profitable from the shameful, for true glory cannot be achieved by deceptive and dishonest ends.[22] *De Officiis*, an influential work of "pragmatic ethics designed to guide the élite Roman through his everyday life," situated the *exemplum* firmly within the landscape of stoic moral philosophy[23] and set the stakes of studying commendable precedents: "the best inheritance that fathers leave to their children, and more worth than all livelihood, is the glory of virtue and worthy deeds."[24]

Shakespeare would have understood the book's importance for handling *exempla* by way of English humanist schooling, which Erasmus established earlier in the century and Thomas Elyot promoted soon afterward. Erasmus espoused a strong intellectual commitment to *exempla* but it did not derive just from his more formalistic account in *De Copia*, where over half of book II unpacks the compositional method of exemplification.[25] It is actually driven by Cicero's *De Officiis*, the first in a long line of annotated editions of classical works that Erasmus would publish.[26] The endorsement of *De Officiis* from Erasmus and later Elyot no doubt contributed to the book's significant role in Tudor education—at the level of court, university, and grammar school.[27] As Peter Mack observes, "Pupils were expected to admire *De Officiis*, not merely as a source of ethical teaching but also for the way it employed moral *exempla*."[28] And so when Erasmus explains to a friend how the book inspired him to implement Pliny's advice of carrying it about oneself every day and learning it by heart,[29] he does so because of its lasting benefits: it is "the divine fountain of honour," which like the Aonian springs gives immortality to those who drink its waters.[30]

Based upon a historical narrative from Plutarch's *Life of Antony*, Pompey's scolding of Menas dramatizes the careful vigilance that stewarding one's own exemplarity entails and, as such, underscores the Roman devotion to honor, embodied by Octavius Caesar, the play's primary foil to Antony.[31] Upon making his first entrance with Lepidus who defends Antony's vices, Caesar insists that Antony deserves to be rebuked for not observing his public duty as "we rate boys who, being mature in knowledge, / Pawn their experience to their present pleasure / And so rebel to judgment" (1.4.31–33). Caesar sounds like a humanist educator here for good reason. Antony, he claims, is "the abstract of all faults / That all men follow" (9–10), an abstract being an epitome or abridgment of text or a document, often distilling Greek, Roman, or other scholarly writings. A true pupil should be an "abstract of all virtues" insofar as his studies involved drawing idealized behavior from classical works and compendia that humanist teachers would make available through print products, namely, commonplace books, florilegia, histories, mirrors, emblem books, and other collections during the period, all of which extended Erasmus's own ambitious project of compiling adages, apopthegms, and similar pedagogical compendia.[32] By reading, collecting, and internalizing *exempla* of honorable deeds, the pupil would build up his memory—that is, his mental storehouse or *inventio* of narratives, adages, commonplaces, parables, etc.—and cultivate his character, so that when confronted with situations demanding politico-ethical action, he could summon up appropriate models for making worthy decisions.[33]

Later in the play, Antony corroborates Caesar's assessment by behaving exactly like a pupil who, despite "his mature knowledge," pawns his experience to the present and rebels against judgment. After accusing Cleopatra of betrayal, he invokes his tutelary deity and putative ancestor, Hercules. "Teach me," he cries out. But instead of requesting a lesson in Stoic self-control, he asks to be schooled in the insane "rage" that overcame Hercules when he donned the poisoned shirt of Nessus (4.13.43–44).[34] Antony's recollection of a wayward *exemplum* to stoke, not quell, his murderous fury parodically distorts the common procedure that educators, such as Kempe, advocated for their readers and students. If Antony had wanted to emulate his ancestor, who, Plutarch says, "through the excellency of [his] virtue did put off mortality and took immortality upon [him]," the fictional narrative he should be recalling is the celebrated parable "the choice of Hercules."[35] Upon reaching maturity, the legendary hero faced a momentous decision at a crossroads, where he considered which of the two allegorical paths to take for his life and opted for the arduous one leading to Virtue rather than the easy one leading to Pleasure. Shakespearean criticism has long grappled with the parallels between Antony and Hercules, noting the latter's famous choice, originally mentioned in Xenophon.[36] But what I want to point out is that Antony fails to remember a crucial *exemplum*, the script for gaining everlasting fame that makes Hercules exemplary for posterity. Humanist students who read the *De Officiis* might have remembered that Cicero recounts the very same "choice of Hercules" and later asserts that the hero for "his great travails and pains," secured a place in the "company" of the gods.[37] To highlight Antony's poor decision-making, which, in effect, has sacrificed a Herculean apotheosis for pleasure, Shakespeare earlier modifies Plutarch's account of the inauspicious event in which Bacchus withdraws his favor from Antony: the Second Soldier upon hearing the supernatural music believes the omen betokens Hercules's abandonment of him (4.3.15–16).

Antony and Cleopatra are notorious for the moral failings of their memories, and, to their distractedness, cognitive lapses, self-forgetting, and nepenthe-induced lethargy, we must add their periodic obliviousness to exemplarity. Their ignorance or neglect of the *exemplum*'s capacity to immortalize noble images may be a function of the kind of orators that they are. Plutarch characterizes their speech as sophistical and manipulative,[38] tacitly setting them against the ethical dimension of Ciceronian rhetoric. Antony and Cleopatra do not know what it means to obey the call of duty, the cornerstone of the stoic program outlined in the *De Officiis*. They are willing to sacrifice their debts to friends, familial commitments, military responsibilities, and princely obligations at the altar of their lascivious relationship so much so that it may be said that their duty is really to themselves—and certainly not their rational selves, but their co-dependent appetites and addictions. They act as though they were licentious gods, periodically asserting their moral and mortal exceptionalism.[39] The numerous and well-known instances of their outrageous behavior need not be rehearsed but the audience cannot ignore its relevance for their immortal longings. The ways in which the protagonists mishandle their exemplarity generates some of the play's rich dramatic irony. At the moment of recounting an *exemplum*, they fail to comprehend the lasting implications of what they are saying, while the educated spectator ascertains their misguidance and ineptitude in aligning their actions with the virtuous outcomes of humanist teaching. When trying to find amusing distractions for coping with Antony's absence, Cleopatra decides to go fishing so she can imagine each fish drawn up "an Antony, / And say, 'Ah ha, you're caught'" (2.5.14–15). The pastime immediately reminds Charmian of a merry prank that Cleopatra had once played on the angling Antony: her mistress commanded a diver to affix a salted fish to his hook (ll. 15–18). The incident fondly remembered through a silly *exemplum* is devoid of any ethically worthy content. Whereas humanist-trained nobles fortify their civic duties by sculpting their actions according to recollected moral narratives, Cleopatra, Egypt's ruling queen, neglects matters of statecraft to restage her petty narcissistic triumphs as a consolation for her self-absorbed despondency. The dramatic irony perceived by the audience yields an *ars moriendi* lesson on how not to prepare for death, since Cleopatra gives no thought to her legacy of virtue at the moment she should be attending to and reflecting upon *exempla*.

But aside from inducing thoughts of *memento mori*, Shakespeare prohibits the audience from settling into a morally superior and complacent position over his characters. His end game is not to shame Antony and Cleopatra by holding them up as examples of depravity and consigning them to the ranks of notorious tyrants the likes of Semiramis, Sardanapalus, Nero, Caligula, and Commodus.[40] Scholarship on the play has long steered away from dogmatic interpretations, which all too often misrepresent the complex experience that readers and spectators have of the fiery, charismatic protagonists.[41] Along these lines, the play does not portray the Ciceronian economy of honor in an uncritical light. Caesar, Antony's envious rival, flagrantly tampers with exemplarity, when recounting an astonishing story recorded by Plutarch: during a brutally tough campaign, Antony was forced to drink puddle water and to feed upon tree bark and strange animal flesh, Plutarch admitting, "it was a wonderful example to the soldiers."[42] By contrast, Shakespeare's Octavius Caesar, who relates the story to Lepidus, refrains from mentioning how it commanded the respect of Antony's men and uses it, instead, to denigrate his rival's current reputation: "It wounds thine honor that I speak it now" (1.4.69). As the play progresses, Caesar's increasingly cynical manipulation of his reputation and that of his rivals leads us to question the extent to which the humanist model of exemplarity has been fabricated by the mighty.[43] To that end, chorus-like, Antony's general Ventidius voices the danger of politically upstaging the master (3.1.12–27).

Another richer kind of dramatic irony makes the audience less judgmental of the protagonists insofar as their ultimate lack of control over how they are remembered arises, we discover, more from the vicissitudes of the exemplary image than from any personal wicked deed. The play's monumental vision posits the discrepancy between the images by which Antony and Cleopatra want to be immortalized and the actual images received by future generations. The climactic illustration of this discrepancy occurs when Cleopatra makes her famous meta-theatrical declaration after meeting with a glib Caesar. She voices her fear that, if she and Iras are taken to Rome, they will end up staged in a comedy where "Antony / Shall be brought drunken forth, and [she] shall see / Some squeaking Cleopatra boy [her] greatness / I'th' posture of a whore" (5.2.214–216). She expresses her horrific disgust with being memorialized by a degrading surrogate, a boy comedian who, the audience realizes, projects her posthumous image on the very stage before them. Shakespeare foregrounds the forensic or evidentiary fact that commemoration depends not merely on the desire and efforts of the individual but on posterity, the contingent destination of the posthumous image.

This oft-quoted episode of self-reflexivity is by no means the only one that makes the spectators aware of their historical distance from the characters portrayed. Throughout the play, Shakespeare generates dramatic irony with his deployment of *exempla*, the vehicles of humanist monumentalization. When he weaves a Plutarchan *exemplum* into a character's discourse rather than dramatizing the narrative's action, he invites the audience to entertain two temporal perspectives on the rhetorical monument: the moment of inscription and the moment of decipherment. During the first moment, the spectators watch a character narrate and reflect upon the *exemplum* as part of everyday speech as if they were witnessing a conversation taking place for the first time. No different from any other history play, *Antony and Cleopatra* transports the spectators into the past through the artifice of imitation and impersonation.

During the moment of decipherment, however, audience members assume a second temporal location, far removed from the historical figures. The *exemplum* hails and addresses audience members no longer as witnesses, but as posterity. That is our ultimate relationship to, for instance, Shakespeare's abbreviated fishing *exemplum* raised by Charmian and taken from Plutarch, who uses the story to represent "all the foolish sports they made."[44] Rather than theatricalizing the story, Shakespeare retains its narrative form, which would have been recognizable by the humanist-educated spectator. Dramatic irony thus arises from our awareness of the temporal disjuncture between Charmian's utterance and its reception by us. Her words no longer belong to a living dialogue with her mistress but unwittingly inscribe the epitaphic—an *exemplum* about a fatuous prank. Put another way, Cleopatra does not know that she is already dead. Throughout the play, Antony and Cleopatra do not know that their posthumous images ossified by *exempla* like the fishing tale have already been passed down through the generations. But we, of course, do.

As posterity, not witnesses, we register the discrepancy between Antony and Cleopatra's immortal longings and their actual posthumous images and, through the long view, ascertain the transience and vanity of memorials, not only physical monuments, rituals, and Triumphs, but more significantly the humanist model of exemplarity. Given such a discrepancy, how can we describe the way in which we cognitively handle the posthumous images of the protagonists? The pair has not slipped out of our minds into utter oblivion. "Antony" and "Cleopatra," after all is said and done, have still been passed down to Shakespeare's audience; though, technically speaking, not forgotten in name, they have hardly secured, however, anything remotely near the monumentalization that they had hoped for. Only if they could see themselves now! Neither forgotten nor remembered, the images of Antony and Cleopatra inhabit the faculty beside the memory in the premodern brain. Dramatic irony makes us aware of posterity's inclination to apprehend the *exemplum* with its imagination.

Enobarbus's shrewd commentary on Cleopatra's *exemplum* about her Venerian barge on the Cydnus and her breathless dash through the Alexandrian streets captures the spectator's mental apprehension of her posthumous image:

> Age cannot wither her, nor custom stale
> Her infinite variety. Other women cloy
> The appetites they feed, but she makes hungry
> Where most she satisfies. For vilest things
> Become themselves in her, that the holy priests
> Bless her when she is riggish. (2.2.233–238)

The passage references much more than the sexual appeal of a historical Cleopatra. In a play whose protagonists are preoccupied with leaving a legacy, it describes how auditors never tire of hearing *exempla* about her, just as the audience presumably thirsts for more, after Enobarbus tells his two salacious stories. "Infinite variety" characterizes the way in which her image has been passed down to posterity. Noteworthy too in this regard is Cleopatra's ascription to Antony of "infinite virtue," (4.9.17) the gendered correlative of her own "infinite variety." Later in the play, Antony confesses that like the ever-changing cloud, "the black vesper's pageants," he "cannot hold this visible shape" (4.15.14), going one step further than her earlier accusation that he is an anamorphosis, a turning picture of a Gorgon and Mars (2.5.117–118). "Infinite" meant during the period boundless and indeterminate in addition to immensely long. For early modern readers, the examples of the plural and plastic image would have resonated with faculty psychology. The "infinite variety" of Cleopatra that stimulates the audience's concupiscent appetites corresponds to the ungoverned imagination with its potentially endless stream of images, which could keep provoking and feeding a person's desires. As George More laments in *A Demonstration of God in his Works*, "The Leopard is not so changeable in the spots of his skin, as man is variable in the affections of his mind. Innumerable are his fancies, unspeakable his conceits, infinite his devices and desires."[45] Motivating Burton and others to describe its proliferation as "infinite," the imagination's capacity to multiply phantasms through fusing and feigning sensory impressions was the primary cause of stirring up the passions and having them run amok.[46]

What was the imaginative source, then, of Cleopatra's infinite variety and Antony's infinite honor, which, in turn, stimulated the fantasies of auditors and readers? Can anyone doubt that it was the steady stream of *exempla* issuing not only from Shakespeare's play but also from classical, medieval, and especially contemporaneous writers? As posterity, literate audiences would have known that the innumerable *exempla* of Antony and Cleopatra scattered throughout sixteenth- and seventeenth-century books, pamphlets, and performances have resulted in a welter of confused and contradictory images that for all intents and purposes bury if not lose whatever legacy the historical figures had hoped for. Cleopatra has been grouped with constant wives[47] and with whores.[48] She is a byword of lust and lechery[49] in addition to being an emblem of pride.[50] And we must not forget that she is the queen of excessive banqueting and prodigality. Her motivations for committing suicide vary as well: loyalty to Antony,[51] sorrow over his demise,[52] heroic disdain for death under dire circumstances,[53] courage to conquer Caesar,[54] and fear to escape impending humiliation and ridicule.[55] Should we follow Turberville who says that she has earned immortal praise[56] for her steadfastness? Or should we agree with *A Dial for Dainty Darlings* and Nashe's *Anatomy* that characterize her as a contemptus-mundi figure for the vanity of beauty?[57]

In the print record, the plasticity of Cleopatra's posthumous image is matched by Antony's. He has been remembered on his own for his military and political exploits. Richard Rainolde places Antony on the same level as Lepidus and Caesar: "loftye and ambitious Princes" whose aspirations led them to betray each other—such are the broils of worldly power.[58] Other chroniclers have been less generous in their assessment of the triumvirate.[59] Moreover, Antony's exemplary actions stretch from his liberality and frank nature to the treachery of ordering Cicero's assassination.[60] Gascoigne appears to see nothing amiss with this "worthy Romain Knight" except that he fell for a "hard-favoured" woman, when he had his pick of Roman beauties.[61] That said, Antony's *exempla*, often circling around his spectacular military losses, convey infinite dishonor much more readily than infinite honor. What personal failing precipitated the shame of his ignoble end? His intemperance and looseness?[62] His extraordinary drunkeness?[63] His desperation for Cleopatra[64] upon learning of her suicide? Should he then be remembered for his foolish adoration of Cleopatra, his Egyptian lover?[65] But then again their prodigal revelry and riot, especially their competition to outdo each other's banquets, has become proverbial.[66] Even Jack Wilton, Nashe's cony-catching traveler, likens himself and his concubine to the feasting lovers when Surrey overtakes them in Florence.[67] But Antony and Cleopatra don't always take center stage. *Exempla* also cast each of them as ignoble props supporting the memorials of others.[68]

My small sampling of the *exempla* attests to heterogeneity in the print record. A half-century ago Marlyn L. Williamson put to bed the erroneous assumption that the tradition of recounting the lovers' escapades displays uniformity: "As one witnesses the variety of artistic responses to the story of Antony and Cleopatra through the ages, he cannot but wonder at the inclusivity of Shakespeare's play, which contains somewhere within it virtually every major interpretation of character and action one encounters in the tradition."[69] In her recent survey of the conflicted depictions of Cleopatra, Yasmin Arshad reaches similar conclusions.[70] Umberto Eco's incisive argument that forgetting can be produced by an excess and not by a deficiency of semiosis explains the difficulty of recollecting Antony and Cleopatra's legacy.[71]

Such "infinite variety" during the early modern period arose, no doubt, from the commercial demand of catering to public taste. The culture industry guided by humanist-educated craftsmen who recycled sayings, commonplaces, and narratives leveraged novelty and salaciousness to make the past palatable for middle-class audiences and readerships.[72] Writers could not rehash the same textual fragments and expect their works to receive sustained interest from publishers and readers. They had to exercise their inventiveness—no matter how minimal—in varying their material within the constraints of the prevailing commonplace-book method of composition. Erasmus's own humanist project acknowledges this marketing principle in his educational handbook *De Copia*, Shakespeare's tag "infinite variety" being another way of designating copia so much so that Enobarbus may very well be invoking the principle with reference to Cleopatra's manifold representation. In theory and in practice, Erasmus realized the psychological importance of varying one's discourse so that one's readers would not suffer from the intellectual fatigue of monotony. He hammers out his lesson rather mechanically by generating 200 variations on a single epistolary line of remembering a friend.[73] The same strategy works with the *exemplum*, to which Erasmus devotes more than half of his treatise's second book. At one point, he raises the illustrative example of the death of Socrates, which, he says, could be turned to praise and blame and, in effect, serve many purposes.[74] Earlier in *Antony and Cleopatra*, Enobarbus's declaration that he has seen Cleopatra die "twenty times upon far poorer moment" (1.2.122–123) takes on a new meaning when we consider her textual evocation to be a site of changing rhetorical exemplification.

Shakespeare's play clearly taps into the unintended consequences of the Erasmian educational agenda, which prepared its students as readers and writers for the marketplace of print. In the humanist project, the two Ciceros—the moral philosopher of *De Officiis* and the rhetorician—cannot be fully reconciled. Subject to the imaginations of writers in their quest to vary their material, *exempla* lack the fixity required for recollection, losing the posthumous image in a welter of contradiction, ambivalence, and distortion, somewhere between fable and history, somewhere between desire and memory. In this regard, *Antony and Cleopatra* problematizes humanism's desire of utilizing the printing press to ensure the stability of commemoration. The prospect that readers will acquire edification and eventually memorialization from pursuing virtue through a noble precedent justified and incentivized English humanists and their print products. In the service of humanist education—or at least according to its advocates—the press permitted the development and the extension of human memory for the purposes of monumentalization. These assumptions about remembrance are cogently expressed by John Day's printer's device, wherein an old nobleman points out to a young man a skeleton recumbent on a sarcophagus (see Fig. 5.1.) The old man appears to speak the words inscribed above him, "although death hastens on from day to day," while the skeleton, out of which grows a tree of honor, seems to complete the old man's sentence with the principal clause, "after burial virtue nevertheless will live on."[75] Punning on his name, the motto credits Day[76]—the preeminent sixteenth-century printer, who published Foxe's *Book of Martyrs*—with preserving a more lasting tomb than stone or marble. The visual emphasis upon a flourishing tree shifts the accent from genealogical branches and heraldic lineage to virtue's ongoing legacy, also communicated by the three states of man: the corpse, the old, and the young. The dead live on through the remembrance of posterity facilitated by the press.

The sixteenth-century cultural industry in appealing to the imagination of audiences and readers through copia preyed upon the infirm side of cognition and properly speaking could not sustain the Ciceronian economy of honor so dear to humanism. Perhaps images of paragons could be transmitted without distortion in an ideal world where future generations—writers and readers—would dedicate themselves to training disciplined and virtuous memories, but not so in Shakespeare's dramatized world, where gossip and slander regularly interfere with how people are remembered. Early modernity did not regard the imagination as a

Fig. 5.1 John Day's printer's mark (final leaf in John Foxe's *Acts and Monuments*)

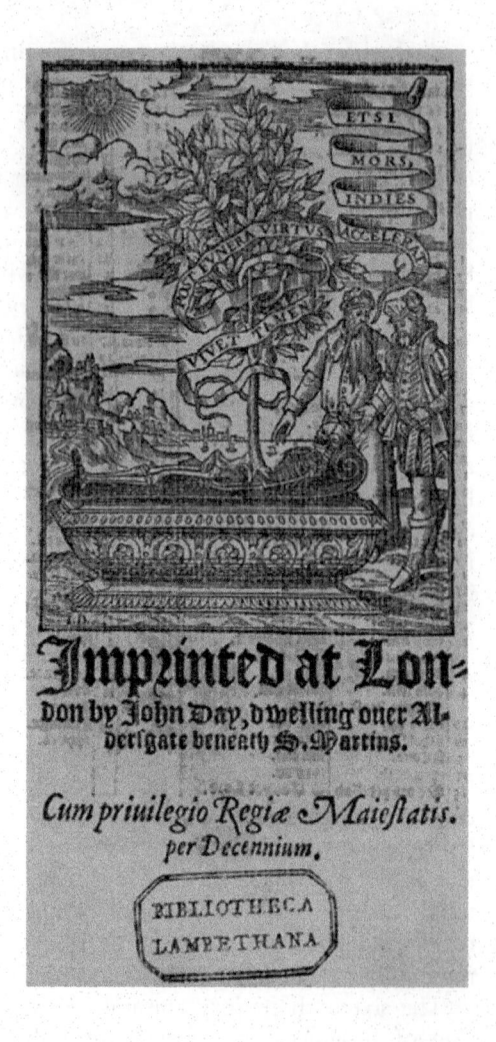

noble organ adequate to or worthy of monumentalizing the great, for Tudor education had no interest in developing this faculty directly in its students unless it meant marshaling the resources of the first stage of rhetoric, inventio, and, under these circumstances, inventio resembled a treasury of stable topoi for supplying the student with the elements of an oral and written discourse. From the imagination arose, at best, opinion, certainly not the elevated idea sublimated by the intellect and conveying knowledge and truth. This imaginative product is, as Pierre Charron claims, "a vain, light, crude and imperfect judgement of things drawn from the outward senses and common report."[77] The play chimes with Charron's description in its repeated demonstration of the vulnerability of an individual's public persona to the hearsay of others: Cleopatra's menacing wrath compels her messenger to diminish the charms of Octavia, her rival (3.3.11–33); as mentioned, Enobarbus regales his fellow martial men with salacious tales about Cleopatra's sexual appeal (2.2.190–231); and Pompey hungrily seeks from Antony and Enobarbus confirmation on exotic tales of the Egyptian court, particularly the notorious ruse of Cleopatra to have herself rolled up in a mattress and secretly carried to Julius Caesar (2.6.64–72).[78]

Contrary to humanism, which sought to locate one's legacy within the memory of posterity, Shakespeare directs our attention to the cognitive verity that Antony and Cleopatra's posthumous *exempla* are enfleshed in posterity's actual imagination—an untrustworthy faculty that proliferated and distorted images according to affect. In premodern faculty psychology, the imagination as one of the three inner senses was viewed with suspicion because of its proximity to the five outer senses and the emotions, both known for their unhealthy and volatile sway over the individual's decision-making capacity. "For fantasy being near the outward senses, / Allures the soul to love things bodily," says John Davies of Hereford.[79] The imagination gave people carnal pleasure because it was a sensuous and sensual organ. Ideally, it was expected to subordinate its activity to the rule of rational judgment, sending its images to the memory, reason, and intellect for further processing, but when the individual did not rein it in, it dominated the mind with its sensuous images in order to extract from them maximum enjoyment.[80] The monumental problems afflicting Antony and Cleopatra thus amount to much more than a mnemotechnic miscarriage. Posterity is exploiting their posthumous images for its personal delectation.

The Plutarchan *exemplum* most expertly handled by Shakespeare sheds light on how his audience apprehends his protagonists' images.[81] It concerns the first and storied meeting of the lovers, when Antony invited Cleopatra to Cilicia and she appeared on her magnificent barge. Shakespeare's skillful yet subtle revision of the narrative highlights its distinct cognitive appeal. Plutarch uses the *exemplum* to communicate the excessive wealth Cleopatra lavishes on her attempt to sexually and politically win Antony over as she did Julius Caesar and Pompey years before.

Antony, who does not see the floating spectacle, finally meets her at an even more extravagant venue: the spectacle of the feast with its "sumptuous fare" and "infinite number of lights and torches," which tacitly surpasses that of the barge, since, Plutarch claims, Antony found the sights profoundly ineffable.[82] Only after describing barge and feast does Plutarch mention Cleopatra's beauty, which, he emphasizes, was not so extraordinary, her appearance benefitting more from her graceful behavior and eloquence.[83]

In contrast, Shakespeare uses the *exemplum* to illustrate how "she pursed up his heart upon the river Cydnus" (2.2.185–186), which seems like an odd thing to say, given that Antony never sees Cleopatra on her barge, having remained seated on his throne alone in the forum. Perhaps, that does not matter, insofar as the conjured scene is really for Enobarbus, his homosocial auditors, and, by extension, us the audience. If in Plutarch the *exemplum* records Cleopatra's regal opulence, in Shakespeare, it exults her irresistible charms. Shakespeare turns Plutarch's *ekphrasis* of the pleasure craft into a blazon of the Egyptian Queen. He saturates the original physical description with sensual appeal, ascribing to the floating court an erotic magnetism that propels the craft forward by subduing the inanimate world. The rhythmical oar strokes made the water, as if in love, "follow faster" (2.2.195); the silken tackle swell with the touches of the "flower-soft hands" of the mermaids; and the "winds were lovesick with" a perfume wafting from the barge (l. 209). It is this strangely alluring fragrance that empties the city of its inhabitants. Sitting upon her throne with the fans of the Cupid boys unable to cool her sultry lust, Cleopatra appears to be the epicenter of the barge's sensual attraction. And yet when Enobarbus comes to depict her, he invokes the topos of ineffability, which Plutarch had reserved for the feast: "For her own person, / It beggared all description: she did lie / In her pavilion—cloth-of-gold of tissue— / O'erpicturing that Venus where we see / The fancy outwork nature" (ll. 196–200). The lines do not tally with Plutarch, where Cleopatra was "appareled and attired like the goddess Venus, commonly drawn in picture."[84] The sight witnessed by Enobarbus doubly surmounted nature and art, but we have to take his word for it, since this blazon of the erotic effects Cleopatra has on her environs finally leaves us with no visual image of her appearance.

At the end of the play, Cleopatra's blazon of Antony, the complement of Enobarbus's blazon of the Egyptian Queen, stimulates our minds in the very same manner. Cleopatra creates a new phantasm of him out of her imagination, since this organ operated unchecked during sleep,[85] when the reason no longer had it under control. However, after tantalizing us with preposterously sensible details of Antony's god-like stature and god-like magnanimity, Cleopatra concludes that no "dreaming" can measure up to her image of his superlatively tumescent size (5.2.96). Just as Cleopatra according to Enobarbus "overpictures" an artwork, whose painter's fancy outperforms nature, Antony as Cleopatra imagines him also surpasses the matchless phantasms produced by the imagination: "Nature wants stuff / To vie strange forms with fancy; yet t'imagine / An Antony were nature's piece 'gainst fancy, / Condemning shadows quite" (ll. 96–99).

In each blazon—an *exemplum* slowed to a narrative stasis—the protagonist's phantasm excites our sensorium while resisting a determinate form within our imagination. That is to say, it is supersensible but not superimaginative (it cannot be confused with an abstract or angelic entity, an object of the intellect). With both *exempla*, Shakespeare primes our sensual imagination, daring us to imagine the protagonists, while denying us the possibility of ever seeing them in our mind's eye. Shakespeare's play sets up a proto-consumer situation in which readers and spectators are prompted to seek out greater and greater pleasure from imaginative stimulation without the assurance of fulfillment. Such cognitive insatiability surely fuels the production of the press and the theater. Antony and Cleopatra's posthumous images have been placed out of reach of monumentalization. In effect, they have become playthings or toys of our insatiable fancies.

This last point is worth emphasizing since it expresses the most sardonic irony grasped by Shakespeare's spectator whose status as posterity fully dawns upon him or her. Cleopatra's disgust for the lower orders is visceral. While warning Iras how Caesar will parade them as trophies in his Triumph, Cleopatra grows hysterical at the thought that the mob's brute physical presence will overwhelm their sensorium: "mechanic slaves" whose "thick breaths, rank of gross diet" shall encloud and force them "to drink their vapour" (5.2.205–209), and "saucy lictors" who will catch at—that is, grab and feel—them "like strumpets" (ll. 210–211). This fear of sensory harassment in a crowded spectacle blurs into another fear of being commemorated in base media: they will be sung about in discordant ballads by "scald rhymers" and portrayed on stage by "quick comedians"—players and ballad mongers, by the way, occupying a socioeconomic position far below that of tradesmen and civil servants. Ironically enough, little do Cleopatra and Iras know that their posthumous images are circulating within the early modern culture industry of print and performance even as they speak. With respect to *exempla*, this industry has widened posterity from the urbane minds of the humanist educated aristocracy to the hungry fancies of the vulgar multitude. There is certainly no roll call of honor, no marble inscription on a triumphal arch, no idolizing minds of future patricians. Impressed upon the flesh and feeling of the Jacobean playhouse's rabble and the prurient frequenters of fairs and bookstalls, Antony and Cleopatra are phantasmatic residue, cognitive toys and playthings groped and smothered by the base imaginations, appetites, and fantasies of commoners.

The play's concern with the plasticity and plurality of images, which scholars have often interpreted as valorizing a decentered, fragmentary, and multiple self, finds a more historically attuned explanation in the problematic of the *exemplum*'s proliferation through cultural production.[86] In privileging a modern view of identity as fluidity, scholarship on the play overlooks the threat that posterity's imagination stimulated by the press and the theater poses to monumentalization. Humanism used the exemplary images of historical figures to advance civic virtue among the elite, but the emergent public sphere, despite its agents' insistence on conforming to educational ends, could not help but tailor these images to a cognitive ecosystem compatible with commercial demands. Shakespeare does not attempt to smooth over this rhetorical conflict and instead magnifies the dissonance between the protagonists' immortal longings and their actual afterlife—the clash between the *exempla* advocated by Cicero's *De Officiis* and those the spectators consume in real time. By addressing the audience as posterity, the play accrues dramatic irony at the expense of the protagonists' visions of leaving a grand legacy.

The period's commitment to the death arts compels us to read Shakespeare's dramatic ironies around commemoration from the perspective of *memento mori*. Why can posterity not provide the secular monumentalization that Antony and Cleopatra crave? Is Shakespeare criticizing the inadequacies of the humanist code of honor? Or is he gesturing toward the theater's—and his own—complicity with marketplace forces? And we must not forget an implicit criticism of the audience's indulgence in the imagination to the neglect of remembering the dead. Finally, is Shakespeare indirectly commenting upon the narcissistic craze of aristocratic tomb-making in his own time? Perhaps, the real triumph of the play occurs for the audience who understand that they are the carnal vessels of immortality for Antony and Cleopatra. Shakespeare gives comfort to the faceless commoner who, without the hope of ever having the opportunity of being lavishly entombed and constellated, witnesses great historical personages failing to achieve their hoped-for apotheosis.

Whoever is to blame for the failure of the protagonists' monumentalization, the play underscores the vanity of striving to leave a mark on the world. By urging us to reflect upon how the protagonists' images of themselves do not measure up to their legacies, the play's dramatic irony makes us aware of the frailty and the contingency of the *exemplum* in the age of mass-produced posterity. In reviewing Erasmus's and Montaigne's skepticism of the universal validity and applicability of the *exemplum*, Michel Jenneret argues that recycling ancient texts with a critical eye did not spell a "crisis of exemplarity" but a dynamic and transformative engagement with the past. What I have been arguing is that the creative plasticity Jenneret articulates came at a cost. It sounded the death knell for the *exemplum* as a vehicle of humanist commemoration. Shakespeare's play helps us to hear that bell, for, although Antony and Cleopatra will be buried together, so to speak, their actual memorial site remains unknown: they reside somewhere in our mass-produced fantasies.

Notes

1. Many thanks to Travis DeCook and Bill Engel, who read over this chapter and provided helpful feedback. Quotations from Shakespeare follow *The New Oxford Shakespeare* hereafter cited parenthetically.
2. *Julius Caesar*, 1.2.136–139.
3. "The list that we know today only became fixed in the Renaissance" but the first forms of the seven wonders emerged in the fifth century BCE. See Clayton and Price, "Introduction" in *Seven Wonders of the Ancient World*, p. 5ff. For an English example before Shakespeare, see Alley, *Ptōchomuseion*, H4^r–H6^r.
4. The phrase comes from *Hamlet*, 5.1.259.
5. I regard the protagonists as wanting to be remembered forever, not as expressing "an ecstatic *desire of death*," according to the psychoanalytic reading of Lisa S. Starks, "'Immortal Longings': The Erotics of Death in *Antony and Cleopatra*," p. 245. Furthermore, I concur with Gordon Braden, "Fame, Eternity, and Shakespeare's

Romans," p. 49, that their actions are not aiming for the afterlife but for worldly fame.
6. C. C. Barfoot, "News of the Roman Empire," p. 111, rightly observes, "Characters are prompted to become their own memorialists and historians, and the memorialists of others, both for their own benefit and for ours." Michael Neill, *Issues of Death*, pp. 305–327, builds a compelling argument around Cleopatra's "act of transcendent self-fashioning" (p. 322), while Garrett Sullivan Jr., *Memory and Forgetting in English Renaissance Drama*, pp. 88–108, demonstrates how Cleopatra, Circe-like, transforms Antony's self-oblivion into an alternative to Rome's memorialization of heroic masculinity. Raphael Lyne, *Memory and Intertextuality in Renaissance Literature*, recognizing full well how the play "features famous figures struggling to deal with their memories and how they will be remembered" (p. 160), investigates Shakespeare's intertextual indebtedness to Plutarch's life of Marcus Antonius.
7. See Daniel 2.
8. *The Pride of King Nabuchadnezzar*, sig. B4[r]. I have silently modernized this quotation and those from other early modern texts in this chapter.
9. Suetonius, *The History of Twelve Cæsars Emperors of Rome*, p. 45. Plutarch, *The Lives of the Noble Grecians and Romans*, p. 1010, says that Caesar "commanded she should be nobly buried and laid by Antonius."
10. Ibid., pp. 998–999, 1010.
11. Ibid., p. 1005.
12. For a study of Shakespeare's rejection of monumentalization in the sonnets, see Grant Williams, "Monumental Memory and Little Reminders: the Fantasy of Being Remembered by Posterity."
13. In Thomas's *Dictionarium Linguae Latinae et Anglicanae*, sig. OO3[r], under the Latin "monimentum," a monument meant a "remembrance of some notable acte, as tombes, sepulchers, books, images, and a memorial, a token, a sign, a testimony, a monument, a record, a chronicle, an history."
14. Kempe, *The Education of Children in Learning*, sig. E2[r].
15. Cicero, *De Inventione*, I.19.27.
16. Geoffrey Fenton, *The Golden Epistles*, sig. L5[r].
17. Kempe, sig. E2[r].

18. In his conduct book for courtiers but for a wider literate audience, *Hērō-paideia*, James Cleland asserts, "There are no rules of moral philosophy so sure and certain as those, which we learn by other men's examples" (L1^r).
19. See Miriam Joseph, *Rhetoric in Shakespeare's Time*.
20. Aristotle, *Rhetoric*, 1356b, designates just two rhetorical techniques for engendering belief: example (*paradeigma*) and enthymeme.
21. John D. Lyons, *Exemplum*, pp. 10, 29.
22. See the primary Tudor translation, *Marcus Tullius Cicero's Three Books of Duties*, sig. P4^{r-v}, sig. K8^r.
23. Rebeca Langland, *Roman Exempla and Situation Ethics*, p. 103.
24. *Marcus Tullius Cicero's Three Books of Duties*, sig. F8^r. Thomas Elyot, *The Book Named the Governor*, sig. L4^v, quotes the same passage.
25. Ignoring the *De Officiis*, Lyons's *Exemplum* focuses exclusively on *De Copia*, about which more will be said below.
26. Erasmus published his edition in Paris around 1501.
27. For the court, see Aysha Pollnitz, *Princely Education in Early Modern Britain*, pp. 53–54. For grammar school, see Thomas Baldwin, *William Shakespeare's Small Latine and Lesse Greeke*, vol. 1, passim. Patrick Gerard Walsh, "Introduction," p. xliv, summarizes the book's influence: "The *De officiis* was prescribed reading at the University of Oxford from 1517, and Ciceronian studies flourished likewise at Cambridge from the same era." Elyot, sig. E6^v–E7^r, advocates three central texts for educating young gentlemen: Plato's works, Aristotle's *Ethics*, and *De Officiis*.
28. Mack, *Elizabethan Rhetoric*, p. 35.
29. Pliny, *Natural History*, vol. 1, para. 23. Erasmus, "Letter 152," ll. 20–23.
30. Ibid., ll. 55–57.
31. Plutarch, p. 984.
32. Here is just a sampling of print texts that reflect upon the importance of exempla to improve moral behavior: Painter, *The Palace of Pleasure*, sig. *3^v–*4^r; Chelidonius, *A Most Excellent History*, sig. K2^v–K3^r; Lodowick, *The Pilgrimage of Princes*, sig. S2^r.
33. Even though Cicero's *De Officiis* seems to get short-shrift in Erasmus, *The Education of a Christian Prince*, p. 251, the latter

regards every text as a potential mine for exempla and teaches the prince the importance of accumulating a store of wisdom (p. 220).
34. See Soellner, "The Madness of Hercules and the Elizabethans."
35. Plutarch, p. 317, says both Hercules and Bacchus took on immortality.
36. On the comparison with Hercules in scholarship, see Deats, "Shakespeare's Anamorphic Dream," pp. 29–30. Xenophon, *Memorabilia*, 2.1.21–34.
37. *Marcus Tullius Cicero's Three Books*, sig F6^v, sig. O5^v.
38. Plutarch, pp. 971, 982.
39. 1.1.39–42; 1.3.34–37; 2.3.5; 2.5.77–79; 2.5.95–96; 3.13.162–169.
40. Whetstone, *The English Mirror*, sig. A4^v, expresses the relationship between negative and positive exemplarity well in comparing Marcus Aurelius with his son Commodus.
41. On the way in which critics have overturned the moralizing hostility toward the protagonists, see Lyne, *Memory and Intertextuality*, pp. 160–161, and Deats, pp. 1–12.
42. Plutarch, pp. 977–978.
43. 5.1.64–66; 5.1.73–77; 5.2.124–129.
44. Plutarch, p. 983.
45. More, *A Demonstration of God*, p. 50.
46. Rossky, "Imagination in the English Renaissance," p. 57.
47. Chaucer, *The Legend of Good Women*, sig. QQ3^r–QQ4^r. Munday, *A Courtly Controversy*, sig. D6^v. Gibson, "A Very Proper Ditty."
48. Batman, *The Golden Book*, sig. E2^v-E3^r. Nashe, *Pierce Penniless*, sig. G1^r.
49. Castiglione, *The Courtier*, sig. FF4^r. Boccaccio, *Amorous Fiammetta*, sig. D2^r.
50. Rankins, *The English Ape*, sig. B1^v. Spenser, *The Faerie Queene*, 1.5.50.7–8. Lodowick, sig. BBB4^r.
51. Boaistuau, *Certain Secret Wonders*, sig. R3^r.
52. Boccaccio, *Amorous Fiammetta*, sig. GG4^r–HH1^r. Bullien, *Bullein's Bulwark*, sig. EEE1^v.
53. Greene, *The Spanish Masquerado*, sig. D4^r.
54. Lodowick, sig. D1^v.
55. Rainolde, *A Chronicle of All the Noble Emperors*, sig. C1^v.
56. Turberville, "To His Friend to Be Constant After Choice Made," sig. D3^v.

57. Averell, *A Dial for Dainty Darlings*, C1^r. Nashe, *Anatomy of Abuses*, sig. A4^v.
58. Rainolde, sig. B6^v.
59. Serres, *The Three Parts of Commentaries* [...] *the Civil Wars of France*, sig. N1^v.
60. Plutarch, *The Lives*, p. 970; Huloet, *Huloet's Dictionary Newly Corrected*, sig. I1^r.
61. Gascoigne, "In Praise of a Gentlewoman."
62. La Primaudaye, *The French Academy*, sig. O2^r.
63. Bishop, *Beautiful Blossoms*, sig. CC3^r. Mexía, *The Forest or Collection of Histories*, sig. LL3^v.
64. Rogers, *A Philosophical Discourse*, sig. J5^v–J6^r. Allott, *Wit's Theater of the Little World*, sig. MM2^v.
65. Garzoni, *The Hospital of Incurable Fools*, sig. M2^r.
66. Elyot, sig. DD5^v. Bishop, sig. H4^v, sig. I2^v.
67. Nashe, *The Unfortunate Traveler*, sig. H2^r.
68. Erasmus, *Apophthegmes*, J1^r. La Primaudaye, sig. LL4^v.
69. Williamson, *Infinite Variety*, p. 15.
70. Arshad, *Imagining Cleopatra*, p. 18.
71. Eco, "An *Ars Oblivionalis?* Forget It!" p. 259.
72. For the aphoristic fragment as an instrument of social mobility, see Crane, *Framing Authority*, p. 4.
73. Erasmus, *De Copia*, pp. 348–365.
74. Ibid., p. 639.
75. This is a translation of the Latin inscription: "Et si mors, indies accelerat, Post funera virtus vivet tamen."
76. On John Day' colophon, see Engel, *The Printer as Author in Early Modern English Book History*, chapter 1.
77. Charron, *Of Wisdom*, sig. F2^v.
78. See Barfoot, "News of the Roman Empire."
79. Davies, *Mirum in Modum*, sig. C2^v. On the relationship between the senses and the imagination, see Smid, *The Imagination in Early Modern English Literature*, pp. 16–24.
80. Rossky, pp. 51–53.
81. Plutarch, pp. 981–982.
82. Ibid., p. 982.
83. Ibid., p. 982.
84. Ibid., p. 981.
85. Rossky, pp. 60–61.

86. See, for instance, Marshall, "Man of Steel Done Got the Blues," p. 391, 401. Neill, pp. 313–315, and Sullivan, p. 105.

References

Alley, William. *Ptōchomuseion [sic]. = The Poor Man's Library*. London: 1565; STC 374.
Allott, Robert. *Wit's Theater of the Little World*. London: 1599; STC 381.
Aristotle. *Rhetoric*. In *The Complete Works of Aristotle*. Edited by Jonathan Barnes. 2 vols. Princeton, NJ: Princeton University Press, 1984. vol. 1.
Arshad, Yasmin. *Imagining Cleopatra: Performing Gender and Power in Early Modern England*. London: The Arden Shakespeare, 2019.
Averell, W. *A Dial for Dainty Darlings*. London: 1584; STC 978.
Baldwin, Thomas Whitfield. *William Shakespeare's Small Latine and Lesse Greeke*. 2 vols. Urbana, IL: University of Illinois Press, 1944.
Barfoot, C. C. "News of the Roman Empire: Hearsay, Soothsay, Myth, and History in *Antony and Cleopatra*." In *Reclamations of Shakespeare*. Edited by A. J. Hoenselaars. Amsterdam: Rodopi, 1994. pp. 105–208.
Barroll, J. Leeds. "Enobarbus' Description of Cleopatra." *Texas Studies in English* 37 (1958): 61–78.
Batman, Stephen. *The Golden Book of the Leaden Goddess*. London: 1577; STC 1583.
Bishop, John. *Beautiful Blossoms*. London: 1577; STC 3091.
Boaistuau, Pierre. *Certain Secret Wonders of Nature*. London: 1569; STC 3164.5.
Boccaccio, Giovanni. *Amorous Fiammetta*. London: 1587; STC 3179.
Braden, Gordon. "Fame, Eternity, and Shakespeare's Romans." In *Shakespeare and Renaissance Ethics*. Edited by Patrick Gray and John D. Cox. Cambridge: Cambridge University Press, 2014. pp. 37–55.
Bullien, William. *Bullein's Bulwark*. London: 1579; STC 4034.
Castiglione, Baldassarre. *The Courtier*. Translated by Thomas Hoby. London: 1561; STC 4778.
Charron, Pierre. *Of Wisdom*. Translated by Samson Lennard. London: 1608; STC 5051.
Chaucer, Geoffrey. *The Legend of Good Women*. In *The Works of Geoffrey Chaucer*. London: 1542; STC 5069.
Cicero. *De inventione, De optimo genere oratorum, and Topica*. Translated by H. M. Hubbell. London: William Heinemann, 1949.
———. *Marcus Tullius Cicero's Three Books of Duties*. Trans. by Nicholas Grimald. London: 1556; STC 5281.

Clayton, Peter A. and Martin J. Price. "Introduction." In *Seven Wonders of the Ancient World*. Edited by Peter A. Clayton and Martin J. Price. London: Routledge, 1988, pp. 1–12.

Cleland, James. *Hērō-paideia, or the Institution of a Young Noble Man*. London: 1607; STC 5393.

Crane, Mary Thomas. *Framing Authority: Sayings, Self, and Society in Sixteenth-Century England*. Princeton, NJ: Princeton University Press.

Davies, John. *Mirum in Modum*. London: 1602; STC 6336.

Deats, Sara Munson. "Shakespeare's Anamorphic Dream." In *Antony and Cleopatra: New Critical Essays*. Edited by Sara Munson Deats. New York and London: Routledge, 2005. pp. 1–93.

Eco, Umberto. "An *Ars Oblivionalis*? Forget It!" Translated by Marilyn Migiel. *PMLA* 103.3 (1988): 254–261.

Elyot, Thomas. *The Book Named the Governor*. London: 1537; STC 7636.

Engel, William E. *The Printer as Author in Early Modern English Book History: John Day and the Fabrication of a Protestant Memory Art*. New York and London: Routledge, 2022.

Erasmus. *Apophthegmes*. Translated by Nicholas Udall. London: 1541; STC 10443.

———. "Letter 152." In *The Correspondence of Erasmus: Letters 142 to 297*. Vol. 2. Translated by R. A. B. Mynors and D. F. S. Thomson. Toronto: University of Toronto Press, 1975.

———. *De Copia*. Translated by Betty I. Knott. In *Antibarbari: Parabolae; De Copia; De Ratione Studii*. Edited by Craig R. Thompson. University of Toronto Press, 1978.

———. *The Education of a Christian Prince*. In Desiderius Erasmus, *Panegyricus: Moria; Julius Exclusus; Institutio Principis Christiani; Querela Pacis; Ciceronianus; Notes; Indexes*. Translated by Neil M. Cheshire and Michael J. Heath. Toronto: University of Toronto Press, 1986.

Fenton, Geoffrey. *The Golden Epistles Containing Variety of Discourse Both Moral, Philosophical, and Divine*. London: 1575; STC 10794.

Garzoni, Tomaso. *The Hospital of Incurable Fools*. Translated by Edward Blount. London: 1600; STC 11634.

Gascoigne, George. "In Praise of a Gentlewoman." In *A Hundreth Sundry Flowers*. London: 1573; STC 11635. N3^v-N4^r.

Gibson, Leonard. "A Very Proper Ditty." London: 1571; STC 11836.

Greene, Robert. *The Spanish Masquerado*. London: 1589; STC 12310.

Huloet, Richard. *Huloet's Dictionary Newly Corrected*. London: 1572; STC 13941.

Joseph, Miriam. *Rhetoric in Shakespeare's Time; Literary Theory of Renaissance Europe*. New York: Harcourt, Brace & World, 1962.

Kempe, William. *The Education of Children in Learning*. London: 1588; STC 14926.
La Primaudaye, Pierre. *The French Academy*. Translated by Thomas Bowes. London: 1586; STC 15233.
Langland, Rebecca. "Roman *Exempla* and Situation Ethics: Valerius Maximus and Cicero *de Officiis*." *The Journal of Roman Studies* 101 (2011): 100–122.
Lodowick, Lloyd. *The Pilgrimage of Princes*. London: 1573; STC 16624.
Lyne, Raphael. *Memory and Intertextuality in Renaissance Literature*. Cambridge: Cambridge University Press, 2016.
Lyons, John D. *Exemplum: the Rhetoric of Example in Early Modern France and Italy*. Princeton, N.J: Princeton University Press, 1989.
Mack, Peter. *Elizabethan Rhetoric: Theory and Practice*. Cambridge: Cambridge University Press, 2002.
Marshall, Cynthia. "Man of Steel Done Got the Blues: Melancholic Subversion of Presence in *Antony and Cleopatra*." *Shakespeare Quarterly* 44 (1993): 385–408.
Mexía, Pedro. *The Forest or Collection of Histories*. London: 1571; STC 17849.
More, George. *A Demonstration of God in his Works*. London: 1597; STC 18071.5.
Munday, Anthony. *A Courtly Controversy between Love and Learning*. London: 1581; STC 18268.
Nashe, Thomas. *Anatomy of Abuses*. London: 1589; STC 18364.
———. *Pierce Penniless his Supplication to the Devil*. London: 1592; STC 18373.
———. *The Unfortunate Traveler*. London: 1594; STC 18380.
Neill, Michael. *Issues of Death: Mortality and Identity in English Renaissance Tragedy*. Oxford: Oxford University Press, 1997.
Pliny. *Natural History*. Volume I: Books 1–2. Translated by H. Rackham. Loeb Classical Library 330. Cambridge, MA: Harvard University Press, 1938.
Plutarch. *The Lives of the Noble Grecians and Romans*. Translated by Jacques Amyot and Thomas North. London: 1579; STC 20066.
Pollnitz, Aysha. *Princely Education in Early Modern Britain*. Cambridge: Cambridge University Press, 2015.
Rainolde, Richard. *A Chronicle of All the Noble Emperors*. London: 1571; STC 20926.
Rankins, William. *The English Ape*. London: 1588; STC 20698.5.
Rogers, Thomas. *A Philosophical Discourse*. London: 1576; STC 21239.
Rossky, William. "Imagination in the English Renaissance: Psychology and Poetic." *Studies in the Renaissance* 5 (1958): 49–73.
Serres, Jean de. *The Three Parts of Commentaries [...] the Civil Wars of France*. Translated by Thomas Timme. London: 1574; STC 22241.5.

Shakespeare, William. *The New Oxford Shakespeare: The Complete Works*. General edited by Gary Taylor, John Jowett, Terri Bourus, and Gabriel Egan. Oxford: Oxford University Press, 2017.

Smid, Deanna. *The Imagination in Early Modern English Literature*. Leiden: Brill, 2017.

Smith, Henry. *The Pride of King Nabuchadnezzar, Dan. 4.26.27*. London: 1591; STC 22688.

Soellner, Rolf. "The Madness of Hercules and the Elizabethans." *Comparative Literature* 10.4 (1958): 309–324.

Spenser, Edmund. *The Faerie Queene*. London: 1590; STC 23081a.

Starks, Lisa S. "'Immortal Longings': The Erotics of Death in *Antony and Cleopatra*." In *Antony and Cleopatra: New Critical Essays*. Edited by Sara Munson Deats. New York and London: Routledge, 2005. pp. 243–258.

Suetonius. *The History of Twelve Cæsars Emperors of Rome*. Translated by Philemon Holland. London: 1606; STC 23422.

Sullivan, Garrett A. *Memory and Forgetting in English Renaissance Drama: Shakespeare, Marlowe, Webster*. Cambridge: Cambridge University Press, 2005.

Thomas, Thomas. *Dictionarium Linguae Latinae et Anglicanae*. Cambridge: 1587; STC 24008.

Turberville, George. "To his Friend to be constant after choice made." In *Epitaphs, Epigrams, Songs, Sonnets*. London: 1567; STC 24326. sig. D3ᵛ.

Walsh, Patrick Gerard. "Introduction." In Cicero. *On Obligations*. Oxford: Oxford University Press, 2000. pp. ix–xlvi.

Whetstone, George. *The English Mirror*. London: 1586; STC 25336.

Williams, Grant. "Monumental Memory and Little Reminders: The Fantasy of Being Remembered by Posterity." In *The Routledge Handbook of Shakespeare and Memory*. Edited by Andrew Hiscock and Lina Perkins Wilder. New York: Routledge, 2018. pp. 297–311.

Williamson, Marilyn L. *Infinite Variety: Antony and Cleopatra in Renaissance Drama and Earlier Tradition*. Mystic, CT: Lawrence Verry, 1974.

Xenophon. *Memorabilia. Oeconomicus. Symposium. Apology*. Translated by E. C. Marchant et al. Revised by Jeffrey Henderson. Loeb Classical Library 168. Cambridge, MA: Harvard University Press, 2013.

CHAPTER 6

Ash, Rust, and Ooze: Funereal Rituals and Tombs in *Pericles*

Dorothy Todd

In "An Ode. To Himself," Ben Jonson bemoans the tastes of playgoers, lamenting that they would rather see "no doubt some mouldy tale / like *Pericles*" than one of his own witty works.[1] In calling *Pericles* a "mouldy tale," Jonson uses this image of decay to criticize the play as "[w]orn out with old age, decrepit; outmoded, antiquated; (also) tediously academic."[2] Yet, as Kurt A. Schreyer demonstrates in "Moldy *Pericles*"—his excellent article focusing on how the tombs of dead writers function as a prosthesis of literary authority that affords medieval and early modern writers fertile ground for stories and poetic identity—the label "moldy" is not entirely condemnatory.[3] Because "moldy" can also mean "[o]f the nature of mould; esp. of the nature of fine or loose soil; earthy, dirty" and "of the nature of a grave or graveyard," to call *Pericles* a "mouldy" tale is not only to point to its antiquated style and well-worn

D. Todd (✉)
Texas A&M University, College Station, TX, USA
e-mail: dtodd@tamu.edu

© The Author(s), under exclusive license to Springer Nature Switzerland AG 2022
W. E. Engel and G. Williams (eds.), *The Shakespearean Death Arts*, Palgrave Shakespeare Studies,
https://doi.org/10.1007/978-3-030-88490-1_6

plot, but also to suggest its fecundity, to highlight both its dependence on convention and its proclivity for innovation.[4]

While Schreyer's conception of mold as "both decayed remains and fecund soil, a locus of death and birth" provides a framework for interrogating *Pericles*'s complex relationship to authorship and textual authority, I argue that this same schema can also aid in conceptualizing the play's enactment of, and engagement with, the death arts. Building upon the divergent meanings of mold that Schreyer outlines, this chapter will trace three distinct but related images of simultaneous decay and fecundity—ash, rust, and ooze—that emerge in *Pericles*. Like the polysemic mold of Jonson's complaint, ash, rust, and ooze in *Pericles* signify in multiple ways simultaneously, calling to mind both decomposition and creation, death and new life. Paired with the play's multiple literal and metaphorical entombments, including Gower's emergence from his tomb to serve as the play's choric figure, these images illuminate the power of funereal rituals in the early modern period both to mark the end of one's life and to preserve the memories of the deceased. Furthermore, objects and characters' repeated emergences from these literal and figurative tombs in *Pericles* reveal both the theater's unique relationship to the death arts—the theater remembers and revives through performance—and the power of the death arts themselves to celebrate, preserve, and reanimate memories of the deceased.[5]

Rising from the Ash

The tomb that frames both the play and this chapter's interpretation of entombment in *Pericles* belongs to the medieval poet Gower, who functions as the play's choric figure. In his opening speech, Gower explains his appearance on the stage as a revivification from the tomb, thus establishing the play's complex relationship to authorship and textual authority. Additionally, the poet's rising from the tomb suggests that the processes of Gower's entombment and monumentalization have in fact provided the fertile ground for Shakespeare's retelling of an old tale. Similar to Gower rising from the tomb to assist in the refashioning and retelling of the ancient tale, both Marina and Thaisa, whom Pericles believes are dead at various points within the action of the play, emerge from their entombment in order to restore and reanimate the family unit at the play's end. Pericles throws Thaisa's casket into the sea, and yet she emerges alive from both casket and sea. Marina's entombment, on the other hand, is initially metaphorical as Pericles sends his infant daughter to live with Cleon and Dionyza, and in doing so, seals off Marina, the constant reminder of his dead wife, from his heart. Yet when Cleon and Dionyza report to Pericles that his daughter has died, he attempts once again to put an ocean between himself and his past. At the play's end, however, Marina is alive and looking forward to marrying Lysimachus, in effect preparing to extend the lineage of Pericles. What is so startling about the play's entombments, as I have mentioned above, is that individuals emerge revivified from their literal and symbolic tombs. In *Pericles*, the entombment of characters who are not dead, and their reanimation from tombs in spite of supposed death, articulates the stage's unique relationship to the death arts. While the death arts in life only allow for meditation and memorialization, the death arts on the stage enact revivification, both of characters and of stories themselves. The play demonstrates the efficacy of the death arts in the process of memorial preservation, but it takes one step further by connecting these moments of apparent death to the continuance and renewal of life on the stage. The death arts in *Pericles* do not simply help us remember; they revive and recreate.

As Gower opens the play, he immediately draws attention to the fact that while he was dead in the past, he now finds himself reanimated though not fully alive. He frames his appearance within the present moment of the stage as a revivification from the tomb: "from ashes ancient Gower is come" (1.0.2).[6] While "ashes" undoubtedly points to burial and to the tomb through the co-existing meanings of ash as "dust of the ground" and "mortal remains, buried corpse," a point to which I will return below, I wish to pause and acknowledge the associations between ash, life, and death in the image of the phoenix to emphasize that Gower does not figure himself here as rising from the ashes with renewed youth.[7] Gower does not appear on stage as a man untouched by the passage of time or as some sort of incorruptible saint; instead he emphasizes that he is "assuming man's infirmities" (1.0.3), taking on a mortal form that is weak and broken by its very nature. He further emphasizes both his past and future as ash—evoking *The Book of Common Prayer*'s phrase, "ashes to ashes, dust to dust"—through his reference to "ember eves" (1.0.3) and by envisioning himself as a "taper light" (1.0.16), willing to burn himself out in the process of enlightening the audience. Combined with the words "old" in line one and "ancient" in line two, which could grammatically modify either "ashes" or "Gower," Gower's initial lines reiterate that both he and his story arise from the medieval past and from beyond the grave in order to appear to, and engage with, early modern audiences. This connection to the ancient past and to death—the traces of a different temporal and spiritual realm—allows Gower and the ancient tale of the Prince of Tyre to provide the play with a framework that looks to the past, and to death, as integral to moving forward in life. Schreyer argues that Gower's resurrection from the tomb is "more than rhetorical" because his appearance on the stage "bears witness to theater's miraculous power of bodily revivification."[8] To this point, I add that Gower's reanimation in the play's opening lines also confirms the power of the death arts' memorialization of the dead to usher in new creation.

The ashes from which Gower emerges call to mind the actual tomb from which the dead poet would have had to emerge in order to make himself visible on the Globe's stage. Almost all critical engagement with the play's opening report that John Gower's tomb lay in St. Mary Overie's—later named St. Saviour's—in Southwark, just a few blocks from the Globe Theater. While it is of course possible that Shakespeare knew of this tomb simply due to the playhouse's proximity to the site of Gower's final resting place, Katherine Duncan-Jones emphasizes the fact that Shakespeare's brother Edmund was buried at St. Saviour's close to the time of the play's composition, thus suggesting a connection between Shakespeare's possible encounter with the recumbent effigy and the play's interest in memorializing and mourning the dead.[9] Schreyer is quick to point out that in addition to Shakespeare's familiarity with the tomb due to its proximity to the playhouse, or due to attending services at the church, Gower's tomb—and the tombs of many medieval authors—had a long literary history, a history with which the play's authors were almost undoubtedly familiar. By evoking Gower's tomb in the play's opening line, Shakespeare makes use of the multiple simultaneous temporalities of the tomb both to demonstrate "a profound investment in, and a sense of connectedness to, the past," and to show that the present continues to be shaped and revived by that which appears to be dead or otherwise beyond reach.[10] Gower accordingly becomes the dead medieval poet, celebrated in death through the monumental tomb, brought back to life to restore the audience through the retelling of an ancient story that has already been retold many times before.

The Temporalities of Tombs

As the physical and literary tomb of Gower demonstrates, tombs and the processes of entombment occupy a temporal multidimensionality in the early modern world. While tombs, specifically the monumental kind featuring ornate carvings, have a long history that stretches back to the medieval period, they became more numerous in Renaissance Europe as the ways in which society thought about death became increasingly focused on the individual. Mass graves gave way to personalized burial practices such as coffins and individual burials, thus populating churches and graveyards with more tombs and monuments.[11] Death became increasingly visible, reminding individuals of its inevitability at every turn in life.

Yet, it is not just the constant presence of death in life that makes tombs and monuments multitemporal; the specific design details and conditions of construction of many tombs in the medieval and early modern periods also contributed to their polytemporality. *Transi* tombs were extremely fashionable in the fifteenth and early sixteenth centuries.[12] *Transi* tombs, according to Catherine Belsey, juxtapose two temporalities for the purposes of contrast, showing the deceased in life and in death:

> These equally double-decker constructions showed the deceased, fully and formally dressed, recumbent on a tomb chest, while below the commemorative effigy lies a corpse in a state of decay. Stripped to their shrouds, often contorted, sometimes verminous, the gaunt cadavers throw into relief the transitory nature of the grandeur shown above them.[13]

Amplifying this temporal disjunction between the deceased's past in life and future in decay is the timing of construction of many of these funeral monuments. As numerous scholars have demonstrated, the Protestant Reformation, and with it the obliteration of Purgatory, drastically impacted the trajectory of the death arts in early modern England.[14] Scott L. Newstok argues that the theological erasure of Purgatory precipitated widespread "anxiety that proper remembrance would not be paid after one's death," which in turn "contributed to an increased valuation of memorialization while living."[15] The concern was that when survivors no longer needed to purchase indulgences or continue to pray for those in Purgatory, the deceased would simply be forgotten. The result of this increased emphasis on memorialization in life was that individuals proactively contracted the building of their own tombs proactively prior to their deaths. It was, therefore, not uncommon to walk past the tombs and monuments of individuals who were still alive. William E. Engel captures the complex temporality of the prematurely constructed tombs when he describes the death arts as capturing the "always ready-at-hand possibility of one's own implied future absence."[16] The monumental tombs, memorializing the life of a still-living individual, encapsulate the past (the moment in time when the monument was constructed and upon which the recumbent figure was based), the present (the moment in time when one walks past the tomb that monumentalizes the still-living individual), and the future (the moment in time when the corpse of the deceased will resemble the decomposing effigy). So commonplace was the temporal disconnect of the memorial constructed for the still-alive individual that in *Much Ado About Nothing*, Benedick criticizes the building of one's tomb in one's own lifetime and the self-interest that perhaps fuels this construction when he remarks, "[i]f a man do not erect in this age his own tomb ere he dies, he shall live no longer in monument than the bell rings and the widow weeps" (*Ado* 5.2.69–72).[17] The temporal complexity of the monumental tomb is epitomized in the construction, in one's own age, of a monument that will mark for future ages the life of someone who has not yet passed.

The common design and construction of monuments prior to the death of those that the monuments aim to memorialize allow individuals to participate actively in the construction of their own memorial. As individuals made choices about the fashioning of their monuments, they also "self-fashioned."[18] Even as burial practices increasingly emphasized the individual rather than the community in the early modern period, the tombs and monuments of individuals still served the important function of emphasizing the continuity, even in death, of bloodlines and families. As David Cressy explains, through carved depictions of spouses and children, as well as embellishments such as coats of arms, these tombs both marked the finite life of the individual and emphasized the continuance of the individual's impact on the world:

> The gentlemen who requested such memorials projected themselves as husbands and fathers, heads of households, rather than as mere individuals. With their heraldic arms representing the past, and their progeny pointing

to the future, the dead man took a crucial place in the maintenance of gentle dynastic continuity.[19]

These self-fashioned and self-fashioning monuments, like the *transi* monuments described above, evoke multiple temporalities simultaneously as they destabilize the distinctions between honoring in life and memorializing in death.

Though the tomb of Gower is never visible on stage, the specter of Gower's tomb inflects the entirety of *Pericles*. On the level of plot, it is presumably from his tomb, just around the corner from the Globe Theater, that Gower has emerged in order to "pleasure bring" through the recounting of his tale (1.0.14). Gower's tomb also helps articulate the lineage of Shakespeare's text as it, like the tombs of early modern individuals that simultaneously point to one's ancestors and offspring, represents the *auctoritas* from which Shakespeare drew in the retelling of the tale of the Prince of Tyre. Lastly, Gower's tomb guides us to see *Pericles*'s literal and figurative tombs as multi-temporal spaces that blur the lines between life and death, between remembering and forgetting, and between celebration and mourning.

Watery Tombs

The sea that Pericles crosses numerous times is the most obvious tomb in the play, in part because the sea frequently serves, both in the early modern period and today, as a final resting place for those who die at sea. Notably, in *Pericles*, the sea functions as both a literal and figurative tomb. Of even greater import is this tomb's inability to keep enclosed what it at first entombs. Like Gower's grave, the sea cannot contain its dead. In the play's opening scenes, the sea first functions as a tomb in which Pericles can bury unwanted information and hide himself temporarily to avoid a worse fate. After solving the riddle of Antiochus and finding himself burdened with information that will result in his death regardless of whether or not he shares the King's secrets, Pericles decides to flee Antioch by sea: "by flight I'll shun the danger which I fear" (1.1.143). Upon returning to his home in Tyre, however, Pericles quickly finds himself once again fleeing Antiochus and attempting to divest himself of his knowledge of Antiochus's incestuous relationship after Helicanus advises him that staying in Tyre would most likely spell death: "Therefore, my lord, go travel for a while, / Till that [Antiochus's] rage and anger be forgot" (1.2.104–5). Implicit in Helicanus's counsel for Pericles are two overlapping notions: that with the passing of time comes forgetting, and that the sea Pericles will cross can also aid in this forgetting. In these ways, the sea functions more like an unmarked grave than a monumental tomb. The sea appears to become a space of forgetting, not remembering.[20] Additionally, the sea stands in as a sort of temporary tomb—a hiding space not unlike the Capulets' tomb in *Romeo and Juliet*—that Pericles must occupy so that he is not found and killed by Antiochus. Though Pericles's initial sailing from Tyre to Tarsus is uneventful, the sea quickly shows that despite Pericles's attempts to bury his knowledge of Antiochus's incestuous secret through sea travel and to entomb himself in the safety of the vast sea, danger still follows him. When an assassin lands in Tyre and Helicanus sends word to Pericles that he must not tarry in Tarsus any longer, it becomes clear that the watery tomb of the sea has not managed to keep its secrets hidden.

The sea becomes more literalized as a tomb at the beginning of Act Two when Gower describes the storm that destroys Pericles's ship on its escape from Tarsus:

> For now the wind begins to blow;
> Thunder above and deeps below
> Makes such unquiet that the ship
> Should house him safe is wracked and split,
> And he good prince, having all lost,
> By waves from coast to coast is tossed.
> All perishen of man, of pelf,
> Ne aught escapend but himself;
> Till Fortune, tired with doing bad,
> Threw him ashore to give him glad. (2.0.29–38)

Following Gower's narration of the deadly sea storm, Pericles emerges on the stage, having been tossed up from the sea that drowned his entire crew. In a direct address to the ocean itself, he recounts what has transpired, and alternating between first and third person, he describes how the "seas hath cast me on the rocks" (2.1.5) and laments, "having thrown him from your watery grave, / [h]ere to have death in peace is all he'll crave" (2.1.10–11). As Pericles uses both "me" and "he," he sees himself both as the living subject and as the seemingly dead—and soon-to-be-dead again—memorialized object. Not unlike the men and women who oversaw the design and building of their own tombs, or even the play's reanimated Gower, Pericles finds himself narrating his own story and thus actively participating in the construction of his own memorial.

Pericles's craving for a peaceful death is cut short by the appearance of three fishermen whose frequent references to whales, alongside the scene's repeated language of consumption and regurgitation, call to mind the biblical story of Jonah, and by extension, point to the further convergence of the sea's literal and figurative tombs. In the midst of the fishermen's lively conversation prior to spotting Pericles, the first fisherman compares a wealthy but miserly man to "a whale […] / driving the poor fry before him, and at last devour[ing] / them all at a mouthful" (2.1.30–33). The second fisherman, meanwhile, imagines that if he were to be swallowed by this hypothetical miser whale, he would eventually find himself belched up from the whale's belly: "Because he should have swallowed me too, and when I had been in his belly I would have kept such a jangling of the bells that he should never have left till he cast bells, steeple, church and parish up again" (2.1.39–42). The third fisherman further imbues this conversation with Jonahic imagery when he comments that King Simonides would "purge" from the community those who steal (2.1.45). Swallowed by a whale but eventually cast back out of the beast's belly, the biblical Jonah faces certain death only to be given a second chance to lead a righteous life. What appears to be Jonah's literal tomb becomes a figurative tomb when, after spending three days and three nights inside the stomach of the whale, Jonah is regurgitated. Through the figurative tomb of the whale's belly—though Jonah was quite literally inside the whale—the Bible teaches that Christians can emerge from the literal tomb of death through eternal life, which is promised to the followers of Jesus Christ. Similarly, Pericles, having been seemingly swallowed by the sea and facing death, is presented another chance at life. Adopting the fisherman's cetacean images of consumption and purging, Pericles reveals himself to the fishermen and amidst exhaustion explains, "May see the sea hath cast upon your coast" (2.1.55). Emphasizing Pericles's escape from the sea's watery tomb, the second fisherman, practically repeating Pericles's words, declares, "What a drunken knave was the sea to cast / thee in our way" (2.1.55–6). Fewer than 100 lines later, the sea casts up more from its watery tomb.

Rusty Armor

Shortly after promising Pericles food and shelter, the fishermen pull in their nets, initially thinking they have caught a fish with "bot on't" (2.1.114). Upon closer inspection, they realize they have hauled in "rusty armour" from the sea (2.1.115). As we soon discover, this armor belonged to Pericles and to his father before him. Through its connection to monumental tombs in the early modern period and due to its rusty condition, this armor represents yet another one of the play's engagements with early modern death arts.

Tombs and armor have long been connected in the memorial practices of medieval and early modern England. Peter Stallybrass contends that tombs often depicted men in their armor due to the fact that "the most privileged markings of identity are those of the knight" in medieval and early modern aristocratic societies.[21] A subset of the popular *transi* tomb displayed the armored body above the decaying cadaver, further establishing the way in which the armor, like the tomb itself, preserved the memory of the monumentalized individual despite the decay of the individual's flesh. In addition to the tombs that depicted men in armor as a primary component of their designs, tombs and armor were often staged as a single memorial tableau with helms, gauntlets, and even swords hanging above or positioned next to individuals' tombs.[22] In *The Second Part of Henry the Sixth*, Iden describes how he will hang over his own tomb the sword he used to slay Cade: "Sword, I will hallow thee for this thy deed / And hang thee o'er my tomb when I am dead" (*2H6* 4.9.67–8). Like the tombs carved from stone, the armor and weapons function as significant material objects in Renaissance death arts, calling attention to the physical absence of the dead individual while also demonstrating, through the survival of material objects, the enduring qualities of memories of the individual. Ironically, with the development of gunpowder, armor became virtually useless on the battlefield with the result that its signification became increasingly ceremonial and theatrical.[23]

Even if ancestral armor did not decorate or embellish a tomb, the fact that plans for armor and plans for tombs often coexisted in the same document—the legal will—further establishes their symbolic overlap. Wills frequently laid out specific instructions for both how armor would be bequeathed and how monuments for the dead were to be constructed. Tombs, armor, and wills all worked in concert to materialize memory in the early modern period.[24] Yet, just as tombs often point both to the past through their representations of the deceased and to the future through their depictions of offspring, armor—and funereal armor in particular— also points to the continuance of the family. When a knight bequeaths his armor to his son, he acknowledges that his heraldic insignias will continue to be seen on the battlefield and in court even after he has passed. What Stallybrass calls "the fantasy of armor," the belief that the metal—unlike cloth or even stone monuments—would not decay, further supports a reading of armor as a powerful image of both memorialization of the dead and continuance of life.[25]

Like Gower emerging from the grave, not in renewed youth but with "man's infirmities" (1.0.3), the armor the fishermen drag from the sea does not appear "bright," "glittering," or "lustrous"—just some of the many words that describe armor and weapons in Shakespeare's canon— but is instead covered in rust.[26] The rust on Pericles's armor, like the mold examined above, suggests an intimate, unbreakable connection to the past, even in the emergence of new life. Additionally, the rust on the armor seems to chastise Pericles for not keeping his father's memory in the forefront of his mind and actions as he crosses the sea, running from the secret of Antiochus rather than fulfilling his duties as the Prince of Tyre. Through a survey of early modern plays, Richard Levin demonstrates that weapons that are put to use do not rust. On the contrary, armor and weapons rust on Shakespeare's stage "when they remain *out of use*, and the longer they remain out of use, the more they rust."[27] Though Pericles, describing his affinity for the armor, remarks, "It kept where I kept, I so dearly loved" (2.1.126), presumably it would not have rusted had Pericles properly put it to use as a memorial to his father.

Once the sea casts up the armor, however, Pericles embraces the armor's representative significance as an element in the elaborate system of death arts, using it both to remember his father and to secure the continuance of his father's lineage through the tournament in which he wins the hand of Thaisa. His own close encounter with death precipitates a new way of thinking about the function of the death arts. Having nearly been lost in the sea himself, he now bonds with the armor, claiming that it provides him with access to the memories of his deceased father. Pericles's description of the armor as both his and his father's—"it was mine own, part of my heritage, / Which my dead father did bequeath me"— echoes the dual function of the armor. Like the tomb, the armor serves as both a monument to the dead and a reminder to the living (2.1.119–20). Further highlighting the multiple temporalities of the armor is Pericles's use of the adjective "dead" to describe the bequeathing father. The construction of the phrase suggests a simultaneity of action; the father continues to give even in death, just as the monumental tomb allows the memories of the deceased to live on even as the corpse decays within its walls. Immediately after acknowledging the armor's function as a keeper of his father's memories, Pericles accesses a memory and recounts the moment his father bequeaths the armor to him: "'Keep it, my Pericles, it hath been a shield / 'Twixt me and death', and pointed to this brace, / 'For that it saved me, keep it'" (2.1.122–4). Pericles models the ways in which tombs and armor function to keep alive the memories of the dead. The father's words, by which he describes the armor's literal function of protecting him from death, in turn underscores the symbolic function of the armor in keeping the memories of the deceased alive. The repetition of "keep" and its cognates in these lines further emphasizes the continuity of life and of memories that this armor represents.[28]

THE POWER OF OOZE

This chapter has primarily considered *Pericles*'s symbolic deaths or deaths that occur off-stage and removed from the action of the play but now will pivot to the play's central and most literal deaths—the deaths of Pericles's wife and daughter. This distinction might seem tenuous since we know that neither Thaisa nor Marina is actually dead, but the difference between the apparent deaths of these characters and the play's other gestures at death lies in the fact that the play shows Pericles in real time participating in practices of mourning and memorialization in these scenes when he believes that Thaisa, and later, Marina are dead. In other words, it is through the putative deaths of the female characters, and through Pericles's responses to their apparent deaths, that the play most directly demonstrates the death arts' capabilities in life and on stage.

In these scenes, life, death, forgetting, and remembering powerfully collide as familial lines extend through birth, are broken through death, and ultimately are recuperated through apparent revivification and actual reunification. The first death we encounter in the play's central portion is that of Thaisa; Lychordia breaks the news to Pericles of his queen's death by handing the infant Marina to her father: "Take in your arms this piece / of your dead queen" (3.1.17–8). By figuring the infant as a part of her dead mother, Lychordia blurs the line between the living and the lifeless. The enjambment of these lines further creates this imbrication of loss and new life by framing Marina as a part of her mother, a holy relic of sorts, but also as a piece that through the line break is eternally separate from her mother. That the birth of Marina and death of Thaisa occur in the midst of a fierce storm at sea further emphasizes the sea as a tomb, a site of simultaneous remembering and forgetting. Marina is named after the sea on which she is born, a constant reminder of how she functions symbolically as her mother's tomb; Marina's very presence endlessly signifies her mother's death, but the daughter also serves as a constant reminder of her mother's life.

After the sailors aboard the ship convince Pericles that he must bury his wife at sea, Pericles gives one of the play's most moving speeches, a speech that emphasizes the simultaneity of life and death, that demonstrates the mourning husband's attempt to remember and to forget, and that draws heavily from the play's earlier images of tombs and other death arts:

> A terrible childbed hast thou had, my dear,
> No light, no fire. Th' unfriendly elements
> Forgot thee utterly, nor have I time
> To give thee hallowed to thy grave, but straight
> Must cast thee, scarcely coffined, in the ooze,
> Where, for a monument upon thy bones
> And aye-remaining lamps, the belching whale
> And humming water must o'erwhelm thy corpse,
> Lying with simple shells. O, Lychorida,
> Bid Nestor bring me spices, ink, and paper,
> My casket and my jewels, and bid Nicander
> Bring me the satin coffin. Lay the babe
> Upon the pillow. Hie thee, whiles I say
> A priestly farewell to her. (3.1.56–69)

By pointing to the elements that have forgotten Thaisa, Pericles suggests he will remember. The reference to the "belching whale" points back to the whale discussed in act 2, scene 1 when Pericles found himself revived from the sea (3.1.62). The "humming water" (3.1.63) calls to mind Gower's first line in the play: "to sing a song that old was sung" (1.0.1). By saying he cannot construct Thaisa a monument or tomb, he creates one, "coffin[ing]" her with his words (3.1.60). The word choice and images in Pericles's farewell address to his wife echo several of the play's scenes that emphasize the intimate intertwining of death and revivification. It would be reasonable, at this point in the play and based on all he has seen and experienced, for Pericles to second-guess the permanence of apparent death. Nonetheless, when Pericles seals Thaisa into the bitumened casket and delivers it to the sea, he believes that he will never see her again. His actions say one thing while his words say another. Even as he mourns the loss of Thaisa, he gestures to the impermanence of her fate.

Central to Pericles's funereal address is ooze, which like the ash and rust of previous scenes provides a polysemic engagement with decay and fecundity. While not able to provide Thaisa with a traditional "grave," Pericles does place her in "ooze" (3.1.59, 60), a substance that has powerful revivifying properties throughout Shakespeare's canon. In *Antony and Cleopatra*, Antony uses the word "ooze" in his discussion of the Nile to explain how the annual floods prepare the flood plain to grow more abundant crops:

> The higher Nilus swells,
> The more it promises. As it ebbs, the seedman
> Upon the slime and ooze scatters his grain,
> And shortly comes to harvest. (*Ant.* 2.7.20–3)

Through his use of the word "ooze" to mean "wet mud or slime; *esp.* that in the bed of a river, estuary, or sea," Antony hints at the Nile's dual powers of destruction and renewal. In *Henry V*, the Archbishop of Canterbury similarly evokes the duality of "ooze" through his image of treasure, previously lost to the sea, springing forth from the slime: "And make her chronicle as rich with praise / As is the ooze and bottom of the sea / With sunken wreck and sumless treasuries" (*H5* 1.2.163–65). In both of these quotations, ooze conveys loss, destruction, or absence followed shortly by new growth or plentitude.

In Shakespeare's romances, including *Pericles*, ooze continues to function as mud or slime that simultaneously takes and gives, but it also signifies more symbolically as Shakespeare deploys the term repeatedly in scenes in which characters *appear* to be dead. To put it another way, ooze becomes a sort of stand-in for the process of supposed death and subsequent reanimation. In *Cymbeline*, Belarius uses the image of ooze to express the depth of his woe following the death of Fidele, who is actually a drugged—not dead—Imogen in disguise: "O melancholy, / Whoever yet could sound thy bottom, find / The ooze, to show what coast thy sluggish crare / Might easiliest harbor in?" (*Cym.* 4.2.204–7). Though

Belarius's grief seems to extend to the bottom of the deepest ocean in this moment, the play's conclusion ushers in the reunification of families, the forgiveness of past sins, the return of good governance, and of course the revelation that Fidele—who is really Imogen—is alive. In *The Tempest*, like in *Pericles*, a shipwreck figures prominently in the romance's plot. Perhaps not surprisingly, ooze, with its connections to water, loss, and recuperation, also appears in the play on more than one occasion. The first time "ooze" appears in the play, it functions purely as slimy mud. Later in the play though, this mud assumes symbolic resonances of loss and restoration. Fearing that his son Ferdinand has drowned in the shipwreck, Alonso mourns for his son in a lament that, through its images of ooze, echoes Pericles's elegy for Thaisa: "Therefor my son i'th' ooze is bedded, and / I'll seek him deeper than e'er plummet sounded, / And with him there lie mudded" (*Tem*. 3.3.95–102). While both Pericles and Alonso conceive of ooze as the substance into which their loved ones have sunk, Alonso is unique in his desire to enact familial restoration by joining his son in the ooze. In the play's final act, Alonso once again expresses his desire to join his son in death through images of ooze: "I wish / Myself were mudded in that oozy bed / Where my son lies!" (*Tem*. 5.1.175–8). However, when Prospero reveals everything that has transpired on the island, Alonso and Ferdinand are reunited in life rather than in death.

Though *Cymbeline*, *The Tempest*, and *Pericles* all make use of images of ooze in their depictions of presumed death and familial reunification, *Pericles* is unique among these romances because audiences share in Pericles's experience of Thaisa's death. There is an immediacy to her death that is absent in both *The Tempest* and *Cymbeline* because audiences know, even if the other characters do not, that Fidele and Ferdinand are actually alive. Since audiences and Pericles alike believe that Thaisa is dead, memorializing her through her entombment in the ooze assumes an urgency that is absent from the death arts in Shakespeare's other romances.

In *Pericles*, the memorial practices of the death arts demonstrate their immediacy and efficacy as Cerimon revives Thaisa just one scene after her supposed death. Language depicting the sea as a watery tomb that regurgitates its holdings permeates the scene as gentlemen appear on stage with Thaisa's bitumened chest. They speak of a sea that "did [...] toss up upon our shore this chest" (3.2.50), ask if the sea "cast [...] up" the chest (3.2.53), and hypothesize that if "the sea's stomach be o'ercharged with gold, / 'Tis a good constraint of fortune / It belches upon us" (3.2.56–8). This language echoes the earlier scene in which Pericles narrowly escapes the shipwreck, suggesting in turn that Thaisa might also emerge alive from her watery tomb. Given what we know about watery tombs, ash, rust, and ooze, Cerimon's revivification of Thaisa in this scene should not come as a total surprise. Yet when Cerimon looks upon Thaisa and declares "[s]he is alive" (3.2.96), audiences cannot help but sense that both Cerimon's ministering and Pericles's (and the audiences') memorializing of Thaisa has brought the dead Queen back to life.

The ash, rust, ooze, and tombs of *Pericles*'s first four acts pave the way for the play's climactic revivification: the reunification and restoration of the familial unit when Pericles discovers that both his daughter and his wife are alive. Strikingly, the language that Pericles employs as he attempts to make sense of the seeming re-emergence of his wife and daughter from their graves blurs the lines between life and death. When Pericles discovers that Thaisa is alive, he commands her to "be buried / a second time within these arms" (5.3.43–44). His embrace becomes a sort of tomb, but it is tomb that enacts and monumentalizes the restoration of the family. Through its emphasis on reunion, the final tomb in *Pericles* brings us full circle to the play's first tomb, the tomb of the poet Gower. In his opening speech, Gower reports that lords and ladies read his stories "for restoratives" (1.0.8). Through its performance of the early modern death arts, specifically the funereal rituals associated with entombment, *Pericles* demonstrates the death arts', and the theater's, power to remember, memorialize, reanimate, and restore.

Notes

1. Jonson "An Ode. To Himself."
2. *OED*, s.v. "mouldy."
3. Schreyer, "Moldy *Pericles*," pp. 209–214.
4. *OED*, s.v. "mouldy."
5. In *Performances of Mourning in Shakespearean Theatre and Early Modern Culture*, Döring examines the performativity involved in mourning and commemoration by considering the cultural strategies of Shakespeare's theater.
6. Quotations from *Pericles*, unless otherwise noted, refer to the Arden Shakespeare edited by Suzanne Gossett.
7. *OED*, s.v. "ash."
8. Schreyer, p. 215.

9. Duncan-Jones, *Ungentle Shakespeare*, pp. 202–203.
10. Schreyer, p. 212.
11. Gittings, *Death, Burial and the Individual in Early Modern England*, p. 120.
12. Belsey, "In Defiance of Death: Shakespeare and Tomb Sculpture," p. 2.
13. Ibid.
14. See Appleford, *Learning to Die in London*; Cummings, "Remembering the Dead in *Hamlet*;" Walsh, "'A Priestly Farewell': Gower's Tomb and Religious Change in *Pericles*."
15. Newstok, *Quoting Death in Early Modern England: The Poetics of Epitaphs Beyond the Tomb*, p. 19.
16. Engel, *Mapping Mortality: The Persistence of Memory and Melancholy in Early Modern England*, p. 4.
17. Quotations from Shakespeare—other than *Pericles*—follow *The Oxford Shakespeare*, hereafter cited parenthetically with play abbreviations as given in *The MLA Handbook* (2016).
18. Here, I borrow Stephen Greenblatt's term "self-fashioning" from *Renaissance Self-Fashioning: From More to Shakespeare*.
19. Cressy, *Birth, Marriage, and Death: Ritual, Religion, and the Life-Cycle in Tudor and Stuart England*, p. 471.
20. Baldo, "Recovering Medieval Memory in Shakespeare's *Pericles*," p. 175.
21. Stallybrass, "Hauntings: The Materiality of Memory on the Renaissance Stage," p. 288.
22. Ibid., p. 291.
23. Harlan, "'Certain condolement, certail vails': Staging Rusty Armour in Shakespeare's *Pericles*," p. 132.
24. Stallybrass, p. 289.
25. Ibid., p. 297.
26. Levin, "Rusting, Bright, and Resting Weapons: A Textual Crux, and Closure in *Romeo and Juliet*," p. 211.
27. Ibid., p. 210.
28. Dubrow, in *Shakespeare and Domestic Loss* (p. 189), reads this repetition of "keep" as functioning to draw attention to the "stability and shielding that home should provide but too often does not," especially with the loss of a parent.

References

Baldo, Jonathan. "Recovering Medieval Memory in Shakespeare's *Pericles*." *South Atlantic Review* 79.3–4 (2014): 171–189.

Belsey, Catherine. "In Defiance of Death: Shakespeare and Tomb Sculpture." *Memoria di Shakespeare* 6 (2019): 1–20.

Cressy, David. *Birth, Marriage, and Death: Ritual, Religion, and the Life-Cycle in Tudor and Stuart England*. Oxford: Oxford University Press, 1997.

Döring, Tobias. *Performances of Mourning in Shakespearean Theatre and Early Modern Culture*. Houndsmill, Basingstoke, UK: Palgrave Macmillan, 2006.

Duncan-Jones, Katherine. *Ungentle Shakespeare*. London: Arden, 2001.

Dubrow, Heather. *Shakespeare and Domestic Loss: Forms of Deprivation, Mourning, and Recuperation*. Cambridge: Cambridge University Press, 1999.

Engel, William E. *Mapping Mortality: The Persistence of Memory and Melancholy in Early Modern England*. Amherst, MA: University of Massachusetts Press, 1995.

Greenblatt, Stephen. *Renaissance Self-Fashioning: From More to Shakespeare*. Chicago, IL: University of Chicago Press, 1980.

Gittings, Clair. *Death, Burial and the Individual in Early Modern England*. London: Croom Helm, 1984.

Harlan, Susan. "'Certain condolements, certain vails': Staging Rusty Armour in Shakespeare's *Pericles*." *Early Theatre* 11.2 (2008): 129–140.

Jonson, Ben. "An Ode. To Himself." In *The Broadview Anthology of Seventeenth-Century Verse and Prose*. Edited by Alan Rudrum, Joseph Black, and Holly Faith Nelson. Peterborough, Canada: Broadview, 2001.

Levin, Richard. "Rusting, Bright, and Resting Weapons: A Textual Crux, and Closure in *Romeo and Juliet*." *The Shakespearean International Yearbook* 10 (2010): 207–229.

Newstok, Scott L. *Quoting Death in Early Modern England: The Poetics of Epitaphs Beyond the Tomb*. Houndmills, Basingstoke, UK: Palgrave Macmillan, 2009.

Schreyer, Kurt A. "Moldy *Pericles*." *Exemplaria* 29. 3 (2017): 209–214.

Shakespeare, William. *The Oxford Shakespeare: The Complete Works* (2nd ed.). Edited by John Jowett, William Montgomery, Gary Taylor, and Stanley Wells. Oxford: Oxford University Press, 2005.

Shakespeare, William. *Pericles*. Edited by Suzanne Gossett. New York: Arden Shakespeare, 2004.

Stallybrass, Peter. "Hauntings: The Materiality of Memory on the Renaissance Stage." In *Generation and Degeneration: Tropes of Reproduction in Literature* and *History from Antiquity to Early Modern Europe*. Edited by Valeria Finucci and Kevin Brownlee. Durham, NC: Duke University Press, 2001.

Walsh, Brian. "'A Priestly Farewell': Gower's Tomb and Religious Change in *Pericles*." *Religion & Literature* 45.3 (2013): 81–113.

CHAPTER 7

Empathetic Reflections on Love, Life, and Death Art in *Othello*

Jessica Tooker

My chapter concerns how *Othello* implicates the interlocutors of the tragedy in an early modern death art involving empathetic performative language. In what follows, for the purposes of my analysis, I will be referring to this as "thana-rhetoric." Thana-rhetoric showcases the way in which the transformative energies associated with lived experience and intimacy counterbalance abject violence, mortality, and death. I contend that thana-rhetoric holds out the possibility of an erotic life force that gives death a run for its money in *Othello*. Consistent with the aims of this volume, my chapter on the Shakespearean death arts analyzes how empathy and shame are felt by the audience through and by means of thana-rhetoric.

Tormented by Iago's insinuations—"Thou hast set me on the rack!" (3.3.338),[1] Othello exclaims—consumed with jealousy, and convinced of

---

J. Tooker (✉)
Indiana University, Bloomington, IN, USA

© The Author(s), under exclusive license to Springer Nature Switzerland AG 2022
W. E. Engel and G. Williams (eds.), *The Shakespearean Death Arts*, Palgrave Shakespeare Studies,
https://doi.org/10.1007/978-3-030-88490-1_7

Desdemona's faithlessness, he needs only hear the lie of Cassio's confessed complicity to "fall into a trance" (4.1.43):

> Lie with her? lie on her? We say lie on her when they belie her! Lie with her, zounds, that's fulsome! –Handkerchief! confessions! handkerchief! – To confess, and then be hanged for his labour! First to be hanged, and then to confess: I tremble at it. Nature would not invest herself in such shadowing passion without some instruction. It is not words that shakes me thus. Pish! Noses, ears, and lips. Is't possible? Confess! handkerchief! O devil! (4.1.35–42)

Othello's seizure shocks because, prior to the moment when he convulses, the audience was ignorant of his complete surrender to Iago's "dangerous conceits" (3.3.329). The abrupt exposure of what is probably Othello's medical condition—"My lord is fallen into an epilepsy," (4.1.50) Iago explains to Cassio—heightens its dramatic impact. More subtly, by keeping audience members in the dark—and then bludgeoning them with the spectacle of Othello's loss of bodily and linguistic control—Shakespeare stages the seizure as a microcosmic representation of the task that the play demands of its protagonist and Desdemona: the injunction to speak truthful words which have the desired effect upon interlocutors. The corollary interpretive challenge falls to the offstage audience whose members understand precisely why words such as "handkerchief," "confessions," and "noses, ears, and lips" are associatively strung together in Othello's seemingly incoherent speech.

On the level of what we might call "affective impression," then, (the audience's imaginative suturing of Othello's fragmented words into coherent discourse), the speech reveals the supreme effectiveness of Iago's "little art upon the blood" (3.3.331), the remarkable potency of words to infiltrate, and ultimately to overwhelm Othello's tortured psyche. Shakespeare's summa exploration of the stunning impact of what Judith Butler calls "injurious words" which—"not only name a social subject, but construct that subject in the naming, and construct that subject through a violating interpellation—*Othello* challenges the audience to experience phenomenologically how words hurt, shame, and alienate, and importantly how they provoke and foreclose empathy.[2] To be sure, were he not in the midst of a seizure, Othello's claim to auricular imperviousness would appear naïve. He may protest, "It is not words that shakes me thus," (4.1.41–42) but Shakespeare never wrote a play where words, words, words are exactly what do.

To this end, I want to argue that the Shakespearean theater—a singular performative laboratory where what Eva-Maria Engelen conceives of as an affective "space of possibility" is generated and "fellow-feeling" can be cathartically experienced en masse—engages the offstage audience in the undoing of what I call "wounding words": injurious speech that affectively, even traumatically impacts audiences onstage and off.[3] I suggest that *Othello* engages interlocutors in this process by deploying the death art of empathetic, and frequently artful, performative language (or what might be termed "thana-rhetoric") showcasing how the transformative energies of love and life serve to ballast dynamically against pain, separation, and mortal death. Thana-rhetoric demonstrates the ultimate possibility of an erotic life force that combats, endures, and imaginatively speaking, conquers death. In keeping with the end goal of this volume, which the editors William Engel and Grant Williams argue to be a fresh critical intervention into Shakespeare's corpus "inviting new ways of assessing the significance of his individual plays and plots where dying, death, and the dead are regularly staged and verbally represented," my chapter on *Othello* analyzes how the experiences of love, life, and death interpenetrate each other and are artfully expressed via the theatrical mechanism of thana-rhetoric.[4]

Of course, in terms of physiological responsiveness, Othello's insistence to Iago that words shouldn't have totalizing power over him makes sense. Ellen MacKay observes that the play tantalizingly posits questions which, as they are applied to Othello's body, remain unanswerable: "How is it that an imaginary sin convulses Othello's body with epileptic seizures? What causes the *absence* of truth—the groundless slander of Desdemona—to manifest such measurable, medical effects?"[5] However, "sensible" (that is, phenomenological and kinesthetic) answers to these questions emerge when they are imaginatively put to members of the offstage audience who feel the intense force of wounding words upon their bodies and minds. Naturally, empathy doesn't always involve articulated expression. In fact, body language and other non-verbal cues are essential when analyzing the behavior of others or communicating that we understand another person's perspective. But language is key to empathetic responsiveness as it relates to the construction of personal identity. As Engelen explains, "Both the way I empathize and the limits of what emotional situations and states I can comprehensibly imagine depend on how my emotional sensations have been semanticized in the process of acquiring language."[6]

If outside of the theater walls, the conditions which we can imagine are constrained by factors mostly beyond our control (personalities, intellectual and emotional capacities, socio-economic status, social class, race, and the society where we grew up), theatrical performance transiently presents a way to substitute the heterogeneity of personal experience with the homogeneity of collective response. Because despite obvious differences amongst empathizers, all empathetic responses are conditioned by the shared understanding of what it means to be and act humanely, to embrace as Engelen puts it, "a fundamental and shared human tenor that sets the space of meaning and thus the 'space of possibility' for what we can see as a certain basic emotion and how we can feel about it."[7] Shakespeare successfully triggers this "shared human tenor" within the audience, and in the case of *Othello*, its negative ramifications. For in this magnificent tragedy which analyzes the profound impact of language upon human beings, the playwright repeatedly stages situations where the audience's empathy is stimulated—and blocked.

Of course, the character who is most aware of the power of words to provoke and debar empathy is Iago. Stephen Greenblatt argues that Iago's genius resides in his superlative empathy, his skillful ability to burrow parasitically into the psyches of others.[8] However, for Iago, empathy is not so much a feeling as a methodological tool, an interpretive waystation to somewhere else. Thus, we might further classify his brand of empathy as what Fritz Breithaupt calls "empathetic sadism," an affective mode defined by, "a manipulation of another that allows one to predict or anticipate the other's feelings in order to more easily simulate or understand him or her. [Sadistic] empathy ranges from knowing *that* the other will have an emotional reaction to a precise estimation or simulation to predicting exactly *what* he or she will feel."[9] The "self-affirming effect" that an empathetic sadist experiences by inducing the pain of another ranges from self-empowerment to intellectual kudos for having accurately surmised and provoked the other's response. Empathetic sadism occurs when an individual imagines "the other fellow's situation" in order to participate in an ethically bad way. What could be labeled the "sadistic urge" allows the empathizer to emotionally manipulate because he or she understands the other person's feelings. As we might expect, intellectually and/or emotionally based games are crucial to empathetic sadism because games allow us to predict what others will do. Games can also be played without immediate repercussions because the violence of gaming can be argued away as "just a game." Therefore, we might conceive of the skilled empathetic sadist as the realizable version of what James Carse describes as "Master Players"—individuals who always win a "finite game" (one with a winner and a loser)—because they are "so perfectly skilled in [their] play that nothing can surprise [them], so perfectly trained that every move in the game is foreseen at the beginning."[10] Of course, Carse's Master Players are aware of the essence of manipulation—they understand it's often necessary to pretend that the "foreseen" was "unforeseen" in order to win the game. However, this cognizance doesn't mean that Master Players are by default manipulative, or, if so, in the negative sense. Rather, Carse argues that a Master Player always "wins the game" due to the successful understanding and management of situations, events, and people. The key difference between Carse's fantasy of Master Players and the real empathetic sadist is that although the latter cannot foresee every move in the game, he or she is a fantastic improviser who possesses as Greenblatt puts it, "the ability both to capitalize on the unforeseen and to transform given materials into one's own scenario."[11]

The traumatic upshot of what Greenblatt dubs Iago's "improvisatory freedom" is the affective phenomenon which Breithaupt terms "empathetic blocking": the distressing experience of an empathetic response being successfully stimulated—and blocked.[12] When this happens, we are transiently prevented from feeling with another human being. To be clear, empathetic blocking isn't inherently negative. In real life, some degree of emotional blocking shields us from the dangers of "hyper-empathy" with others. Besides preserving psychological welfare, empathetic blocking also serves as a defense response mechanism allowing humans to empathize with others by filtering out unnecessary, distracting, or dangerous stimuli. As it turns out, in order to lead productive lives, we must instinctually jettison most of what we "receive" from others in terms of their appeal for an empathetic response. Empathy is the exceptional emotional state rather than the normatively self-centered rule. Moreover, it operates as an affective counterpoint against the Freudian death drive pulsing throughout *Othello*. To be sure, over its duration, "Shakespeare makes us see the many deaths punctuating life's intense experiences."[13] Yet if as William Engel remarks, "Love may well reign in death," Shakespearean empathetic thana-rhetoric showcases how, in this tragedy, what may ultimately be "figured forth is the triumph of life, not death."[14]

In terms of theatrical performance, the problem arises when the human urge to empathize is altruistic, healthy, and present, but blocked by the structural dictates of the scene. In *Othello*, the most obvious example of this unnerving experience occurs throughout the often discussed "temptation scene" of 3.3, where Iago, masterfully rouses Othello to violent jealousy with words alone. Famously, Iago's "medicine" (4.1.45) works efficaciously upon Othello's psyche and leads to his onstage seizure by means of what Patricia Parker calls "close dilations," or "targeted insinuations summoning the specter of that which is, 'secret' or 'private'—the opposite of what is displayed or 'shown' [...] [that] convey the sense of partial opening and partial glimpses of something closed or hid."[15] As members of the offstage audience witness Othello's rising jealousy and shame—set on by Iago's targeted deployment of wounding words progressively leading the other man to draw his own devastating suppositions about Desdemona's faith—they become increasingly aware that their empathetic responses are neither desired nor required for the scene to progress to its tragic conclusion. Significantly, *Othello* stages anti-cathartic empathetic blocking. Pivoting upon the sadistic exploitation of audience members' permeability to violent language (and pitting their emotional responses against them), the play compels the audience to experience what it's like to be shamed by others and ashamed of ourselves—to see, and ultimately to feel, the tragedy of Othello's "Otherness" as our own.

Shame permeates the core of individual consciousness, miring the shamed individual in a self-reflexive "feedback loop" where in personal misery is propagated by awareness of outside judgment. Felt on the interior as the horrified inward gaze of, as Silvan Tomkins puts it, "the experience of the self by the self," shame engenders affective discomfort exterior to it, pained awareness generated by the collective gaze of a real or imagined multitude that witnesses, judges, and finds fault.[16] While the phenomenological experience of shame is private and interiorized, its conceptual basis is public, exteriorized, and, I would argue, "theatrical," in that shame is engendered by the individual's belief that they somehow have "failed" to perform according to the dictates of society. Shame requires the individual to understand and agree that a social performance essential to the normal functioning of society was called for—and has been spoiled, flouted, or negated. So critical is the accuracy of this first performance to the "general good" that the very idea of a "bad show" provokes, within the collective, what Michael Morgan describes as "a 'web of interlocking shame' or a 'community of shame,' whereby each of us feels shame before all others, for what we have collectively become."[17] Shared social shame confirms societal norms by concretizing acceptable social behavior. Unsurprisingly, in order to displace the unwanted experience of vicarious shame, the group frequently turns the individual's failed performance into a humiliating encore: the cathartic ritual of scapegoating. As René Girard argues, the term "Scapegoat indicates both the innocence of the victims, the collective polarization in opposition to them, and the collective end result of that polarization."[18] Labeling the crowd persecution of an individual "the scapegoat mechanism," Girard observes "When violence is at the point of threatening the existence of the community [...] communal violence is [...] projected upon a single individual [...] The person that receives the communal violence is a 'scapegoat.'"[19] However, over the course of the play, Othello cannily reverses the profound violence of this mechanism (branding him an exotic "Other" to Venice) by deploying artful language triggering the empathy of audiences onstage and off.

This is the Achilles Heel of shame: the *act* of shaming can actually stimulate empathy *for* the victim and—if collective empathy is roused—the "Othered" scapegoat ironically becomes (transiently or permanently) an honorary member of the shaming community. Humanely executed, then, shame can be socially and morally productive for the shamed individual and society at large. In fact, we can encourage ourselves to feel shame in order to improve our lives and those of others, and as Tomkins observes it's possible to do so with "models" (or actors) who experience it "for us": "The human being is capable of being shamed by another whether or not the other is interacting with him in such a way as to intentionally shame him, or interacting with him at all. The human being is capable through empathy and identification of [...] being shamed by what happens to others."[20] If shame is inherently "theatrical" because it necessitates "the gaze of the other"—the phenomenon of actors and audience who understand their mutually "being seen" as also receptively performing for each other—nowhere is shame more manipulable (and arguably more educative) than in the theater, where the exact similitude between actors and audience matters less than the shared affective response between them. In performance, the reaction of onstage actors and offstage audience to each other allows its members to imagine and experience the emotional states of being of characters with whom they might otherwise never identify. Through the playwright's skillful utilization of thana-rhetoric—language establishing the primacy of human love and life over mortal death—and performative displays of shame, audience members are stimulated to feel with, and not simply for Othello. For example, when Othello credits Iago's false reportage of Desdemona's infidelity branding her as—rather than "The Jewel of Venice," quite the reverse, "The Faux Strumpet of Cyprus"—he is mortified by the excruciating spectacle of shaming cuckoldry and we empathize with the tragic protagonist as he articulates his emotional pain.

Within Shakespeare's corpus, *Othello* stands as a remarkable test case for exploring how words, that so often and easily incite shame, are rarely successful in erasing its deepest wounds. Beginning with Iago's observation to Roderigo that he has been unfairly passed over for promotion (and his implication that he has been shamed by Othello, and Othello should be ashamed of himself), revolving around the false accusation of Desdemona's infidelity (the source of Othello's pain, shame, and rage), and ending with Desdemona's murder and Othello's suicide (his final attempts to purge himself of shame), the play pivots upon the display, sanctioning, and expression of shame. In between these events are multiple instances of overt shaming (Brabantio's realization that Desdemona has married and eloped with Othello and subsequent decision to haul him before the Venetian senate, Cassio's drunken brawl with Roderigo and ensuing loss of reputation, the entirety of the "temptation scene," and Othello's verbal and physical abuse of Desdemona in the latter acts of the play). The variations of shame, the many ways in which it can be witnessed and deployed as personal and public punishment, illustrate why Shakespeare selected it as "affect of choice" for a tragedy about the power of words to wound. Shame operates as a short, sharp shock to our system which, as Morgan observes, "provok[es] reflection and self-examination, both in order to assess who we are and in order to assess our relationships with certain others."[21] Ironically, it's members of the offstage audience's normally positive capacity for empathy that ricochets the painful experience of shared social shame back onto them.

In her discussion of the potential for injurious words to annihilate personal identity, Butler argues that by socially shaming the subject, hate speech instantiates "self-loss": "To be injured by speech is to suffer a loss of context, that is, not to know where you are […] Exposed at the moment of such a shattering is precisely the volatility of one's 'place' within the community of speakers; one can be 'put in one's place' by such speech, but such a place may be no place."[22] *Othello* begins with precisely this experience: of finding that one's place in the world—shattered by "injurious words"—has become no place. Assuring Roderigo of his hatred for "The Moor" (1.1.38), Iago complains that Othello, by appointing Cassio as his lieutenant, has displaced him within the Venetian "community of speakers":

> I know my price, I am worth no worse a place.
> But he, as loving his own pride and purposes,
> Evades them, with a bombast circumstance
> Horribly stuffed with epithets of war,
> And in conclusion
> Nonsuits my mediators. For "Certes," says he,
> "I have already chose my officer." (1.1.10–16)

The play begins with a double denunciation (Othello displaces Iago for Cassio, Iago displaces Othello within Venice) showcasing the power of language to alter perception. In his critique, Iago calls attention to Othello's status as simultaneously Venice's best general—and its inarguable "Other." Of course, Iago can deride Othello's "horribly stuffed" language as little more than "bombast circumstance" because the other man depends upon genteel language in order to maintain his position as what Ania Loomba terms Venice's "honorary white."[23] Exhorting Roderigo to determine if he has any reason to love Othello, Iago simultaneously puts the interpretive challenge to the offstage audience by tacitly reminding its members that how we speak of ourselves in the world—and how others speak of us—confers an understanding of our place within it.

Othello's blackness is the most obvious marker of his Otherness. But his problem is as much social as racial, as much a question of cultural conditioning, as skin of a different color. Inarguably, it's "The Gaze of Venice" that determines how Othello must manifest himself. To this end, the force of a speech act to contour personal identity is artfully displayed in Othello's stories: his wooing tale and the retroactive "history-narrative" of the handkerchief. For despite professions to the contrary Othello is, of course, a magnificent storyteller. But if Othello's stories are to function as performances successfully concretizing his identity as a Venetian general (and Desdemona's husband), he must also consciously perform his past, intentionally re-creating himself as an exotic alien to the state and "the man who did these things." Poignantly, Othello's trust in his interlocutors is coupled by the faint anxiety we hear pulsating beneath his words. Listening to Othello recount his travels, we acknowledge our collective role as spectators who (like the assembled Venetians) become empathetic witnesses to—and judges of—Othello's past, present, and decision to marry and elope with Desdemona.

Reflective of a breach of—and a "theft" within—the Venetian "social contract," of course, the choice was hers as well. Confronted by the Duke's loaded question—"What would you, Desdemona?" (1.3.248)— she answers, "That I did love the Moor to live with him / My downright violence and scorn of fortunes / May trumpet to the world. My heart's subdued / Even to the very quality of my lord: / I saw Othello's visage in his mind" (1.3.249–253). As Stanley Cavell observes, Desdemona's remarkable claim is a moment of profound empathy: "She saw his visage as he sees it... she understands his blackness as he understands it, as the expression (or in his word, his manifestation of his mind—which is not overlooking it)."[24] Rivaling Iago in her ability to imaginatively "see into" the mind of another, Desdemona demonstrates how empathy may be turned toward positive or negative ends, and consequently might become profound misrecognition. However, perfect empathy does not equal perfect understanding, (which is not overlooking its potency). Desdemona's moving expression of empathy for Othello compels her to successfully articulate her subjectivity as the rationale for her love—and here is where her efforts fall short. Although Desdemona's subjectivity has no impact upon what her identity is permitted to mean, the tragedy is she thinks, from beginning to end, that it does. As Linda Charnes explains the difference between *identity* and *subjectivity*: "To 'identify' someone is to attempt to secure meaning, to erase multiplicity and eliminate indeterminacy—to 'fix' that person, so to speak [...] [Subjectivity] means the subject's experience of his or her relationship to his or her 'identity.'"[25] Desdemona's mistaken belief that her subjectivity (how she experiences her identity) matters in Venice, that she can easily substitute it *for* her identity (how she is understood and "fixed" within Venetian society) is interwoven with her conviction that Othello's does as well, that their dual identities will be successfully re-fashioned and strengthened by their connection (she no longer a dutiful daughter but a loving wife, he no longer Venice's "black Other" but just its noble general) their love for each other, and her empathetic response to him. Empathizing with Othello, Desdemona radically de-privileges the gaze of the Venetian patriarchy tout court and deprives them of the power to shame her. As Tomkins would observe, Desdemona "stands at the curb of [Venetian] shame, confident that s[he] knows when to commit [herself] to the risks of passage"—and decides to step off.[26]

Ironically, Desdemona's rejection of what Brabantio thinks ought to shame her (her marriage and Othello himself) poignantly, if understandably, strikes her black husband *as* shaming. Because she interprets Othello's "very quality" (1.3.252) based upon her own perceptions and desires, Desdemona also misunderstands—or at the very least ignores—what Othello would actually like her to say. Unsurprisingly therefore, when he supports her request to accompany him to Cyprus, Othello alters the highly sexed, transgressive focus of her argument to address his carefully crafted social identity. Safeguarding his reputation, Othello rebuffs Desdemona's claim that she can accurately envision his psychological mindset, and immediately debars her from receiving empathy from the senators and him. But if Desdemona's defense doesn't receive the response it deserves from the onstage audience, it's a striking example of "how to empathize" for the offstage one. We are encouraged to see Othello's visage in our minds—to empathize with an "Other" who cannot conceive of the connection himself.

Of course, the fact that Othello cannot is to Iago's advantage. Famously, Iago is remarkably skilled in shaping the actions of those around him into a series of contiguous events that he has psychically visualized in advance. As Marjorie Garber observes, Iago "never really *says* anything, but uses language instead to insinuate, to imply, to pull out of people's imaginations the dark things that are already there."[27] And of course, Iago emerges as the play's primary agent of shame. Or perhaps as Ewan Fernie argues, "Iago *is* shame."[28] The rub is that, for the first two acts, we are involved with Iago's plotting, which includes the off-loading of staged shame onto certain characters (such as Cassio and Desdemona) and—in the case of the former's spectacular shaming and demotion—the offstage audience. Consequently, its members become increasingly aware that they require a substitutive body onto which they can imaginatively offload the rising kinesthetic revulsion generated by the growing awareness of collective shame, of their own too, too sullied flesh. (As Slavoj Žižek observes, "The hatred of the Other is the hatred of our own excess of enjoyment").[29] Tragically, that absorptive body is Desdemona's. To what extent, *Othello* asks, are we supposed to be unsettled by our enjoyment of ugly spectacles? How are we positioned to experience and sanction the play's off-loading of shame, and thus to minimize and/or negate our empathetic responses by allowing someone else to take the affective hit for us?

Othello's internal shame is artfully externalized in the striking banter between Iago, Desdemona, and Emilia in Act 2 where Iago "renames" both women. Generally ignored or denigrated in literary criticism (M.R. Ridley calls it "one of the most unsatisfactory passages in Shakespeare" and a "piece of cheap backchat"), the conversation demonstrates how—long before Othello is convinced of her infidelity—Desdemona becomes a victim of spectatorial and verbal violence and unknowingly sets herself up to become a receptacle of public shame.[30] Throughout the hypnotic dialogue (and similarly to *Hamlet*), the audience detects, "a persistent and ineluctable hum betokening the omnipresence of death in life and life in death."[31] Awaiting Othello's arrival in Cyprus—and intervening with Iago and Emilia's marital bickering—Desdemona asks Iago to "write her praise." Critically, Iago is not the first to praise Desdemona. Before she arrives on stage, in response to the general Montano's query, "Is your general wived?" (2.1.60), Cassio launches into a rhapsodic, markedly opaque blazon of Desdemona: "Most fortunately: he hath achieved a maid / That paragons description and wild fame; / One that excels the quirks of blazoning pens / And in th'essential vesture of creation / Does tire the inginer" (2.1.61–65). While it's easy to ascribe Cassio's courtly language to his Florentine etiquette, his attempt to describe "the divine Desdemona" (2.1.73) foreshadows the problem of definition that will afflict her throughout the play: there is always a separation between what we see and how we speak of it. Cassio's generalizing language presages the disconcertingly artful "praise game" that Iago will play with the women and encourages Desdemona to think of herself in allegorical terms—or at least to request them from Iago. Of course, reducing others to allegorical two-dimensionality is a psychological coping mechanism for dealing with emergent selves, people, and situations for which we are not adequately prepared, for transforming that which is unfamiliar into something familiar and under control. In *Othello*, this type of allegorization brings clarity to confusion and signals an attempt to displace personal shame onto others.

Iago's game begins when Emilia (irritated by his misogynist generalizations) informs him, "You shall not write my praise" (2.1.116) to which Iago replies, "No, let me not" (2.1.116). At this point, Desdemona interjects by asking Iago, "What wouldst thou write of me, if thou shouldst praise me?" (2.1.117). In her hypothetical request, Desdemona initiates a mode of "polite" conversation that Erving Goffman calls "remedial work," a series of gestures "chang[ing] the meaning that otherwise might be given to an act, transforming what could be seen as offensive into what can be seen as acceptable."[32] Of course, Desdemona is attempting to stop the domestic squabble between Iago and Emilia. But I think she is also fishing for a compliment. Strikingly, Desdemona's admission of identificatory openness to improvisation echoes Iago's declaration of occluded selfhood ["I am not what I am" (1.1.64)]: "I am not merry, but I do beguile / The thing I am by seeming otherwise" (2.1.122–123). Her acknowledgment of a "secret self" (much like Cressida's) licenses Iago to engage in what Kevin Groark calls "empathetic insight" which he observes is a dynamic and active process of 'seeing within' in order to access "those dimensions of self that are actively hidden from view."[33]

Dangerously, Desdemona allows Iago empathic in-sight into her interior; she permits him to see her visage in his mind. However, by changing the scope of Desdemona's request for affirmation into a perversion of remedial work, Iago ensures that each move the players make will be based upon his responses—none of which Desdemona can predict in advance or are what she expects. While the praise game begins as a diversion, Iago's aestheticized rejoinders are also oblique references to Desdemona and Emilia's allegorical positions as, respectively, fair and virtuous, black and witty. Iago's responses are successful because—past the first hypothetical which he offers that is clearly intended to praise Desdemona ["If she be fair and wise, fairness and wit, / The one's for use, the other useth it" (2.1.129–130)]—*no one* openly acknowledges the similarity between Iago's hypothetical generalizations and the women standing before him. The game conceals an "open secret" that is obvious to audiences onstage and off: Iago's increasingly sexual analogies "could" refer to the women—but the connection is never made explicit. Good empathetic sadist and Master Player that he is, Iago understands that there must be polite distance between people and comparisons for his wounding words to work effectively upon the psyches of others. As Iago's answers become more sexually crude, they also begin to apply more blatantly to Desdemona. By his third rhyme, as he will later do with Othello, Iago baldly plays the mouthpiece of Venetian society as he unambiguously hypothesizes about (fair/white) Desdemona's (foolish) marriage to (black) Othello: "She never yet was foolish that was fair, / For even her folly helped to an heir" (2.1.136–137). By dialogue's end, Desdemona, Emilia, and Iago have flirtatiously showcased how,

"Every activity, every gesture, and every expenditure of energy potentially direct themselves toward mortifying ends—'mortifying,' etymologically speaking, as 'making death'".[34] Ultimately, Iago emerges as the victor of the praise game. Refusing to provide the remedial aid that Desdemona requests, Iago puts her in the distressing position of being unnamed— without being immediately renamed.

Ironically, when Desdemona receives a new title, it's Iago whom she asks to bequeath it, and once again he disappoints. Distraught over Othello's recently incomprehensible behavior, Desdemona asks:

> DESDEMONA Am I that name, Iago?
> IAGO What name, fair lady?
> DESDEMONA Such as she said my lord did say I was. (4.2.119–121)

In this brief, heartbreaking exchange, Iago mockingly echoes Desdemona's question, refuses to acknowledge the "name" that she cannot bear to say, and intensifies her pained self-perception. Desdemona sees her visage in Othello's mind and understands that he sees a whore. In the same scene, as Othello (punning on his title, "The Moor of Venice") puts it to Desdemona with searing cruelty: "I cry you mercy then, / I took you for that cunning whore of Venice / That married with Othello" (4.2.90–92). When in an instance of supremely black comedy, Desdemona tells Iago, "I cannot say whore: / It does abhor me now I speak the word" (4.2.164–164), she unconsciously verbalizes her shame by accidentally saying the word "~~whore~~" twice; her slip of the tongue solidifies her surrender of identity to Iago's improvisations and transformation into the second scapegoat or, as Loomba argues, the "honorary black" of the play.[35] Stunned by the lingering effects of verbal abuse, Desdemona illustrates Butler's observation that, "to be injured by speech is to suffer a loss of context, that is, not to know where you are."[36]

Presciently deploying thana-rhetoric countermanding Iago's wounding words, in Act 3, Othello explains the significance of his first love gift to Desdemona: her ill-fated handkerchief, an everyday item that slips, all too easily, from hand to ground, from hand to hand, from hand to beard. As Michael Neill argues, "In Othello's imagination, the handkerchief is invested with the same magical significance as a wedding-ring [...] Though it ostensibly represents the power of the wife to 'subdue [the husband]' [...] that power is revealed as wholly contingent upon the husband's gift."[37] Crucially, Desdemona devalues the symbolic worth of the handkerchief because she understands its material significance as subordinate to Othello's aestheticized narration of its magical properties, his utilization of storytelling thana-rhetoric invoking what Joan Pong Linton observes as the affective potency of Early Modern trifles—"their mysterious power of creating desire in individuals" and compelling engagement with "the intersubjective dynamics of magical manipulation."[38] With stunning verbal artistry, Othello confesses to Desdemona:

> 'Tis true, there's magic in the web of it.
> A sibyl that had numbered the world
> The sun to course had two hundred compasses,
> In her prophetic fury sewed the work;
> The worms were hallowed that did breed the silk,
> And it was dyed in mummy, which the skilful
> Conserved of maidens' hearts. (3.4.71–77)

Of course, the passionate relationship drama unfolding between the couple demonstrates their mutual belief that as Charnes argues, "Nothing is more important than what we *do* with our histories."[39] Furthermore, this logic of joint action, and belief, in the future, is borne out in the tragic revelation of Desdemona's innocence. For ultimately, she—embodying her role as The Sublime Object of Martyrology—remains pure, unsullied, virtuous, and a scarring sacrifice upon the altar of Othello's shame. Witnessing Othello's final speech and suicide where he asks that others "Speak of me as I am" (5.2.340), the audience hears and empathetically sanctions the moving request for the purgation of his "Otherness"; that is, we imaginatively memorialize and cathartically purify the scapegoat as he desires. Additionally, by establishing Othello as a *moriens* figure scripted in the *ars moriendi* tradition of the "death arts," audience members participate in learning how to live a good life and die a good death. Shakespeare's striking refusal to provide an easy answer as to how to interpret Othello allows us to recognize how our formerly blocked empathy (transformed into felt and shared pain) allows us to surmount the conditions of empathetic sadism, and to understand what it's like to be traumatically "Othered" ourselves. Of course, we must empathize with Othello in order to tell his story correctly.

In the end, the audience remains aware that it can never fully do so. As MacKay observes of the affective "hurt" that its members sustain at the end of the play, "*Othello* seems bent on proving that the impact of performance is a suffering that only increases with the knowledge that it is, at its core, 'a nothing that hath no being.'"[40] This is a remedy that revokes the promise of catharsis in any traditional Aristotelian way. Because *Othello* illuminates how the space between ourselves, another, and an Other is bridged by the human capacity to empathize, and the humane responsibility to do so. We understand that, as Amy Cook puts it, "Theater teaches us to see and feel for nothing, and that is something."[41] Within the playhouse walls, we empathetically bear witness to the stories of those who (rendered nothing by their societies) afflict us with their suffering, teach us to see and to feel for them, and help us to know that we have transformed this "nothing that hath no being" into something—the acknowledgment not only of the humanity in the "Other," but of the Otherness in each human making us humane. Love, as it is in so many of Shakespeare's plays, is the key to this connection with others—felt perceptibly on our bodies, in our minds, and in our hearts. For the tragedy of Othello is also the tragedy of Desdemona: she who loved too wisely and too well. I'faith, *Othello* is a tragedy about the failure to believe in unconditional love.

NOTES

1. All quotations from *Othello* are from the third edition of The Arden Shakespeare, ed. E.A.J. Honigmann, introduction. Ayanna Thompson (London and New York: Bloomsbury Arden Shakespeare, 2016), and are cited in the text by act, scene, and line.
2. Judith Butler, *Excitable Speech: A Politics of the Performative*, p. 49.
3. Eva-Maria Engelen, "Empathy and Imagination," p. 12.
4. William Engel and Grant Williams, Introduction to *The Shakespearean Death Arts: Hamlet Among the Tombs*.
5. Ellen MacKay, *Persecution, Plague, and Fire: Fugitive Histories of the Stage in Early Modern England*, p. 119.
6. Engelen, "Empathy and Imagination," p. 6.
7. Ibid., p. 12.
8. For more on Iago's empathy, see Greenblatt's chapter on Shakespeare, "The Improvisation of Power," in *Renaissance Self-Fashioning: From More to Shakespeare*.
9. Fritz Breithaupt, "Empathetic Sadism: How Readers Get Implicated," in *The Oxford Handbook of Cognitive Literary Studies*, p. 5.

10. James Carse, *Finite and Infinite Games: A Vision of Life as Play and Possibility*, p. 21.
11. Greenblatt, *Renaissance Self-Fashioning*, p. 227.
12. Ibid. See also Breithaupt, "The Blocking of Empathy, Narrative Empathy, and a Three-Person Model of Empathy," p. 2.
13. Engel and Williams, Introduction to *The Shakespearean Death Arts*.
14. Engel, *Death and Drama in Renaissance England: Shades of Memory*, p. 82, p. 166.
15. Patricia Parker, "*Othello* and *Hamlet:* Dilation, Spying, and the 'Secret Place' of Woman," p. 61.
16. Silvan Tomkins, *Shame and Its Sisters: A Silvan Tomkins Reader*, p. 136.
17. Michael Morgan, *On Shame*, p. 56.
18. Rene Girard, *The Scapegoat*, p. 39.
19. "René Girard," entry on the Internet Encyclopedia of Philosophy, accessed December 1, 2020. https://iep.utm.edu/girard/#H3.
20. Tomkins, p. 159.
21. Morgan, *On Shame*, pp. 42–43.
22. Butler, p. 4.
23. Ania Loomba, *Gender, Race, Renaissance Drama*, p. 52.
24. Stanley Cavell, *Disowning Knowledge in Seven Plays of Shakespeare*, p. 129.
25. Linda Charnes, *Notorious Identity: Materializing the Subject in Shakespeare*, p. 8.
26. Tomkins, p. 169.
27. Marjorie Garber, *Shakespeare After All*, p. 606.
28. Ewan Fernie, "Shame in Othello," p. 21.
29. Slavoj Žižek, *Tarrying with the Negative*, p. 203.
30. Ayanna Thompson, Introduction to *Othello*, p. 42.
31. Engel and Williams, Introduction, *The Shakespearean Death Arts*.
32. Erving Goffman, *Relations in Public: Microstudies of the Public Order*, p. 119.
33. Kevin Groark, "Social Opacity and the Dynamics of Empathetic Insight Among the Tzotzil Maya of Chiapas, Mexico," p. 249.
34. Engel and Williams, Introduction, *The Shakespearean Death Arts*.
35. Loomba, p. 59.
36. Butler, p. 4.

37. Michael Neill, *Issues of Death: Mortality and Identity in English Renaissance Tragedy*, p. 165.
38. Joan Pong Linton, *The Romance of the New World: Gender and the Literary Formations of English Colonialism*, p. 86.
39. Charnes, "Shakespeare, and belief, in the future," p. 77.
40. MacKay, p. 120.
41. Amy Cook, "Staging Nothing: *Hamlet* and Cognitive Science," p. 97.

REFERENCES

Breithaupt, Fritz. "Empathetic Sadism: How Readers Get Implicated." In *The Oxford Handbook of Cognitive Literary Studies*. Edited by Lisa Zunshine. Oxford: Oxford University Press, 2014. pp. 440–462

Breithaupt, Fritz. "The Blocking of Empathy, Narrative Empathy, and a Three-Person Model of Empathy." *Emotion Review* 20.10 (2011): 1–8.

Butler, Judith. *Excitable Speech: A Politics of the Performative*. London and New York: Routledge, 1997.

Carse, James P. *Finite and Infinite Games: A Vision of Life as Play and Possibility*. New York: Ballantine Books, 1987.

Cavell, Stanley. *Disowning Knowledge in Seven Plays of Shakespeare*. Cambridge: Cambridge University Press, 1987; rpt. 2003.

Charnes, Linda. "Shakespeare, and Belief, in the Future." In *Presentist Shakespeares*. Edited by Hugh Grady and Terence Hawkes. London and New York: Routledge, 2007. pp. 64–77.

Charnes, Linda. *Notorious Identity: Materializing the Subject in Shakespeare*. Cambridge, MA.: Harvard University Press, 1993; rpt. 1995.

Cook, Amy. "Staging Nothing: *Hamlet* and Cognitive Science." *SubStance* 35. 2, Issue 110: Nothing (2006): 83–99.

Engel, William E. *Death and Drama in Renaissance England: Shades of Memory*. New York: Oxford University Press, 2002.

Engel, William and Grant Williams. Introduction to *The Shakespearean Death Arts: Hamlet Among the Tombs*. London and New York: Palgrave Macmillan, 2022. XX.

Engelen, Eva-Maria. "Empathy and Imagination." Conference Paper. Universität Konstanz, Germany. April 2011.

Fernie, Ewan. "Shame in Othello." *The Cambridge Quarterly* 28.1 (1999): 19-45.

Garber, Marjorie. *Shakespeare After All*. New York: Anchor Books, 2004; rpt. 2005.

"Gerard, René" as an entry in the Internet Encyclopedia of Philosophy. Accessed December 1, 2020. https://iep.utm.edu/girard/#H3.
Girard, René. *The Scapegoat*. Translated by Yvonne Freccero. Baltimore: The Johns Hopkins University Press, 1982; rept. 1986.
Goffman, Erving. *Relations in Public: Microstudies of the Public Order*. New York: Harper and Row, 1972.
Greenblatt, Stephen. *Renaissance Self-Fashioning: From More to Shakespeare*. Chicago and London: University of Chicago Press, 1980; rpt. 2005.
Groark, Kevin P. "Social Opacity and the Dynamics of Empathetic Insight Among the Tzotzil Maya of Chiapas, Mexico." *Ethos* 36. 4 (2008): 427–48.
Honigmann, Ernst Anselm Joachim. Introduction. *Othello*. London and New York: Bloomsbury Arden Shakespeare, 1997. pp. 1–111
Linton, Joan Pong. *The Romance of the New World: Gender and the Literary Formations of English Colonialism*. Cambridge: Cambridge University Press, 1998.
Loomba, Ania. *Gender, Race, Renaissance Drama*. Manchester and New York: Manchester University Press, 1989.
MacKay, Ellen. *Persecution, Plague, and Fire: Fugitive Histories of the Stage in Early Modern England*. Chicago and London: University of Chicago Press, 2011.
Morgan, Michael L. *On Shame*. New York: Routledge, 2008.
Neill, Michael. *Issues of Death: Mortality and Identity in English Renaissance Tragedy*. Oxford: Clarendon Press, 1997.
Parker, Patricia. "*Othello* and *Hamlet*: Dilation, Spying, and the 'Secret Place' of Woman." *Representations* 44 (Autumn 1993): 60–95.
Shakespeare, William. *Othello*. Revised Edition (3rd). Edited by E.A.J. Honigmann. Introduction by Ayanna Thompson. London and New York: Bloomsbury Arden Shakespeare, 2016.
Thompson, Ayanna. Introduction. *Othello*. Revised Edition (3rd). Edited by E. A. J. Honigmann. London and New York: Bloomsbury Arden Shakespeare, 2016. pp. 1–116.
Tomkins, Silvan. *Shame and Its Sisters: A Silvan Tomkins Reader*. Edited by Eve Kosofsky Sedgwick and Adam Frank. Durham and London: Duke University Press, 1995.
Žižek, Slavoj. *Tarrying with the Negative*. Durham: Duke University Press, 1993.

CHAPTER 8

Othello's Speaking Corpses and the Performance of *Memento Mori*

Maggie Vinter

Othello's suicide invokes and re-performs an earlier death. Immediately before he stabs himself, he announces

> [...] that in Aleppo once,
> Where a malignant and a turbaned Turk
> Beat a Venetian and traduced the state,
> I took by th' throat the circumcised dog
> And smote him – thus![1]

Many readers have noted the importance of this passage to *Othello*'s exploration of alienation and assimilation.[2] Reminding his listeners of his service to the city, while simultaneously positioning himself as a threat from which it must be protected, Othello acknowledges, accepts and

M. Vinter (✉)
English Department, Case Western Reserve University, Cleveland, OH, USA
e-mail: mlv28@case.edu

© The Author(s), under exclusive license to Springer Nature Switzerland AG 2022
W. E. Engel and G. Williams (eds.), *The Shakespearean Death Arts*, Palgrave Shakespeare Studies,
https://doi.org/10.1007/978-3-030-88490-1_8

then annihilates the paradoxical status of "the Moor of Venice," both citizen and outsider, that he has inhabited within the white world of the play. Less remarked is how this speech stands at the end of a series of untimely and destabilizing encounters between the living and the dead. Yet these two features are connected. Othello can characterize himself as both enemy and defender of Venice in the moment of death because he evokes a literary and artistic tradition of corpses who engage in social critique. In *memento mori*, the dead rise up to claim kinship with the living and remind them of their ends. Juxtaposing their bare bones to the trappings of worldly success, they insist that titles and goods cannot be taken into the grave, and distinct identities will be overwhelmed by the leveling experience of death. *Othello* evokes this tradition repeatedly over the course of acts Four and Five, as the dead revive to speak back to those who survive them in ways that expose and disrupt social demarcations based on race, class, religion and gender. Furthermore, the play suggests that a corollary of Death's role as a leveler is that destabilizing encounters between self and other which initially seem to have little to do with mortality can function as *memento mori*. When the opposition between Turkish attacker and Venetian defender collapses into a paradoxical similitude, it prefigures Othello's particular demise, but also evokes something of the dislocation, self-loss and untimeliness of death.

To produce this effect of the dead speaking back, *Othello* exploits conventions developed in the tradition of performed *memento mori*. Unlike visual and narrative reminders of finitude, theatrical and musical ones require living performers to assume the role of the dead and to speak both to and as the departed. Performance traditions like the *danse macabre* have the living and the dead confront one another in postures of mutual, reciprocal imitation that undermine distinctions between original and copy, self and other, and past and future. Similarly, the play's speaking corpses turn to performance to wrench characters, players and audiences out of the normal flow of life. Well before Othello's death, the play alludes to performed *memento mori* in Desdemona and Emilia's vocalizations of the Willow Song and Desdemona's brief resurrection from her deathbed. These moments evoke mortality using the distinct affordances of mimetic representation. When the voices of Barbary, Desdemona and Emilia echo and layer over one another from both sides of the grave, the gap between the representational and presentational qualities of the Willow Song becomes audible. When the suffocated Desdemona revives to speak again after what not just Othello, but also the audience, has assumed was her murder, she draws attention to the implicit pact between players and watchers that stillness will stand for lifelessness. Viewed one way, such reminders of the artificiality of dramatic and musical performance confirm the difference between staged death and real death and by extension mark how human arts inevitably fail to offer a true vantage on mortality. Viewed another, though, gestures to the mediated and artificial nature of performance can generate what Rebecca Schneider describes as a kind of double negative; this is not death, but it is also not not death.[3]

The speaking corpses in *Othello* draw attention to the imbrication of early modern death arts with other practices of self-cultivation and representation employed inside and outside the theater. The play's specular mimetic encounters between the dead and the living can direct our attention to the various strategies through which individual characters define their own social positions and identities in the face of alterity. Yet while death can be conceived as a type of performance or practice, it is also an intrusion of the real that threatens to shatter performance. It thus draws attention to the fabric of the theater and the boundaries and limits between different dramatic and performative strategies governing (among other things) staged music, the representation of gender and race, the discipline of actors' bodies, and the relationship between word and spectacle. The corpses that speak back through the theater cannot tell us of the truth of the grave. But as their voices carry out to the audience, they become reminders of how proximate death is, and how easily it can intrude into the world of the living.

"As You Are, so Once Was I. As I Am, so Shall You Be"

The motto *tu fui, ego eris* [as you are, so once was I. As I am, so shall you be] delineates the project of *memento mori*: to anticipate one's own death in the death of another. As you contemplate my corpse, you attempt to imagine it as your own. The collapse of distinctions between self and other is achieved through a disruption of linear time. You and I become images of one another because my past is your future. My memorial doubles as your script in a specular confrontation where the balance of power, and the viewer's perspective, continually shift.

As Eileen Sperry observes elsewhere in this volume, this exercise is almost impossible. The paradox of *tu fui* continually threatens to collapse into either pure difference or pure identity, each of which evades the full scandal of life's proximity to death. Some writers, like Christopher Sutton, whose treatise *Disce Mori* (1600) Sperry discusses, present this collapse itself as morally significant; a prideful soldier's refusal to identify with a corpse can serve as an occasion for lamenting worldly venality.[4] Other artists and authors from the medieval and early modern eras, however, are more optimistic that the particular affordances of different media can force their consumers to acknowledge and sustain the paradox of *tu fui*. Visual *memento mori* like transi tombs and vanitas paintings use lurid depictions of putrefaction and decay to shock their viewers into acknowledging mortality. Poetic dialogues between the living and the dead can manipulate readers' entry points into texts to shift their identification from living person to corpse, or use sonic echoes and rhymes to hold difference and identity in tension.[5] While using these same visual shocks and verbal strategies, performed *memento mori* also exploit the doublenesses inherent in mimetic enactment to sustain the *tu fui* paradox. The imperfect superimposition of player and role, and the permeable barriers between performer and auditor, can figure the uncanny proximity of the living and the dead.

This possibility becomes evident in the *danse macabre*, an expansion of the dyadic *tu fui* encounter in which companies of grinning skeletons claim dance partners from casts of pontiffs down to peasants and lead them off to the grave. Such an augmented assembly increases opportunities for connecting *tu fui* to social critique. Hierarchically ordered human estates square off against deindividuated corpses who seek to strip away their particularities. The larger scale of the *danse macabre* additionally generates an arresting theatrical spectacle. Today, the motif is associated largely with visual imagery (and to a lesser degree, poetry). Originally, though, it was also a performance tradition, danced by enactors who took on the parts of the living and the corpses.[6] While the ephemerality of performance makes surviving records scarce, Elina Gertsman argues persuasively that in many of its painted manifestations, the *danse macabre* encodes "vestiges of performances," designed to draw viewers into the scene.[7]

The text of the most widely disseminated English language version of the *danse macabre*—John Lydgate's *Dance of Death* (c. 1426), which circulated in manuscript and was illustrated in a mural on the cloister of St Paul's Cathedral—also contains performance vestiges that hint at how such dances could have worked in practice. Lydgate's poem, like many forms of medieval theater, minimizes separation between observers and enactors, in this case by dramatizing the transformation of nonperformers into performers. Death accosts a sequence of reluctant participants with ironic reference to their worldly professions and preoccupations. Addressing the Sergeant, for instance, he appropriates his victim's power of arrest:

> Come forth, Sir Sergant with youre statly mace;
> Make no defence ne no rebellioun.
> Not may availe to grucche in this cace,
> Though ye be deynous of condicioun,
> For nouther pele ne proteccioun
> May yow fraunchise to do nature wrong.
> For ther is no one so sturdy champioun;
> Though he be myghty, another is as stronge.[8]

The mimicry here is at once mocking and sincere. In part, Death, appears as a social reformer, characterizing the Sergeant's "statly mace" not as a symbol of justice but rather as a trapping of worldly vanity, which is impotent in the face of death. His demand that the Sergeant "Make no defence" is a mockery of the office. Yet Lydgate also takes the analogy between Death and the Sergeant seriously. Death's assertion that "nouther pele (appeal) ne proteccioun / May yow fraunchise to do nature wrong" expresses his absolute power over humanity. The Sergeant's social role is exposed as mere illusory performance through a mimetic satire that reveals Death to be the true arresting agent. Appreciating the full of effect of the stanza requires recognizing the analogy between Death and the Sergeant as reversible—ironic in one direction and serious in the other. The sergeant's reply displays something of the same doubleness:

> Howe dare this Dethe sette on me areste,
> That am the kinges chosen officere,
> Wiche yesterday bothe west and este.
> Min office dide ful surquidous of chere?
> But nowe this day I am arestid here
> And may not flee, though I hadde it sworn.[9]

The sergeant initially resists Death's assertion of similitude, but then affirms it by mournfully echoing back the summons. As he joins the dancing skeletons, following their steps, the direction of imitation switches. Performer mimics observer who mimics performer. Tenor and vehicle, original and copy, become reversible as death mocks life and life anticipates death. *Tu fui* is sustained through reciprocal patterns of imitation that repeatedly overlay sincerity with irony, and success with failure, in order to hold difference and identity in tension.

Like the ranged estates on display in the *danse macabre*, images of racial difference were also appropriated, on and off stage, to represent confrontations between the living and the dead. Kim Hall notes that traditional Christian iconography associating blackness with "death and mourning, sin and evil [...] become infused with ideas of Africa and African servitude" in the sixteenth and seventeenth centuries. She cites a posthumous portrait in which an image of the dead subject, Lord Willoughby d'Eresby, is accompanied by a African servant holding a *memento mori*.[10] Similar associations of blackness with sin and death are reflected in dramatic representation of devils as black and also in African villains like Shakespeare's Aaron the Moor.[11] These theatrical stock figures participated as fully as visual images in consolidating racist ideologies that subordinated the personhood of Black individuals to semiotic systems that aligned blackness with evil. But as I will discuss in the case of *Othello*, when binary oppositions between black and white intersected with *memento mori* tropes in the theater, they could sometimes be unsettled temporarily. In much the same way as Lydgate's Sergeant and Death resemble one another seriously and in jest, encounters between representatives of the living and the dead who are marked as racially distinct can expose the highly conventional nature of performances of race on the early modern stage, while also encouraging audiences to see deeper affinities between characters of different backgrounds based on shared exposure to mortality.

These representational and performance strategies survived Reformation attacks on Catholic religious iconography and ritual, even as some of the motifs that spawned them became marginalized. The St. Paul's Dance of Death mural on which Lydgate's poem appeared was razed in 1549, and similar images around the country were destroyed over the following decades. Though Stephen Greenblatt may be right to suggest that the Protestant reforms often increased the perceived distance between the living and the dead, the abolition of traditional institutions to circumscribe death could also sometimes make mortality more proximate.[12] From Erasmus onwards, the art of dying as defined in *ars moriendi* texts was increasingly conceived less as a discrete set of deathbed practices than as a call to cultivate awareness of death throughout life.[13] Scott Newstok argues that the destruction of church memorials loosened the connection between specific interred bodies and the epitaphs attached to them, which subsequently became portable as universal reminders of death.[14] Similarly, even as dance of death murals in English churches were razed, other dramatic forms of the *tu fui* confrontation that they illustrate persisted. Delocalized, and sometimes secularized, imitative performances of reciprocal identification between the dead and the living retained their power to shock audiences into acknowledging their proximity to the grave.

Hearing Death

Othello has no graveyard scene. Compared to plays like *Hamlet*, *The Duchess of Malfi* and *The Revenger's Tragedy*, which stage explicit, extended confrontations between living characters and imagined or real corpses, its engagement with *memento mori* can seem somewhat incidental. In *Othello*, the dead speak from the bedchamber, not the cemetery. And rather than shock and horror, their eruption into the world of the living initially produces evasion and embarrassment. Yet precisely because their voices emerge only fleetingly and tentatively within the play, they illuminate the flexibility of *tui fui* tropes, their intimate connection to performance practices in drama and music, and their complex interaction with social hierarchies, particularly those organized around race, class and gender.

In Act Four Scene Three, while preparing for bed with the help of Emilia, Desdemona complains of mental distraction which leads her "foolish" mind to contemplate being shrouded in her wedding sheets (4.3.21). She then narrates to Emilia the story of her mother's maid Barbary, who was abandoned by a lover and subsequently died singing a song that "expressed her fortune" with the refrain "Willow, willow, willow" (4.3.27). Desdemona seemingly tells Barbary's story in order to disavow the Willow Song and distinguish herself from her mother's maid. Still, she finds herself repeating snatches of it, not only recounting to Emilia the occasion under which she first heard it, but also performing it, and reviving the voice of the dead woman to whom it was attributed.

What exactly are we hearing when we hear Desdemona sing Barbary's Willow Song? As he commonly did, Shakespeare here appropriates a ballad that predates *Othello*, a fact that Desdemona nods to when she describes it as "an old thing" (4.3.26). Printed copies of very similar songs appear in lute collections and broadsides dating from the 1580s onwards.[15] The closest surviving analogue to Shakespeare's version is a 1615 ballad titled "A Louers complaint being forsaken of his Loue."[16] Like Desdemona's rendition of the song, this opens with a description of "The poor soul [who] sat sighing by a sycamore tree" (4.3.39), from whose perspective the rest of the lyrics are sung. The framing establishes a distance between the complainer and the singer. Yet since the frame is never closed, the two personae converge over the course of the lyrics, culminating in the final verse:

> Farwell faire fals-hearted, plaints end in my breath.
> O Willow, etc.
>
> Thou dost loath me, I love thee though cause of my death:
> O Willow, willow, willow,
> O Willow, willow, willow,
> Sing O the greene Willow shall be my Garland.[17]

The rhyme of "breath" with "death," punctuated by the last reprisal of the refrain, aligns the ending of a vocal performance of the song with the expiration of the character whose thoughts it voices. Singer and persona merge in the moment of cessation.

In *Othello*, the nameless protagonist of the lyric and the undefined position of singer are both overlaid, first with the person of Barbary and then with that of Desdemona. This process suggests that the correct question might not be *what* are we hearing, so much as *who* are we hearing. Barbary fulfills the full ballad text's anticipation that heartbreak will be fatal even as her final moments become pure swan song. Her demise while singing literalizes the text's alignment of the end of the song with the end of the persona, but overwrites the generic, featureless "poor soul," with a particularized absent figure. And Barbary's personal characteristics are highly significant in a play so concerned with categories of identity. As the Willow Song passes from its ballad source to Barbary, and then from Barbary to Desdemona, it crosses lines of gender, race and class. Bruce R. Smith observes that all other extant versions of the song assume a male subject and singer; in attributing the song to Barbary, Shakespeare switches the gender of its implied subject.[18] Shifts in subject position also mark the passage of the song from Barbary to Desdemona. Within the play, Desdemona's description of Barbary stresses characteristics that distinguish her from Desdemona herself. Barbary is a social inferior and family servant. In addition, her name, which evokes the Barbary coast and echoes Iago's description of Othello as a "Barbary horse" (1.1.110), aligns her with Africa and places her, if perhaps only associatively, on the other side of a racial divide to her mistress's daughter.[19] The scene twice iterates the pattern found in the ballad where initial disavowal of identity is followed by subsequent appropriation that merges singer and song. And it encourages its audiences to connect this movement to the play's ongoing exploration of attempts at differentiation, assimilation, empathy and identification between people of different backgrounds.

How we understand Desdemona's appropriation of the Willow Song depends on whether we place more emphasis on the who or on the what—on the interpersonal and psychological processes by which it moves between singers or on the song itself. Desdemona's initial resistance to Barbary's song and subsequent repetition of it are often interpreted psychologically. As Erin Minear observes, what Desdemona describes as an intrusion from outside, a hijacking of consciousness, paradoxically serves as a strategy to enhance the character's psychological realism since it offers the audience evidence of multiple levels of mental interiority.[20] The song allows Desdemona to evaluate her own faltering marriage against the precedent of Barbary's abandonment and could suggest that she anticipates a similarly dire fate for herself. In such an interpretation, Barbary's song functions primarily as a stand-in for Barbary's biography. However much the two women differ in status and background, shared experiences of suffering and betrayal connect them and explain how both can use the same ballad to lament their unhappy situations. The song, therefore, facilitates empathic identification across social divides. And insofar as it portends death, it does so as a memento of a particular dead individual whose precedent helps Desdemona recognize her own danger.

In equally important respects, however, the Willow Song is distinguished from Desdemona's psychology and Barbary's person as alien and invasive matter. Desdemona complains that it "Will not go from [her] mind" and that she has "much to do / But to go hang my head all at one side / And sing it like poor Barbary" (4.3.29–31). The song is contagious, an earworm that Desdemona cannot help vocalizing. Its intrusive qualities evoke a set of artistic protocols, quite different to those of psychological realism, which deny the autonomy and boundedness of individual characters and instead force performers and observers to adopt one another's attributes.

In dramatizing this earworm, Shakespeare exploits distinctively automatic qualities of sonic memory that can make mental echoes of songs appear autonomous. As Elizabeth Margulis puts it, under the influence of an earworm "I seem not to remember, but rather to *rehear* the entire thing, note by note, in clear temporal sequence, and over an amount of time that roughly matches the duration its actual performance might have had. In this sense, it is more like an imaginative reconstruction than a memory" [original emphasis].[21] Recent theoretical accounts of earworms tend to align their inhuman dimensions with the technological and economic forces of modernity that render repetitive, highly memorable music so ubiquitous. Discussing the contemporary music industry, Peter Szendy, for instance, notes how popular hit songs exploit catchiness as "an essential hinge [...] between the market and the psyche," effectively turning their hearers into unwilling recording and amplifying devices in order to increase the circulation of particular tracks and drive sales.[22] This insight can illuminate how the Willow Song holds power because of how it fails to align fully with Desdemona's interior and instead reflects a nonhuman cooption of human powers of iteration. The song itself, rather than any particular singer, is the agent in this scenario, capable of replicating itself along pathways that may be unchosen, and that have little or nothing to do with the interior lives of the parties involved.

Where Szendy aligns the inhuman qualities of viral and self-replicating music with capitalism, I want to suggest that early modern audiences of *Othello* hearing the Willow Song would be more inclined to connect them to mortality. "Willow, willow, willow," the repeated refrain which renders the song recognizable and memorable, evokes the willow tree as a conventional symbol of lamentation. More generally, Scott Trudell notes that early modern writers often associated the invisibility and ephemerality of song with nothingness.[23] Like the servant in the portrait of Willoughby d'Eresby, Barbary can be seen as a vehicle for *memento mori*. Details of her biography—in particular her death and the name that connects her to blackness through Africa—might function less as reminders of an actual dead person whom Desdemona has known than as a framing device that intensifies the Willow Song's depersonalized connection to mortality. The inhuman qualities of the song do not just replicate themselves through Barbary; they also appear to hijack details of her distinct existence in order to intensify the atmosphere of lamentation associated with "Willow, Willow." Barbary the particularized individual is overtaken by a general reminder of mortality in a process that analogizes the deindividuating force of the grave. And the song's jump to Desdemona promises to consign her to a similar fate.

Peculiarities of early modern theatrical performance heighten this effect. The fulcrum between human and nonhuman produced by the earworm coincides with a shift between different protocols of representation and presentation. Situating the Willow Song in the context of early modern debates about gender and performance, Clare McManus emphasizes how the boy actor playing Desdemona must move repeatedly between spoken dialogue (which encourages the audience to discount the player's male gender in favor of the character's female one) and song (which spotlights the distinctive qualities of the boy singer's voice).[24] Something similar could be happening with the representation of race here. Barbary's association with Africa raises the possibility that Desdemona is performing a kind of musical blackface, instantiating and then crossing a sonic color line as she first evokes Barbary and then sings her song.[25] The scene showcases the virtuosity of its performers, who are able to move capably between different performance modes associated with blackness, whiteness, men, women, representation and presentation. But in the process, it reminds audiences of the highly stylized strategies used to represent gender and race in the Jacobean theater; women are played by boys, and black characters by white actors adopting conventional signifiers like blackface makeup. Hearing Barbary's song and Desdemona's dialogue in a boy's voice draws attention to the layers of artifice that make up the performance. Like the song embedded within it, the play as a whole is an artistic construction that at best mimics reality.

Any diminution of verisimilitude should not be seen only as a failure of realism, however. Discussing performances of the bugle piece "Taps" during Civil War reenactments—a performance practice far more committed to ideals of authenticity than Shakespeare's stage—Rebecca Schneider notes that:

> in playing music, one does not (or does not only) *represent* playing it, which is not to say that music is never mimetic, but that the act of playing music is not, or not only, mimetic of music. Though one may be posing "as if" a Civil War bugler while playing, and arguably *representing* the Civil War, one is simultaneously *making* the music [...] Both are true—real *and* faux—action and representation—and this both/and is the beloved and often discussed conundrum of theatricality in which the represented bumps

uncomfortably (and ultimately undecideably) against the affective, bodily instrument of the real.[26]

On the one hand, "Taps" makes the rest of the enactment look more fake by comparison. On the other, it might allow an encounter with the real to emerge out of fiction. *Othello* achieves a comparable conjunction in the Willow Song. But since the esthetic of Jacobean drama is more stylized than that of reenactment, the relative values of real and faux are far less stable. The song of the dead enters into *Othello* as something both more and less artificial than the action in which it is embedded. As in the *danse macabre*, mortality is evoked in unstable confrontations between reality and simulacrum.

This, then, is what we are hearing when we hear Desdemona sing the Willow Song: a song that is continually disavowed as belonging to someone else by those who come reluctantly to sing it; a song that marks particularities of race, class and gender through its viral propensity to surmount them; a song that validates psychological interiority and facilitates empathy while also reducing characters to automatic recording and playback devices; a song that imbues the theater with a realism that threatens to make everything else look fake; and, as a consequence, a song that bridges the gap between the living and the dead. When Desdemona attributes the song she finds herself singing to a dead woman she transforms herself into a conduit between the worlds of the living and the dead. She at once resurrects the departed and foreshadows her imminent murder. Beyond the genealogy associated with the lyrics, the shift into music is crucial to creating the effect of mortality intruding into the domestic space. The Willow Song functions as a *memento mori* in Act Four Scene Three of *Othello* because of how it sits between a who and a what—how it at once memorializes a particular dead woman whose future predicts Desdemona's own and also functions as an impersonal, generic occasion of lamentation that can be repeated indefinitely.

The Corpse Talks Back

Throughout Act Four Scene Three, the macabre dimensions of the Willow Song are associated with constraint. Desdemona's unchosen imitation of Barbary reflects her entanglement in a disintegrating marriage and anticipates her imminent murder. The ballad captures her like the skeleton that arrests Lydgate's Sergeant. Associations created between performance and mortality fold Desdemona's specific tragedy into a universal experience of finitude. As the bodies pile up in Act Five Scene Two, the connections between performance and mortality that the Willow Song primes us to recognize only intensify. But their implications for understanding, practicing and performing death shift significantly. During and after death, Desdemona and Emilia take on some of the agency displayed by corpses in the *tu fui* motif. The precedent of specular confrontation between corpse and living person allows both women to speak back as if from the grave to confront their murderers.

At the beginning of the scene, Othello asserts that death is something he can bring to someone else. As he contemplates the sleeping body of the woman he is about to murder, he emphasizes the finality of killing:

> Put out the light, and then put out the light!
> If I quench thee, thou flaming minister,
> I can again thy former light restore
> Should I repent me. But once put out thy light,
> Thou cunning'st pattern of excelling nature,
> I know not where is that Promethean heat
> That can thy light relume. (5.2.7–13).

The extinction of a torch is reversible, that of a woman, terminal. The speech presents homicide as an action that moves in only one direction, temporally and causally, from Othello as the killer to Desdemona as the killed. This transitive movement grants Othello not just power, but also (he believes) moral authority. "She must die" (5.2.6) points dually to the inevitability of mortality and the irresistibility of the patriarchal code that demands this honor killing.

Yet the scene overall will suggest that the distinction between living and dead is more unstable, and less controllable, than Othello chooses to believe. Even within this speech, Othello's comparison of Desdemona's skin to "monumental alabaster" (5.2.5) connects her still-living form with funeral effigies and statues of saints. The body of the living woman gestures backwards to past memories of holy martyrdom and forwards to her future interment. As was the case in Lydgate's satirical exchange between Death and the Sergeant, and in Desdemona's appropriation of Barbary's Willow Song, the specular confrontation of living and dead draws attention to social hierarchies even as it promises to dissolve them in the indeterminate space of the grave. On the one hand, Desdemona's death emerges as a tragic consequence of Othello's jealousy and misogynistic honor code, which reinforce cultural associations of death with blackness and masculine force. On the other, as Othello's simile locates this deathliness in Desdemona's white skin color and feminized smoothness, it suggests that mortality can alter the cultural associations and hierarchical positions of different identity categories.

From this point on, Othello struggles to keep control of the scene. Desdemona wakens and refuses to perform the role that he has scripted for her. Instead of confessing her sins and giving Othello proof of adultery, she resists. Then, after Othello is convinced that he has killed her, she revives to announce her murder to Emilia. Her medically implausible resurrection is accompanied by a series of disjointed pronouncements. She asserts that she is "falsely, falsely murdered," announces "A guiltless death I die," and finally claims the blame lies with "Nobody. I myself. / Commend me to my kind lord—O, farewell!" (5.2.115, 120, 121–22). These statements are strictly incompatible with one another, and lead Othello to conclude that Desdemona is "like a liar gone to burning hell" (5.2.127). By reading his wife's contradictions as further evidence of her falsity and sinfulness, he seeks to transform ambiguity into certainty, and to consign her conclusively to the grave.

As in Act Four Scene Three, though, we have a choice to focus less on the interpersonal and psychological dynamics that condition Desdemona's death and more on how it functions formally as a *memento mori*. The contradictions of Desdemona's final words perhaps position her less as a coherent, psychologically realized character than as an avatar of death. Like the skeletons in the *tu fui* trope, she confuses past and future and cause and effect. Shifting from past to present tenses and locating the blame for her end both inside and outside herself, she becomes an emblem of mortality that cannot be localized. Furthermore, like the virtuosic shift from dialogue into song in Act Four, Desdemona's unexpected revival can draw the audience's attention to the conventions and assumptions underlying the theatrical representation of mortality. Over the course of the scene, the performer playing Desdemona has been called upon to imitate death in multiple ways, which exist in some tension with one another. First, we see Desdemona asleep, in a state of insensibility that (as Hamlet observes) simulates and anticipates death, but is not yet the thing itself. Then, we see her after her strangulation, as a corpse. In these two moments, the character exists in two distinct ontological states. But if we stop to think about what the *player* is doing, the distinction threatens to collapse. A performance of Desdemona's corpse will not only resemble a performance of sleep; it will repeat it. Whether playing sleep or death, the actor lies inertly, doing nothing except what he or she is not supposed to be doing—namely, being alert, alive. That stillness can stand for sleep, insensibility or death is such an excepted theatrical convention that it only typically comes to audience awareness in situations like this where the status of an inert body is in doubt. When Trinculo assesses Caliban's prone form in *The Tempest* or when Juliet simulates death by drinking the potion, the similarity of performance conventions used to represent different states of unconsciousness becomes more visible to audiences. But since the ambiguity in each case is a plot point, it can easily be reconciled to the realist project of the plays. Desdemona's unexpected revival, by contrast, breaks the audience's trust, and so draws attention both to the similar nature of performances of sleep and death, and to their constitutive falsity. It overwrites realism with a quite different protocol for representing death: that of the speaking corpse, which announces its own fate and promises a similar future to its listeners by wrenching them out of their settled assumptions.

Emilia's final speech weaves together many of the patterns that Desdemona has established. She too speaks from different moments in time, while also voicing the Willow Song. Her behavior seems to confirm that notable features of Desdemona's behavior toward the end of the play are best understood less as consequences of Desdemona's distinct personality than as strategies to represent mortality as such. Gratiano records Emila's death before it occurs: "sure he hath killed his wife [...] his wife's killed" (5.2.234–236). His determination of fatality positions Emilia's final words in the same liminal space, between life and death, as Desdemona's last lines. Like Othello, Gratiano presents death as a caused action, inflicted by a man upon a woman. And like Desdemona, Emilia answers back from the other side of the pronouncement of her murder:

> What did thy song bode, lady?
> Hark, canst thou hear me? I will play the swan
> And die in music. [*Sings.*] Willow, willow, willow.
> —Moor, she was chaste, she loved thee, cruel Moor,
> So come my soul to bliss as I speak true!
> So speaking as I think, alas, I die. (5.2.244–49).

Emilia speaks at once as a member of the living to one of the dead and as a member of the dead to one of the living. Her questions to Desdemona seek guidance about what is to come from her already dead mistress. Her "true" speech asserting Desdemona's chastity—a counter to Othello's assertion that she is "like a liar gone to burning hell"—appropriates the authority of departed saints to instruct mortal sinners. The Willow Song, now attributed to Desdemona rather than Barbary, is the fulcrum between these two moments.

Conclusion

Schneider suggests that "errors in theatricality [...] are generative of a relationship to history that partakes of the double negative: a reenactment *both* is *and* is not the acts of the Civil War. It is *not not* the civil war. And, perhaps, through the crack in the "not not," something cross-temporal, something affective, and something affirmative circulates" [original emphasis].[27] The final two acts of *Othello* draw attention to their own artificiality in order to facilitate a similar effect of "not not" in relation to tragedy and mortality. Tragedy is not death. But it is also not not death. When subversions of established artistic protocols and shifts between different modes of performance coincide with reminders of human finitude, they do not only break the illusion. Like the speaking corpses in *tu fui* motifs and the *danse macabre*, they can sometimes produce the effect of a starker reality breaking into the world of the play to shock characters and audiences out of their complacency. The chains of automatic sonic memory that connect different performances of the Willow Song, like the rapidly shifting tenses and perspectives that characterize Emilia and Desdemona's final speeches, reproduce the disturbing effect of a corpse reaching out to the living from the past and the future simultaneously. The dead speak and sing through *Othello* to register the characters' particular tragedies, and in doing so offer social commentary on the divides of race, class and gender out of which they emerge. But they also transform those particular tragedies into more general *memento mori*. Hearing them, we hear the distinctive power of early modern death arts, echoing from the seventeenth century into the present.

Acknowledgements I am grateful to Eileen Sperry and Gavin Hollis for their thoughtful responses to earlier versions of this argument.

NOTES

1. William Shakespeare, *Othello*, Revised Edition, ed. E.A.J Honigmann and Ayanna Thompson (London: Arden, 2016), 5.2.350–54. Further line references given parenthetically.
2. For instance, see Lupton, *Citizen Saints: Shakespeare and Political Theology*, pp. 120–22; Bartels, *Speaking of the Moor: From Alcazar to Othello*, p. 187.
3. Schneider, *Performing Remains: Art and War in Times of Theatrical Reenactment*, p. 43.
4. See Eileen Sperry, "'As Thou Art, I Once Was;'—Death and the Bodies in *2 H IV*," in this volume, Chapter 3.
5. For examples of this effects in medieval poetry, see Steel, *How Not to Make a Human: Pets, Feral Children, Worms, Sky Burial, Oysters*, pp. 79–85; Smith, *Arts of Dying: Literature and Finitude in Medieval England*, pp. 230–38.
6. Elina Gertsman discusses the surviving records of two *danse macabre* performances in *The Dance of Death in the Middle Ages*, p. 81. Many more, presumably, have left no lasting trace.
7. Ibid., p. 15.
8. John Lydgate, *The Dance of Death*, A Version (Selden), ll. 362–63.
9. Ibid., ll. 368–74.
10. Hall, *Things of Darkness: Economies of Race and Gender in Early Modern England*, pp. 4–5.
11. See Loomba, *Shakespeare, Race and Colonialism*, p. 17.
12. Greenblatt, *Hamlet in Purgatory*.
13. See Pabel, "Humanism and Early Modern Catholicism: Erasmus of Rotterdam's *Ars Moriendi*," pp. 26–45.
14. Newstok, *Quoting Death in Early Modern England: The Poetics of Epitaphs Beyond the Tomb*, pp. 16–19.
15. See Smith, "Female Impersonation in Early Modern Ballads," p. 284.
16. "A Louers complaint being forsaken of his Loue."
17. Ibid.
18. Smith, "Female Impersonation," p. 284.
19. See Chakravarty, "More Than Kin, Less Than Kind: Similitude, Strangeness, and Early Modern English Homonationalisms," p. 26.

20. Minear, *Reverberating Song in Shakespeare and Milton: Language, Memory and Musical Representation*, p. 53.
21. Margulis, *On Repeat: How Music Plays the Mind*, p. 75.
22. Szendy, *Hits: Philosophy in the Jukebox*, p. 80.
23. Trudell, *Unwritten Poetry: Song, Performance, and Media in Early Modern England*, p. 20.
24. McManus, "'Sing it Like Poor Barbary:' *Othello* and Early Modern Women's Performance," pp. 99–120, esp. pp. 107–8.
25. Stoever develops the concept of a sonic line in *The Sonic Color Line: Race and the Cultural Politics of Listening*.
26. Schneider, p. 41.
27. Ibid., p. 43.

References

"A Louers complaint being forsaken of his Loue." London: 1615? Pepys Library. EBBA 20167.
Bartels, Emily C. *Speaking of the Moor: From* Alcazar *to* Othello. Philadelphia, PA: University of Pennsylvania Press, 2008.
Chakravarty, Urvashi. "More Than Kin, Less Than Kind: Similitude, Strangeness, and Early Modern English Homonationalisms." *Shakespeare Quarterly* 67.1 (2016): 14–29.
Gertsman, Elina. *The Dance of Death in the Middle Ages*. Turnhout: Brepols, 2010.
Greenblatt, Stephen. *Hamlet in Purgatory*. Princeton, NJ: Princeton University Press, 2001.
Hall, Kim. *Things of Darkness: Economies of Race and Gender in Early Modern England*. Ithaca, NY: Cornell University Press, 1995.
Loomba, Ania. *Shakespeare, Race and Colonialism*. Oxford: Oxford University Press, 2002.
Lupton, Julia. *Citizen Saints: Shakespeare and Political Theology*. Chicago, IL: University of Chicago Press, 2005.
Lydgate, John. *The Dance of Death*. Edited by Megan L Cook and Elizabeth Strakhov. Kalamazoo, MI: Medieval Institute Publications, 2019.
Margulis, Elizabeth Hellmuth. *On Repeat: How Music Plays the Mind*. Oxford: Oxford University Press, 2014.
McManus, Clare. "'Sing it Like Poor Barbary:' *Othello* and Early Modern Women's Performance." *Shakespeare Bulletin* 33.1 (2015): 99–120.

Minear, Erin. *Reverberating Song in Shakespeare and Milton: Language, Memory and Musical Representation*. Burlington, NH: Ashgate, 2011.
Newstok, Scott. *Quoting Death in Early Modern England: The Poetics of Epitaphs Beyond the Tomb*. Houndmills, Basingstoke, UK: Palgrave, 2009.
Pabel, Hilmar M. "Humanism and Early Modern Catholicism: Erasmus of Rotterdam's *Ars moriendi*." In *Early Modern Catholicism: Essays in Honour of John W. O'Malley, S. J.* Edited by Kathleen M. Comerford and Hilmar M. Pabel. Toronto: University of Toronto Press, 2001, pp. 26–45.
Schneider, Rebecca. *Performing Remains: Art and War in Times of Theatrical Reenactment*. Abingdon, UK: Routledge, 2011.
Shakespeare, William. *Othello*. Edited by E.A.J Honigmann and Ayanna Thompson. London: Arden, 2016.
Smith, Bruce R. "Female Impersonation in Early Modern Ballads." In *Women Players in England 1500–1600: Beyond the All-Male Stage*. Edited by Pamela Brown and Peter Parolin. Burlington: Ashgate, 2008.
Smith, D. Vance. *Arts of Dying: Literature and Finitude in Medieval England*. Chicago, IL: Chicago University Press, 2020.
Sperry, Eileen. "'As thou art, I once was'—Death and the Bodies in *2 Henry IV*." In *The Shakespearean Death Arts: Hamlet Among the Tombs*. Edited by William E. Engel and Grant Williams. London and New York: Palgrave Macmillan. Chapter 3.
Steel, Karl. *How Not to Make a Human: Pets, Feral Children, Worms, Sky Burial, Oysters*. Minneapolis, MN: Minnesota University Press, 2019.
Stoever, Jennifer Lynn. *The Sonic Color Line: Race and the Cultural Politics of Listening*. New York: New York University Press, 2016.
Szendy, Peter. *Hits: Philosophy in the Jukebox*. Translated by Will Bishop. New York: Fordham University Press, 2012.
Trudell, Scott. *Unwritten Poetry: Song, Performance, and Media in Early Modern England*. Oxford: Oxford University Press, 2019.

PART II

Hamlet and the Death Arts

PREFACE TO PART II

Shakespeare's *Hamlet* is a privileged expression and enactment of the Renaissance death arts so much so that it could be called a handbook or even a compendium of the *memento mori*. But, as with his depictions of other rituals and iconographies, this play does not passively register the stamp of tradition. Shakespeare puts his imprimatur on the death arts, retooling them into his own theatrical vernacular, what Isabel Karremann calls a "dramaturgy of mortality" in Chapter 14 of this volume.

The chapters of the second part broadly speaking explore Hamlet's dramaturgy of mortality, bringing into focus a problematic poignantly articulated by Roland Frye decades ago. Frye sought out iconographical analogues for the skull and the skeletal in Renaissance pictorial art in order to defend Hamlet's graveyard meditation from the charge of being sickly morbid. He argued that the play traces the Danish Prince's growing maturity as he comes to terms with his mortality.[1] For Frye's landmark study on the subject—temporally bound though it is—we recognize the perennial utility of his book and, in fact, pay homage to his precedence with our collection's subtitle, which echoes one of his chapter headings.

These seven chapters, which—for reasons that will become apparent in what follows—are not addressed in the order listed, shed new light on the cultural complexities of Frye's question by adding the lens of the death arts to their scrutiny. Behind Hamlet's decision-making and actions is an artifice not "acceptable" to modern readers. His struggles are couched in the schematic and scripted predispositions of medieval and Renaissance culture, not a transhistorical existential condition often read into the "to be or not to be" soliloquy (3.1.57–3.1.89).[2] And they tacitly export the gender assumptions of his society, betrayed by Frye's unreflective emphasis upon the painting of a young man holding a skull. Coming to terms with one's mortality in *Hamlet* must be channeled through an understanding of the period's death arts if we are not to repeat the anachronistic error of taking our modern notion of death to be universal, an error which Phillippe Ariès, as mentioned in the Introduction, worked so hard to correct in his historical account.

Isabel Karremann's chapter spins out the full implications of the *danse macabre*, perhaps the most curious and most recognizable death art from the period. Building upon Frye's attention to the visual traditions informing *Hamlet*, Karremann advances a more ambitious argument with detailed, illuminating analysis: the play owes its memento-mori theatricality to this arresting death art—at once, mural, narrative, and iconographic system—whose assimilation into the play's fabric enables spectators to meditate on the many bad deaths depicted on the stage. Our eponymous hero not only struggles with his mortality over the arc of the plot, but is also an *ars moriendi* instrument in helping the audience come to their own terms with death. Karremann's examination attests to the way in which the early modern theater perpetuates the didactic ends of the medieval *danse macabre*, thereby leading her to contest critics who, overdramatizing the break between Catholic and Protestant ritual, regard the play as endorsing "modern secularized individualism." In this respect, Karremann, as with several other contributors to the volume, also builds upon the literary sleuthing of Stephen Greenblatt, whose *Hamlet in Purgatory* popularized the issue of the "boundary dispute" of the Reformation for interpreting the period's texts as well as Shakespeare's.[3] The entanglement of the death arts within confessional continuities and discontinuities challenges contemporary scholarship to sort out their subtle politico-religious inflections.

Jonathan Baldo's inquiry into *Hamlet* hinges more on memory than on *memento mori* per se, taking his point of departure from Greenblatt's contention that Catholic ritual and doctrine haunt the play. Baldo concerns himself with older death arts, such as the Norse *minne*, that extend beyond medieval Catholicism into England's early history with

PART II: *HAMLET* AND THE DEATH ARTS   175

Danish and Norman conquerors. *Hamlet* unearths disturbing memories—along with their suppressed practices—for the protagonist and for the Elizabethan and later Jacobean spectator, who are also meant to feel the unbearable weight of the past. As with much of the spadework in this part, Baldo's investigation invites us to revisit the graveyard scene, the most iconic of Shakespeare's *memento-mori* tableaux. This scene is the turning point in Hamlet's tribulations with remembrance, for it is a kind of anti-memory theater, where the burden of history is finally laid to rest. What makes all the difference is the ancient death art of riddling, which helps the Prince to shed the reverential aura around his father's memory. With their rhetorical finality, riddles bring relief and closure to the play's relentless interrogation of the past.

Zackariah Long puts an innovative spin on Hamlet Senior's injunction "Remember me." The death arts that Long observes operating in the play are two symbolic topographies, the theater of memory, exemplified by Camillo's "Theatro," and the theater of God's judgments, illustrated by Dante's *Divine Comedy*. These two designs were manifested by the Globe itself, the canopy above the stage standing for heaven and the cellar beneath for hell—as first analyzed by Francis Yates's pioneering monograph, *The Art of Memory*.[4] Even more importantly, they were mental schema by which practitioners could order their thoughts and their world. Hamlet, as Long explains, employs a blending of the theaters in his soliloquies to make sense of his father's death and his mother's remarriage. They enable him to come to grips with his own mortality in that their cosmological breadth imposes a moral framework—God's judgments—upon life's inherently random actions and events. However, these artificial modes of thinking, these cognitive artifacts, change with Hamlet's evolving self-awareness until he abandons their puritanical severity, learning to suspend his judgments with a Stoic stance of accepting how things are rather than trying to stage-manage the fates of others.

It is only fitting that Michael Neill's chapter should have the last word in this collection. His groundbreaking work *Issues of Death* established the importance of death studies for Shakespearean and Renaissance tragedy and has influenced a generation of literary scholars. His chapter's placement is also appropriate because it directly deals with the wished-for "closure" that no death art can ever truly deliver. Every drama's drive toward a finale constitutes a death art in that the narrator tries to shape the protagonist's life into a coherent totality from the beginning through the middle to the end, as Aristotle prescribes in the *Poetics*. But mortals are, Neill reminds us, thrown into the midst of things and their deaths take place in this "middest." *Hamlet* exploits such a structuring principle of temporal interruption and dislocation, denying its characters the comfort of closure. Neill takes the reader on a dizzying tour of the play's "succession of abrupted narratives" and inevitably turns to a consideration of Shakespeare's own handling of the plot with its loose ends. Though Hamlet wants a good death, the consolatory arts of Catholicism that formerly made this exit possible are no longer permissible among those schooled in Protestant Wittenberg, and, as a result, he suffers the same fate as his father, now forgotten when Hamlet dies.

The deeply rhetorical construction of the Shakespearean death arts is implied by the work of several of the collection's chapters. Like Neill's, Amanda K. Rudd's essay grapples with the consolatory strategies of textuality. Particularly, she ascertains the form and function of description in revenge tragedy. As well as being one of the elemental exercises in the *progymnasmata*, description covers a set of figures under the concept of *enargeia*, that is, those figures that create lively and vivid word pictures. According to Rudd, elegiac description is a death art insofar as it allows the protagonist to respond to traumatic loss and enables the playwright to communicate that loss to audiences. This rhetorical technique achieves the effect of conveying the feelings of mourning by conjuring up the experience of presence with a powerful image of a loved one only to highlight the image's illusory status and have it fade into nothingness. In doing so, it enacts the painful process of loss on the level of language. Shakespeare, moreover, uses elegiac description as a way of suspending the plot's momentum and proffers it as an "alternative to vengeful action." This salient feature of *Hamlet* is also a feature seized upon for great effect by Thomas Kyd's *Spanish Tragedy*, reminding us that the Shakespearean death arts grow up in the soil of early modern theatrical composition.

Two of the chapters in this part challenge the androcentric assumptions of prioritizing Hamlet's involvement in the death arts. The feelings, thoughts, and motivations behind Ophelia and Gertrude's possible suicides are ignored by Shakespeare's theatrical interest in Hamlet's angst over his father's death and Claudius's betrayal. The question of how the female protagonists come to terms with their mortality seems left by the wayside. And yet it should be all the more pressing because, as Pamela Royston Macfie and Lina Perkins Wilder suggest, Ophelia and Gertrude are the ones who actually "resolve [themselves] into a dew." They are the ones who act upon Hamlet's brooding speculations. Where the women are concerned, readers do not have the benefit of soliloquies but only second-hand accounts, allusions, gaps, and ultimately silences with which to puzzle out the female dimension of the death arts in the play.

If critics have regularly sought out answers from the gravedigger, Macfie turns, instead, to Gertrude's description of the wateryburial of Ophelia, whose iconography first became a critical touchstone with Bridget Gellert Lyons's compelling essay on the topic.[5] For Macfie, sifting through fluvial sediment rather than excavating dirt becomes the proper mode of investigation for understanding the play's gendered responses to mortality. Macfie reads Ophelia's drowning through the pastoral commonplace of the *locus amoenus*, the logic of which posits a geo-humoral outlook on existence whereby the elemental body shares a porous reciprocity with the elemental world. In Ophelia's waterburial, Gertrude's account recognizes the associations of mud with the primal— "storied matter" replete with mystery and possibility. It contrasts significantly, even philosophically, with Hamlet's musings in the graveyard scene, where dust signifies nothing but annihilation and randomness evocative of Democritean atomism.

Wilder's chapter shifts the focus to Gertrude's potential suicide. Though theatrical representations of killing oneself can definitely be grouped under the death arts, actual suicide, we must not forget, was legally speaking well outside the SimpleParameters of what the early modern church considered to be the *ars moriendi*. But the audience does not know for sure whether or not Gertrude—or for that matter Ophelia—has taken her own life because Shakespeare denies the audience access to her inwardness as distinguished from Hamlet's richly available introspection. Female opacity prompts male suspicion, which Wilder develops by unpacking the play's dense allusive relations to the classical and historical figure Agrippina, as well as to her husband Claudius and son Nero. Hamlet's distrust of his mother leads him to probe into her sexual life—a violent intrusion that Wilder likens to the rape of anatomization and other invasive medical technologies whereby Hamlet tries to discover whether or not she carries Claudius's heir. Gertrude's suicide, along with Ophelia's, may very well be precipitated by an unwanted pregnancy that suggests a courageous defiance surpassing anything that Hamlet can dream of. Wilder's essay demonstrates both the perplexing continuities and backwardness of the Shakespearean death arts within our own contemporary moment.

Grant Williams

Notes

1. Frye, p. 206.
2. This quotation is taken from The New Oxford Shakespeare, The Complete Works.
3. Greenblatt, pp. 244–248.
4. Yates, pp. 342–367.
5. Lyons, "The Iconography of Ophelia."

References

Ariès, Phillipe. *The Hour of Our Death: The Classic History of Western Attitudes Toward Death Over the Last One Thousand Years*. Translated by Helen Weaver. 2nd edition. New York: Vintage Books, 2008.

Frye, Roland Mushat. *The Renaissance Hamlet: Issues and Responses in 1600*. Princeton, NJ: Princeton University Press, 1984.

Greenblatt, Stephen. *Hamlet in Purgatory*. Princeton, NJ: Princeton University Press, 2001.

Lyons, Bridget Gellert. "The Iconography of Ophelia." *English Literary History* 44.1 (1977): 60–74.

Neill, Michael. Issues of Death: Mortality and Identity in English Renaissance Tragedy. Oxford: Clarendon Press, 1997.

Shakespeare, William. *The New Oxford Shakespeare, the Complete Works*. General edited by Gary Taylor, John Jowett, Terri Bourus, and Gabriel Egan. Oxford: Oxford University Press, 2017.

Yates, Francis. *The Art of Memory*. 1966. Chicago, IL: University of Chicago Press, 1974.

CHAPTER 9

"Must I Remember?": The Burden of the Past Tense in *Hamlet*

Jonathan Baldo

Dwelling on his mother and father's mutual tenderness, Hamlet asks in his first soliloquy, "Heaven and earth, / Must I remember?" (1.2.142–3).[1] It is a resonant question in a play that, I shall argue, repeatedly brings the experience of arduous and uncomfortable memories directly to audiences. Spectators are invited to share Hamlet and Denmark's uneasy relations with the past by means of glancing but powerful reminders of

---

This essay was written originally for the "Shakespearean Death Arts" seminar (organized by William E. Engel and Grant Williams) which was to have been held at the Shakespeare Association of America meeting in Denver. Although that meeting was canceled due to the global pandemic, I want to express my deep appreciation to both organizers and to Zachariah Long and Amanda Ruud for their thoughtful and helpful comments on earlier drafts.

J. Baldo (✉)
Eastman School of Music, University of Rochester, Rochester, NY, USA
e-mail: jbaldo@esm.rochester.edu

© The Author(s), under exclusive license to Springer Nature Switzerland AG 2022
W. E. Engel and G. Williams (eds.), *The Shakespearean Death Arts*, Palgrave Shakespeare Studies,
https://doi.org/10.1007/978-3-030-88490-1_9

both the Norman and Danish conquests of England. If allusions to these entwined conquests were too remote historically from the play's London audiences to be experienced as harrowing, they could at the very least alienate audiences from the pleasurable aspects of remembering, thereby reinforcing the play's sense of memory as a "heavy burden" (Claudius, 3.1.53) for Prince and King alike. The sense of spiritual privation that pervades *Hamlet* stems from the loss not only of a father but also of a profitable relation to the past and to the faculty that connects us to the past: memory, which sometimes acquires a purgatorial dimension in the play.

The sense of loss that accompanies remembering in *Hamlet*, as Stephen Greenblatt has elegantly established, issues in large part from the many reminders of the Catholic faith that England had recently left behind, reminders of which still haunted the nation.[2] As Eamon Duffy and others have persuasively argued,[3] to recall Catholicism in early modern England was to remember forgotten or suppressed practices of remembering itself, especially for remembering the dead. For recusant Catholics and church papists, those who outwardly conformed to the new religion but who remained inwardly devoted to the traditional faith,[4] "Must I remember?" would have carried a powerful contemporary application. The anguished question serves as a reminder of the sense of loss undergirding a "Tudor language of nostalgia" that, as Harriet Phillips has recently written, "travelled beyond polemic into the common imagination: not driven by the ideological imperatives of reformers, but as part of the shared world of everyday usage and appropriation."[5]

Largely unremarked in criticism of the play are connections between its remnants of Catholicism and other triggers of historical memory, including the Norman Conquest and the Danish Conquest. It is no accident that Denmark should be the setting for a play in which looking to the past should bear so much more pain than pleasure. Taking my cue from the gravedigging scene, I propose to explore ways in which *Hamlet* is a play about buried pasts. It invites us to follow the gravedigger's example and take up a spade, as it were. "He who seeks to approach his own buried past," writes Walter Benjamin, "must conduct himself like a man digging. Above all, he must not be afraid to return again and again to the same matter; to scatter it as one scatters earth, to turn it over as one turns over soil."[6] In the Graveyard Scene, Hamlet does indeed "conduct himself like a man digging," turning over the meaning of earth if not actual spadefuls of soil. Hamlet remembers Yorick bearing

9 "MUST I REMEMBER?": THE BURDEN OF THE PAST TENSE IN *HAMLET* 181

him on his back, an apt symbol of the way in which one memory carries another on its back. By remembering Yorick, Hamlet recovers a fragment of his own childhood. In what follows, I will explore the ways in which *Hamlet* similarly enticed its early modern English audiences to turn over the soil of their history and uncover early remnants. It is a history whose individual episodes inevitably carry others on their backs, as the fleeting references to the Norman horseman Lamord and the Danish demand of tribute from England show. One of the first memories triggered by the play concerns a practice intended to keep alive remembrance of the dead, the month-mind.

"A LITTLE MONTH"

Widely practiced in pre-Reformation England, month-minds and years-minds or obits, also known as minding days or minnying days, were special days of remembrance on which commemorative services and feasts for the departed took place, one month and one year after their deaths.[7] These acts of commemoration could be elaborate. As Christopher Daniell writes in this regard: "It was not uncommon in wealthy households for the month's mind to be as grand as the original burial."[8] The annual celebration of the year-mind, writes Peter Marshall, "involved an exact re-creation of the funeral rites on the anniversary of the death, with the bell-man going forth once more, candles, mass and *dirige*, doles to the poor, even the presence of a hearse in the parish church."[9] According to David Cressy, "Though repudiated by the Reformation, the traditional month-mind and year-mind had a customary half-life in many parts of England as far apart as Lancashire and Essex."[10] Although observance of year-minds and month-minds persisted in some English parishes for decades beyond the Elizabethan Settlement of 1559, for a Catholic exile like Cardinal William Allen, observance of prayers for the dead was waning even before the accession of Elizabeth, that "pitifull overthrowe of vertue." Such prayers were reduced to, "for the most parte, but twelve monthes-myndes, or monthes for the most: and that commonly but for the first yere of theyre rest: and then afterwarde ether cleane forgotten, or openly not often remembered."[11] Reformers considered the lingering tradition of month-minds and year-minds to be "means for priests to fleece the laity."[12] They belonged to an arsenal of devices, including trentals,[13] another popular pre-Reformation practice related to the first month after death, that stood in need of suppression and rooting out.

Edmund Grindal, Archbishop of York and a puritan sympathizer, ordered in 1571 that "no month-minds or yearly commemorations of the dead, nor any other superstitious ceremonies be observed or used which tend either to the maintenance of the prayer for the dead or of the popish purgatory."[14] Although purgatory ceased to be a part of church doctrine, the practice of saying prayers for the dead lingered on for decades.[15]

The thirty "minding days" following the loss of a loved one, the formal thirty-day period in which the survivor was expected to perform obsequies, was an ancient practice: a survival "of the Norse *minne* or ceremonial drinking to the dead."[16] The *minne* or ritual draughts and their accompanying memory toasts are referred to in the Norse Eddas, where they are frequently dedicated to individual Norse gods. After the advent of Christianity, the Scandinavian practice survived in the form of memory-cups dedicated to Christ, Mary, or the saints as well as to departed family members and friends. According to Edward Burnett Tylor, "The 'minne' was at once love, memory, and the thought of the absent, and it long survived in England in the 'minnying' or 'mynde' days, on which the memory of the dead was celebrated by services or banquets."[17] Although rampant at Elsinore, ceremonial drinking seems linked to oblivion rather than remembrance. It occupies the background of Act 1, scenes 2 and 4, while in the foreground Hamlet and Horatio remember the former king. The background and foreground of these scenes are out of joint. A few lines before he tells Horatio that he sees his father in his "mind's eye," Hamlet ironically assures his friend, "We'll teach you for to drink ere you depart" (1.2.174). Presumably he means that his friend, a partner in remembrance, will be invited to join the Danish fraternity of forgetting. Claudius's heavy drinking in the wake of his recent coronation and marriage might be viewed as a Scandinavian *minne* turned upside down. Decried by Hamlet as "a custom / More honoured in the breach than the observance" (1.4.15–16), Claudius's ceremonial draughts are dedicated not to the past but to the present, not to the dead but to the living. Rather than memory-cups seeking to revive the memory of the departed, Claudius's "stoups of wine" (5.2.244) are agents of oblivion, the center of a court ritual of forgetting.

Although no ceremonies that might be described as popish are performed over Ophelia's corpse—no bell-ringing, lighting of wax candles, singing of psalms, holy water, or prayers for the dead—allusion to the officially forbidden observance of the month-mind, still in need of suppression in parts of England during Shakespeare' youth, might be

9 "MUST I REMEMBER?": THE BURDEN OF THE PAST TENSE IN *HAMLET* 183

heard in a particularly insistent manner in Hamlet's soliloquy in Act 1, scene 2. Hamlet decries the speed of his mother's remarriage in terms in which the word "month" itself acts as a tolling remembrance of his father: "But two months dead—nay, not so much, not two—"; "And yet within a month / (Let me not think on't—Frailty, thy name is Woman), / A little month"; "Within a month, / Ere yet the salt of most unrighteous tears," 1.2.138, 145–7, 153–4).[18] Of Hamlet's six references to the period of a "month" or "months" in the play, five allude to the lack of remembrance accorded his father's death. Allusion to the traditional observance of the month-mind might also be heard in Claudius's reference in the same scene to a fixed term of filial obligation to a departed parent: "the survivor bound / In filial obligation for some term / To do obsequious sorrow" (1.2.90–2). "Some term" most likely refers to the month-mind, a period that expired shortly after the marriage of Gertrude and Claudius ("within a month"). In his study of the play's complex negotiations of confessional differences, Stephen Greenblatt refers to Shakespeare's "remarkable gift for knowing exactly how far he could go without getting into serious trouble."[19] Like Ophelia's body, those religious differences are not yet entombed and laid to rest. In particular, the proscribed practice of the month-mind is everywhere present "by indirection" (2.1.63), not only in the play's evocation of the Scandinavian *minne*, the ancestor of the month-mind or period of thirty minding days, but also in Hamlet's insistent references to the period of the month.

Allusions to the month-mind arguably link Old Hamlet's death to Polonius's and to a strange figure of death alluded to near the end of the play. Hamlet mockingly tells Claudius of the location of Polonius's body, "But if indeed you find him not within this month you shall nose him as you go up the stairs into the lobby" (4.3.34–6). Here the traditional period of mourning, perhaps tied to a belief that the spirit of the dead lingers on earth for a period of thirty days, becomes a period of corporeal putrefaction. A different sort of corporealizing is evident in the King's description of the Norman knight, whose name, Lamord, is supplied by Laertes:

KING Two months since
Here was a gentleman of Normandy—
I have seen myself, and served against, the French,
And they can well on horseback, but this gallant
Had witchcraft in't; he grew unto his seat
And to such wondrous doing brought his horse

> As had he been incorpsed and demi-natured
> With the brave beast. So far he topped my thought
> That I in forgery of shapes and tricks
> Come short of what he did.
> LAERTES A Norman was't?
> KING A Norman.
> LAERTES Upon my life, Lamord!
> KING The very same. (4.7.80–90)

This curious exchange between Claudius and Laertes, dropped into a scene in which the King persuades Laertes to fence with Hamlet and thereby make him a corpse, has seemed to many critics a strangely irrelevant digression. In his edition of the play, Dover Wilson comments that it "does not arise naturally out of a context in which the accomplishment dwelt on is fencing, not horsemanship."[20] However, I would suggest that the speech resembles others in the play by virtue of its historical-emotional triggers. "Incorpsed" or made one body with his horse, this Norman whose name echoes that universal maker of corpses, "la mort," was seen in Denmark "two months since": the length of time that Hamlet assigns to his father's death at the staging of The Mousetrap ("die two months ago and not forgotten yet?" 3.2.123–4). Might the knight Lamord, who rides into our imaginations just before the Graveyard Scene, represent older practices regarding death, *la mort*, practices that still lived on in France in the religion officially banished in England?

Shakespeare's curious neologism "incorpsed," usually glossed as "made into one body,"[21] seems assured to prick up the ears of auditors who had never before heard the word. The word sums up one side of the controversy over the Eucharist that several commentators locate at the heart of the play, particular in the Ghost's enjoining his son, "Remember me," an echo of Christ's words at the Last Supper: "Take, eat: this is my body, which is broken for you: this do you in remembrance of me."[22] According to Mark Sweetnam, "Hamlet's remembrance of his father, with its stubborn insistence on the flesh, on the body of the king, becomes a Eucharist, privately partaken of, the sort of 'private, churlish breakfast' so repugnant to the reformers."[23] It brings Hamlet's training at Wittenberg, the origin of the Protestant Reformation, "into an intriguingly close connexion with the traditional Eucharist of transubstantiation."[24] The son's "relentlessly fleshy commemoration of his father" stands in stark contrast with "the incorporeality of the Ghost."[25] The end of the play, argues Sweetnam, "revisits the Eucharist" in the form of a false communion designed by Claudius, in which Gertrude drinks not salvation but damnation to herself. After his death, Hamlet's physical remains become the center of a sacramental observance, "publicly uplifted for remembrance and [...] veneration": "the old order seems to have been restored, a true Eucharist reinstated."[26] Late medieval culture, writes Miri Rubin, experienced a crisis over the use and meaning of the Eucharist, which was "fought over regionally and nationally." In the process, the "Eucharist became identified as a controversial object, a militant emblem of a struggle unto death."[27] Like a symbol in a dream, Lamord is an overdetermined sign. The figure of the Norman horseman, incorpsed or made into one body with his horse, may very well have represented to English audiences in 1600 a dream of the past: of chivalric knighthood if not of the traditional faith to which it was tied, with its ritual and liturgical emphasis on "incorpsing."[28]

Within that dream, was there embedded a nightmare? The ghost of the past most likely to return at the mention of Normandy would undoubtedly have been the Norman Conquest, especially in light of the king's earlier allusion to the Danish Conquest of England (3.1.168–9), which led directly to the Norman invasion. Without claiming that Lamord functions simply as an avatar of William the Conqueror, who brought so much death and destruction to England,[29] it might be noted that this Norman warrior was famous for his horsemanship. His chaplain and biographer William of Poitiers records an "account of Duke William riding across Normandy in the late summer of 1053 at such speed that the horses of his companions collapsed with exhaustion."[30] According to William's biographer David Bates, the contemporary soldier Geoffrey Martel, Count of Anjou, held him to be "peerless as a warrior and a horseman."[31] The Battle of Hastings represented the first time in their history that the English faced mounted cavalry in battle, and horsemen (as well as archers) seem to have been key to the Norman success at Hastings. A few years after the battle, William "employed an equestrian image on the obverse of his double-sided seal."[32] In 1087, William would die as a result of being thrown from his horse. The life and career of this most infamous of Normans (to the English, at least) was indeed "incorpsed" with his horse.

In his Arden Third Series edition of the play, Harold Jenkins calls the name of the Norman knight "a presage of fatality," noting the likely play on "La Mort."[33] Rather than, or perhaps in addition to, a portent or forewarning, I would suggest that the name looks *backward* to two fatalities: a historically remote one that an English audience would likely associate with Normandy; and a much more recent one, the sometimes violent disruption of ritual practices and spiritual life known as the Reformation, one result of which was increased tensions with Catholic France.[34]

England as Tributary

The likelihood that Lamord might trigger historical memory of the Norman Conquest is enhanced by the King's earlier glancing reference to the Viking conquest (3.1.168–9), which led directly to the Battle of Hastings. Both antagonists at Hastings had Danish ancestors. Harold Godwinson had a Danish mother, and his opponent William the Conqueror was descended from a Danish chieftain. Normandy itself was named for the Norsemen who raided the coasts and eventually settled there. The Viking threat also had the indirect effect of intertwining the Anglo-Saxon bloodline with a Norman one. Seaports in Normandy often served as havens for Viking ships. It was to prevent their use that in 978 King Æthelred II of England took as his second wife Emma of Normandy, producing a son who was to become Edward the Confessor, King of England beginning in 1042 and last king of the House of Wessex. (In addition to being the mother of Harathcnut, her son by Cnut, and Edward the Confessor, her son by Æthelred, Emma was the great aunt of William the Conqueror.) The protracted struggle against the Danes therefore caused Norman and Anglo-Saxon bloodlines to be mingled, eventually causing William to advance a case for his legitimacy as ruler of England.

Although it makes a delayed entrance in the play, like Hamlet himself, England is mentioned by name nineteen times in *Hamlet*—Denmark, twenty.[35] In light of this, it is somewhat surprising that Anglo-Danish relations, which extend from 793–1066 and beyond, rarely figure in discussions of the play. The Ghost, whom Harold Bloom describes as "a warrior fit for Icelandic saga,"[36] offers the first cue to audiences to cast their imaginations back to early medieval England. The first mention of England occurs in the middle of the play, after a sequestered Claudius and Polonius witness Hamlet's cruel rejection of Ophelia. Originally having decided that it is less dangerous to have Hamlet remain in court under his watchful eye rather than pursuing his studies at Wittenberg, Claudius has decided that his own safety depends on Hamlet's exile: "He shall with speed to England / For the demand of our neglected tribute" (3.1.168–9). The revelation that Claudius's Denmark is engaged

9 "MUST I REMEMBER?": THE BURDEN OF THE PAST TENSE IN *HAMLET* 187

in extortion, demanding what is essentially protection money of England, would certainly be enough to turn audiences against him even before it is confirmed later in the act that he committed fratricide. Furthermore, the reference to a "neglected tribute" hints that under Claudius's predecessor, Old Hamlet, demands for tribute from England may have been forgiven or forgotten.[37]

This first reference to England recalls a period in Anglo-Saxon England following the Vikings' victory at the Battle of Maldon in 991, which resulted in King Æthelred the Unready paying the invaders a massive tribute of 10,000 pounds of silver in order to end the fighting. A few years later, in 994, a Danish siege of London led to a second payment, followed by regular Viking invasions and ever-increasing demands for tribute money until the Danish King Sweyn Forkbeard conquered England, becoming its king in 1013. A second conquest followed, by Sweyn's son Cnut the Great, King of England after 1016. From 1013–1042, most of England belonged to a North Sea Empire that also comprised Denmark, Norway, and part of Sweden. Heaven and earth, must we remember?

The invasion of England in the south by William's victorious Norman force in 1066 was preceded by an invasion in the same year by a Norwegian force in the north led by Harald Hardrada.[38] The Norwegians were defeated by Harold Godwinson, the last of the Anglo-Saxon Kings of England, before the latter fell to William at the Battle of Hastings. Together, Claudius's reference to England's "neglected tribute" in Act 3 and his extravagant praise of the Norman knight's horsemanship in Act 5 evoke the series of interrelated invasions in the tenth and eleventh centuries by the Vikings and eventually by the Normans, particularly the twin invasions of 1066 occasioned by the death of the childless Edward the Confessor. England had seen more than its share of warlike Danes in its past, and it is a mistake to overlook the play's reminders of that history: reminders consistent with other ways in which looking to the past is revealed to be a potentially harrowing experience. David Bates notes that the historian David C. Douglas "was once moved to speculate why Shakespeare did not write a play about the Norman Conquest."[39] Perhaps, by indirection, he did.

Turnings in the Grave

> Men have always had a presentiment that there must be a realm in which the answers to questions are symmetrically combined—a priori—to form a self-contained system.—Ludwig Wittgenstein, *Tractatus Logico-Philosophicus*. 5.4541[40]

It may seem inevitable that a play that so richly explores the tribulations of memory should eventually take audiences to a graveyard. The Danish court with its practice of heavy drinking is a space of forgetting, one in which Denmark actively seeks to lose sight of its last ruler. By contrast, the graveyard seems a dismal memory theater. Banished from the court, memory takes refuge in the graveyard, and Hamlet is memory's preeminent refugee. It is a place where Hamlet and the gravedigger may share their respective (and quite different) private recollections of a "mad rogue" (5.1.169),[41] and where the lowly are remembered more vividly than the high and mighty. In this place of remembrance, Hamlet's distant yet living memory of the jester gives the lie to his caustic observation to Ophelia about the impermanence of his father's memory, "O heavens—die two months ago and not forgotten yet? Then there's hope a great man's memory may outlive his life half a year!" (3.2.123–5). In keeping with the spirit of both the living jester, the gravedigger, and the dead one, Yorick, remembrance sheds the reverential aspect that it bears when the question is Hamlet's father.

But memory is not simply offered refuge in this deeply memorable scene. In a sense, it is memory itself that is ultimately laid to rest there. As Delver goes about his work of digging Ophelia's grave while being questioned by the prince, immaterial as well as material relics of the past, names as well as skulls, are flung about: Caesar, Alexander, even Adam. In the process, the faculty of memory gets handled as roughly as Yorick's skull. As in an archaeological dig, successive layers of the ancient past are verbally uncovered and tossed in the air. But these layers quickly become indistinguishable, like bones in a graveyard that are dug up to make way for new burials. Elsinore's graveyard is a place where difference itself goes to die: differences of rank (as Adam, the ur-delver, becomes "the first that ever bore arms," 5.1.33) as well as the casuistical distinctions of lawyers.[42] Like their bodies, historical memories of Caesar and Alexander become reduced to a kind of intellectual and affective dust.

Caesar, already dishonored by Polonius's recollection of having played the role, becomes the subject of a rhyme about "stop[ping] a hole to keep the wind away," as Alexander was the subject of speculation that the loam into which he might have been transformed could now be stopping a beer-barrel (5.1.201, 203). Caesar and Alexander are not so much remembered as they are exhumed so as to be forgotten: their immense achievements buried, as it were, beneath twin mounds of silence.

Delver's riddle unearths differences in burial practices and beliefs about the dead that lie at the heart of the play. Riddles were a vital part of both Anglo-Saxon literature (the Exeter Book features over ninety examples[43]) and the Norse poetic tradition.[44] In the *Eddas*, riddle contests are a means for the gods to test the cunning and wisdom of mortals. One of the earliest forms of wordplay, riddles have an impressive history that is of interest to anthropologists and historians of religion as well as literary scholars.[45] In primitive cultures, riddles were a common feature of ritual practices. They often held a sacred import because of their association with esoteric knowledge, magical power, and a sense of mystery. Walter Benjamin writes, "Riddles appear where there is an emphatic intention to elevate an artifact or an event that seems to contain nothing at all, or nothing out of the ordinary, to the plane of symbolic significance."[46] In tragedy, which originated in ritual, the fate of heroes may hinge on their interpretive skills, especially on their ability to wrench a secret from the gods. Oedipus, the salient example, becomes a monarch by solving the riddle of the Sphinx, only to fall victim to the enigmatic gods by failing to solve the conundrum of his own existence. The riddle proper may not seem as prominent a feature of that modern Oedipus-play, *Hamlet*, but in a broad sense, Hamlet riddles throughout the play, beginning with his first cryptic aside ("A little more than kin, and less than kind," 1.2.65[47]) and his first rejoinder to Claudius ("Not so much, my lord, I am too much in the 'son,'" 1.2.67).[48]

The riddle in the strict sense makes a late entrance, in the banter of Goodman Delver with his companion. Its appearance on so solemn an occasion as Ophelia's burial may have offended neoclassical critics,[49] but Delver's riddle, I maintain, is in fact perfectly placed. Galit Hasan-Rokem writes of the appearance of riddle tales in the fifth- or sixth-century Midrash on the book of Lamentations, "Only readers who overlook the centrality of playfulness in midrashic practice would find their presence there out of place [....] [P]lay and humor may be the most powerful modes of spiritual survival in moments of utter stress."[50]

The darkly comical exchange between the gravedigger and his companion may seem remote in many ways from the riddle-contests of legend and myth, in which a riddle is commonly used either to test a suitor's aptness, as in the first act of Shakespeare and Wilkins's *Pericles,* or to test the fitness of a ruler. Nevertheless, it resembles those contests in at least two important ways. First, the riddle must have one and only one answer. In the riddle-contest, Johann Huizinga writes, "Should it prove that a second answer is possible, in accord with the rules but not suspected by the questioner, then it will go badly with him: he is caught in his own trap."[51] A second feature of the riddle-contest is its potential danger. In ancient Hebrew, Greek, Egyptian, and Scandinavian tales alike, answering the riddle correctly is often a matter of life or death. Huizinga informs us, "The riddle contest with life at stake is one of the main themes of Eddic mythology."[52] The graveyard scene alludes to both of these features in comic form.

> GRAVEDIGGER   I'll put another question to thee. If thou answerest me not to the purpose, confess thy self.
> 2 MAN   Go to.
> GRAVEDIGGER   What is he that builds stronger than either the mason, the shipwright or the carpenter?
> 2 MAN   the gallows-maker, for that outlives a thousand tenants.
> GRAVEDIGGER   I like thy wit well, in good faith. The gallows does well. But how does it well? It does well to those that do ill. Now, thou dost ill to say the gallows is built stronger than the church. Argal, the gallows may do well to thee. To't again, come.
> 2 MAN   Who builds stronger than a mason, a shipwright or a carpenter?
> GRAVEDIGGER   Ay, tell me that and unyoke.
> 2 MAN   Marry, now i can tell.
> GRAVEDIGGER   To't.
> 2 MAN   I cannot tell.
> GRAVEDIGGER   Cudgel thy brains no more about it, for your dull ass will not mend his pace with beating. And when you are asked this question next, say a grave-maker. The houses he makes lasts till doomsday. Go get thee in and fetch me a stoup of liquor. (5.1.33–56).

As in a riddle-contest, the riddle must have a single answer. The gravedigger must therefore turn away his companion's answer, "the gallows-maker," even though it fits the question well. In fact, it is probably the gravedigger who unwittingly suggests this answer to his companion when, introducing the riddle to his companion, he warns, "If thou answerest me not to the purpose, confess thy self" (5.1.34–5): most likely shorthand for the proverbial "confess thyself and be hanged."[53] The gravedigger alludes to the threat of death that hangs over the riddle contestant, should he or she fail to answer correctly. Of course, no particular threat hangs over the companion, but only the reminder of humanity's universal death warrant that issues from the setting and the conversation.

Just before the gravedigger poses the riddle, he and his companion have the following exchange: "There is no ancient gentlemen but gardeners, ditchers and grave-makers. They hold up Adam's profession." "Was he a gentleman?" his companion asks, to which the gravedigger answers, "'A was the first that ever bore arms" (5.1.29–33). The exchange amounts to a riddle in reverse, in which the answer comes before the question (Who was the first to ever bear arms?). The back-to-back, forward and backward riddling of the gravedigger and his companion therefore serves to uncover at least two buried pasts. The riddles of Anglo-Saxon literature and the riddle contests of the Old Norse Eddas are made to lie side by side, as it were, with that of the biblical Adam.[54]

The exchange of riddles in the graveyard bears a striking resemblance to cultural practices described by the Scottish anthropologist and folklorist James G. Frazer in *The Golden Bough* (1890). Frazer surmises about the custom of asking riddles on certain ritual occasions, "Perhaps enigmas were originally circumlocutions adopted at times when for certain reasons the speaker was forbidden the use of direct terms."[55] *Hamlet* is a virtual encyclopedia of such occasions. In Elsinore "the use of direct terms" is ill-advised, if not actually taboo. Nearly everyone approaches others on the "bias," seeking "By indirections [to] find directions out" (2.1.62–3). In this respect the graveyard, a place where the use of direct terms would ordinarily be avoided, functions as an emblem of all of Denmark.

In many cultures, riddles have been integral to burial customs. According to Frazer, "They appear to be especially employed in the neighborhood of a dead body. Thus in Bolang Mongondo (Celebes) riddles may never be asked except when there is a corpse in the village [....] In the Aru archipelago, while a corpse is uncoffined, watchers propound riddles to each other."[56] "In Brittany," closer to Shakespeare's home, "after a burial, when the rest have gone to partake of the funeral banquet, old men remain behind in the graveyard, and having seated themselves on mallows, ask each other riddles."[57] According to Annikki Kaivola-Bregenhø, "many researchers have observed riddling during a wake."[58]

Galit Hasan-Rokem and David Shulman write of the practice of riddling in the presence of a dying tribal member among the Gonds of Central India: "the adult men divide into two groups and gather at the boundary of the village; one group chants riddles to the beat of a drum, and the other group searches for answers."[59] Robert Elliott conjectures that the cultural practice of riddling in the graveyard is a means of "unlocking and controlling powers which lie mysteriously at the heart of things."[60]

Posing a question to this interrogative form, "Why sing riddles at the moment of dying?" Hasan-Rokem and Shulman surmise, "The transition between realms seems to be articulated by this form. The riddle is poised on the boundary between domains, at the edge of life and death, where each issues into the other. Both are somehow contained and made present through the challenge posed by the riddling question and addressed by its solution."[61] Similarly, Eleanor Cook observes in her study of the literary riddle, "Boundaries, borders, crossings. The association of riddle and enigma with birth and death is longstanding. Not so much with the results of birth and death, but rather with the process of crossing the boundary into life or into death."[62] A play that begins at thresholds of both space and time—it is midnight on the battlements—takes us to the ultimate boundary, that separating the living from the dead: after the Reformation, no longer a threshold that could be easily crossed. It is a "bourn" (3.1.78), as Hamlet's most famous soliloquy would have it, that the Reformation has transformed from a certainty to a question.

James Kelso surmises that the practice in Brittany of posing riddles in the presence of a corpse "is evidently rooted in animism, and enigmatical language may be used to puzzle the spirit of the departed" and delay its departure from this world.[63] In early modern England, a residual belief of the old faith that souls of the dead lingered for a period after death may have been related to the observance of the month-mind. It may therefore have born a kinship to the practice of riddling in the graveyard among the people of Brittany. According to historian David Cressy,

> Some people believed that the soul lingered in the vicinity of the body during the first thirty days after burial, a liminal situation requiring great ritual caution. During the Elizabethan period, especially in the early part of the reign, some testators continued to provide for this 'triginal' period by ordering a black cover for their coffin or grave during this month's mind,

or arranging for another service, dole, and funeral feast when it came to an end.[64]

In pre-Reformation England, practices related to the first thirty days after death included a "trigintal" of daily masses, the daily practice of bell-ringing, or a daily *Placebo* and *Dirige*.[65] The particular popularity of the month-mind, according to Christopher Daniell, may derive from the traditional belief that "the soul was still regarded as lingering in the vicinity of the body during the first thirty days after burial, a situation needing extreme caution."[66]

Whether or not Delver's riddle leads back, by subterranean means, to the abolished practice of the month-mind and the related belief that souls of the dead lingered for a period of thirty days after burial, it undoubtedly has the effect of helping to silence the interrogative mood that wanders at will throughout most of the play. The riddle is the inverted image of most interrogative exchanges in the play. After all of the play's unanswered questions and questions with multiple answers, this discursive form that promises to yield a perfect one-to-one correspondence between question and answer must hold enormous appeal. In the riddle, the question becomes an instrument of closure. Furthermore, unlike most questions posed in the play, riddles project mastery and control by the one who speaks them, for the riddler is uniquely possessed of the answer to the question, inverting the dominant pattern wherein the questioner seeks knowledge of which he or she is ignorant. The graveyard in *Hamlet* is, among other things, a burial ground for the interrogative mood.

Questions in *Hamlet* pertain overwhelmingly to the past, not the present or future, a pattern broken by the gravedigger. Throughout the play, questions are deeply implicated in the play's exploration of both the ethics and pathology of memory. Delver's riddle has the effect of silencing both the interrogative mood and the posture of remembering. Delver ends his riddling discourse with two nods to the future ("when you are asked this question next" and "doomsday") and a request for that Danish agent of oblivion, "a stoup of liquor." In a heavier mood, Hamlet will similarly reveal before he dies his twin emancipations from the interrogative mood and the burden of the past that comes to him in "such a questionable shape" (1.4.43). To Horatio, he explains why he is prepared to overlook any misgiving about the challenge to fence with Laertes:

We defy augury. There is special providence in the fall of a sparrow. If it be, 'tis not to come. If it be not to come, it will be now. If it be not now, yet it will come. The readiness is all, since no man of aught he leaves knows what is't to leave betimes. Let be. (5.2.197-202)

At the end of the play, the past tense appears to have yielded to the present and future in these elaborately choreographed sentences in which future and present alternate positions. In these same lines, the perturbed spirit of the interrogative mood, faithful companion and confidant of the past tense, "hies / To his confine" (1.1.153–4).

Notes

1. All citations from *Hamlet* refer to the Arden Third Series Revised Edition, ed. Ann Thompson and Neil Taylor (London: Bloomsbury Publishing, 2016). William E. Engel has reminded me that what he calls a "pseudo-oath," Hamlet's "Heaven and earth," echoes the biblical warning against taking oaths (*Geneva Bible*, James 5:12): "But before all things, my brethren, swear not, neither by heaven, nor by earth, nor by any other oath: but let your yea, be yea, and your nay, nay, lest ye fall into condemnation."
2. Greenblatt, *Hamlet in Purgatory*.
3. Duffy, *The Stripping of the Altars: Traditional Religion in England*.
4. See Walsham's groundbreaking study, *Church Papists: Catholicism, Conformity and Confessional Polemic in Early Modern England*.
5. Phillips, *Nostalgia in Print and Performance*, p. 16.
6. Benjamin, "Excavation and Memory," p. 576.
7. *The Monthly Mirror: Reflecting Men and Manners* contains the following entry under "A Month's Mind": "days which our ancestors called their *monthe's mind*, their *year's mind*, and the like, being the days whereon their souls (after their deaths) were had in special remembrance, and some office or obsequies said for them; as *obits, dirges*, & c. This word is still retained in Lancashire" (240).
8. Daniell, *Death and Burial in Medieval England, 1066–1550*, p. 56.
9. Marshall, *Beliefs and the Dead in Reformation England*, pp. 20–1.
10. Cressy, *Birth, Marriage & Death: Ritual, Religion, and the Life-Cycle in Tudor and Stuart England*, p. 398.
11. Allen, *A Defense and Declaration of the Catholike Churches Doctrine touching* Purgatory, p. 169; cited in Marshall, p. 115.

12. Marshall, p. 55.
13. For an account of the popular medieval "Trental of St. Gregory," see Greenblatt, p. 129.
14. Cited in Cressy, p. 400.
15. Cressy, p. 56; Lucy Wooding, "Remembrance in the Eucharist," p. 25.
16. *Encyclopaedia Britanica*, p. 786. More broadly, the word *minne* designates the memory of a person or a memento.
17. Tylor, *Primitive Culture*, p. 96.
18. The word "months" also chimes in the exchanges between Ophelia and Hamlet just before the staging of "The Mousetrap": "Nay,'tis twice two months, my lord" (Ophelia, 3.2.121) and "O Heavens— die two months ago and not forgotten yet?" (Hamlet, 3.2.123–4).
19. Greenblatt, p. 237.
20. *Hamlet*, ed. by John Dover Wilson, pp. 228–9. The mysterious nature of the reference to Lamord has led to much speculation about his identity. Wilson suggests that Claudius's account of Lamord may be a topical reference to the playwright's patron the Earl of Southampton, whom Devereaux created Master of his Horse in the previous year, 1599. More recently, Steve Sohmer discerns a different topical reference, reading the Norman knight as "a personal allusion honouring the Careys, whose line was ennobled by the defeat of a French champion" (*Shakespeare for the Wiser Sort*, p. 136). Avi Erlich associates Lamord with King Hamlet, noting "peculiar similarities" between the two (*Hamlet's Absent Father*, p. 133). Cherrell Guilfoyle reads Lamord as an apocalyptic figure of death, like the rider Death in The Book of Revelation ("Not Two: Denial and Duality in *Hamlet*,", p. 311). Michael Ovens suggests a different sort of French connection with Lamord than the one I am proposing. He associates his nationality with a Francophilic love of the rapier in early seventeenth-century England, an expression of a desire for revenge within a culture of honor: a "madness" that has overtaken the country, which, the play suggests, must return to the native English chivalric values represented by Old Hamlet ("France and the Norman Lamord in *Hamlet*," pp. 79–86). Ovens's intriguing argument strikes me as consistent with the generally retrospective spirit of the play.
21. *Hamlet*, ed. Ann Thompson and Neil Taylor, p. 430n.

22. *Geneva Bible*, 1 Corinthians 11:24. See Catherine Gallagher and Stephen Greenblatt, Chapter 5, "The Mousetrap"; Mark S. Sweetnam, "*Hamlet* and the Reformation of the Eucharist"; and Roberta Kwan, "Of Bread and Wine, and Ghosts: Eucharistic Controversy and Hamlet's Epistemological Quest.".
23. Sweetnam, p. 16.
24. Sweetnam, p. 16.
25. Sweetnam, p. 18, p. 15.
26. Sweetnam, pp. 24–6.
27. Rubin, *Corpus Christi*, p. 347.
28. It was certainly possible to express nostalgia for chivalrous knighthood without nostalgia for medieval Catholicism, as the example of the Earl of Essex demonstrates. In "Prothalamion" Spenser described the controversial Earl, a militant Protestant, as the "flower of chivalry".
29. David Bates shows how William was portrayed in biographies and poetry both as a peacemaker and as "the destroyer of lives, the bringer of a disaster of unnecessary proportions to the English" (p. 526).
30. Bates, p. 131.
31. Bates, p. 93.
32. Boulton, "Classic Knighthood as Nobiliary Dignity," p. 52, n.45.
33. *Hamlet*, ed. Harold Jenkins. p. 369. See also his "Longer Note," pp. 543–4.
34. Four years before the premiere of the play, those tensions eased when England entered the Triple Alliance with France and the United Netherlands, against Spain. The alliance effectively ended two years later, when France signed a peace treaty with Spain.
35. Compare the frequency of "Norway" (twelve) and "Poland" (three).
36. Bloom, *Shakespeare and the Invention of the Human*, p. 187.
37. The numerous references to Rome and Caesar in the play might have reminded audiences of another period when England owed tribute to a conqueror.
38. King Harald III of Norway, also known as Harald Hardrada, failed in his attempt to reclaim the Danish throne lost by his half-brother, Olaf Haraldsson, to Cnut the Great, as well as in his attempt to claim the throne of England in 1066. His defeat by Harold Godwinson, the last crowned Anglo-Saxon King of

England, is often thought to mark the end of the Viking Age. In *Hamlet*, Norway is persuaded by diplomatic means not to seek to reclaim its lands lost to Denmark, but ends up claiming the throne of Denmark at the end of the play by happenstance. Since the play refers to tribute owed by England to Denmark, presumably England will now pay tribute to Norway.
39. Bates, p. 7; Douglas, *The Norman Conquest and British Historians*, p. x. Bates himself takes not of "parallels between the lives of Edward the Confessor and Hamlet" (p. 7). He speculates, rather improbably, "that Shakespeare might have chosen Hamlet and Lear because their stories were rather less complicated to stage than Edward's and William's. With both Edward and William, so much was taking place within their minds and the minds of others that the roots of the drama are ultimately unknowable" (p. 7).
40. Wittgenstein, *Tractatus Logico-Philosophicus*, p. 46.
41. Yorick, of course, does not fall under the category of a "great man" in any conventional sense. The gravedigger calls him a "whoreson mad fellow," and his defining memory is of Yorick dousing his head with "a flagon of Rhenish" (5.1.166, 170).
42. After debating the question whether Ophelia drowned herself in self-defense, the gravedigger muses over one of the countless inequities in the world: gentle folk, who enjoy countless liberties denied the poor, also have more leave "to drown or hang themselves [...] than their even-Christen," 5.1.27–9). Like the first question, which derides the act of making finer and finer distinctions as practiced by lawyers ("an act hath three branches—it is to act, to do, to perform," 5.1.11–12), the second makes a mockery of difference, in this case, difference in social rank, an issue that leads him back to the beginning of time: "There is no ancient gentlemen but gardeners, ditchers and grave-makers. They hold up Adam's profession."
43. See Baum (trans.), *Anglo-Saxon Riddles of the Exeter Book*.
44. Burrows, "Enigma Variations: Hervarar saga's Wave-Riddles and Supernatural Women in Old Norse Poetic Tradition," p. 194.
45. On the latter, see the marvelous study by Eleanor Cook, *Enigmas and Riddles in Literature*.
46. Benjamin, "Riddle and Mystery," p. 267.
47. John Dover Wilson (ed.) notes that the line is a riddle of sorts (*Hamlet*, p. xl).

48. Harry Levin writes, "The somber legend of Hamlet has been traced back to an enigma in the Old Norse Eddas; and in the play, as Dover Wilson notes, the very first line of Hamlet's part is a riddle" (*The Question of* Hamlet, p. 38).
49. Even the celebrated eighteenth-century actor-manager David Garrick, who led the effort to restore Shakespeare's original texts, swore that he "would not leave the stage till [he] had rescued that noble play from the rubbish of the fifth act." Cited in Stone, Jr., "Garrick's Long Lost Alteration of *Hamlet*," p. 893.
50. Hasan-Rokem, "'Spinning Threads of Sand': Riddles as Images of Loss in the Midrash on Lamentations," p. 109.
51. Huizinga, *Homo Ludens*, p. 110.
52. Huizinga, p. 109.
53. Thompson and Taylor (eds.), p. 442n.
54. In an essay that traces the character of Hamlet to an even earlier Gaelic source, Lisa A. Collinson writes, "*[I]t is agreed that Shakespeare (probably indirectly) borrowed much material, including the core of his central character, from the early thirteenth-century Danish pseudo-history, Gesta Danorum, attributed to Saxo Grammaticus. Second, the Gesta Danorum character, Amlethus—on whom Hamlet is partially based—is held to be related to a figure called Amloði*" ("A new etymology for Hamlet? The names Admlithi, Amloði, and Amlethus," p. 675). The Old Norse name *Amloði appears a single time in the Snorra Edda; Saxo's Amlethus may be a Latinized version of that Old Norse name.*
55. Frazer, *The Golden Bough*, p. 69.
56. Frazer, p. 69.
57. Frazer, p. 69.
58. Kaivola-Bregenhø, "Riddles and Their Use," p. 11.
59. Galit Hasan-Rokem and David Shulman, *Untying the Knot: Riddles and Other Enigmatic Modes*, p. 3.
60. Elliott, *The Power of Satire*, p. 62.
61. Hasan-Rokem and Shulman, p. 3.
62. Cook, p. 246.
63. James Kelso, "Riddle," p. 770.
64. Cressy, p. 398.
65. Loades, "Rites of Passage and the Prayer Books of 1549 and 1552," p. 209.
66. Daniell, p. 56.

References

Allen, William. *A Defense and Declaration of the Catholike Churches Doctrine touching Purgatory*. Antwerp: 1565.
Bates, David. *William the Conqueror*. New Haven: Yale University Press, 2016.
Baum, Paull F. (trans.). *Anglo-Saxon Riddles of the Exeter Book*. Durham, NC: Duke University Press, 1963.
Bloom, Harold. *Shakespeare and the Invention of the Human*. London: Fourth Estate, 1998.
Boulton, D'A. J. D. "Classic Knighthood as Nobiliary Dignity: The Knighting of Counts and Kings' Sons in England, 1066–1272." In *Medieval Knighthood V: Papers from the Sixth Strawberry Hill Conference*. Edited by Stephen Church and Ruth Harvey. Woodbridge: The Boydell Press, 1995: 41–100.
Benjamin, Walter. "Excavation and Memory." In *Selected Writings, vol. 1, 1913–26*. Edited by Marcus Bullock and Michael W. Jennings. Translated by Rodney Livingstone. Cambridge, MA: Harvard University Press, 1996.
———. "Riddle and Mystery." In *Selected Writings, vol. 1, 1913–26*. Edited by Marcus Bullock and Michael W. Jennings. Translated by Rodney Livingstone. Cambridge, MA: Harvard University Press, 1996.
———. *Selected Writings, vol. 2, part 2, 1931–34*. Edited by Michael W. Jennings, Howard Eiland, and Gary Smith. Translated by Rodney Livingstone et al. Cambridge, MA: Harvard University Press, 1999.
Burrows, Hannah. "Enigma Variations: Hervarar saga's Wave-Riddles and Supernatural Women in Old Norse Poetic Tradition." *The Journal of English and Germanic Philology* 112 (2013): 194–216.
Collinson, Lisa A. "A New Etymology for Hamlet? The names Admlithi, Amloði, and Amlethus." *The Review of English Studies* 62 (2011): 675–94.
Cook, Eleanor. *Enigmas and Riddles in Literature*. Cambridge: Cambridge University Press, 2006.
Cressy, David. *Birth, Marriage & Death: Ritual, Religion, and the Life-Cycle in Tudor and Stuart England*. Oxford: Oxford University Press, 1997.
Daniell, Christopher. *Death and Burial in Medieval England, 1066-1550*. London and New York: Routledge, 1997.
Douglas, David C. *The Norman Conquest and British Historians*. D. Murray Lecture. Glasgow: The University of Glasgow, 1971.
Duffy, Eamon. *The Stripping of the Altars: Traditional Religion in England*. New Haven, CT: Yale University Press, 1992.
Elliott, Robert. *The Power of Satire: Magic, Ritual, Art*. Princeton, NJ: Princeton University Press, 1960.
Encyclopaedia Britanica: A Dictionary of Arts, Sciences, Literature and General Information. 11th ed. Vol. 18. New York: The Encyclopaedia Britanica Co., 1911.

Erlich, Avi. *Hamlet's Absent Father.* Princeton, NJ: Princeton University Press, 1977.
Frazer, James G. *The Golden Bough: A Study in Magic and Religion*, 2nd ed. Vol. 3. London: Macmillan and Co., 1900.
Gallagher, Catherine and Stephen Greenblatt. *Practicing New Historicism.* Chicago, IL: University of Chicago Press, 2001.
Geneva Bible [*The Bible Translated According to the Hebrew and Greek*]. London: 1599.
Greenblatt, Stephen. *Hamlet in Purgatory.* Princeton, NJ: Princeton University Press, 2001
Guilfoyle, Cherrell. "Not Two: Denial and Duality in *Hamlet.*" *Comparative Drama* 23 (1989): 297–313.
Hasan-Rokem, Galit. "'Spinning Threads of Sand': Riddles as Images of Loss in the Midrash on Lamentations." In *Untying the Knot: Riddles and Other Enigmatic Modes.* Edited by Galit Hasan-Rokem and David Shulman. Oxford: Oxford University Press, 1996.
Hasan-Rokem, Galit and David Shulman (eds.). *Untying the Knot: Riddles and Other Enigmatic Modes.* Oxford: Oxford University Press, 1996.
Huizinga, Johann. *Homo Ludens: A Study of the Play-Element in Culture*, International Library of Sociology 86. London: Routledge, 1949; rpt. 1998.
Kaivola-Bregenhø, Annikki. "Riddles and Their Use." In *Untying the Knot: Riddles and Other Enigmatic Modes.* Edited by Galit Hasan-Rokem and David Shulman. Oxford: Oxford University Press, 1996.
Kelso, James. "Riddle." In *Encyclopaedia of Religion and Ethics.* Edited by James Hastings. Vol. 10. Edinburgh: T. and T. Clark, 1918. pp. 765–70.
Kwan, Roberta. "Of Bread and Wine, and Ghosts: Eucharistic Controversy and Hamlet's Epistemological Quest." *Journal of Language, Literature, and Culture* 62 (2015): 3–18.
Levin, Harry. *The Question of Hamlet.* New York: The Viking Press, 1959; rpt 1961.
Loades, David M. "Rites of Passage and the Prayer Books of 1549 and 1552." *Studies in Church History* 10 (1994): 205–15.
Marshall, Peter. *Beliefs and the Dead in Reformation England.* Oxford: Oxford University Press, 2002.
Ovens, Michael. "France and the Norman Lamord in *Hamlet.*" *Cahiers Élisabéthains* 87 (2015): 79–86.
Phillips, Harriet. *Nostalgia in Print and Performance, 1510-1613: Merry Worlds.* Cambridge: Cambridge University Press, 2019.
Rubin, Miri. *Corpus Christi: The Eucharist in Late Medieval Culture.* Cambridge: Cambridge University Press, 1991.
Shakespeare, William. *Hamlet.* Edited by John Dover Wilson. New Cambridge Shakespeare. 2nd edition. Cambridge: Cambridge University Press, 1936.

———. *Hamlet*. Edited by Harold Jenkins. Arden Third Series. London: Methuen, 1982.

———. *Hamlet*. Edited by Ann Thompson and Neil Taylor. Arden Third Series Revised Edition. London: Bloomsbury Publishing, 2016.

Sohmer, Steve. *Shakespeare for the Wiser Sort*. Manchester, UK: Manchester University Press, 2007.

Stone, Jr., George Winchester. "Garrick's Long Lost Alteration of *Hamlet*." *PMLA* 49 (1934): 890–921.

Sweetnam, Mark S. "*Hamlet* and the Reformation of the Eucharist." *Literature and Theology* 21 (2007): 11–28.

The Monthly Mirror: Reflecting Men and Manners. Vol. XVII. London: J. Wright, 1804.

Tylor, Edward Burnett. *Primitive Culture: Researches into the Development of Mythology, Philosophy, Religion, Language, Art and* Custom. Vol. 1. Mineola, NY: Dover Publications, 1873; rpt. 2016.

Walsham, Alexandra. *Church Papists: Catholicism, Conformity and Confessional Polemic in Early Modern England*. London: The Royal Historical Society, 1993.

Wittgenstein, Ludwig. *Tractatus Logico-Philosophicus*. Translated by D. F. Pears and B. F. McGuiness. London: Routledge and Kegan Paul, 1961.

Wooding, Lucy. "Remembrance in the Eucharist." In *Remembrance in Early Modern England: Memorial Cultures of the Post Reformation*. Edited by Andrew Gordon and Thomas Rist, 2013; rpt. London and New York: Routledge, 2016.

CHAPTER 10

The Theater of Hamlet's Judgments

Zackariah Long

The symbolic topography of the English Renaissance playhouse was one of the most powerful aesthetic resources available to playwrights for representing, remembering, and working through death. The theater's vertical scheme, with its canopy and galleries above the stage, colloquially referred to as the "heavens," and the crawl space beneath the stage, correspondingly known as "hell," framed the action of each play as unfolding between two afterworlds.[1] The plots of plays often exploit this feature of symbolic topography by instigating traffic between these worlds. Such traffic could be literal, with gods descending from the heavens to visit characters in dreams or devils ascending from hell to tempt characters to action. Or, it could be figurative, gestural, or rhetorical, with characters invoking these eschatologically charged spaces as they struggle with important decisions or ponder the spiritual significance of their thoughts. While both forms of traffic take advantage of the Renaissance playhouse's symbolic topography, they do so in different ways, the former trading

Z. Long (✉)
Ohio Wesleyan University, Delaware, OH, USA
e-mail: zclong@owu.edu

© The Author(s), under exclusive license to Springer Nature Switzerland AG 2022
W. E. Engel and G. Williams (eds.), *The Shakespearean Death Arts*, Palgrave Shakespeare Studies,
https://doi.org/10.1007/978-3-030-88490-1_10

203

on its metaphysical implications and the latter privileging the subjective experience of the speaker. In *Hamlet*—the early modern period's most quintessential expression of its fascination with the world beyond the grave—we get both: a ghost that rises from beneath the stage to scramble our eschatological expectations and a title character who struggles to sort out the resulting confusion in soliloquies addressed to an audience that sits and stands across every level of the playhouse's vertical scheme.

In this chapter, I would like to consider a death art that Hamlet practices in these soliloquies that takes full advantage of the Renaissance playhouse's symbolic topography: his habit of rhetorically placing characters within different otherworldly locations, depending upon his judgments of them. This practice of sorting characters into a cosmographic scheme is indebted to two different kinds of premodern theater: first, "theatres of memory," architectural schemes for the organization of knowledge modeled on the *theatrum mundi*; and, second, "theatres of God's judgments," topographically organized tours of the afterlife from visionary literature. Both of these species of theater participate in the death arts in the sense that they are driven by a desire to transcend or come to grips with mortality—in the former case, by achieving a Godlike perspective on the universe that robs death of its sting; in the latter case, by vividly imagining the next life as a spur to reform in this one. However, in adapting these theaters' organizational and justicial practices for his own purposes, Hamlet transforms them, turning the Renaissance playhouse into a screen for his own ambivalent determinations. For this reason, while the theater's symbolic topography provides him with a framework for thinking through his moral intuitions, it never fulfills its promise as a taxonomic system for imposing order on the world. The story of Hamlet's theater of judgments is therefore also the story of its eventual abandonment. In what follows, I track this process through close readings of three of Hamlet's soliloquies, those in which he addresses the topography of the theater most directly.

"Heaven and Earth"

Hamlet's inaugural attempt at arranging his family members into a moral and topographic hierarchy occurs in his first soliloquy. At the foundation of this hierarchy are distinctions among persons, his father put forth as a paragon of virtue, his mother and uncle as fallen creatures. However,

10 THE THEATER OF HAMLET'S JUDGMENTS 205

because the iconography through which Hamlet represents these distinctions is invested with cosmic significance, what begins as a pecking order quickly expands into a kind of private cosmography. We can observe this sequence in miniature in Hamlet's opening characterization of the difference between his father and uncle:

> That it should come to this,
> But two months dead, nay, not so much, not two,
> So excellent a king, that was to this
> Hyperion to a satyr.[2]

Hamlet Senior, likened to Hyperion, progenitor of wisdom and light, clearly belongs to a higher order of existence, whereas satyr-like Claudius belongs to a lower. These orders of existence, in turn, map onto different cosmographic regions, Hyperion hailing from the celestial world and the satyr from the terrestrial one. This matching of character to locus obviously takes on special significance in a playhouse whose symbolic topography reflects the structure of the universe. With a skyward glance, Hamlet may "look up" to his father both literally and figuratively, reinforcing the idea of the stage's starry canopy as a fit habitation for a godlike figure. At the same time, this topographic association serves as a reminder of the fact that Hamlet Senior has passed from "this world" (l. 134), a world that in his absence has grown to reflect its goatish new king: "'tis an unweeded garden / That grows to seed" (ll. 135–36). In this way, the playhouse's vertical scale also takes on a temporal dimension. The idealized past of Hamlet's memory is "up there," in the heavens, while the debased present of Claudius's reign is "down here," on the stage. The result is a symbolic edifice that finds its objective correlative in the theater of the world that encircles the prince, so that when Hamlet calls out, "Heaven and earth! / Must I remember?" (ll.142–43), it is impossible to tell whether he is referring to the theater inside his mind, to the one outside it, or to the *theatrum mundi* that encloses them both.

Those familiar with the arts of memory may recognize in Hamlet's theater of judgments glimmers of one of the most quintessential Renaissance expressions of the architectural mnemotechnic, the theater of memory.[3] Like other memory arts, the Renaissance memory theater was a system of places and images designed to assist in the preservation, organization, and recollection of knowledge. By translating the content one wished to remember into symbolic figures and then depositing those figures within imagined spaces, practitioners of the memory arts created storehouses of knowledge that could be called upon at need. What distinguished the Renaissance memory theater from other mnemonic systems was its purpose and form. Channeling the humanist aspiration for universal knowledge into a tangible structure, the memory theater empowered its operator to view the entirety of human wisdom in a single glance, as the cosmos in the mind of God.[4] The theater was considered an apt vessel for such an enterprise because its circular form already mirrored the shape of the *orbis terrarum*. Moreover, its microcosmic character suggested an abundance of conceptual schemes for organizing and marking its contents, especially from cosmology and mythology. Thus, for example, Italian polymath Giulio Camillo superimposed atop his semicircular Vitruvian theater several overlapping conceptual schemes: a "vertical" scheme for his auditorium's ascending rows of seats based on the phases of creation; a "horizontal" scheme based on the planets that divided each row into qualitatively distinct loci; and a repertory of images based on the planetary gods and their attributes that marked the contents of these loci.[5] By inspecting the auditorium, mnemonists could not only consult the theater in the manner of an encyclopedia, but also avail themselves of its contents to create rhetorical or literary compositions. However, the ultimate purpose of Camillo's theater was to tap into the hidden structures of reality itself, so that its operator could wield control over its contents in the manner of an alchemist-magus or even a god.[6]

Of course, in turning to the "theatre of the world" that surrounds him, Hamlet is not attempting to build a system of universal knowledge or perform alchemical magic. Instead, he is grappling with a series of personal and political crises, namely the death of his father and king and his mother and queen's remarriage. Yet, Hamlet's response to these crises takes a similar shape to Camillo's—the attempt to order the objects of his memory by arranging them into a stable form. This is because, on a fundamental level, Hamlet and Camillo are responding to a similar challenge—the challenge of trying to impose a sense of coherence on a world made out of confusing and potentially contradictory elements. In Camillo's case, this challenge is to knit together his Christian, Classical, and Kabbalistic sources into an integrated scheme lest the unity of Truth be fragmented. In Hamlet's case, it is trying to restore a sense of moral order, if only imaginatively, to a world that seems indifferent to the quality of persons. In undertaking this effort, the prince draws on compositional strategies that also inform Camillo's theater. Like a memory artist, Hamlet borrows a conceptual scheme from cosmography, adopting the heavens and earth as loci for his memories. He also transforms what he wishes to remember into iconographic images and places them where they belong within this cosmographic scheme, as we see with Hamlet Senior and Claudius. And finally, this cosmographic scheme maps neatly onto the symbolic topography of the Renaissance playhouse itself. By superimposing atop this playhouse a symbolic topography that both reflects and represents the world, the prince constructs an imaginative edifice that can stand as a counterpoint to the "unweeded garden" that surrounds him.

There is obviously an important difference between the structure of this imaginative edifice and that of the playhouse that surrounds it. Namely, Hamlet only activates the top two levels of the Renaissance theater's symbolic topography, heaven and earth, while leaving the crawl space beneath the stage—conventionally known as hell—unremarked upon. Given the play's clever use of the understage cellarage elsewhere in *Hamlet*, this omission is clearly intentional; it is meant to reflect something about the character of Hamlet's judgments. To understand what, though, one must go beyond Hamlet Senior and Claudius to consider the third figure in Hamlet's memory gallery, a figure who has the distinction of being the only one to appear on both upper and lower levels. I speak, of course, of Gertrude, who functions in each case as a kind of lateral complement and counterpoint to her husband and king. In the heavens, she joins Hamlet Senior in an idealized domestic scene—his father "so loving to my mother / That he might not beeteem the winds of heaven / Visit her face too roughly" (ll. 140–42), while his mother "would hang on him, / As if increase of appetite had grown / By what it fed on" (ll. 143–45). Then, on earth she joins Claudius for what Hamlet depicts as a hurried coupling of sub-human ("satyr") and sub-animal ("a beast that wants discourse of reason / Would have mourned longer" (ll. 150–51)). In considering this juxtaposition, it is striking that the contrast between Hamlet Senior and Claudius is framed in terms of body versus spirit, whereas the difference between Gertrude-Past and Gertrude-Present is characterized primarily by appetite—not its presence or its absence, but rather its object. So long as Gertrude is with Hamlet Senior, the prince can imagine this appetite in salutary terms—indeed, perhaps it was Gertrude's superhuman passion, apparently exempt from the ordinary laws of consumption and satiation, that made her a fit companion for a superhuman husband. It is only when she turns that desire on Claudius that it becomes a sign of perversity. What it doesn't become a sign of, though, is something demonic, just as Claudius's association with satyrs doesn't imply devilishness, but goatishness. The distinction the soliloquy develops between the heavenly and earthly realms is thus between regulated and unregulated appetite, or between a prelapsarian and postlapsarian world. Hell is not an appropriate locus because the prince does not yet see his uncle and mother as malevolent, but only as imperfect. And in this sense, the conceptual and topographic dimensions of Hamlet's symbolic edifice fit each other perfectly.

Where Hamlet's theater of judgments finds itself on shakier ground is on the other side of the mnemonic equation—the repertory of images that Hamlet entrusts to his theatrical environment. As we have noted, the art of memory directs its practitioners to translate those things they wish to remember into symbolic images. Since all memory theorists agree that images are easier to remember than bare concepts, these images serve a practical purpose. But, just as importantly, they serve a hermeneutic purpose, for to translate something into a symbolic image requires that one distill it into its essence, so that, to mix metaphors, it "wears its meaning on its sleeve." This, no doubt, partially explains why Hamlet is attracted to the memory arts, because in a world of misleading appearances—where what "seems" may be different from what "'tis" (1.2.76–77)—such images are supposed to denote things truly, so they can be confidently assigned a place. (Titans, gods, and apotheosized heroes belong in the heavens; therianthropes and animals belong on earth.) But these taxonomic assignments only make sense if the acts of symbolic translation on which they depend are grounded in reality; otherwise, they don't attach to the world outside the artificer's head but are only projections of his mind. And it is the mythographic translation of Claudius, Hamlet Senior, and Gertrude to which critics have often objected.[7] After all, whatever his uncle's crimes, his rhetorically measured and politically shrewd opening speech makes it clear that he is not a mere satyr. And despite the prince's association of his father with Hyperion, the fact that the play's opening scene finds his spirit tarrying "below" on earth suggests that he is not as separate from the dross of fallen humanity as his son would like to think. Most telling of all, though, is Gertrude, who suffers Hamlet's unrealistic projections from both idealizing and debasing directions. When Hamlet Senior was still alive, her desire for her husband was assumed to be infinite ("As if increase of appetite had grown / By what it fed on" (1.2.144–145)); then, when he died, it was assumed she would grieve in perpetuity, like Niobe the mythical queen whose grief was so intense it transformed her to stone (l.149). But it is no more possible for passion to stay indefinitely affixed to an absent object with the same degree of intensity than it is for passion to stay affixed to a present object with an ever-increasing degree of intensity. To be human means to be subject to the vicissitudes of time and change. If Gertrude falls short of Niobe's example, it is because she is flesh and blood.

Nevertheless, of all the figures in this first iteration of Hamlet's theater of judgments, Gertrude most strongly suggests the possibility of a more capacious symbolic framework. First, because she occupies multiple levels of Hamlet's cosmographic scheme, she signifies the possibility for dynamism—a kind of positive indeterminacy. And, second, because she serves as a counterpoint to her husband on each level, she suggests a range of possibilities for what it means to be "heavenly" or "earthly." These patterns of arrangement are not unique to Hamlet's symbolic schema. As we have seen, Camillo's theater also possesses a lateral dimension, with contents that belong to the same phase of creation differentiated by distinct figures. Moreover, Camillo places the same figures on different levels of his theater in order to demonstrate how they change over time. In positioning Gertrude on both levels of his memory gallery and then tracking her "fall" from the heavens of her former marriage to the earth of her current one, Hamlet comes close to acknowledging such capacity for change, albeit under the sign of frailty. Yet, only a few lines after recalling how Gertrude "followed my poor father's body / Like Niobe, all tears" (1.2.149), Hamlet changes his mind about even this, clarifying that these were "most unrighteous tears" (l. 154), implying duplicity and corruption where before there was only weakness. The suggestion seems to be that if Gertrude truly loved his father, then she could not have remarried so quickly; the fact that she remarried so quickly, then, proves that she was false. That this reinterpretation threatens to undo the entire distinction between the idealized world of Elsinore-Past and the debased world of Elsinore-Present on which Hamlet's symbolic system depends is not something the prince seems to grasp. Yet, he certainly feels it. Gertrude is therefore left to flicker between these two models of imperfection—frailty and corruption, mutability and duplicity—quietly disordering her son's taxonomic structure. But before Hamlet is even able to acknowledge such indeterminacy, he must first confront a challenge to his theater's symbolic topography from a different direction.

"And Shall I Couple Hell?"

That something has changed in Hamlet's theater of judgments is apparent from the opening of his second soliloquy.[8] Still reeling from the Ghost's revelations and turning over in his mind the implications of his parting words ("Remember me"), Hamlet attempts to collect his thoughts (1.5.91). In doing so, his first impulse, tellingly, is to locate himself in space. Moving downstage and addressing himself to the audience, Hamlet recapitulates the symbolic topography of his first soliloquy, but this time with a notable addition: "O all you host of heaven! O earth! What else? / And shall I couple hell?" (1.5.92–93). In the first soliloquy, the prince invokes "Heaven and earth" and then likens his family members to mythographic figures from these worlds. It is this matching of figure to locus that activates the mnemonic dimension of his theater of judgments. A natural question, then, is whether or not the activation of hell as a new locus signals a corresponding change in the organization of Hamlet's memory. The lines that follow make it clear that Hamlet continues to view his father as an exalted figure, declaring that he will separate the Ghost's words from "baser matter" and vowing "by heaven" to remember his commandment (l. 104): his father is still "above." Gertrude, meanwhile, is largely passed over: while Hamlet rails against her as a "most pernicious woman" (l. 105), this is no worse than his castigations in soliloquy one; presumably, then, she remains on earth. The language surrounding Claudius, however, does undergo an important shift. Having learned from the Ghost that his uncle has committed a mortal sin, Hamlet apostrophizes Claudius in infernal terms: "O villain, villain, smiling, damned villain!" (l. 106). In the theater of Hamlet's judgments, loci are recruited to accommodate persons; one therefore would expect a change in the evaluation of a character to correspond with a change of locus. If Hamlet's judgment of his uncle has changed from satyr to "damned villain," then the most appropriate locus for Claudius would be the one just introduced: hell.

The activation of the bottommost level of the Renaissance playhouse introduces an eschatological dimension into Hamlet's theater of judgments not present in soliloquy one. Although that soliloquy hinges on a contrast between heaven and earth, the heaven of Hamlet's imagination is, there, mostly a classical pantheon; to the extent that it evokes the Four Last Things, it is only by implicit contrast to postlapsarian earth. Hell is different. It reframes the cosmographic contrast between "above" and "below" in explicitly Christian terms and introduces a penitentiary element into Hamlet's theater of judgments, especially as the Ghost has commanded Hamlet to wreak vengeance upon Claudius. More importantly, though, hell brings with it a new species of indeterminacy.

As with Gertrude in the first soliloquy, this indeterminacy centers on a particular figure. However, unlike with Gertrude, it is not grounded in that figure's iconography; instead, it stems from its placement. I speak, obviously, of the Ghost. We have noted that Hamlet continues to speak of his father's spirit in elevated terms in soliloquy two, treating his injunction as sacrosanct. However, within the fictional and theatrical universe of the play, the Ghost's topographic associations are quite different. First, the Ghost tells Hamlet that by day he is "confined" in a "prison house" of "sulph'rous and tormenting flames" "Till the foul crimes done in my days of nature / Are burnt and purged away" (1.5.11–14), a thinly veiled description of purgatory that underlines its similarities to hell. Second, the Ghost enters the play through the stage trapdoor and then later calls out to Hamlet and his companions from the understage area conventionally known as "hell." The contrast between the prince's topographic assignment of his father and the play's is therefore striking. We do not find this disjuncture of conceptual and topographic space in soliloquy one—or, if we do, it is the audience who finds it and not Hamlet: so far as Hamlet knows at the beginning of the play, his father *is* "above" in the heavens, and Gertrude and Claudius are obviously "below" on earth. Hamlet's theater of judgments does not seek to change this symbolic topography but only to impose meaning upon it. In the second soliloquy, in contrast, the prince's inner and outer topographies begin to pry apart. Claudius walks the earth but "belongs" in hell, whereas the Ghost "belongs" in heaven but seems to reside in hell. Claudius's reassignment makes sense insofar as it reflects new information about his character. But what do we make of the gap between Hamlet's placement of his father and the play's?

To untangle this question, it is helpful to look at the second species of premodern theater that informs Hamlet's theater of judgments, which for symmetry's sake I shall call "theatres of God's judgments": topographically organized tours of the otherworld from medieval and early modern visionary literature.[9] Unlike memory theaters, these are not symbolic topographies that take inspiration from actual performance spaces. Instead, they are "theatres" in the more ancient sense of "places for seeing:" symbolic environments where the visionary traveler can meditate upon otherworldly representations of punishment and reward in order to better understand the ways of God to man.[10] Moreover, with the exception of the work in which this tradition finds its triumphant expression, Dante's *Commedia*, these otherworlds are not meticulously organized spaces like memory theaters.[11] Instead, they tend to follow the logic of dreamscape rather than landscape, insisting on the tantamount importance of *placement* while leaving the precise coordinates of *places* unmapped.[12] Yet, it is this attitude toward space that provides a link to *Hamlet*. After all, while the Ghost refuses to provide the kind of otherworldly tour so popular in visionary literature, he nevertheless takes care to repeatedly drop hints about his provenance. His place, the play strongly suggests, expresses his meaning. Yet, Hamlet is either unable or unwilling to take these hints, whereas he reclassifies Claudius instantaneously. Understanding the evolving place of purgatory within the medieval and early modern Eschaton may illuminate this puzzle.

Although purgatory is by definition "the middle place," one of the ironies of medieval visionary literature is that it rarely appears in perfect equidistance between heaven and hell. Instead, from an early time, even before the consolidation of purgatory into a single unified zone, sites of otherworldly purification tended to lean to one side or the other, toward the infernal or supernal pole. In the early vision of Tundale, for example, there are two locations designated for those who fall between the extremes of good and evil: a field of wind and rain for those who are "evil but not very evil" and a field of rest for the "good but not very good."[13] Yet, despite the evil of the former and the good of the latter, both sites clearly fall on the "heavenly" side of the boundary between heaven and hell. In contrast, in the later vision of Evensham, there are also two places of purifying torment—a marsh of variegated punishments and a mountain that ferries souls between extremes of hot and cold— but these sites of purgation are characterized by infernal imagery and are directly adjacent to the pit of hell.[14] In the visionary literature of the Middle Ages, the Evensham model proved the more durable, with Purgatory's center of gravity steadily migrating closer to hell, to the point where it can be difficult to tell them apart.[15] You have to know *where* you are to know *what* you're looking at. This spatial conflation permeated visual representations of the Eschaton in the late Middle Ages, which often depicted purgatory and hell with nearly identical iconography; it also left its mark on medieval theater, which typically assigned both locations to the understage area.[16] Which isn't to say that medieval art had no way of distinguishing these areas: although visual representations of purgatorial and hellish torment were often identical, artists did make use of structural distinctions, like ministering angels or tormenting devils, to set them apart, and plays of the Last Judgment employed speech, costume, cosmetics, and stage mechanics—such as dual trap doors—to establish "horizontal" distinctions between them. In this way, medieval art managed to sustain a structural distinction between hell and purgatory even while underscoring their topographic resemblance.[17]

In some ways, this topographic history of purgatory makes Hamlet's treatment of the Ghost more legible while in other ways deepening its mystery. The fact that purgatory was at least sometimes imagined as adjacent to heaven gives Hamlet license to imagine his father's spirit in heavenly terms and to continue to talk and think about him as though he is "above." At the same time, the gradual infernalization of purgatory and its spatial conflation with hell makes his persistence in doing so all the more remarkable, since it requires pushing against the accumulated weight of cultural tradition, including the inherited symbolic topography of the Renaissance stage. The inevitable question, then, is why Hamlet continues to insist on his father's exaltation against the internal evidence of the play and the external evidence of theatrical convention. While there is obviously not one answer, the prince's attitude toward the occupants of his theater of judgments provides a clue.

Although Hamlet admits to Horatio that his father is, in the end, merely a man, his first soliloquy makes it clear that he feels his father is cut from different cloth than Claudius. And following millenia of deeply ingrained orientational metaphors that associate virtue with loftiness and vice with lowness, Hamlet cannot help but understand this difference in spatial terms.[18] If Hamlet Senior is "up," then Claudius must be "down"; and if Claudius is "down," then Hamlet Senior must be "up." Accepting his father's relegation to the cellarage would require that his father share imaginative space with Claudius—a topographic equivalency he cannot tolerate. And with purgatory having been banished from the Eschaton by the Reformation and matters of religion having been banished from the public stage by the state, Renaissance theater offers considerably fewer representational resources for managing this spatial conflation than its medieval predecessor. In a nutshell, the dual trapdoors have been replaced by a single. In the absence of such a saving "horizontal" distinction, Hamlet doubles down on the vertical distinction between his father and uncle, even if it means turning the conventional symbolic topography of the Renaissance playhouse on its head.

Where does this leave Hamlet at the end of his second soliloquy? In many ways, in the same kind of position that he ended his first. That is to say, Hamlet doesn't appear to grasp the significance of the incoherence he has introduced into his theater of judgments. And the reason he doesn't is that he is unable to connect Claudius and Hamlet Senior in his mind. He is too busy thinking about them independently—his uncle's guilt on the one hand, and his father's commandment on the other. Yet, like the contradictory figurations of Gertrude that haunt his first soliloquy, the contradictory localizations of his father and uncle that haunt his second soliloquy threaten to surface whenever the prince veers too close to the question of where they belong; and, as with Gertrude, these moments of incipient crisis are marked by sudden emotional outbursts. Thus, at the opening of the soliloquy, the introduction of hell as a locus triggers a sudden and violent reaction that almost topples the prince: "O, fie! Hold, hold, my heart, / And you, my sinews, grow not instant old, / But bear me stiffly up" (ll. 93–95). Rather than following his disgust, though, the prince suddenly pivots to the Ghost and his sacred vow. Then a little further down the same pattern repeats itself, but this time in reverse: having just sworn "by heaven" to uphold the Ghost's commandment, Hamlet suddenly erupts in anger at Claudius, proclaiming him a "damned villain" and reaching for his writing tables to scribble some shallow invective on his hypocrisy (ll. 107–110). It is almost as though the spaces themselves are trying to speak to the prince through their juxtaposition, yet in both cases the prince merely toggles between them, reinforcing his father's and uncle's compartmentalization. What finally leads Hamlet to connect these dots is the subject of Hamlet's final microcosmic soliloquy.

"Seasoned for His Passage"

There is a long interval between Hamlet's second and sixth soliloquies, so by the time the prince articulates the final version of his theater of judgments, his thinking about the Ghost and Claudius has undergone several revolutions. It has occurred to the prince that the Ghost may be a devil, assuming a "pleasing shape" in order to lure him to damnation (2.2.539); he has devised the Mousetrap as a way of testing the veracity of the Ghost's claims (ll. 528–44); and the Mousetrap has convinced him of those claims and of Claudius's guilt (3.2.281–82). Given this chain of events, one might think that Hamlet would feel vindicated in his imaginative consignment of his uncle to hell and his father to heaven. However, the next time he grapples with these issues in soliloquy, it is the opposite possibility he is forced to confront. The reversal is triggered when Hamlet stumbles upon Claudius alone in prayer, a sight sufficiently unexpected to arrest Hamlet's initial impulse toward violence:

> Now might I do it pat, now a is a-praying,
> And now I'll do't. And so he goes to heaven,
> And so am I revenged. That would be scanned.
> A villain kills my father, and for that,
> I, his sole son, do this same villain send
> To heaven.
> O, this is hire and salary, not revenge.
> A took my father grossly, full of bread;
> With all his crimes broad blown, as flush as May;
> And how his audit stands who knows save heaven?
> But in our circumstance and course of thought,
> 'Tis heavy with him; and am I then revenged,
> To take him in the purging of his soul,
> When he is fit and season'd for his passage?
> No.
> Up, sword, and know thou a more horrid hent.
> When he is drunk asleep, or in his rage,
> Or in th' incestuous pleasure of his bed,
> At game-a-swearing, or about some act
> That has no relish of salvation in't—
> Then trip him, that his heels may kick at heaven,
> And that his soul may be as damned and black.
> As hell, whereto it goes. (3.3.73–95)

As in the earlier microcosmic soliloquies, this final incarnation of Hamlet's theater of judgments is framed by the question of who belongs where, and the answer to this question is framed in terms of the match between the soul and its destination—or, put it in the language of the memory arts, between figure and place. Despite these similarities, the dynamic of Hamlet's sixth soliloquy is profoundly different, and this is due to the fact that Hamlet is forced to directly confront evidence that challenges his topographic assignments. In his first soliloquy the prince proceeded as though his father's soul was already in heaven, and in his second soliloquy as though his uncle's soul was as good as in hell. However, the sight of Claudius praying shakes these assumptions, as the prince is forced to contemplate for the first time that his uncle's moral trajectory could be different—that he could ascend to heaven—which in turn leads him to admit, for the first time, of the opposite possibility for his father. In doing so, Hamlet does not explicitly point to the bottommost level of the theater, where purgatory shares a locus with hell. However, his reference to the gravity of his father's predicament is clear enough in its import: "[I]n our circumstance and course of thought, /'Tis heavy with him." In this way, the hazy outlines of a different theater of judgments begins to take shape, with Claudius above and Hamlet Senior below.

That these potential relocations of Claudius and Hamlet Senior should come bundled together is not an accident, since the possibility for ascent is also the condition for descent. It also makes sense that recognition of the one should trigger the other, since it is the prospect of inadvertently dispatching Claudius to heaven during prayer that calls to Hamlet's mind the very different circumstances of his father's death—how he was taken "grossly, full of bread; / With all his crimes broad blown, as flush as May" (ll. 80–81). Still, coming as it does after two soliloquies of Hamlet assiduously imagining his father in elevated terms and his uncle in debased ones, this broadening of eschatological possibilities is striking. First, it allows for dynamism in Hamlet's theater of judgments—not the foreclosed dynamism of Gertrude's topographic assignments from soliloquy one, but the authentic dynamism of Camillo's memory theater. Second, it clears a path for Hamlet to think about his father and uncle from within the same imaginative space—something he resolutely avoided in soliloquy two, but which he now undertakes willingly. Third, it loosens the binaries that have characterized all of Hamlet's assignments of figures to places from the beginning of the play—after all, if neither Claudius nor Hamlet Senior can assuredly be assigned "above" or "below," then that means the center of gravity must shift to the center—that is, to say, to earth, the locus of potential, or as Hamlet puts it, of "passage." And, fourth, it reconfigures the relationship between Hamlet's inner and outer worlds, for whereas Hamlet's first impulse in previous soliloquies has been to fashion an imaginative universe in correcting an unsatisfying reality, he now seems willing to accommodate his theater of judgments to reality whether he finds it satisfying or not.

10 THE THEATER OF HAMLET'S JUDGMENTS 217

Of course, what the prince decides to do with this newfound open-mindedness is to accommodate his vengeance. For no sooner has Hamlet acknowledged the possibility of a different trajectory for Claudius then he sets out to correct it—not by adjusting his internal topography to account for a repentant Claudius, but by engineering reality to match his internal topography. Specifically, he decides to wait to kill Claudius until such time that his passage to hell is guaranteed. In this new twist on dynamism, Hamlet posits that although Claudius may be penitent in the present, it is inevitable that he will eventually backslide into vice. Matching his soul to its proper locus, then, is just a matter of waiting until the right moment: "Then trip him, that his heels may kick at heaven, / And that his soul may be as damn'd and black / As hell, whereto it goes" (ll. 93–95). There is obviously great irony in this decision, since as soon as Hamlet departs Claudius confesses that his prayer has been unsuccessful. But Hamlet doesn't know this, leaving the audience to contemplate Hamlet's eagerness to extend his vengeance into the permanent hereafter. If there is a moment when the dark side of the analogy between the memory artist and God comes to the fore, this is it, for in seeking to remake the *theatrum mundi* in the image of his theater of judgments Hamlet is playing God. At the very moment that Hamlet's theater of judgments seems to open itself to new possibilities, it snaps shut again.

Although Hamlet does not articulate another version of his theater of judgments in soliloquy, this "two steps forward, one step back" dynamic continues to be characteristic of the prince's thinking about his family circle as he stumbles toward the play's catastrophe. That is to say, Hamlet continues to toggle back and forth between differently inflected topographic and iconographic models, sometimes regressing to earlier formulations while at other times grasping toward new ones. In the closet scene, for example, Hamlet finally confronts his mother about her remarriage, and in the course of trying to drive home to her the difference between her husbands, he launches into an ekphrastic passage inspired by two portrait miniatures:

> Look here upon this picture, and on this,
> The counterfeit presentment of two brothers.
> See, what a grace was seated on this brow:
> Hyperion's curls, the front of Jove himself,
> An eye like Mars, to threaten and command,
> A station like the herald Mercury
> New lighted on a heaven-kissing hill—

> A combination and a form indeed
> Where every god did seem to set his seal
> To give the world assurance of a man.
> This was your husband. Look you now what follows.
> Here is your husband, like a mildew'd ear,
> Blasting his wholesome brother. Have you eyes?
> Could you on this fair mountain leave to feed,
> And batten on this moor? (3.4.53–67)

Notably, the uppermost organizational schema of this speech is not the vertical scale of the prince's typical theater of judgments, but instead a horizontal comparison of the two kings side by side, not unlike the horizontal juxtapositions of Camillo's auditorium or the medieval stage's juxtaposition of damned and purgatorial souls. Nevertheless, within this horizontal frame, there is still a strong vertical hierarchy that reinscribes the heaven-to-earth polarities of soliloquy one. Hamlet Senior is, once again, associated with a classical celestial pantheon ("Hyperion's curls," "the front of Jove," "an eye like Mars," "a station like the herald Mercury / New lighted on a heaven-kissing hill") while Claudius is likened to marshy land ("this moor") and blasted crops ("mildewed ear") appropriate to earth as a locus—but not to hell. It is almost as though the eschatologically inflected vertical scheme of soliloquies two and six has suddenly vanished. Yet one hundred lines later, when Hamlet confronts Gertrude about the possibility of her own moral improvement, it suddenly reasserts itself:

> Good night—but go not to my uncle's bed.
> Assume a virtue, if you have it not.
> That monster, custom, who all sense doth eat
> Of habits devil, is angel yet in this,
> That to the use of actions fair and good
> He likewise gives a frock or livery
> That aptly is put on. Refrain tonight,
> And that shall lend a kind of easiness
> To the next abstinence; the next more easy;
> For use almost can change the stamp of nature,
> And either lodge the devil, or throw him out
> With wondrous potency. (3.4.159–70)

Now Gertrude finds herself, like Claudius in soliloquy six, suspended between heaven and hell, with the possibility of ascent or descent before her, so long as she can transform the "devil" of custom into the "angel" of habit. There are ways, perhaps, of making sense of such vacillations. It could be that confronting Gertrude about the differences between her two husbands throws Hamlet back into the world of soliloquy one, whereas confronting her about the difference between what she is and what she could be triggers the frame of soliloquy six. But ultimately there is something irreducibly mysterious about Hamlet's toggling back and forth between these models.

The safest generalization one can make about the final stretch of Hamlet's journey is that whatever drove the prince to want to arrange the members of his family into a topographic hierarchy has apparently dissipated. Instead, when Hamlet invokes the idea of the *theatrum mundi*, he increasingly associates it not with stage-managing others' destinies but allowing himself to be stage-managed by the heavens:

> [L]et us know
> Our indiscretion sometimes serves us well
> When our deep plots do pall, and that should learn us
> There's a divinity that shapes our ends,
> Rough-hew them how we will— (5.2.7–11)

If, as we have observed, one of the broad trends across the prince's various articulations of his theater of judgments is his growing acceptance of dynamism and indeterminacy—the sense that other characters' fates may not be sealed but in progress—then it would make sense if at some point Hamlet simply gave up the project altogether, deferring to the heavenly playwright above. Seen in this light, Hamlet's theater of judgments is a kind of self-consuming artifact, an edifice raised so that it can eventually be abandoned. As a death art, this is less paradoxical than it seems. If the art of living is to learn to die, then perhaps the art of judgment is learning to suspend judgment. The rest is silence.

Notes

1. Stern, "'This Wide and Universal Theatre': The Theatre as Prop in Shakespeare's Metadrama."
2. All in-text citations on the play are taken from William Shakespeare, *Hamlet* ed. A. R. Braunmuller (New York: Penguin, 2016), 1.2.137–140.
3. For overviews of Camillo's and Fludd's theatres, see Yates, *The Art of Memory*, pp. 129–172, pp. 320–367.
4. Peters, "Theatre and Book in the History of Memory: Materializing Mnemosyne in the Age of Print," p. 186.
5. Giulio Camillo, *L'Idea del theatro* (1550), translated in Wenneker, "An Examination of *L'Idea del theatro* of Giulio Camillo."
6. Bolzoni, "The Memory Theatre of Giulio Camillo: Alchemy, Rhetoric, and Deification in the Renaissance."
7. For an overview of classic treatments, see Russell, *Hamlet and Narcissus*, p. 228, n.4. For a more recent treatment, see Cousins, "*Hamlet* and *Of Truth*: Humanism and the Disingenuous Soliloquy," p. 95.
8. The opening of this section condenses but then quickly expands upon my essay "Shakespeare, Memory, and the Early Modern Theatre."
9. For a convenient overview of medieval visionary literature, see Gardiner (ed.), *Visions of Heaven and Hell Before Dante*.
10. West, *Theatres and Encyclopedias in Early Modern Europe*, pp. 1–2.
11. Marshall, "The Map of God's Word: Geographies of the Afterlife in Tudor and Early Stuart England."
12. Greenblatt, *Hamlet in Purgatory*, pp. 90–93.
13. "Tundale's Vision," in Gardiner (ed.), pp. 180–182.
14. "The Monk of Evensham's Vision," in Gardiner (ed.), pp. 203–208.
15. Jacques LeGoff, *The Birth of Purgatory*.
16. Greenblatt, pp. 52–55; Schreyer, *Shakespeare's Medieval Craft: Remnants of the Mysteries on the London Stage*, p. 118, pp. 120–126.
17. Schreyer, p. 118.
18. Lakoff and Johnson, *Metaphors We Live By*, pp. 14–21.

REFERENCES

Bolzoni, Lina. *The Gallery of Memory: Literary and Iconographic Models in the Age of the Printing Press*. Translated by Jeremy Parzen. Toronto: University of Toronto Press, 2001.

———. "The Memory Theatre of Giulio Camillo: Alchemy, Rhetoric, and Deification in the Renaissance." In *Lux in Tenebris: The Visual and the Symbolic in Western Esotericism*. Edited by Peter Forshaw. Boston: Brill, 2017. pp. 66–80.

Cousins, A. D. "*Hamlet* and *Of Truth*: Humanism and the Disingenuous Soliloquy." In *Shakespeare and the Soliloquy in Early Modern English Drama*. Edited by A. D. Cousins and Daniel Derrin. Cambridge: Cambridge University Press, 2018. pp. 93–104.

Gardiner, Eileen (ed.). *Visions of Heaven and Hell Before Dante*. New York: Italica Press, 1989.

Greenblatt, Stephen. *Hamlet in Purgatory*. Princeton, NJ: Princeton University Press, 2001.

Lakoff, George, and Mark Johnson. *Metaphors We Live By*. Chicago, IL: University of Chicago Press, 1981.

LeGoff, Jacques. *The Birth of Purgatory*. Translated by Arthur Goldhammer. Chicago, IL: University of Chicago Press, 1984.

Long, Zackariah. "Shakespeare, Memory, and the Early Modern Theatre." In *The Routledge Handbook of Shakespeare and Memory*. Edited by Andrew Hiscock and Lina Perkins Wilder. New York: Routledge, 2018. pp. 11–22.

Marshall, Peter. "The Map of God's Word: Geographies of the Afterlife in Tudor and Early Stuart England." In *The Place of the Dead: Death and Remembrance in Late Medieval and Early Modern Europe*. Edited by Bruce Gorman and Peter Marshall. Cambridge: Cambridge University Press, 2000. pp. 110–130.

Peters, Julie Stone. "Theatre and Book in the History of Memory: Materializing Mnemosyne in the Age of Print." *Modern Philology* 102.2 (2004): 179–206.

Russell, John. *Hamlet and Narcissus*. Newark, DE: University of Delaware Press, 1995.

Schreyer, Kurt. *Shakespeare's Medieval Craft: Remnants of the Mysteries on the London Stage*. Ithaca, NY: Cornell University Press, 2014.

Shakespeare, William. *Hamlet*. Edited by A. R. Braunmuller. New York: Penguin, 2016.

Stern, Tiffany. "'This Wide and Universal Theatre': The Theatre as Prop in Shakespeare's Metadrama." In *Shakespeare's Theatres and the Effects of Performance*. Edited by Farah Karim-Cooper, Tiffany Stern, and Andrew Gurr. London: Bloomsbury, 2013. pp. 11–32.

Wenneker, Lu Berry. "An Examination of *L'Idea del Theatro* of Giulio Camillo." PhD diss. University of Pittsburgh, 1970.

West, William. *Theatres and Encyclopedias in Early Modern Europe*. Cambridge: Cambridge University Press, 2002.

Wilder, Lina. *Shakespeare's Memory Theatre: Recollection, Properties, and Character.* Cambridge: Cambridge University Press, 2010.

Yates, Frances. *The Art of Memory*. Chicago, IL: University of Chicago Press, 1966.

CHAPTER 11

Death, Loss, and Description in Early Modern Rhetoric and Drama

Amanda K. Ruud

The humanist art of rhetoric, which was central to the education of Renaissance poets and playwrights, cultivated the powers of description. Figures such as *descriptio* and *enargeia* were praised for their ability to achieve vivid illusions of presence, offering orators a way of wielding verbal invention against absence and even against death.[1] For early modern dramatists, descriptive figures from classical rhetoric offered, on the one hand, an opportunity to defy the limitations of the stage and make the absent seem present.[2] Employing *enargeia*, playwrights absorb their audiences in a rhetorical-theatrical illusion in which events that are absent or imagined arouse responses as if they were present and real. Description is the "crooked figure" by which, the Prologue to *Henry V* asserts, a playwright "may / Attest in little place a million" and "cram" an empty stage with armies.[3] At the same time, descriptive speech in

A. K. Ruud (✉)
University of Southern California, Los Angeles, CA, USA
e-mail: ruud@usc.edu

© The Author(s), under exclusive license to Springer Nature Switzerland AG 2022
W. E. Engel and G. Williams (eds.), *The Shakespearean Death Arts*, Palgrave Shakespeare Studies,
https://doi.org/10.1007/978-3-030-88490-1_11

drama has a tendency to delay action, to slow the progress of narrative as a speaker summons or meditates on persons or things that are meaningfully absent. In this chapter, I argue that the tensions implicit in this figure provided playwrights with a powerful poetic tool for representing moments of loss and grief. Description, as a figure that represents both absence and presence, became a key rhetorical device for depicting mourning in early modern drama. When early modern playwrights turn to description at moments of loss, they reflect and amplify an implicit association between elegy and description in ancient rhetorical texts. Meanwhile, applying ancient rhetorical lessons to the problem of representing grief and death allowed playwrights to press toward innovations in their own form. Drawing on a sub-text in rhetorical handbooks, Shakespeare and other playwrights use descriptive scenes to make space for grief and offer an alternative to narrative action in the context of loss.

The power of rhetorical description to navigate a tension between absence and presence is intensely on display in *Hamlet*, and the play explicitly turns to descriptions, visions, and images as responses to loss. Grief itself is a form of present absence for prince Hamlet who "sees" his dead father in his "mind's eye" long before he encounters the King's ghostly image.[4] But however vivid it may be, Hamlet's phantasmic vision of his father only amplifies his feeling of loss.[5] Like the "crooked figure" of description, Hamlet's bereaved imagination summons an experience of presence only to declare it illusory and lost. In *Hamlet*, vivid pictures frequently perform this disappearing act. The Player's vision of a grieving Hecuba, the miniature portraits of King Hamlet and Claudius, Gertrude's image of the dying Ophelia suspended on the water of the brook: all of these images (themselves occasioned by loss) appear vividly in the rhetoric of Shakespeare's characters only to dissipate. For Shakespeare, these evanescent images represent an inventive means by which to represent loss on the level of the figure. Described images produce the immediacy or presence for which a griever longs combined with a pivotal absence: pictures represent things that aren't there. As these illusory images disappear, the losses they represent are repeated. Like the mind of a mourner, these scenes of description call up images of absent things or persons in what is, at best, a temporary form of consolation.

Using description as a poetic form in which to embody responses to loss is also part of a larger literary-historical transformation at the turn of the seventeenth century. In using description for mourning, Shakespeare adapts the humanist art of rhetorical description from its primary purposes. This poetic innovation, while keeping with this period's copious and generative modes of responding to death, is specifically occasioned by loss. Out of joint with rhetoric's primary function of persuading men to belief or action, the vivid pictures that appear and disappear in this play do little to advance the goals of Shakespeare's characters and they more than once interrupt the narrative trajectory of the play as a whole. If description, as Claire Preston has argued, is a figure that arouses emotion in order to produce action, the descriptions in *Hamlet* seem to do the opposite: the play's lingering images—like Pyrrhus's sword in the Player's speech—seem "in th'air to stick," and for a while do nothing (2.2.417).[6] And while Stephen Pender has shown that early modern orators used rhetorical descriptions and examples in order to console grievers and compensate for experiences of loss, the descriptions in this play seem rather to amplify grief.[7] The mourning dramatized through Shakespeare's use of description is, then, part of a larger early modern literary project explored by scholars including Lynn Enterline and Jenny C. Mann, in which the forms of rhetoric (in this case, rhetorical *enargeia*) are appropriated for poetic ends.[8] In this particular poetic appropriation of rhetoric, pictorial and descriptive speech is used variously to amplify or dramatize grief, to resist narrative progression, to make the dead vividly present, and even to imagine oneself as dead.

While these melancholic uses of description are genuinely innovative, they also draw on a deep well of rhetorical knowledge, reflecting and intensifying a preoccupation with loss in ancient rhetorical texts about description. In perfecting the skills of amplification and verbal *copia* the poets and humanists of early modern England systematically turn to stories of loss, memories of absent places and persons, and examples of elegiac speech in ancient rhetoric. Many of these examples appear when rhetoricians are expounding the uses of rhetorical descriptiveness (when defining *enargeia* for example), or when they are attending to how an orator can arouse passion in their audience to the end of persuasion, as Quintilian encourages a speaker to do during the peroration or conclusion of a persuasive speech.[9] Many and diverse, however, are the uses of these death and loss-oriented examples in the rhetorical tradition handed down from Cicero and Quintilian to Erasmus, Peacham, Hoskins, Puttenham, and other early modern poet-orators. Henry Peacham turns to a description of a sacked city, borrowed from Erasmus and Quintilian, to demonstrate the art of amplification, noting that amplification is "mighty to delight and perswade the mindes of men to the purpose and drift of the speaker."[10] Philip Sidney finds an ultimate model of heroic speech in Virgil's lines "Shall this land see Turnus in flight? Is death so very sad?"[11] George Puttenham argues that "noble poets" choose primarily to depict "death and burials" and other grievous events in order to temper their readers' sorrow with a Paracelsan dose of sorrow.[12] And many samples of highly effective word- or clause-level tropes are heightened with a sense of loss. Erasmus's definition of synecdoche, for example, appeals to lines from Virgil in which "one thing is understood from another," such as "'they did live,' for they are dead. 'We too did flourish,' and 'we were Trojans.'"[13] Quintilian similarly praises the quick potency of Virgil's line describing the death of Antores: "and dying, he remembered sweet Argos."[14] These examples carry all the elegiac force of the *et in arcadia ego* motif. They pack mourning for a lost past into a neat rhetorical parcel. Quintilian, and Erasmus after him choose them because of their ability to communicate efficiently, persuade, or describe, but both rhetoricians also seem keenly attracted by the element of elegy that allows these brief clauses to accomplish even more. I submit that the preponderance of rhetorical examples that carry this double weight—both accomplishing rhetorical aims and modeling verbal responses to loss—is a highly suggestive source for how Shakespeare and others will eventually put these figures of speech to work.

A popular example of *enargeia*, Quintilian's description of a sacked city, performs rhetoric's tendency to elegize at the same time that it describes. Rather than saying, "the city was stormed," Quintilian urges an orator to amplify:

> If you expand everything which was implicit in the one word, there will come into view flames racing through houses and temples, the crash of falling roofs, the single sound made up of many cries, the blind flight of some, others clinging to their dead ones in a last embrace, shrieks of children and women, the old men whom an unkind fate has allowed to live to see this day; then will come the pillage of property, secular and sacred, the frenzied activity of plunderers carrying off their booty and going back for more, the prisoners driven in chains before their captors, the mother who tries to keep her child with her, and the victors fighting one another wherever the spoils are richer. "Sack of a city" does, as I said, comprise all the parts. We shall succeed in making the facts evident, if they are plausible; it will even be legitimate to invent things of the kind that usually occur.[15]

Quintilian's description is repeated in whole or significant part by multiple early modern rhetoricians. The passage's images are memorably horrific. A reader with a keen imagination may even find them unbearable. And this is precisely Quintilian's point. An orator who employs *enargeia* to amplify a plain relation of facts will, he writes, "seem not so much to be talking about something as exhibiting it. Emotions will ensue just as if we were present at the event itself."[16] As this particular model of rhetorical effectiveness was handed down between rhetoricians and poets, so too was its emphasis on illuminating detail, on vivid imagery, and perhaps smuggled among these emphases, apostrophizing absence and articulating loss.

In this key example, a scene of loss is somehow made liminally present by way of readers' ability to participate in the author's image-eliciting power. In other words, *enargeia* enlists the reader's imagination to summon specters or ghosts. Word-painting or verbal image making is a kind of demonstrative rhetoric that thrives upon the invention of details that amplify a sense of absence or memorialization, that are summoned only to be declared dead or lost or imagined. Just as painting mediates between absence and presence, the descriptive force of *enargeia* pulses between invention and loss.

There is, of course, an element of enjoyment in even the most grievous and mournful examples of description in rhetorical handbooks. The rhetorician takes delight in layering vivid verbal images to produce effective speech. Among the rhetoricians of the Renaissance, Erasmus seems particularly keen to acknowledge the triangulation between pleasure, invention, and elegy in rhetorical description. For example, in *De Copia*, Erasmus's example of *delectatio*—a figure of dilation meant to give delight and pleasure—retells Andromache's last conversation with Hector and the grieving of the women who were certain of his forthcoming death. The force of the example rests in its simultaneous ability to provide delightful sensory details and appeal to the emotions. The details Erasmus celebrates (Hector's "gleaming helmet" and Andromache's "sweet-smelling bosom") amplify the affective force of the narrative's conclusion: "And so," Erasmus writes, "though he was still alive, they mourn him as dead."[17] The amplified details offer a sense of fullness but delighting in them also constitutes them as worthy to be mourned. As in ancient monodies for the dead, which often contained detailed physical accounts of the departed, vivid particulars amplify the emotional experience of the grievers as they attend to the minutiae of the beloved's presence in the world.[18] In the midst of his treatise, Erasmus takes a significant amount of time to relay this narrative passage in detail. He does not quote Homer directly, but retells the story himself, as if reliving and inviting his own reader to participate in the pleasure he takes from the account. Erasmus's evident delight and the space he affords to the dilation, like the generative detail included within the narration itself, carve out poetic and descriptive speech as a space of pleasure held in equipoise with the sense of loss created by the description itself.

What is one to do with a figure that is so rhetorically effective, stimulating, and also interruptive and haunting? Another frequently cited passage from Quintilian demonstrates early modern authors' sensitivity to the larger possibilities of description. When Erasmus and Peacham introduce the figure of *chronographia* or description of a time, they turn to an illustrative passage from the *Aeneid*. What is striking about this example is the emphasis both authors place upon its usefulness, even while the exact nature of that "use" remains rather open-ended. As Erasmus writes, this kind of description is "for the sake of giving pleasure [...] although even another purpose ought not to be completely lacking."[19] Both Erasmus and Peacham, however, follow Quintilian in suggesting that the main result of the description is to amplify the effect of Dido's sorrow. Here is Erasmus's version (as translated by Donald B. King):

> "It was night, when the stars turn
> In mid-flight, when every field lies still;
> And tired bodies over the earth
> Were enjoying peaceful sleep; the woods
> And wild seas were still,
> The beasts and varicolored birds, those that far
> And wide haunt the limpid lakes, and fields rough
> With brambles, lay in sleep under the silent night,
> Healed their cares, and hearts forgot their toil."
> For this description of nocturnal quiet tends to emphasize the grief of Dido who was not resting even when all things else were resting. For immediately it follows: "But not the distressed Phoenician queen, not ever was she lulled to sleep."[20]

Here, as Erasmus and Peacham both celebrate, Virgil deploys descriptive materials to the poem's other ends. The repeated appeals to stillness, quiet, and sleep act as a kind of charm, lulling the passage to motionlessness. This is effective rhetoric in its own right, for, to borrow from a later passage in Erasmus, its "pleasing charm holds the hearer."[21] But what is more remarkable about this passage in the minds of these rhetoricians is that the charm is not the final point. It is a means to an end. As Peacham writes, the descriptive charm acts "to amplifie the dolorous sorrow of Dido who could by no meanes finde rest at that time, when everie creature enjoyed rest."[22] The stillness and quiet of the night exaggerate the felt length of Dido's grief amplify her loneliness and make space for a reader to join her in that isolation. The descriptive passage, which is not exactly about Dido, somehow acts to make Dido's grief more important and central to the poem. The passage forges the poem into a space of navigation between Dido's isolated sorrow and a narrative world that drives toward empire. *Descriptio* becomes a pivotal tool for commenting on the project of the epic as a whole.

In ancient rhetoric and poetry, description's association with loss and mourning is implicit but essential. Classical texts and the early modern rhetorical handbooks that employ them depict the moving power of *descriptio* and *enargeia* as essentially elegiac.[23] Meanwhile, models of effective descriptive speech repeatedly return to scenes of loss and lament, and a majority of the literary examples drawn from ancient epic contain evocative descriptions of figures and places that are absent, dead, or dying. The spoken pictures of early modern poetry and rhetoric, then, depend upon a kernel of elegy and become a means of reflecting on language's ability to represent loss and grief.

When playwrights like Shakespeare take up the challenges of representing loss and death, they draw on this association to adapt the old form of descriptive rhetoric to a new purpose. The difficulties of depicting grief and suffering send early modern playwrights back to their schoolbooks, but they also offer playwrights an opportunity for further innovation. Using description as a means for mourning, especially in the midst of a familiar or generic plot, provides playwrights with a poetic alternative to narrative drive or action. This possibility of *enargeia* is key to Shakespeare's construction of the Ghost in *Hamlet*. King Hamlet's Ghost offers descriptions that bring their subjects vividly before Hamlet's mind's eye. Striking here is Shakespeare's choice to take rhetorical features that were praised for their "vitality" and "lifelikeness" and place them in the mouth of a ghost. The vitality of the Ghost's descriptions has all the more power over the grieving Hamlet because the speaker is dead. The Ghost's descriptions dwell on suffering but are leveraged toward a specific, active response—that is, revenge. Much as classical forensic orators would use quick, ekphrastic images to persuade a jury to rule in their favor, the Ghost uses vivid description in the hope of coercing Hamlet to act. If, as Claire Preston argues, *ekphrasis* is "a trope of enforcement," which uses the form and placement of a description to elicit a specific reaction, the Ghost is clear in the behavior he means to enforce: "Revenge [my] foul and most unnatural murder" (1.5.25).[24] Clad in armor and urging revenge, the Ghost establishes a set of generic expectations that are heroic, active, and ultimately tragic.

As urgent as his command may be, however, the Ghost's descriptions also occupy a striking amount of space and they struggle to resolve fully into a call to action. Just as the ekphrastic scene of Dido's grief interrupted Virgil's epic poem, bringing action to an apparent stand-still, the Ghost's description of the "leperous distilment" with which he was poisoned "even in the blossoms" of his sin forges a still space in the midst of a revenge tragedy (1.5.42–91). The near fifty-line image of the king's death pangs extends the play's first act. Despite the Ghost's repeated statements of concern over time—"Brief let me be" (1.5.59), "My hour is almost come" (1.5.2)—he indulges in multiple diversions and dwells on the details of his suffering:

> Upon my secure hour thy uncle stole
> With juice of cursed hebona in a vial
> And in the porches of my ears did pour
> The leperous distilment whose effect
> Holds such an enmity with blood of man
> That swift as quicksilver it courses through
> The natural gates and alleys of the body
> And with a sudden vigour it doth possess
> And curd like eager droppings into milk
> The thin and wholesome blood. So did it mine
> And a most instant tetter barked about
> Most lazar-like with vile and loathsome crust
> All my smooth body.
> Thus was I sleeping by a brother's hand
> Of life, of crown, of queen at once dispatched,
> Cut off even in the blossoms of my sin.
> Unhouseled, disappointed, unaneled,
> No reckoning made but sent to my account
> With all my imperfections on my head.
> O horrible, O horrible, most horrible! (1.5.61–80)

The Ghost's concluding *gradatio* would render it difficult for anyone, but especially a grieving son, to fulfill one of the first instructions he gives to Hamlet: "Pity me not, but lend thy serious hearing / To what I shall unfold" (1.5.5–6). Rather, like Quintilian's description of the sacked city, the Ghost's *enargeia* amplifies details that increase the horror of the scene, eliciting emotions from his son as if he were witnessing a death.

The Ghost's speech and his stated desire create the central rhetorical tension of this scene, a tension that exemplifies Shakespeare's inventive, even critical, use of *enargeia*. As clearly as the description is crafted to elicit action and move a plot forward, it also elicits, and indeed enacts, mourning. Borrowing the resources of rhetorical amplification and dilation, the scene makes King Hamlet's suffering vividly present in a poetic representation of pain and death. It forges an aesthetic space within the drama that is capacious enough to hold the pain of the father, the horror of his death, and the mourning of the son even though the action the Ghost requests aims to break off the scene of suffering, turning it into a catalyst for pitiless political action. In other words, the Ghost hopes to use his own powers of pictorial poetry to produce a revenge drama and cast himself as the key victim and Hamlet as revenging agent, but the play resists following these generic directions.

There is, of course, a flaw in the Ghost's rhetorical plan, which he acknowledges by showing an emphatic concern with Hamlet's pitying response. King Hamlet refuses to offer the typical Senecan description of his sufferings in the afterlife because he is sure that Hamlet will be overwhelmed by it.[25] The Ghost claims to be wary of description—though perhaps not wary enough—because he suspects that describing his present pain will make Hamlet so full of pity and grief that he will be able to do nothing. To hear an "eternal blazon," or lengthy description of the underworld, he tells Hamlet, would "harrow up thy soul, freeze thy young blood," and "Make thy two eyes like stars start from their spheres" (1.5.16–20). What the Ghost wants is to perform rhetoric that moves Hamlet to action but not pity. One imagines that this might work were it not that, as a ghost, his very presence elicits a certain amount of pity, and, more to the point, if he had not chosen to use description. Pity for the Ghost, stirred by his description of suffering, does not inspire retributive action, but rather encourages emotional reflection.

The Ghost's description of suffering and his imperative of vengeance induce clashing feelings in Hamlet. Hamlet's famed "delay" is a perfectly reasonable response to the poetic pictures of loss and suffering that are put before his mind's eye. A key feature of *enargeia* is that it compels an emotional response in the hearer. Hamlet must choose then, between two kinds of response to the Ghost's suffering. One is to obey the coercive command that follows the Ghost's *ekphrasis* and act as a heroic revenger. But another response, also compelled by the Ghost's powerful rhetoric, is to "lose the name of action" and pause to grieve (3.1.87). The Ghost's rhetorical position, then, straddles two articulations of the aims of descriptive rhetoric. He offers both the call for action (even at the expense of pity) and the arresting and plaintive force of one who speaks for the dead. Put differently, he offers description as an act of rhetorical persuasion at the same time that he uses it to mourn.

In the face of this contradiction, which the Ghost seems at pains to navigate, one wonders why Shakespeare would choose to make his ghost a compelling enargeist who turns to poetic description to accomplish his rhetorical goal. For the purposes of a revenge plot, the proverbial Senecan ghost roaring "Hamlet, Revenge!" would have been a bit more efficient. Given the awkward position into which Shakespeare thrusts both his Ghost and his protagonist, it seems that the Ghost's presence is not meant merely to launch a revenge tragedy, but rather to interrogate the uses of a rhetorical device that might complicate such a tragedy.

At this point, readers of *Hamlet* will likely recall the descriptive scenes that punctuate the rest of Shakespeare's play, including the Player's speech and Gertrude's explicitly mournful description of Ophelia. These scenes plainly employ description as a force that slows or resists action, even if the counterpoints they offer to narrative drive are ultimately subsumed in a tragic plot. The Player's speech, which draws on Virgil's *Aeneid*, uses description as a means of mourning that quite literally interrupts an epic plot. The Player, whose tears ultimately lead Polonius to cut off the speech, assertively employs description to slow down and resist the narrative of Pyrrhus's vengeful murder of Priam and amplify the scene's pathos:

> For, lo, his sword
> Which was declining on the milky head
> Of reverend Priam seemed i'th' air to stick.
> So as a painted tyrant Pyrrhus stood
> Like a neutral to his will and matter,
> Did nothing. (2.2.415–420)

This lingering image carries the same critical energy that Erasmus attributed to the Dido scene, which slowed an epic trajectory to amplify a woman's grief. Here, however, mournful description is placed in tension with both Virgil's epic and the present revenge plot. The image interrupts the narrative to make space for pitying and mourning Priam at the same time that it slows down *Hamlet*.

Hearing the Player's speech recapitulates the first instance in which Hamlet was haunted by a descriptive poetic image and so reiterates the tension he experiences between an active and a reflective response, between rhetoric as a motive and cue for action and rhetoric used for poetic mourning. While Hamlet might ask to hear the speech in order to motivate and justify his own action—his bringing down of justice against the murderer Claudius—the scene as played ultimately stops at inaction, grief, and pity focused on the bereaved Hecuba. Combining specific attention to the visual (a reference to painting) with delay (Pyrrhus's pause, the length of the speech itself), the speech asserts the description of loss as a site of aesthetic attention that invites pity and practices mourning. The Player's speech is troubling to Hamlet, perhaps because the prince finds the interruption of vengeful action with a sympathetic response to be both familiar and attractive.

Hamlet explores the possibility that description can serve as a means of mourning and in doing so appropriates a rhetorical form for poetic ends. If the project of transforming rhetoric into a means for poetry was a pivotal feature of late Elizabethan and Jacobean writing, as Lynn Enterline has proposed, this particular reimagination of the uses of rhetoric arose specifically as a response to the challenges of representing loss and grief.[26] While, as I have shown, Shakespeare and other early modern poets were clearly drawing on ancient precedent in imagining description as an elegiac form apt for representing loss, they also inventively played upon the associations between descriptive rhetoric and loss to apply pressure to their own generic forms. Adapting descriptive rhetoric as a means of representing mourning is, then, a rich example of how early modern writers engaged death and loss as spurs to invention and artistic plenitude. As a "death art," or an aesthetic invention prompted by the challenge of responding to death and mortality, elegiac description became a tool by which early modern playwrights could also reimagine their own narrative conventions and values.

If *Hamlet* poses elegiac description as an alternative to vengeful action in response to loss, a passage added to Thomas Kyd's *The Spanish Tragedy* in 1602 takes up this possibility with even greater conviction. The passage known as "the painter scene" was added to Kyd's play by another hand, and it explicitly appeals to the resources of description in order to fill out the play's representation of mourning and resist the trajectory of dramatic revenge narrative.[27] While the painter scene might anticipate the play's later turn to another form of art, performance, as a means of exacting revenge for loss, I suggest that the scene represents a possible "otherwise," interrupting the revenge plot to explore a different option for how tragedy might articulate and respond to grievous experiences. In any case, the fact that the later addition makes explicit use of visual description as a form for mourning implies that early modern playwrights were increasingly attentive to the resources that the elegiac pictorial imagination could offer their craft.

In Act 3 of the revised 1602 edition of Kyd's play, a painter arrives to visit the bereaved father Hieronimo. As it turns out, both the painter and Hieronimo have recently lost their sons to murder. They meet at a moment of mourning. When Hieronimo first hears of the painter's arrival, he alludes to a notion (or desire) that an image might offer some form of consolation. "Bid him come in," he says "and paint some comfort. / For surely there's none lives but painted comfort."[28] Hieronimo's welcome invokes a kind of solace that might be possible through the painter's art and immediately denies it. The bitter joke of the second line hangs on the mimetic nature of painting: it is not real and cannot—despite the highest claims of Renaissance painters—truly make the absent present. But Hieronimo's first impulse is also to express a kind of hope about what an image could do for him at his moment of loss. Hieronimo goes on to inquire after the painter's skill, asking if he can fulfill a series of increasingly bold demands in the form of an image. When Richard Meek discusses this passage, he ultimately takes the absurd demands Hieronimo makes as a subtle nod toward the superiority of narrative or drama over the frozen image. What Hieronimo describes, Meek points out, does not resemble "any conceivable piece of visual art," but rather shows the character "envisaging himself as a character in a narrative, or even a play."[29] And indeed, it is ultimately a play that Hieronimo will use to exact his revenge on his son's murderer. If we view the passage with an eye to its implicit *paragone*—that is, the debate over visual forms—as Meek does, then it is clear that an image cannot keep up with what Hieronimo desires. But viewed in another way, Hieronimo's increasing demands sketch out the possibilities of description. What if these images—which are possible in verbal art if not in visual art—offer an alternative to revenge? In what sense could the demands he places on description be seen as an attempt at finding consolation through a rhetorical form?

Hieronimo first asks for a painting that might indeed reflect on the claims of consolation offered in early modern commonplaces about visual art. In essence, he asks for an image that returns what he has lost:

> Look you, sir, do you see? I'd have you paint me in my gallery in your oil colours, matted, and draw me five years younger than I am. Do you see, sir? Let five years go, let them go, like the Marshal of Spain. My wife Isabella standing by me, with a speaking look to my son Horatio, which should intend to this or somelike purpose: 'God bless thee, my sweet son'—and my hand leaning upon his head, thus, sir, do you see? May it be done? (3.12A.112–120)

Here, Hieronimo casts the painter as someone with the power to turn back time, to manage who is present and who is absent, and to make a picture appear to speak. Of course, in this moment, it is Hieronimo's speech that accomplishes these things, as his opening question ("do you see?") underscores. The image Hieronimo imagines here does offer some consolation. It returns his lost son and offers him a blessing. But this dream of an image proves inadequate, perhaps because it participates too much in consolatory fantasy rather than active mourning and so leaves him dissatisfied.

Hieronimo's requests of the painter shift as he gets nearer and nearer to naming the nature of his tragedy. His next requests return to the location of his trauma and reflect the images that are seared in his memory. He asks the painter to depict the "very tree" in which his son's body was found and asks if he can draw "a youth, run through and through with villain's swords" (3.12A.130–140). Here the work of the image is not so much to console as to offer a glimpse of the visual memories that haunt him. These concrete visual memories are examples of the kind of *phantasms* that Quintilian argued an orator could employ to make a vivid, enargeic description. These images are best, Quintilian suggests, when they come from reality and observation.[30] In effect, Hieronimo is here calling up— in rhetoric, inventing—the details that will make his vivid ekphrasis appear before the eyes of his listening audience.

Finally, Hieronimo bursts out with the image he truly longs for. As he speaks, he crafts a complex kind of picture that is only possible in verbal form and at the same time offers a strikingly full display of the many roles description can play in the context of loss:

> Hieronimo Well, sir, then bring me forth, bring me thorough alley and alley, still with a distracted countenance going along, and let my hair heave up my nightcap. Let the clouds scowl, make the moon dark, the stars extinct, the winds blowing, the bells tolling, the owls shrieking, the toads croaking, the minutes jarring and the clock striking twelve. And then at last, sir, starting, behold a man hanging, and tottering, and tottering as you know the wind will wave a man, and I with a trice to cut him down. And looking upon him by the advantage of my torch, find it to be my son Horatio. There you may show a passion, there you may show a passion. Draw me like old Priam of Troy, crying 'The house is o'fire, the house is o'fire!', as the torch over my head. Make me curse, make me rave, make me cry, make me mad, make me well again, make me curse hell, invocate heaven, and, in the end, leave me in a trance, and so forth.
> PAINTER And is this the end?
> HIERONIMO Oh, no, there is no end; the end is death and madness. (3.12A.146–159)

Hieronimo's last request is for a full representation of the traumatic event of discovering his son's murder. Even while he adds more and more action and sound to his picture, imagining himself like a character in an epic, the rhetorical frame of the passage (the request for a painting) places all of the description's actions in tension with the stillness of an image. The reader encounters each action like another vignette in a crowded painting. The effect is something like an early modern narrative painting of an epic in which multiple actions take place on the same plane, placing each event in relation to the ones that surround it.

At the same time, Hieronimo's speech could also look like a compelling instance of forensic oratory. Quintilian describes the role of a prosecutor in terms that anticipate Hieronimo's speech. "When I am lamenting a murdered man," he writes, "will I not have before my eyes all the things which might believably have happened in the case under consideration? Will the assailant not suddenly spring out [....] Will I not see the blow and the victim falling to the ground? Will his blood, his pallor, his dying groans not be impressed on my mind?"[31] This, Quintilian writes, is *enargeia* at work. For Quintilian, the occasion for such a speech is a prosecution, even though he describes himself as "lamenting" the murdered victim. The speech then, borrows effects and methods from both rhetoric and the visual arts.

However, I suggest that whoever revised Kyd's play in 1602, whether it was Jonson, Shakespeare, or another unidentified hand, makes the most of this kind of descriptive speech by appropriating it as a space of mourning. Lodged in the middle of the passage is a description of night that carries traces of the Virgilian commonplace that Erasmus and Peacham found so capaciously useful. Here, however, the shrieking owls and croaking toads signify the commonplace landscape of tragedy. They anticipate Hieronimo's horror even while they delay its arrival within the speech. Hieronimo is like Dido in the Aeneid passage—a figure whose affective experience is amplified and made more sympathetic by the description into which he is placed. But by imagining his description as a painting, Hieronimo seems to enact a longing for the kind of stillness to which that celebrated passage attained. Perhaps this grieving father wants not only to perform his madness for revenge but also to be still like a painting himself. "Draw me," he begs, asking to be made motionless like the dead son he mourns and remembers. Or is it rather that Hieronimo imagines himself being made into the matter of poetry? Hieronimo does indeed cast himself as a Virgilian figure. He asks to be drawn "like old Priam of Troy, crying 'The house is o'fire, the house is o'fire!'" To be like Priam would be to have his suffering and loss recorded in the annals of history and epic. But, as Shakespeare's Lucrece acknowledges in her own identification with an image of Hecuba, it would also mean to be rendered as still and silent as a painted or historical figure. For a moment, Hieronimo glimpses the image as a space to memorialize the gravity of his loss and to remain within it rather than to seek revenge. At the same time, he also recognizes that the end of this kind of immersion in a mourning image is "death and madness." As Hieronimo crafts his description, he makes himself like the figures of legend even while he inters himself in the still, imagined image as a space of perpetual mourning. Drawing on epic narrative, on oratory, on painting, and on the complex ontology of described images, Hieronimo demonstrates what one can do with descriptive rhetoric at a moment of loss. Descriptive rhetoric, for this speaker, is a masterful trope for responding to loss; it is, in other words, a death art.

Notes

1. Hoskins, praises description as a way of bringing in "life and luster" in *Directions for Speech and Style*, pp. 47–48.
2. In *The Orator's Education*, a common classroom text in Elizabethan England, Quintilian urges rhetors to amplify descriptions with copious detail. "The result," Quintilian writes, "will be *enargeia*, what Cicero calls *illustratio* and *evidentia*, a quality which makes us seem not so much to be talking about something as exhibiting it" (6.2.31).
3. Shakespeare, *Henry V*, Prologue.
4. Shakespeare, *Hamlet*, ed. by Ann Thompson and Neil Taylor (London: Bloomsbury, 2016) 1.2.183, 184. Quotations from *Hamlet*, hereafter parenthetical, are from this edition.
5. Quintilian writes: "The person who will show the greatest power in the expression of emotions will be the person who has properly formed what the Greeks call *phantasiai* (let us call them 'visions'), by which the images of absent things are presented to the mind in such a way that we seem actually to see them with our eyes and have them physically present to us" (6.2.29).
6. Preston, "Ekphrasis," p. 119.
7. Pender, "Rhetoric, Grief, and the Imagination," pp. 54–85.
8. See Enterline's "Introduction" in *Elizabethan Narrative Poems: The State of Play*, pp. 1–20, and Mann's contribution to the same volume, "Reck'ning with Orpheus," p. 21.
9. Quintilian, 6.1.
10. Peacham, *The Garden of Eloquence*, sig. S1^r.
11. Sidney, "Defence of Poesy," p. 24. The sentence Sidney chooses to place a final period on his argument that poetry is a means of instruction is "*Hic opus, hic labor est*" ("This is the work, this is the labor") (22). It is another striking example of effective rhetoric drawn from a scene of grief, since this is how the dead Anchises describes the labor of making one's way out of the underworld to Aeneas.
12. Puttenham, *Arte of English Poesie*, p. 96.
13. Erasmus, *On Copia of Words and Ideas*, p. 33.
14. Quintilian, 6.2.33.
15. Ibid., 8.3.66.
16. Ibid., 6.2.31.

17. Erasmus, pp. 102–103.
18. On monodies, see Ruth Webb, *Ekphrasis, Imagination, and Persuasion*, p. 216.
19. Erasmus, p. 55.
20. Ibid., p. 55.
21. Ibid., p. 69.
22. Peacham, *Garden of* Eloquence, sig. U2^v.
23. When Quintilian discusses image-making, or the formation of "*phantasiai*," as the most powerful tool for "the expression of emotions," he defines these "visions" as devices "by which the images of absent things are presented to the mind" (6.2.29).
24. Preston, p. 119.
25. On Senecan descriptions of the afterlife see Pearlman, "Shakespeare at Work," pp. 71–84.
26. Enterline, pp. 1–20.
27. The identity of the playwright who wrote the additional lines for the 1602 edition is unknown, though Jonson and Shakespeare have both been suggested. See Bruster, "Shakespearean Spellings," pp. 420–424.
28. Kyd, *The Spanish Tragedy*, 3.12A.73–74. References to this play, hereafter parenthetical, are from this edition.
29. Meek, p. 19.
30. Quintilian, 6.2.
31. Quintilian, 6.2.31–32.

References

Bruster, Douglas. "Shakespearean Spellings and Handwriting in the Additional Passages Printed in the 1602 Spanish Tragedy." *Notes and Queries* 60.3 (2013).

Enterline, Lynn. *The Rhetoric of the Body from Ovid to Shakespeare*. Cambridge and London: Cambridge University Press, 2000.

———. "Introduction: On 'Schoolmen's Cunning Notes'." In *Elizabethan Narrative Poems: The State of Play*. Edited by Lynn Enterline. London: Arden Shakespeare, 2019. pp. 1–20.

Erasmus, Desiderus. *On Copia of Words and Ideas*. Translated by Donald B. King and H. David Rix. Milwaukee, WI: Marquette University Press, 2012.

Hoskins, John. *Directions for Speech and Style*. Edited by Hoyt T. Hudson. Princeton, NJ: Princeton University Press, 1935.
Kyd, Thomas. *The Spanish Tragedy*. Edited by Clara Calvo and Jesus Tronch. Arden Early Modern Drama. London: Bloomsbury, 2013.
Mann, Jenny C. *Outlaw Rhetoric: Figuring Vernacular Eloquence in Shakespeare's England*. Ithaca, NY: Cornell University Press, 2012.
———. "'Reck'ning' with Shakespeare's Orpheus in *The Rape of Lucrece*." In *Elizabethan Narrative Poems: The State of Play*. Edited by Lynn Enterline. London: Arden Shakespeare, 2019. pp. 21–44.
Meek, Richard. *Narrating the Visual in Shakespeare*. Farnham, UK: Ashgate Publishing Company, 2009.
Peacham, Henry. *The Garden of Eloquence*. London: Richard Field, 1593.
Pearlman, E. "Shakespeare at Work: The Invention of the Ghost." In *Hamlet: New Critical Essays*. New York: Routledge, 2013. pp. 71–84.
Pender, Stephen. "Rhetoric, Grief, and the Imagination in Early Modern England." *Philosophy and Rhetoric* 43.1 (2010): 54–85.
Preston, Claire. "Ekphrasis: Painting in Words." In *Renaissance Figures of Speech*. Edited by Sylvia Adamson, Gavin Alexander, and Katrin Ettenhuber. Cambridge: Cambridge University Press, 2007. pp. 115–130.
Puttenham, George. "The Art of English Poesy." In *Sidney's "Defense of Poesy" and Selected Renaissance Literary Criticism*. Edited by Gavin Alexander. London: Penguin Classics, 2004. pp. 55–203.
Quintilian. *The Orator's Education*. Edited and translated by Donald A. Russell. Loeb Classical Library. Cambridge, MA: Harvard University Press, 2001.
Shakespeare, William. *Hamlet*. Edited by Ann Thompson and Neil Taylor. London: Bloomsbury, 2006.
———. *Henry V*. Edited by T.W. Craik. London: Bloomsbury, 1995.
Sidney, Philip. "The Defence of Poesy." In *Sidney's The Defence of Poesy and Selected Renaissance Criticism*. Edited by Gavin Alexander. New York and London: Penguin Classics, 2004.
Webb, Ruth. *Ekphrasis, Imagination, and Persuasion in Ancient Rhetorical Theory and Practice*. New York: Routledge, 2016.

CHAPTER 12

"Native and Indued / Unto that Element": Dissolution, Permeability, and the Death of Ophelia

Pamela Royston Macfie

Although Ophelia's death has been variously interrogated, especially in terms of its floral attributes,[1] scholars have devoted relatively scant attention to that death's liquid process. This essay argues that Ophelia's drowning performs a burial rite that counters her final interment in earth. Though this death by water might seem to parody Christian baptism,[2] its images are steeped in elemental mystery. Gertrude's description of Ophelia's dying radicalizes the literary convention of the *locus amoenus*, defines

---

Quotations from Shakespeare follow *The Riverside Shakespeare*, hereafter cited parenthetically with the play abbreviations as given in *The MLA Handbook* (2016).

P. R. Macfie (✉)
Sewanee: The University of the South, Sewanee, TN, USA
e-mail: pmacfie@sewanee.edu

© The Author(s), under exclusive license to Springer Nature Switzerland AG 2022
W. E. Engel and G. Williams (eds.), *The Shakespearean Death Arts*, Palgrave Shakespeare Studies,
https://doi.org/10.1007/978-3-030-88490-1_12

death as dissolution, and privileges both water and mud as mediums that permit a terra-aqueous embrace that returns a creature to its origins. With these details, Shakespeare draws attention to an ecology of the female body whose final interaction with elemental nature is both permeable and deliquescent; strategically, this interaction provides a foil for Hamlet's declaration in the very next scene that death's processes, turning all to dust, are those of fracture and desiccation.

Gertrude's lyrical meditation, liquid as the scene she describes, mystifies death and affiliates it with beauty:

> There is a willow grows askaunt the brook,
> That shows his hoary leaves in the glassy stream,
> Therewith fantastic garlands did she make
> Of crow-flowers, nettles, daisies, and long purples
> That liberal shepherds give a grosser name,
> But our cull-cold maids do dead men's fingers call them.
> There on the pendant boughs her crownet weeds
> Clamb'ring to hang, an envious sliver broke,
> When down her weedy trophies and herself
> Fell in the weeping brook. Her clothes spread wide,
> And mermaid-like awhile they bore her up,
> Which time she chaunted snatches of old lauds,
> As one incapable of her own distress,
> Or like a creature native and indued
> Unto that element. (5.1.166–180)

Gertrude may idealize the setting in which Ophelia drowns in order to soften the blow she must deal Laertes, who has, after all, returned to court prepared to lead a mob against it. Still, the place she conjures seems nearly numinous. Its glassy stream reflects a willow's silvered leaves; its meadow yields the spring flowers Ophelia turns into garlands; its waters seem both to inspire and intermingle with song. Without exception, the shimmering site in which Ophelia is ferried to death displays the defining features of the *locus amoenus* ("pleasant place") as articulated by Theocritus, Virgil, and Ovid and carried forward in early modernity: greenery, shade, water, and song.[3] The willow shades the brook; the water invites reflection; the green world fills with song. The phrase that initiates Gertrude's speech, "There is a willow," resonates against the rhetorical marker with which Ovid, suggesting a timeless present, introduces the ideal landscapes of the *Metamorphoses*: "locus est" or, more frequently, "est locus" ("there is a place").[4] The tree that distinguishes the site in which Ophelia drowns is the same tree whose beauty—of blossom and sound—fills the paradigmatic *locus amoenus* in Virgil's first eclogue: "hinc tibi, quae semper, vicino ab limite saepes / Hyblaeis apibus florem depasta salicti / saepe levi somnum suadebit inire susurro" ("On this side, as aforetime, on your neighbour's border, the hedge whose willow blossoms are sipped by Hybla's bees shall often with its gentle hum soothe you to slumber").[5] For Virgil's Meliboeus, the susurration of the willow's leaves is enchantingly hypnotic.

Entering the willow's glade, Ophelia discovers in its remote beauty innocence and ease. There, in accordance with the *locus amoenus*'s association with leisure, shelter, and protection, she gathers flowers, offers a flower crown in tribute to the willow, and sings. Her "fantastic garlands" do not merely call to mind funerary and bridal wreaths, anticipating, in this, the "virgin crants" (5.1.232) she is allowed in her abbreviated funeral rites. They link her chaplets with verse, recalling, for instance, the cyclic division of the Greek Anthology into "garlands" and the association of wreaths with verse throughout classical poetry.[6] Like Virgil's shepherd-poets, Ophelia appreciates verdant nature as both her art's source (in the form of "crowflowers, nettles, daisies, and long purples") and its crucial recipient (in the form of the willow, to which she presents her "weedy coronet"). Ophelia's further actions sustain Theocritus's and Virgil's crucial identification of the *locus amoenus* with song.[7] The susurration[8] of Virgil's willow leaves, sounded in onomatopoeic sibilance, finds a liquid equivalent in Ophelia's "melodious lay" (4.7.182), which melts in water and air. Like the willow's leaves, Ophelia's song makes a shaded landscape a place of reverie. In a system of exchange, Ophelia is both transformative of and transformed by the plenitude in which she rests. As she floats, singing, in the brook, Ophelia inhabits the pastoral poet's essential, recumbent posture.[9] Virgil's Tityrus stretches out[10] beneath a beech tree and sings; Ophelia, her garments spread wide, rests on water and chants "old lauds" (4.7.177). For a handful of lines, she seems weightless, a creature of water rather than bone.

Ophelia's pastoral trance is, however, finally revealed to push the *locus amoenus*'s association with *otium* ("ease") beyond the topos's ordinary limits. Characterized "as one incapable of her own distress" (4.7.178), Ophelia drifts unaware to death's kingdom. Her reverie does not achieve the *ataraxia* Lucretius and Virgil identify with the *locus amoenus*: a beatific state, free from mortal anxiety, achieved in a contemplation of nature.[11] It moves by slow degrees to the oblivion of death. When Ophelia is finally bedded in ooze, her death literalizes with eerie absolutism the *locus amoenus*'s original purpose: to unite a person with nature. In Ophelia's case, this union is achieved in matter as well as mind.

Gertrude's presentation of Ophelia's muddy end is not, however, wholly bleak. Achieved in immersion, her death oscillates against the Neoplatonic notion that the soul's origins lie in water. Regarding the emanation of the soul, Plotinus writes in the *Enneads*: "Think of a spring which has no other source, but gives all of itself to rivers while not exhausting itself in the rivers but quietly remaining itself, while the streams which go forth from it are still all together before they flow their separate ways."[12] Plotinus imagines the end of the soul's pilgrimage as the primal source from which it flowed. Describing that source as exhibiting each of the four elements' characteristic agency, he endows it with water's power of cohesion.[13] Exploring the metaphysical question of whether bodies can be completely transfused, he pursues analogies of absorption: "So, when water flows through wool, or, when papyrus exudes the water in it [...] [and] one quality joins another quality, it is not simply the quality it was but is together with another quality [...] [thus] when a magnitude is joined to another magnitude it is not obscured" (2.7.2).

Ophelia's status as "a creature native and indued / Unto that element" (4.7.178–179) is of particular resonance here. "Native," deriving from the Latin *nativus* ("born"),[14] implies that Ophelia has been created, "mermaid-like" (4.7.176), from the element in which she dies. "Indued," which Shakespeare uses in *Othello* to describe that which has been brought to a particular state or condition,[15] suggests her liquid passage to death is orchestrated by external agency and purpose. This suggestion deepens when we consider the word's derivation from the Latin *inducere* ("to lead, bring, or conduct into a place") and its subsequent iteration in the verb "to induct," as in a ceremony or rite.[16] "Indued" unto the element of water, Ophelia is both habituated to and incorporated within its mystery. The process is not haphazard, but ineluctable.

"Indued" yields one final association in the line at issue: that sounded in its phonetic equivalence to the phrase "in dew." Recalling the wish Hamlet expresses in his first soliloquy, that "this too too sallied flesh would melt, / Thaw, and resolve itself into a dew" (1.2.129–130), the pun suggests that Ophelia achieves in primal liquescence the release Hamlet originally desired. In the soliloquy, Hamlet likens spiritual release to the alchemical process that removes impurities from mineral substance in order to turn it into pure vapor. His references to melting, thawing, and resolution variously ply the vocabulary of the alchemical treatise.[17] Notably, the idea of alchemical conversion gathers credence whether we read Hamlet's flesh as "sallied" or "solid." If his flesh is "sallied" ("sullied"), it awaits sublimation into something pure; if it is "solid," it awaits transmutation into a vapor.[18] Gertrude, in words that perform the figurative promise of Deuteronomy 32:2 ("my speech shall flow as doeth the dew"),[19] implies with "indued" (4.7.179) that Ophelia undergoes a similar kind of change. This suggestion, hovering just below the surface of Gertrude's decorated verse, admittedly distills and evaporates in an instant. At the same time, it participates in an imagistic program that maps fluid sympathies between the natural world and the female body.

These sympathies, which exceed pathetic fallacy, are authorized by early modern geo-humoral theory like that unfolded in Helkiah Crooke's monumental 1615 *Mikrokosmographia: A Description of the Body of Man*. Stretching from the writings of Hippocrates, through the works of Galen, and into the early modern treatise, this theory elaborates parallels between human physiology and climatic conditions, studies human embodiment as it is manifest in the four elements, and posits that habitat or environment influences human identity.[20] Early modern geo-humoralism, as Gail Kern Paster has established, is also theory of gender; it links the female body with the element of water, characterizing it as cold and moist, and the male body with fire, characterizing it as hot and dry.[21] The female body's humoral identification as something clammy, congealed, and saturated by cold,[22] which nuances Gertrude's reference to "our cull-cold maids" (5.1.171), is literalized in Ophelia's imbrication in mud.

Paster's study of the humoral system has uncovered in the works of Shakespeare and his contemporaries what she describes as a "psychophysiological reciprocity between the experiencing subject and his or her relation to the world."[23] Such a reciprocity initially links Ophelia, in her decentered madness, and the brook, with its slanted willow. The tree's arcing to the stream mimes Ophelia's movement toward water. Its emblematic association with forsaken love remembers her rejection by Hamlet.[24] Its fragility, manifest in its slender boughs and shallow roots, twins her incapacity to endure. When Thomas Fuller writes in his 1662 *History of the Worthies of England* that the willow is "a sad Tree, whereof such who have lost their love make their *mourning garlands* and we know what *Exiles* hung up their (Psalm 137.2) *Harpes* upon such dolefull *Supporters*,"[25] his words seem a belated commentary on Ophelia's identification with the tree and its abjection.

Our impression of a "psychophysiological reciprocity" between Ophelia and the elemental world deepens when the brook is characterized as "weeping" (4.7.175). For a moment, the stream seems more saltwater than fresh, as if Shakespeare would mine the chemical association he exploits elsewhere in images of "an ocean of salt tears" (*2H6* 3.2.143) and "tears as salt as sea" (*2H6* 3.2.96). The "weeping brook" (4.7.175) figures a palpable transfer between Ophelia's humanity and several lower elements—both aqueous and vegetative—in the cosmic hierarchy; simultaneously, it performs a transfer of poetic expectation. Shakespeare does not name the willow as "weeping," despite that tree's emblematic association with sorrow; he infuses the brook with tears. Doing so, he does more than evoke the fantasy that the brook mourns its part in Ophelia's death; he identifies the brook with the overdetermined liquescence of Ophelia's body as posited by humoral physiology.[26] Ophelia's fall into the brook alters both herself and the environment she enters; here, as Paster would put it, Ophelia's bodily affect expresses itself "environmentally as part of a 'vast system of fluid exchange' between the body and the world."[27] Ophelia becomes "mermaid-like" (5.1.176); the brook flows with tears. The images commemorate a double absorption. Ophelia becomes one with water; the water unites with human suffering.

Gertrude unfolds in the close of her speech one final "psychophysiological reciprocity" between Ophelia and elemental nature: that evinced in "muddy death" (4.7.183). Signaling reversal with a strong, medial "but," Gertrude turns from beautifying Ophelia's death to exposing its materiality:

> But long it could not be
> Till that her garments, heavy with their drink,
> Pull'd the poor wretch from her melodious lay
> To muddy death.   (4.7.180–183)

Corruption takes beauty's place; Gertrude's fluid meditation stops midline; Ophelia's drift in water and song is stilled. The description of Ophelia dragged from "melodious lay / To muddy death" (4.7.182–183) performs cancellation in its very sounds; here, as Michael Neill has noted, Shakespeare repeats the initiating murmur of "melodious" in "muddy," but thwarts the liquid alliteration of "melodious lay" (4.7.182) in "muddy death['s]" dental stutter (4.7.183).[28] Sudden and startling, the image of "muddy death" evokes pollution and shrouds Ophelia's death in uncertainty. Ophelia lies in muck; her death's motives are occluded; her body interacts with an environment that emphasizes her porosity and permeability (and, in this, her susceptibility to corruption). This interaction does not merely accrue meaning from early modern theories of gendered physiology and embodiment. It glances ahead to Julia Kristeva's explanation of death as a process of abjection: a casting out and down that confounds the body's borders and unites it with waste.[29] For Kristeva, "the cadaver, the most sickening of detritus,"[30] represents the threat of complete formlessness; for Gertrude and her audience, a corpse that lies in mud would seem to provoke similar imaginings.

The image of "muddy death" (4.7.183), however, also figures an elemental semiosis. Mud is defined by the *Oxford English Dictionary* as a "soft, moist, glutinous material resulting from the mixing of water with soil, sand, dust, or other earthy material" ("mud," n.1). Created when water and earth meet, it inhabits boundaries under transition. Incorporating various kinds of matter, it is a vehicle of uncanny exchange. Recent eco-critical and feminist theory has explored both mud's vibrant character and its status as that which is haunted. Sonja Boon, Lesley Buter, and Daze Jeffries articulate its signifying potential: its generation of meaning through the matter with which it interacts.[31] Sara Ahmed explores its ghostliness: its power to confound the history of anything suspended or secreted within it.[32] The idea that mud is a spectral source of erasure resonates against Elizabeth Grosz's definition of the "viscous" as "a formlessness that engulfs all form, a disorder that threatens all order."[33] With varying emphases, these writers figure mud as a site of teeming life and ghostly simulacra. The image of mud with which Gertrude seals Ophelia's death is similarly double in meaning. As matter and metaphor, mud realizes, on the one hand, Ophelia's defilement; on the other, her agential (if haunted) mystery. Gertrude does not restrict mud to the dark reality of the cadaver; she also implies its association with primal origins.

Shakespeare, we should note, associates mud with a variety of meanings throughout his canon. At certain turns, he uses it to signify corruption: Lorenzo notes we cannot hear the music of the spheres while we are "grossly" enclosed in "this muddy vesture of decay" (*MV* 5.1.64–65); Prospero uses "muddy" as if it is interchangeable with "foul" when he describes his enemies' moral confusion (*Tmp.* 5.1.82); King Henry IV, regarding York's treasonous son, laments the royal stream that defiles itself "through muddy passages" (*R2* 5.3.62). At other turns, especially in *Antony and Cleopatra*, Shakespeare associates mud with that which is fecund and generative. Thus, Lepidus declares to Antony, "your serpent of Egypt now is bred of your mud by the operation of your sun; so is your crocodile" (*Ant*. 2.7.26–27); more practically, Caesar observes that seeds are best scattered on the Nile's "slime and ooze" (*Ant*. 2.7.22) if they are to thrive. The disconsolate maid described in *A Lover's Complaint* (herself a version of Ophelia) imagines mud will form "sepulchers" (46) for the ruined love tokens she casts to the river's "weeping margent" (38). Mud, Shakespeare understood, interacts with other things. Mixing earth and water, it is an elemental slurry that incorporates in its viscosity heterogeneous forms of life and detritus. It retains the print of the creatures that cross it; it gathers histories unto itself; it memorializes the fall of a leaf or feather. In time, through flood and under evaporation, mud confers new sheens and textures upon all matter (living and dead) that it touches.

Executed in viscosity, mud's union with Ophelia's corpse destabilizes boundaries. In "muddy death" (5.1.84), Ophelia retains, postmortem, a signifying power. Mud, we assume, adheres to her body, but is itself modeled by that body's weight and contours. The mud's density and flow determine where and in what position Ophelia comes to rest. At the same time, the mud is shaped by Ophelia's torso and limbs and threaded by her hair. The moistened earth in which Ophelia lies will retain the indentations left by her body; over time, those indentations will themselves be printed by rain and shaped by flux. The interactions in this palimpsest are intimate and porous; they are also trans-corporeal, demonstrating, as Stacy Alaimo would have it, that "the human is always the very stuff of the messy, contingent, emergent mix of the material world."[34] Until the silhouette of her corpse is fully smoothed away, Ophelia will cause an intermediary zone of water and earth to bear the sign of a body once present, now absent. Mud, Ahmed observes, is always about encounter.[35]

Where Gertrude imagines Ophelia's death within a landscape that is mysteriously receptive to the signifying power of her corpse, the grave diggers who appear in the next scene lay bare her death and interment. The clowns debate Ophelia's guilt as a suicide and describe death as shipping a body into the land, mocking with this metaphor Ophelia's reported passage into mud. Most heartily, they sing of the "pit of clay for to be made / For such a guest" (5.1.89–90). Recalling Laertes's reference to "the profoundest pit" to which he would damn "conscience and grace" (4.5.131), the diggers' pit suggests condemnation. These men describe Ophelia as a "guest" to be housed in earth (5.1.97, 131) much as the Doctor of Divinity imagines Ophelia "lodged" in "ground unsanctified" (5.1.229). The Doctor would have "shards, flints, and pebbles [...] thrown upon her" (5.1.231); the diggers excavate clay littered with skulls and bones.

Though clay, like mud, is a conglomerate, this place of interment does not resemble the fluvial site that initially received Ophelia's body; it is far less receptive. Shakespeare does not present the clay excavated in 5.1 as moist and malleable; it is hard and compacted. The gravemakers must work it, as their irreverent song makes clear, with pickax and spade (5.1.94). With these details, Shakespeare figures Ophelia's grave as a place of compression and confinement. Translated in mud, Ophelia's postmortem body is open to eddies of water and wind; compounded in clay, that same body is contained and invisible. The "pit of clay" (5.1.89) prepared for Ophelia obliterates identity.

As the diggers exhume skulls from the earth that will become Ophelia's grave, Hamlet initiates his commentary on death as disintegration. The skulls inspire his realization that what was once a "fine pate" (5.1.107)— a head distinguished by a subtle rarity of wit—is now "full of fine dirt" (5.1.108). Using "fine" first to signify an excellence of mind and then to describe powdered detritus, Hamlet reproduces the downward turn of that early speech in which he introduces humanity as "noble in reason [...] and infinite in faculties" (2.2.304) only to conclude man ends as a "quintessence of dust" (2.2.308). Early modern alchemical treatises used the word "quintessence" to identify a fifth element: the "aether" above the terrestrial sphere, imagined as "the incorruptible, pure, and original substance of the world magically able to preserve all sublunary things from destruction."[36] Hamlet invokes this elevated meaning only to negate it. His "quintessence of dust" insists we end as waste. In alchemical terminology, "dust" refers to the alchemist's "dregs."[37] In material terms, it signifies a pulverized form of the lowest element in the cosmic scale. Hamlet's discourse before Rosencrantz and Guildenstern uses dust in order to deny the possibility of death as transcendence; his graveside conversation with Horatio reaches an equally annihilating conclusion.

Hamlet's meditation on dust, which imagines how such powder may become the loam used to plug a bunghole or the clay to patch a wall, demystifies our postmortem reincorporation into the animate world. Though dust becomes a paste-like substance by becoming moist (accruing in this process what Plotinus identifies as the cohesive property of water), Hamlet pays scant attention to its metamorphic potential. He concentrates instead on its performance of disintegration. In the play's second scene, Gertrude admonishes her son not to "seek for [his] noble father in the dust" (1.2.71); in the graveyard, Hamlet fixes his gaze on dust and discovers its properties evince our material and metaphysical incoherence.[38] Hamlet sees in dust's unsettled movement and mingling a world ghosted by instability. Dedicated to an annihilating skepticism, his vision anticipates Walter Benjamin's notion of the *Trauerspiel*: a drama of mourning whose focus on disintegration denies even "the faintest glimmer of any spiritualization of the physical."[39] Although "dust" derives from the German noun *dunst*, meaning "vapour,"[40] Hamlet does not imagine its capacity to be airborne or to become one with a cloud. He imagines it in terms of descent. For Hamlet, dust figures not our exhalation into the universe, but our incorporation into baser forms of matter.

Like Gertrude's poetics of dissolution, which accrue meaning from geo-humoral theory, Hamlet's emphasis on our postmortem disintegration and drift participates in a larger field of reference: that of early modern atomism, which explained that changes in nature result from the movement of its tiniest particles. Though it was related to advances in mathematics, optics, and corpuscular physics, atomism also sustained the legacy of Lucretius, whose *De Rerum Natura* described the universe and the atoms of which it was comprised to be incessantly in motion, collision, and fissure. R. A. Shoaf has observed that Hamlet would have encountered atomist thought as a student at the University of Wittenberg, where the example of Lucretian materialism would have encouraged him to interrogate every process and thing within his view.[41]

Although we cannot know if Shakespeare owned the 1563–1564 edition of the *De Rerum Natura* Montaigne held in his own library, Shoaf demonstrates, especially in his close reading of *King Lear*, Shakespeare's familiarity with Lucretius's most arresting images and ideas.[42] Two passages in the *De Rerum Natura* seem implicitly to subtend Hamlet's mapping of dust. The first describes a world whose energies are mobile, chaotic, and devoid of purpose:

> If you think the firstbeginnings of things can stand still, and by standing still can beget new motions amongst things, you are astray and wander from true reasoning. For since the first-beginnings of things wander

through the void, they must needs all be carried on either by their own weight or by a chance blow from one or other. For when in quick motion they have often met and collided, it follows that they leap apart suddenly in different directions; and no wonder, since they are perfectly hard in their solid weight and nothing obstructs them from behind.[43]

Linking every subject's inevitable end to the random dispersal of its atoms, Lucretius here anticipates Hamlet's emphasis on both fissure (manifest in our disintegration into dust) and recombination (performed in our dust's incorporation in loam or clay). The second passage at issue, which closely follows the lines cited above, invites Lucretius's reader to scrutinize "an image and similitude always moving and present before our eyes": that of dust particles shifting "in everlasting conflict" within the light cast by a sunbeam.[44] Here, Lucretius foregrounds the very object of Hamlet's concentration in the graveyard.

Early modern atomist philosophy problematized both the idea of a coherent cosmos and the relationship between the cosmos and the individual.[45] In contrast to geo-humoral theory, which imagined the relationship between elemental nature and the human body as one of porosity, atomism concentrated on all things' unpredictable division, collision, and swerve. This last term (*clinamen* in Lucretius's Latin) is nearly vertiginous in association, especially in *De Rerum Natura*,[46] which links the vagaries of human will to the swerve of the atom. Considering a universe whirled in disorder, Lucretius admits, "so true is it that some hidden power grinds down humanity, and seems to trample on the noble rods and cruel axes, and hold them in derision."[47]

Hamlet's meditation on dust matches Lucretius's contemplation of *primordia* (atoms and the void) in intensity and obsession. When Hamlet asks, "why may not imagination trace the noble dust of Alexander, till 'a find it stopping a bunghole" (5.1.203–204), Horatio cautions him not to consider the problem "too curiously" (5.1.205). Hamlet, however, is determined to interrogate the meaning of minutiae: "No, faith, not a jot, but to follow him thither with modesty enough and likelihood to lead it: Alexander died, Alexander was buried, Alexander returneth to dust, the dust is earth, of earth we make loam, and why of that loam whereto he was converted might they not stop a beer-barrel?" (5.1.207–212). Tracking Alexander's "noble dust" to a decidedly ignoble end, Hamlet offers a document in disordered materiality. When he considers next how even a Caesar, "dead and turn'd to clay, / Might stop a hole to keep the wind away" (5.1.213–214), his jingling couplet reckons the reduction of even the most noble "children of the earth" (2.2.226). Here, like Lucretius, Hamlet imagines how "some hidden power grinds down humanity."[48]

As Hamlet describes our postmortem drift into a granularity whose particles are subject to new combinations, his words do not merely resonate with the terms of Lucretian atomism; they also invoke rhythms and images shaping the early modern burial liturgy. "The Order for the Burial of the Dead" in the 1559 *Book of Common Prayer* ascribes to the priest, at the moment "the earth shall be cast upon the body," the following sentence: "we therefore commit his body to the ground, earth to earth, ashes to ashes, dust to dust."[49] The three-fold organization of these words, creating a sense of the inevitable, is reprised in Hamlet's three-fold intonation: "Alexander died, Alexander was buried, Alexander returneth to dust" (5.1.208–210). Both series end with the words "to dust." Both series invite us to imagine a return to origins: one through the lens of Genesis; the other through the model of atomism. Two passages from Genesis inform the liturgical moment.[50] The first declares, "The Lord God also made the man of the dust of the grounde, and breathed in his face breath of life, and the man was a living soule"[51]; the second mandates, "In the sweat of thy face shalt thou eat bread, til thou returne to earth: for out of it wast thou taken, because thou art dust, and to dust shalt thou returne."[52] The account of human creation emphasizes the universal plenitude of Yahweh's medium; dust is everywhere and multitudinous in quantity. The sentence of death emphasizes man's diminishment in dust, which signs his waste and disintegration. Hamlet's imaginings ignore dust's primal associations and embrace its forbidding significance. Further, though Hamlet echoes a specific turn in the burial liturgy, he denies what follows it: consolation in the "sure and certaine hope of resurrection to eternal life, through our Lord Jesus Christ, who shall change our vile body that it may be like to his glorious body, according to the mighty working wherby he is able to subdue all things to himself."[53] In the place of this mystery, Hamlet tracks a sequence of material change. Postmortem, a hero turns to dust and then (by chance) to loam, which stops a hole until (by chance) the loam itself disintegrates. Hamlet does not, of course, directly entertain clay and loam's eventual degradation. The threat merely hangs in the air. For Hamlet, dust does not signify our return to primal essence; it discloses our endless drift in a void.

Hamlet's materialist conclusion counters Stephen Connor's exploration of dust as "a powerful quasi-object, a magic substance, something to conjure with."[54] Hamlet cannot see dust as a thing of exaltation: a dynamic cloud that makes the air shimmer. Neither can he see it as a veil: a layering of traces that invite interpretation. Connor, who pays particular attention to the ways in which dust is both "dispersive and concentrating," discovers in its trans-shifting a metaphor for the creative process.[55] Carolyn Steedman, recognizing that dust never disappears, discovers in its circulation a metaphor for the work of writing history.[56] Hamlet cancels dust's signifying power even as it sifts through his imagination.

In this detail, Hamlet anticipates Geoffrey Bennington's dismissal of dust as mere scatter. Unlike Connor and Steedman, Bennington denies the capacity of dust to spark and sustain "a phenomenology of the imagination"; for him, dust is "matter with no inner principle of gathering or preservation, subject only to dispersion and loss."[57] Diffused by the tiniest breath or puff of wind, Bennington's dust can maintain neither shape nor sign. Its movement is wayward; its preservation of a trace evanescent. In transient clouds and eddies, dust, Bennington insists, thwarts our search for meaning.[58] Hamlet's graveyard meditation turns upon a similar conviction.

Hamlet's insistence upon death as a process of disintegration sharply contrasts Gertrude's exploration of death as dissolution. In scenes that are contiguous with one another, Shakespeare confronts his audience with two accounts of the postmortem body. Hamlet describes in the graveyard scene how death turns great men—even an Alexander or a Caesar—into grainy matter that may stop a beer barrel or seal a wall. Gertrude imagines in her elegy for Ophelia how death translates a woman within a drift of mud. The issue of gender is crucial here. Hamlet tracks the dust into which the male body fragments; Gertrude draws our attention to the mud that embraces a female body. Hamlet's identification of the postmortem male body with dust surely derives, at least in part, from the early modern geo-humoral assumption that men's bodies were hotter than women's bodies and therefore drier and harder.[59] It makes sense that Hamlet imagines the dry male body desiccating and crumbling after death. Gertrude's meditation, quite differently, imagines the female body (itself moist, cold, and porous) dissolving within mud. Her description gathers full authority from the early modern association of female embodiment with earth as well as water. Crooke implies such linkage in his

Mikrokosmographia, which notes that human seeds must "be sown and as it were buried in the fruitfull Field of Garden of Nature, the wombe of the woman."[60] Friar Lawrence figures the association in observing how "the earth that's nature's mother is her tomb. / What is her burying grave, that is her womb" (*Rom.* 2.3.9–10). Geo-humoral theory described women and earth as similarly cold and moist; considering such description, Paster characterizes "the consequences of women's coldness [as] global."[61]

Fused in water and earth, the "muddy death" Gertrude confers upon Ophelia is far more consoling than the dust with which Hamlet imagines our reduction. Hamlet denies dust's expressive capacity and its biblical association with our origins. Dust does not eddy or rise in his imaginings. Nor does it create a film that invites interpretation. Gertrude, however, imagines Ophelia's death through a medium in which individual and collective histories meet. Mud weds the female body to the elements of earth and water that defined that body's biological plenitude and dynamism. This intimacy, in turn, figures the mud with meaning. As Ophelia's corpse shapes the moistened earth in which she is embedded, Gertrude's witness presents Ophelia and mud as storied matter. Hamlet may, in the next scene, strip both the earth and the crushed bones with which it mingles of their capacity to bear transcendent and transcorporeal meaning. Nonetheless, Gertrude's account of death as a process that is layered, deliquescent, and permeable is not easily forgotten, as the efflorescence of body and brook in Sir John Everett Millais's Pre-Raphaelite "Ophelia" (1851–1852) and Odilon Redon's symbolist *Death of Ophelia* (1905) and *Ophelia Among the Flowers* (1908) would come to underscore.

Notes

1. Ronk, pp. 26–28; Otten, pp. 397–402; Wentersdorf, pp. 413–417.
2. Coursen, p. 28.
3. Theocritus in his *Idylls* valorizes the shaded, rustic settings in which Nature itself seems to sing; Virgil presents in his *Eclogues* shepherds practicing their songs beneath the shade of a beech tree; Ovid explores in the *Metamorphoses* how seemingly ideal groves may yield danger as well as rest. See Curtius, pp. 195–200.
4. Hinds, p. 126.
5. Virgil, *Eclogues*, 1.53–55.
6. Hines, pp. 71–72.

7. On song as *locus amoenus*'s exemplary activity, see Karakasis, pp. 51–53.
8. That is, "susurro," Virgil, 1.55.
9. On the significance of the reclining poet, see Scalabrini and Stimilli, p. 35.
10. That is, "recubans," Virgil, 1.1.
11. On *ataraxia* and the *locus amoenus*, see Giesecke, pp. 1–15.
12. Plotinus, *Enneads*, 3.8.10.
13. Ibid., 6.7.32.
14. Glosses of Latin throughout follow *A Latin Dictionary*, ed. by Lewis and Short.
15. The line, cited by the *Oxford English Dictionary* ("endue / indue, v.," 1.1), reads, "For let our finger ache, and it endues / Our other healthful members even to a sense / Of pain" (*Oth*. 3.4.146–147).
16. *Oxford English Dictionary*, "endue / indue, v.," 1.1.
17. Warhaft, p. 27; Eggert, pp. 53–55.
18. On the textual crux, see Weiss, pp. 219–220; Warhaft, pp. 22–29, uses humoral theory to defend the Folio's "solid" flesh over the Q1 and Q2's "sallied" and J. Dover Wilson's "sullied."
19. *The Geneva Bible*.
20. For an overview of geo-humoral thought, see Schoenfeldt, pp. 1–15.
21. Paster (1987, pp. 44, 47–48; 2004, pp. 77–80).
22. Crooke, p. 275.
23. Paster (2004, p. 19).
24. On the willow's association with lovelorn grief in early modern song, see Brennecke, pp. 35–38.
25. Fuller, p. 144.
26. Paster (1987, p. 4; 1993, pp. 23–63).
27. Paster (2004, p. 42).
28. Neill, p. 233.
29. Kristeva, p. 69.
30. Kristeva, p. 4.
31. Boon, Buter, and Jefferies, pp. 35, 38.
32. Ahmed, p. 91.
33. Grosz, p. 203.
34. Alaimo, p. 11.
35. Ahmed, p. 90.
36. Abraham, p. 75.

37. Abraham, p. 62.
38. On Hamlet's vision of man as dust, see Reno, pp. 109–113.
39. Benjamin, p. 18.
40. *Oxford English Dictionary*, "dust n.1," etym.
41. Shoaf, p. xviii.
42. Shoaf, pp. 9–28; see also Pollack, pp. 122–132.
43. Lucretius, *De Rerum Natura*, 2.80–88.
44. Ibid., 2.114–120.
45. Crane, pp. 8–9, 16–17, 21–22; Mazzio, pp. 238–241.
46. Lucretius, 2.284–287.
47. Ibid., 5.1161.
48. Ibid., 5.1233–1234.
49. Quoted from Booty's edition of the 1559 *Book of Common Prayer*, p. 321.
50. On dust's figurative associations throughout the Old Testament, see Hillers, pp. 77–87.
51. *The Geneva Bible*, Gen. 2:7.
52. Ibid., Gen. 3:19.
53. Booty (ed.), p. 310.
54. Connor, p. 1.
55. Ibid., p. 4.
56. Steedman, pp. 164–165.
57. Bennington, p. 26.
58. Ibid., p. 30.
59. Classen, p. 72.
60. Crooke, p. 271.
61. Paster (2004, p. 85).

References

Abraham, Lyndy. *A Dictionary of Alchemical Imagery*. Cambridge: Cambridge University Press, 1998.

Ahmed, Sara. *The Cultural Politics of Emotion*. New York, NY: Routledge, 2004.

Alaimo, Stacy. *Bodily Natures: Science, Environment, and the Material Self*. Bloomington, IN: Indiana University Press, 2010.

Benjamin, Walter. *The Origin of German Tragic Drama*. Translated by John Osborne. London: Verso, 1998.

Bennington, Geoffrey. "Dust." *Oxford Literary Review* 34.1 (2012): 25–49.

Book of Common Prayer, 1559. Edited by John E. Booty. Charlottesville, VA: The University Press of Virginia, 1976.
Boon, Sonja, Lesley Buter, and Daze Jeffries. *Autoethnography and Feminist Theory at the Water's Edge: Unsettled Islands.* Aldershot: Palgrave Pivot, 2018.
Bowerbank, Sylvia. *Speaking for Nature: Women and Ecologies of Early Modern England.* Baltimore, MD: Johns Hopkins University Press, 2004.
Brennecke, Ernest. "'Nay, that's not Next!': The Significance of Desdemona's 'Willow Song'." *Shakespeare Quarterly* 4.1 (1953): 35–38.
Classen, Constance. *The Deepest Sense: A Cultural History of Touch.* Urbana, IL: University of Illinois Press, 2012.
Coursen, H. R. "Ophelia's Doubtful Death." *Christianity and Literature* 27.3 (1978): 28–31.
Connor, Steven. "Pulverulence: The Power of Powder." *Cabinet* 35 (Fall, 2009). http://www.cabinetmagazine.org/issues/35/connor.php
Crane, Mary Thomas. *Losing Touch with Nature: Literature and the New Science in Sixteenth-Century England.* Baltimore, MD: Johns Hopkins University Press, 2014.
Crooke, Helkiah. *Mikrokosmographia: A Description of the Body of Man.* London: 1615. Early English Books Online.
Curtius, Ernst Robert. *European Literature and the Latin Middle Ages.* Translated by Willard P. Trask. Princeton, NJ: Princeton University Press, 1953; rpt. 1990.
Eggert, Katherine. "*Hamlet*'s Alchemy: Transubstantiation, Alchemy, Belief." *Shakespeare Quarterly* 64.1 (Spring, 2013): 45–57.
Fuller, Thomas. *The History of the Worthies of England.* London: 1662.
The Geneva Bible: A Facsimile of the 1560 Edition. Edited by Lloyd E. Berry. Madison, WI: University of Wisconsin Press, 1969.
Giesecke, Annette Lucia. "Lucretius and Virgil's Pastoral Dream." *Utopian Studies* 10.2 (1999): 1–15.
Grosz, Elizabeth A. *Volatile Bodies: Toward a Corporeal Feminism.* Bloomington, IN: Indiana University Press, 1994.
Hillers, Delbert R. "Dust: Some Aspects of Old Testament Imagery." In *Collected Essays on Ancient Literature.* Edited by F. W. Dobbs-Allsop. Philadelphia, PA: Penn State University Press, 2015. pp. 77–87.
Hinds, Stephen. "Landscape with Figures: Aesthetics of Place in the *Metamorphoses* and its Tradition." In *The Cambridge Companion to Ovid.* Edited by Philip Hardie. Cambridge: Cambridge University Press, 2002. pp. 122–149.
Hines, Caitlin. "Vergilius Florens: Blossoming Intertexts in the *Sphragis* of the *Georgics.*" *Vergilius (1959-)* 66 (2020): 69–86.
Karakasis, Evangelos. *Song Exchanges in Roman Pastoral.* Berlin: De Gruyter, 2011.

Kristeva, Julia. *Power of Horror: An Essay on Abjection*. Translated by Leon S. Roudiez. New York, NY: Columbia University Press, 1982.
Lewis, Charlton T. and Charles Short. *A Latin Dictionary*. Oxford: The Clarendon Press, 1975.
Lucretius. *De Rerum Natura*. Translated by W. H. D. Rouse. Revised by Martin Ferguson Smith. Cambridge, MA: Harvard University Press, 1947; rpt. 1992.
Mazzio, Carla. "Coda: Scepticism and the Spectacular – On Shakespeare in an Age of Science." In *Spectacular Science, Technology and Superstition in the Age of Shakespeare*. Edited by Sophie Chiari and Mickaël Popelard. Edinburgh: Edinburgh University Press, 2017. pp. 237–244.
Neill, Michael. *Issues of Death: Mortality and Identity in English Renaissance Tragedy*. Oxford: Clarendon Press, 1997.
Otten, Charlotte F. "Ophelia's 'Long Purples' or 'Dead Men's Fingers.'" *Shakespeare Quarterly* 30.3 (Summer, 1979): 397–402.
Paster, Gail Kern. "Leaky Vessels: The Incontinent Women of City Comedy." *Renaissance Drama, New Series* 18 (1987): 43–65.
———. *The Body Embarrassed: Drama and the Disciplines of Shame in Early Modern England*. Ithaca, NY: Cornell University Press, 1993.
———. *Humoring the Body: Emotions and the Shakespearean Stage*. Chicago, IL: University of Chicago Press, 2004.
Plotinus. *The Enneads*. Translated by George Boys-Stones, John M. Dillon, Lloyd P. Gerson, R. A. H. King, Andrew Smith, and James Wilberding. Edited by Lloyd P. Gerson. Cambridge: Cambridge University Press, 2018.
Pollack, Jonathan. "Of Mites and Motes: Shakespearean Readings of Epicurean Science." In *Spectacular Science, Technology, and Superstition in the Age of Shakespeare*. Edited by Sophie Chiari and Mickaël Popelard. Edinburgh: Edinburgh University Press, 2017. pp. 119–132.
Reno, Raymond H. "Hamlet's Quintessence of Dust." *Shakespeare Quarterly* 12.2 (Spring 1961): 107–113.
Ronk, Martha C. "Representations of Ophelia." *Criticism* 36.1 (Winter, 1994): 21–43.
Scalabrini, Mossimo and Davide Stimilli. "Pastoral Postures: Some Renaissance Versions of Pastoral." *Bibliothèque d'Humanisme et Renaissance* 71.1 (2009): 35–60.
Schoenfeldt, Michael C. *Bodies and Selves in Early Modern England: Physiology and Inwardness in Shakespeare, Herbert, and Milton*. Cambridge: Cambridge University Press, 1999.
Shakespeare, William. *The Riverside Shakespeare*. Edited by G. Blakemore Evans and J. J. M. Tobin. Boston, MA: Houghton Mifflin Company, 1997.
Shoaf, R. Allen. *Lucretius and Shakespeare on the Nature of Things*. Newcastle upon Tyne, UK: Cambridge Scholars Publishing, 2014.

Steedman, Carolyn. *Dust: The Archive and Cultural History.* New Brunswick, NJ: Rutgers University Press, 2002.
Virgil. *Eclogues*. Translated by H. Rushton Fairclough. Cambridge, MA: Harvard University Press, 1978.
Warhaft, Sidney. "Hamlet's Solid Flesh Resolved." *English Literary History* 28.1 (March, 1961): 21–30.
Weiss, Samuel A. "'Solid,' 'Sullied' and Mutability: A Study in Imagery." *Shakespeare Quarterly* 10.2 (Spring, 1959): 219–227.
Wentersdorf, Karl P. "*Hamlet*: Ophelia's Long Purples." *Shakespeare Quarterly* 29.3 (Summer, 1978): 413–417.

CHAPTER 13

The Soul of Agrippina: Gender, Suicide, and Reproductive Rights in *Hamlet*

Lina Perkins Wilder

Hamlet's (and perhaps English literature's) most famous speech is about suicide, a death that provoked the same anxieties that the art of dying was meant to assuage[1]:

> To be or not to be—that is the question,
> Whether'tis nobler in the mind to suffer
> The slings and arrows of outrageous fortune
> Or to take arms against a sea of troubles
> And by opposing end them? (3.1.55–59).[2]

Hamlet's question sets aside both Christian arguments about the good death and classical debate about the good life. Hamlet denies that there is anything fundamentally important about the *way* one lives or dies,

---

L. P. Wilder (✉)
Connecticut College, New London, CT, USA
e-mail: lwilder@conncoll.edu

© The Author(s), under exclusive license to Springer Nature Switzerland AG 2022
W. E. Engel and G. Williams (eds.), *The Shakespearean Death Arts*, Palgrave Shakespeare Studies,
https://doi.org/10.1007/978-3-030-88490-1_13

whether one exists or does not exist is the urgent thing. It does not matter if one chooses "to suffer [...] Or to take arms." The classical choice between the contemplative life and the active life is simply moot. It is not *to be or to do* but *to be or not to be*. As he rejects the good life, Hamlet also rejects Christian moral thinking about suicide. The ultimate source for the Christian condemnation of suicide in the Middle Ages is St. Augustine, who argues that suicide is sinful because it represents an assertion of the human will against God's will. Along with this moral argument, Hamlet implicitly rejects the entire concept of a good death.

While Hamlet weighs the moral quality of suicide, the only characters in the play who may actually commit suicide are Ophelia and Gertrude. By allowing the duel with Laertes to occur rather than actively seeking it, Hamlet arranges his death as a martyrdom, which is passively suffered rather than actively and sinfully pursued.[3] This is made clear in the dialogue. Hamlet talks about what he's doing. He has witnesses. In contrast, Ophelia and Gertrude are defined, in death as in life, by their opacity. Questions are asked about Ophelia's death that are not asked about Hamlet's; these questions cannot be answered. Gertrude's death is perhaps even more ambiguous. There is no aside where she tells the audience why she drinks the poisoned cup. Her death may simply be an accident. She tells audiences nothing.

Hamlet is often considered a foundational text in the representation of subjectivity, but the play's treatment of subjectivity is strongly gendered.[4] Men in *Hamlet* (and, of course, particularly Hamlet himself) discuss their inner lives; women do not. But while the women do not tell us much about their thoughts, they are not treated as if they do not have such thoughts: the men around them work constantly to figure out what they are thinking. Women's sexual behavior is one very obvious target of this control. Women's deaths are another. But at every turn, Ophelia and especially Gertrude actively refuse to give access to their inner lives.

What seems to motivate investigations into Gertrude's and Ophelia's secrets is an unspoken agreement that the passivity expected of women is not natural and that women may be hiding something behind their gendered behavior.[5] In Ophelia's case, these suspicions intensify after her death. In Gertrude's, the crisis is somewhat different. In the closet scene, Hamlet does something he had done before: he calls up a classical precedent only to reject it, and with the precedent, he rejects a more active role for his mother. I have written previously about the Hecuba episode in the Player's speech.[6] Here, I argue that Hamlet's rejection of "the soul of Nero" is also implicitly a rejection of Nero's mother, Iulia Agrippina, and her open involvement in political questions. Gertrude's death closes off this line of inquiry, and her secrets remain untold. With only silence and inaction open to her, Gertrude intervenes in the final scene by dying. Paradoxically, her death is forced on her by gendered expectations, but it also represents an assertion of selfhood. Questions not only about the choice between active and contemplative life but also about the efficacy of human action lie at the heart of the play; these questions are gendered and best illustrated in the life not of Hamlet but of his mother.

SUICIDE IN EARLY MODERN EUROPE

Medieval Europeans considered suicide and the death arts to be incompatible. Killing oneself displaced the rituals of the *ars moriendi*, particularly if death was sudden. Indeed, it is possible that the rise of the death arts in the Middle Ages intensified negative ideas about suicide.[7] Nonetheless, while nearly all of Shakespeare's contemporaries would agree with Hamlet that suicide was prohibited by God, attitudes toward suicide were changing in this period.[8] Although suicide is not explicitly condemned in the Bible, medieval Christians came to consider suicide to be a form of murder and thus a deadly sin.[9] This view persisted well into the early modern period. The theological sources for this view were Augustine, who in *The City of God* (413–426 CE) condemned suicide as a defiance of the will of God, and Thomas Aquinas, who expanded Augustine's argument in *Summa Theologiae* (ca. 1265 CE).[10] With very few exceptions, European intellectuals of the sixteenth and seventeenth centuries were horrified by suicide, and their horror was shared by most of their plebeian counterparts.[11] Condemnation of suicide was the norm until the eighteenth century.

There is more than one reason for the change. A traditional view is that Enlightenment philosophy produced the first significant change in European attitudes toward suicide, as non-religious thinking began to enable Europeans to accept arguments for suicide like those used in Roman thought and to honor some who chose to die rather than to continue a life no longer worth living.[12] However, shifting legal and ecclesiastical penalties for suicide and literary and dramatic representations of suicide from the sixteenth and seventeenth centuries tell a somewhat more complicated story than one of religious prohibition replaced by non-religious allowance.[13] As Paul S. Seaver notes, beginning with Sir Thomas

More's *Utopia* in 1516, a number of English literary and discursive works, including plays like *Hamlet*, consider the morality of suicide.[14] Rome is prominent in these works but not ubiquitous.[15] While Epicureanism and Neostoicism may lead a few intellectuals, like John Donne, to defend suicide—and while a sympathetic response to suicide may thus seem to be specific to wealthy and educated men—this intellectual framework is not always necessary.[16] Seaver cites the example of the Puritan Nehemiah Wallington's 1632 treatise, *A Memorial of those that laid violent hands on themselves*: Wallington would have rejected the intellectual attitudes of Donne's *Biathanatos*, but advised Christian compassion and trust in God rather than condemnation of suicide.[17] During the seventeenth century, in many places in Europe, including England, there was a gradual decrease in legal penalties for suicide (such as postmortem hurdling, dismemberment, and display of the body; or penalties to their heirs) and ecclesiastical penalties (such as burial in unconsecrated ground).[18]

In England, legal codes beginning with the Tudors required coroners to report all "unnatural" deaths to be adjudicated by coroner's courts. A verdict of *non compos mentis* removed most of the penalties assigned to suicides, but such judgments were rare before the end of the seventeenth century, and a full Christian burial was not always the result: a *non compos mentis* verdict only ensured that the person's property would not be seized and that they might receive normal burial rites.[19] The Book of Common Prayer is silent on the subject.[20] Moreover, *non compos mentis* verdicts were rare: MacDonald finds fewer than 2% of suicide trials between 1485 and 1660 ended with such a verdict.[21] High social status could help to produce a more lenient judgment, but did not always do so.[22] Once a verdict of *felo de se* had been given, a bishop's license might allow for Christian burial.[23] Accidental death was another possible verdict, but even when deaths might have been accidental—and drowning is a central example of such an ambiguous death—juries still sometimes returned verdicts of *felo de se*.[24]

When survivors defend their friends and relatives who died by suicide, they often emphasize reasons for the suicide, such as physical pain or poverty; evidence of penitence before death; and melancholy or distraction.[25] In the 31 petitions discussed by Seaver, only two mention the devil, despite diabolical influence being "a standard trope" in discussions of suicide.[26] Suicides who survived temporarily and thus had time to repent their sins and die in a state of grace could also be defended.[27]

Ophelia's suicide is an almost perfect example of the unanswerable questions and social pressures that characterize early modern English suicides. Critics have read Gertrude's account—particularly the less rhetorically elaborate version in Q1—as similar to eyewitness testimony in a suicide trial.[28] While her intention is, as ever, unclear, Gertrude frames Ophelia's death in multiple ways that could allow her a Christian burial. She describes Ophelia as a passive victim and implies in addition that she was *non compos mentis*: betrayed by a breaking branch and by the heavy clothing that pulls her into the water as it becomes water-logged, Ophelia dies "as one incapable of her own distress" (4.7.176).[29] Even in this state, Ophelia also follows what might be a form of penitence, "chant[ing] [...] old lauds" (4.7.175).

Gertrude's death lacks this kind of postmortem defense and perhaps does not require it. But a gendered, passive suicide is not Gertrude's fate. The passivity that allows suicide to be excused is gendered, and that gendering is reflected in the characterization of Ophelia, but less so in Gertrude.[30] Gertrude contains a range of narrative possibilities in which self-assertive action, not passive suffering, predominates. Shakespeare curtails some of these possibilities when he does not include the detail from Hamlet's historical source that Gertrude, not Old Hamlet, is the inheriting monarch. Avenues for action open up again in the play's classical allusions.

Gertrude and Agrippina

O Hamlet, speak no more!
Thou turn'st my very eyes into my soul
And there I see such black and grieved spots
As will leave there their tinct. (3.4.84–88)

More than once, *Hamlet* evokes and then dismisses the possibility of a more active, more violent Gertrude through classical allusion. The Player's speech (a speech with a woman as audience, "Aeneas's talk to Dido") and the description of Hecuba is one example; the other is Hamlet's rejection of "the soul of Nero."[31] It's not as if a power-wielding Gertrude is unthinkable. In fact, giving Gertrude more power would make her more like the majority of the mature women in Shakespeare's plays, not less: Tamora, Queen Margaret, Queen Elizabeth in *Richard III*, Lady Macbeth, Volumnia, Hermione, and Paulina are only a few examples. The play works hard to eliminate Gertrude's power, and Hamlet's rejection of Nero is part of that process. Even the Ghost, who implicitly blames the Queen for committing incest, orders Hamlet to take revenge without "contriv[ing]" anything against his mother—and even without thinking about her.

As I have argued elsewhere, the description of Hecuba in the Player's speech (2.2.439–458) alludes to the mourning Hecuba of Euripides's *The Trojan Women* but also to the vengeful Hecuba of Ovid's *Metamorphoses* and Marlowe's *Dido, Queen of Carthage*, among others.[32] The Hecuba episode is a folded, complex, and multiple allusion which contains a range of sources, emotional affects, and family structures as well as evoking many different ways in which emotional or physical pain, or both, could be inflicted on Hamlet's family. The allusion contains as many false directions as it does direct parallels with the action of the play, and it invites us to think about the play's action—and in particular, its treatment of death—alongside other, sometimes contradictory possible actions. In particular, it brings to the fore the possibility of a woman taking revenge.

A similar allusive logic can be found in Hamlet's comparison of himself to Nero, an allusion in which his mother is explicitly included:

> O heart, lose not thy nature. Let not ever
> The soul of Nero enter this firm bosom—
> Let me be cruel, not unnatural:
> I will speak daggers to her but use none. (3.2.383–386)

The parallels between Nero's family and Hamlet's have been noted by editors at least since Edward Dowden, in the late nineteenth century. In their note on this passage, Ann Thompson and Neil Taylor write that Nero's famous (and probably apocryphal) examination of his murdered mother's uterus is only part of the story: "Dowden points out that [Nero's mother Iulia] Agrippina was accused of poisoning her husband and living with her brother."[33]

Dowden's account of Agrippina's actions omits some rather intriguing details. The brother whom Iulia Agrippina was accused of "living with" was the emperor Caligula; the husband she is supposed to have poisoned was the emperor Claudius; and she is said to have poisoned Claudius in order to pave the way for her son Nero to become emperor.[34] The gossip about Agrippina's sexual behavior may be further evidence of her power. Judith Ginsburg argues that the persistent rumors about incestuous or adulterous relationships among Agrippina, her sisters, and Caligula and others mask anxiety about their public visibility and political influence, which was highly unusual for Roman women.[35] Agrippina's power was considerable. Once Nero became emperor, Agrippina retained broad power and influence for a short time. Several years after she was ousted from her position of influence, she was assassinated on Nero's orders.[36]

The resonances between the plot of Hamlet and this piece of Roman history are well known: Claudius is "the type of a bad ruler" in Erasmus, and of course, "the incestuous marriage and the uncle-stepfather analogies" also find parallels in *Hamlet*.[37] The parallels line up quite neatly, allowing for the play's habitual double vision when it comes to family relationships: Claudius is the bad ruler Claudius, but also the cruel Caligula; Old Hamlet is Caligula but also Claudius; Hamlet is Nero; Gertrude is Agrippina. The analogy is not particularly kind to Old Hamlet or to Claudius: as Claudius or Caligula, they can each be either feckless or cruel. Hamlet aggressively blames his mother for her disloyalty to Old Hamlet and her marriage to Claudius, but even more than with Hecuba, the allusion to Nero and his mother evokes a less obvious choice of better and worse husbands and a much more active political role for Gertrude.

Curiously, editors and some critics find it difficult to accept the play's parallels with the lives of Agrippina, Nero, and Claudius. One reason is that *Hamlet*'s Claudius is only called by this name in the paratextual apparatus of the second Quarto and Folio texts of the play, not in the dialogue.[38] Because of this, Thompson and Taylor argue that "the analogies [between Shakespeare's Claudius and the emperor Claudius] [...] have never been available for audiences as opposed to readers."[39] Harold Jenkins argues that the mismatches between the events of the Roman emperor Claudius's life and those of Shakespeare's King Claudius should make us cautious: "since the emperor was murdered by his wife, who was murdered by her son, one must resist the temptation to extend" the analogy.[40]

But why should the analogy be false because it is part of the read text and because it rearranges the family relationships and the directions of violence already present in the play? Claudius's name could be evidence of the intervention of readers, actors, or printers rather than as the potential residue of authorial intention. The confusion of kinship relations is a central topic in *Hamlet*, evident in the incest plot and from Hamlet's bitter remarks on it in the second scene of the play ("a little more than kin and less than kind"; "My aunt-mother and uncle-father are deceived"), as well as in the plot of the Mousetrap, where the murderer, whom readers might expect would resemble Claudius, is not brother but "nephew to the king"; and, as I have suggested, in the Player's response to the Troy story. Moreover, rethinking the family relationships of *Hamlet* in light of this piece of Roman history opens up a number of possible narrative directions—versions of *Hamlet*, and of Gertrude's role in it, that might have been.

First is the Queen's potential as a political actor in her own right. In Saxo Grammaticus, it is Gerutha (Shakespeare's Gertrude), not Horwendil (Shakespeare's Old Hamlet) or his brother, who is the inheriting monarch.[41] (Granted, as De Grazia notes, Denmark was an elective monarchy rather than a patrilinear one; nonetheless, family relationships were still a source of power.)[42] Agrippina is in a similar position: while she cannot inherit the throne herself, she is a lineal descendent of the emperor Augustus, and her son Nero is the last of that line. In addition, for Agrippina, political power is not simply a matter of inheritance. As stated above, she is said to have killed for, maneuvered within, and otherwise directly intervened in the political events surrounding the rule of the three emperors. Shakespeare's play does not make clear whether Gertrude participated in or even knew about the murder of Old Hamlet; Old Hamlet himself urges his son to "leave [the Queen] to Heaven" and her own conscience. However, in Hamlet's analogy between himself and Nero, there is an allusion to a more active and powerful mother whose intimate access to kings far exceeds Hamlet's own and whose support for her son's ambitions is matched by her ambition for herself.

Second, and following closely on this, is the possibility of an alliance between Hamlet and Gertrude. Nero's mother poisoned a husband named Claudius; why couldn't Hamlet's mother do the same? There is a very real sense in which Hamlet and Claudius are rivals for Gertrude's love, and this is true even if we set aside Freudian readings of their relationship. One of Hamlet's goals in 3.4 appears to be to separate his mother from Claudius, and this is a goal that he achieves: he tells her to keep the secret of his antic disposition, and she explicitly agrees; he tells her to "go not to [his] uncle's bed" (3.4.157), and she appears to acquiesce.

Finally, there is the rivalry between Hamlet and Gertrude. The Freudian reading notwithstanding, Hamlet and Gertrude are in competition with one another as mourners and as enforcers of family decorum. Hamlet repeatedly attempts to relegate his mother to a more passive role and even to a more passive physical state (that "tame" blood). It might even be possible to suggest that Hamlet does not want to kill his father and sleep with his mother but to sleep with his Hyperion-like father and kill his mother. In fact, killing his mother is precisely the possibility that he rejects when he styles himself as a metaphorical Nero who "speak[s] daggers" but doesn't use them literally. He does hold very closely to the dagger metaphor in 3.4, where he performs a metaphorical vivisection of Gertrude by "set[ting] [...] up a glass / Where [she] may see the inmost part of herself" (3.4.18–19).

Using this "glass," Hamlet works like a sixteenth-century anatomist but also like a twenty-first century one. Seeing the inside of a woman's body was a central obsession of sixteenth-century anatomy, justified and motivated by the need to "know thyself" and to gain visual access to one's own origins in the womb: precisely what Nero is supposed to have done.[43] No less authority than Vesalius enshrined this goal on the title page of *De humani corporis fabrica*, which shows Vesalius himself pointing to the dissected uterus of a female cadaver. Twentieth- and twenty-first-century technology provides all sorts of options for perspective "glasses" that could provide visual access to Gertrude's internal parts: ultrasounds, X-rays, imaging techniques using special dyes, tiny cameras. Sixteenth-century technology does not, of course; but the men who dissected human cadavers were obsessed with seeing (at a remove) their own internal organs and with seeing their mothers' bodies as well. The access that Hamlet claims here implies violence. Certainly, this is how Gertrude and Polonius understand it.

Let me say that again: access to Gertrude's "inmost part" implies violence. This is true whether or not the moment is underlined with physical violence.[44] Hamlet should know that this will be the effect of his words. Hamlet obsessively investigates his own range, depths, and layers, but when Rosencrantz and Guildenstern attempt to gain access, he experiences their questions as violence. When it comes to what is unknowable in other people, Hamlet's rage to gain access to Claudius's inward thoughts is surpassed only by his rage to know what is unstated by his mother and Ophelia.

Even after he accidentally kills Polonius, Hamlet continues to "speak daggers" to his mother. She echoes back his figure of speech (which she does not hear), verbatim: "these words *like daggers* enter in mine ears" (3.4.93). Each of her responses, as Hamlet continues to hound her, expresses the violence of the experience. She feels her eyes turn backward in their sockets; she feels her heart cut into two pieces. It is easy to explain this response as evidence of Gertrude's guilt or shame; the "spots" she sees in herself are very much in line with the long tradition in Christian discourse where dark colors and stains are equated with personal culpability.[45] But the process of exposing that vision of inward self is one of unrelenting torture.

In plays such as *The Spanish Tragedy*, *Women Beware Women*, *The Revenger's Tragedy*, and others, women's suicides are a narrative expedient to avoid the social or legal consequences of behavior outside the norm. In many cases, such behavior includes being a victim of rape, and, implicitly, these Lucretia-imitating narratives seem to suggest that this radical loss of agency is in fact evidence of self-assertion—the rape victim is to blame and must punish herself if she is to be forgiven. Ophelia could fall into this category, if not literally, then figuratively, or even in the terms that Hamlet himself suggests: she may be "pure," but she can't escape rumors (ours). Hamlet's assault on the Queen is staged in front of us, and if it is not literally rape, it is nonetheless a violation. The Queen's culpability in the murder of Old Hamlet is not clear. As far as the audience can see, she never does anything worse than entering the kind of technically incestuous marriage that any Christian monarch might get a papal dispensation for. Her death removes her from the play's final resolution, but she is given no chance to reflect, remark, plan, or exert any control over the circumstances or timing.

Death Rights

Augustine and Aquinas taught Christians to view suicide as an assertion of the will, but the early modern experience of suicide—perhaps in defense against the Church's condemnation—was one of passivity. Whether their state of mind was understood to be caused by melancholy or by the devil, "the affected human body was passive and served merely as the battleground for external forces. Thus self-destructive wishes were found in the body and spirit of an individual but were caused by mechanisms beyond the individual's control."[46] Many people who survived suicide attempts described their state of mind using exactly the terms that Hamlet uses at the end of Act 2: they were in a state of melancholy, and the devil took advantage of this state of mind to influence them to harm themselves.[47]

All of this is gendered. Hamlet, Laertes, Polonius, and others in the play spend a lot of energy making sure that women do not assert their will. Ophelia's "doubtful" death is the culmination of a life controlled by other people's ideas. Her brother and her father dismiss her understanding of Hamlet's actions and her own. She cuts ties with Hamlet at her father's order. In her madness, Ophelia's "speech is nothing, / Yet the unshaped use of it doth move / The hearers to collection. They yawn at it / And botch the words up to fit to their own thoughts" (4.5.7–9). The King, perhaps disingenuously, hears "conceit upon her father" (4.5.45); others, including audience members, hear other motivations. It continues after her death. To her brother, dead Ophelia is an emblem of feminine innocence; to others, she is a scandalous suicide. In the end, her body and her grave are desecrated by Hamlet and Laertes, the two men who, by their own assertion, love her the most and who inflict on this putative suicide what the Church and the law did not.

The insistence on rendering women passive brings me to reproductive rights. I wouldn't be the first person to suggest that Gertrude and Ophelia sacrifice themselves in their capacity as potential mothers and vessels for the continuation of the patriarchy that the Ghost's commands and Hamlet's actions are designed to uphold.[48] This is true on a symbolic level even though actual pregnancies are not directly represented in the play. The possibility of pregnancy is quite close to the surface, however, particularly for Ophelia.[49] Several of the plants that Ophelia carries in Act 4 are abortifacients, a fact that has led a number of readers to argue that she is pregnant. While readers seem deaf to the suggestion that Gertrude could be pregnant, Ophelia's offers of rosemary and rue might imply just that.[50] Hamlet's rivalry with Gertrude herself does not preclude the possibility that Gertrude and Claudius could have a child and that that child could become Hamlet's rival in the succession. This possibility would provide a very concrete reason for Hamlet to urge his mother to "go not to my uncle's bed" (3.4.157).

Pregnancy remains a state that subjects pregnant people to assertions of control that are not, under most circumstances, considered acceptable with non-pregnant persons. These range from relatively benign actions (advice, prognostications) to questionable (unwanted touching) to egregiously invasive and even violent (certain laws regarding elective abortion, domestic partner violence). Like Hamlet, five US States (Kentucky, Louisiana, Tennessee, Texas, and Wisconsin) currently require that pregnant people seeking abortions be confronted with an image of the "inmost part" of themselves in the form of an ultrasound and that the technician describe the image in case the patient refuses to look.[51]

Two more states, Ohio and North Carolina, have similar laws, but court orders currently render them unenforceable.[52]

The goal of the ultrasound is to impart knowledge of a kind that the pregnant person has no access to on their own. That knowledge takes the form of an image. The facilities known as "crisis pregnancy centers" appear to pursue this goal when they offer ultrasounds (if, often, no other medical care) to pregnant people. True Care Women's Resource Center, for example, in Casper, Wyoming, provides an anecdote about a teenager who accepts an ultrasound and gains transformative knowledge: "Our patient's brown eyes grew large and round. 'I never imagined I was that far along!' she said in a shocked voice."[53] With her childlike "round" eyes, this woman is the very picture of innocence disrupted by the "shock" of new knowledge. One imagines that she will act differently now that she has this knowledge. However, evidence suggests that this kind of transformation does not actually happen in many cases: whether they had a positive or negative emotional experience when viewing an ultrasound, and even whether the ultrasound is mandated or not, most pregnant people do not change their minds about abortion after seeing an ultrasound.[54]

Access to knowledge about one's own health is governed by strict ethical rules for the very reason that such knowledge is a source of power. Medical ethicists accuse crisis pregnancy centers of a range of misleading practices, including incorrect information about abortion and contraception; vague information about the qualifications of their employees, who often are not medically trained; and a strategy of targeting vulnerable communities, such as the poor and people of color (thus, perhaps, the dark color of the "patient's" eyes).[55] When Hamlet asserts control over Gertrude's interior, and when he claims to be able to make her "inmost part" visible, he follows the same logic as state legislatures and crisis pregnancy centers who push ultrasounds on pregnant people: Gertrude does not understand herself; he will make her understand. His privileged knowledge takes precedence over her lived experience, and his need to see and know, and for her to see and know, takes precedence over any desire she may have to keep her own counsel.

The right to comprehensive, informed reproductive care is based on the fundamental Enlightenment idea of individual rights, and from the start, many people have found it difficult to accept that these rights extend to anyone other than white men. Wherever readers may place Hamlet with regard to individualism, he does hold his own choices in fairly high regard. He never does the same for Gertrude or Ophelia. When it comes to their reproductive and wifely functions—and Hamlet considers little else—women are at fault, in Hamlet's eyes. They are at fault whenever they do anything other than what he wants them to do. Hamlet may reject Nero as a model for his actions, but he embraces Nero as a metaphor; he uses no daggers, but speaks many.

Denmark's elective monarchy should free Gertrude from some of these pressures. Hamlet is adopted, not born, as his uncle's heir, and the Queen's fertility is not really a topic of discussion. In an inherited monarchy, a queen's pregnancy could be the object of deep anxiety. However, in contrast to Hecuba, with her "lank and all o'er-teemed loins" and her twenty children, Gertrude never seems to act merely as a vessel for the next generation. She has only one child.

However, a non-pregnant Gertrude is not exempt from Hamlet's scalpel. Hamlet lays claim to his mother's interior not only as a potential mother for future monarchs but also, and more obviously, as a place of moral reckoning. He attempts to control her thoughts, motivations, and actions. Her control of that space, and her refusal to reveal its contents, in turn, makes her dangerous. Active intervention in matters of life and death made suicide morally repugnant to medieval and early modern European Christians. It is no mistake that Gertrude—who works so hard, rhetorically, to make sure that Ophelia's death is couched in the passive terms that would make it morally acceptable—dies with an unreasonable, unexplained assertion of will. Claudius tells her not to drink; she defies him: "I will, my lord. I pray you pardon me" (5.2.274).

Notes

1. The relatively few scholarly treatments of Shakespeare and suicide include Wymer, *Suicide and Despair in the Jacobean Drama*; MacDonald, "Ophelia's Maimèd Rites"; Sanderson, "Suicide as Message and Metadrama in English Renaissance Tragedy"; Smith, "Neither Accident nor Intent: Contextualizing the Suicide of Ophelia"; Clare, "'Buried in the Open Fields': Early Modern Suicide and the Case of Ofelia." MacDonald, a historian, has written extensively on the history of suicide (cited below).
2. Quotations from *Hamlet* follow the Arden edition, third series, edited by Ann Thompson and Neil Taylor (London: Thompson

Learning, 2006). I have replaced their semicolon after line 55 with a comma.
3. On Hamlet's death as suicide, see Pollin, "Hamlet: A Successful Suicide."
4. While gender is the most relevant parameter for the purposes of this essay, subjectivity in the play is also marked in terms of class and race. For a summary of the critical conversation regarding Hamlet's (the character's) subjectivity, see Slater in "The Ghost in the Machine: Emotion and Mind–Body Union in *Hamlet* and Descartes," pp. 593–620, esp. pp. 593–595. On Gertrude's subjectivity, see Montgomery, "Enter QUEEN GERTRUDE Stage Center: Re-Viewing Gertrude as Full Participant and Active Interpreter in *Hamlet*."
5. On Ophelia's passivity, see Fischer, "Hearing Ophelia: Gender and Tragic Discourse in *Hamlet*," pp. 1–10, esp. pp. 1–2.
6. Wilder, *Shakespeare's Memory Theatre: Recollection, Properties, and Character*, pp. 114–121.
7. Brown, *The Art of Suicide*, p. 50.
8. On suicide in early modern Europe, see Watt, ed., *From Sin to Insanity: Suicide in Early Modern Europe*; Brown, esp. pp. 49–145, pp. 1–2; Minois, *History of Suicide: Voluntary Death in Western Culture*; Murray, *Suicide in the Middle Ages*.
9. On biblical suicides and medieval visual art, see Brown, pp. 56–72.
10. Primary-source material from many traditions is excerpted in Battin, ed., *The Ethics of Suicide Digital Archive*. Watt, p. 2, p. 4; Brown, pp. 50–51. On Augustine and suicide, see Sato, pp. 135–142; see also Braden, "Fame, Eternity, and Shakespeare's Romans," pp. 37–55, esp. pp. 38–39.
11. Watt, p. 6; Vera Lind, "The Suicidal Mind and Body: Examples from Northern Germany," pp. 64–80, esp. p. 67.
12. Watt, pp. 1–2.
13. Ibid., pp. 4–5. But see MacDonald and Murphy, *Sleepless Souls: Suicide in Early Modern England*, pp. 42–76; MacDonald, "Ophelia's Maimèd Rites," p. 315.
14. Seaver, "Suicide and the Vicar General in London: A Mystery Solved?", pp. 25–47, esp. 39–40.
15. Ibid., pp. 42–45. On suicide in early modern art, see Brown, p. 14, pp. 49–145.

16. On social class, see ibid., p. 49; MacDonald, "Ophelia's Maimèd Rites," pp. 315–316.
17. Seaver, pp. 45–46.
18. Ibid., p. 26; Watt, pp. 4–5; Brown, pp. 88–89. Braden, p. 39, states that penalties *increased* during the early modern period, but the historical evidence discussed in the Watt collection suggests otherwise, at least for the seventeenth century.
19. MacDonald, "Ophelia's Maimèd Rites," p. 310; Seaver, pp. 26–27, p. 47. See also MacDonald, "The Secularization of Suicide in England 1660–1800"; MacDonald and Murphy, *Sleepless Souls*, pp. 24–28, pp. 346–353; MacDonald, *Mystical Bedlam: Madness, Anxiety, and Healing in Seventeenth Century* England, p. 135.
20. Macdonald, "Ophelia's Maimèd Rites," p. 310, pp. 313–314.
21. Ibid., p. 3130.
22. Seaver, pp. 30–32; MacDonald, "Ophelia's Maimèd Rites," p. 313.
23. Seaver, pp. 30–32.
24. Ibid., p. 30, p. 31; MacDonald, "Ophelia's Maimèd Rites," pp. 311–313.
25. Seaver, pp. 32–38.
26. Ibid., pp. 37–38. On the devil and suicide, see also Smith, pp. 102–103.
27. Lind, p. 68.
28. Clare, pp. 246–247.
29. On passivity, see MacDonald, "Ophelia's Maimèd Rites," p. 313.
30. Brown, *Art of Suicide*, p. 92, 94.
31. On *Hamlet* and the Claudius-Agrippina-Nero family, see E. G. Berry, "*Hamlet* and Suetonius," *Phoenix* 2, no. 3 (1948 Autumn): 73–81; Richard Dutton, "*Hamlet* and Succession," in *Doubtful and Dangerous: The Question of Succession in Late Elizabethan England*, ed. Susan Doran and Paulina Kewes (Manchester: Manchester University Press, 2014), 173–191, esp. 183; Catherine Belsey, "Hamlet and Early Modern Stage Ghosts," in *Gothic Renaissance: A Reassessment*, ed. Elisabeth Bronfen and Beate Neumeier (Manchester: Manchester University Press, 2014), pp. 32–54, esp. p. 35; and the Arden editions cited below.
32. Wilder, *Shakespeare's Memory Theatre*, pp. 116–117, 119–121. On Hecuba and revenge, see Sarah Carter, "*Titus Andronicus* and Myths of Maternal Revenge," *Cahiers Elisabéthains* 77.1 (2010

Spring): 37–49; and, with special relevance to *Hamlet*, pp. 44–49. But see also Margreta de Grazia, "*Hamlet*" *without Hamlet* (Cambridge: Cambridge UP, 2007), pp. 11–12, 20.
33. Ann Thompson and Neil Taylor, eds., *Hamlet* (London: Thomson Learning, 2006), p. 325n; and Edward Dowden, ed., *The Tragedy of Hamlet* (Indianapolis: Bowen Merrill, 1899), p. 131n.
34. John Percy Vyvian Dacre Balsdon and Antony J. S. Spawforth, "Iulia Agrippina," Oxford Classical Dictionary (Oxford: Oxford University Press, 2012), https://www.oxfordreference.com/view/10.1093/acref/9780199545568.001.0001/acref-9780199545568-e-3372#. On Agrippina, see Judith Ginsburg, *Representing Agrippina: Constructions of Female Power in the Early Roman Empire* (Oxford: Oxford University Press, 2005).
35. Ginsburg, *Representing Agrippina*, 12–13.
36. Balsdon and Spawforth, "Iulia Agrippina."
37. Harold Jenkins, ed., *Hamlet* (London: Methuen, 1982), p. 163n; and Thompson and Taylor, p. 141n.
38. Jenkins, ed., *Hamlet*, p. 163n; Thompson and Taylor, eds., *Hamlet*, p. 141n.
39. Thompson and Taylor, eds., *Hamlet*, p. 141n.
40. Jenkins, ed., *Hamlet*, p. 163n; see also De Grazia, *Hamlet without "Hamlet,"* pp. 10–12.
41. Jenkins, ed., *Hamlet*, p. 86.
42. De Grazia, Hamlet *without Hamlet*, pp. 87–89.
43. On dissection and taboos, see Jonathan Sawday, *The Body Emblazoned: Dissection and the Human Body in Renaissance Culture* (Cambridge: Cambridge University Press, 1996), pp. 11–12.
44. On violence, see Thompson and Taylor, eds., *Hamlet*, pp. 335–336n.
45. On the spots, see David Sterling Brown, "(Early) Modern Literature: Crossing the Color-Line," *Radical Teacher* 105 (2016 Summer): 69–77, esp. pp. 72–73; Patricia Parker, "Black Hamlet: Battening on the Moor," *Shakespeare Studies* 31 (2003): 127–164.
46. Lind, "Suicidal Mind," pp. 69, 79–80.
47. Lind, "Suicidal Mind," p. 69.
48. Carla Freccero, "Forget *Hamlet*," *Shakespeare Quarterly* 62.2 (2011 Summer): 170–173, esp. p. 173.

49. On Ophelia's pregnancy, see Maurice Hunt, "Impregnating Ophelia," *Neophilogus* 89 (2005): 641–663, esp. pp. 641–642. On plants, see Lucile F. Newman, "Ophelia's Herbal," *Economic Botany* 33, no. 2 (1979 April–June): 227–232; Robert Painter and Brian Parker, "Ophelia's Flowers Again," *Notes and Queries* 41.1 (1994 March): 42; Magin Lasov Gregg, "Reading *Hamlet* 3.1.121 as Remembrance of *Richard II* 5.1.23," *ANQ: A Quarterly Journal of Short Articles, Notes, and Reviews* 22.8 (2010 July): 8–13, https://doi.org/10.1080/08957690903227639; James Persoon, "Hamlet," *The Explicator* 55.2 (1997 Winter): 70–71.
50. In an unpublished paper, my former student, Isabelle Smith, discusses this possibility at length.
51. Guttmacher Institute, "Requirements for Ultrasound," 1 June 2021; https://www.guttmacher.org/state-policy/explore/requirements-ultrasound#. See also Advancing New Standards in Reproductive Health, "Mandatory ultrasound viewing does little to dissuade women from getting abortions," University of California San Francisco, 26 July 2017; https://www.ansirh.org/research/research/mandatory-ultrasound-viewing-does-little-dissuade-women-getting-abortions.
52. Guttmacher Institute, "Requirements for ultrasound."
53. True Care Women's Resource Center, "3 Reasons to Have an Ultrasound before Abortion," https://truecarecasper.org/3-important-reasons-to-have-an-ultrasound-before-an-abortion/. True Care is listed under "ministries" on the website of the Mountain View Baptist Church in Mills, Wyoming. Mountain View Baptist Church, "Ministry Outreach," Mills, WY; http://www.mvbccasper.com/site/ministryteams.asp?sec_id=180014995.
54. Ellen R. Wiebe and Lisa Adams, "Women's perceptions about seeing the ultrasound picture before an abortion," *European Journal of Contraception and Reproductive Care* 14.2 (2009 April): 97–102; https://doi.org/10.1080/13625180902745130. U.D. Upadhyay, K. Kimport, E.K.O. Belusa, N.E. Johns, D.W. Laube, and S.C.M. Roberts, "Evaluating the impact of a mandatory pre-abortion ultrasound viewing law: A mixed methods study," *PLoS One* 12.7 (2017 July 26): e0178871; https://doi.org/10.1371/journal.pone.0178871.

55. Amy G. Bryant and Jonas J. Swartz, "Why Crisis Pregnancy Centers Are Legal but Unethical," *AMA Journal of Ethics* 20.3 (2018): 269–277; https://doi.org/10.1001/journalofethics.2018.20.3.pfor1-1803.

REFERENCES

Advancing New Standards in Reproductive Health. "Mandatory ultrasound viewing does little to dissuade women from getting abortions." University of California San Francisco, 26 July 2017. https://www.ansirh.org/research/research/mandatory-ultrasound-viewing-does-little-dissuade-women-getting-abortions.

Balsdon, John Percy Vyvian Dacre, and Antony J. S. Spawforth. "Iulia Agrippina." In *Oxford Classical Dictionary*. Oxford: Oxford University Press, 2012. https://www.oxfordreference.com/view/10.1093/acref/9780199545568.001.0001/acref-9780199545568-e-3372#.

Battin, Margaret Pabst (ed.). *The Ethics of Suicide Digital Archive*. University of Utah. https://ethicsofsuicide.lib.utah.edu.

Berry, E. G. "*Hamlet* and Suetonius." *Phoenix* 2.3 (1948 Autumn): 73–81.

Belsey, Catherine. "Hamlet and Early Modern Stage Ghosts." In *Gothic Renaissance: A Reassessment*. Edited by Elisabeth Bronfen and Beate Neumeier. Manchester: Manchester University Press, 2014. pp. 32–54.

Braden, Gordon. "Fame, Eternity, and Shakespeare's Romans." In *Shakespeare and Renaissance Ethics*. Edited by Patrick Gray and John D. Cox. Cambridge: Cambridge University Press, 2014. pp. 37–55.

Brown, David Sterling. "(Early) Modern Literature: Crossing the Color-Line." *Radical Teacher* 105 (2016 Summer): 69–77.

Brown, Ron. *The Art of Suicide*. London: Reaktion Books, 2004.

Bryant, Amy G., and Jonas J. Swartz. "Why Crisis Pregnancy Centers are Legal but Unethical." *AMA Journal of Ethics* 20.3 (2018): 269–277. https://doi.org/10.1001/journalofethics.2018.20.3.pfor1-1803.

Carter, Sarah. "*Titus Andronicus* and Myths of Maternal Revenge." *Cahiers Elisabéthains* 77.1 (2010 Spring): 37–49.

Clare, Janet. "'Buried in the Open Fields': Early Modern Suicide and the Case of Ofelia." *Journal of Early Modern Studies* 2 (2013): 241–252.

De Grazia, Margreta. "*Hamlet*" *without Hamlet*. Cambridge: Cambridge University Press, 2007.

Dowden, Edward (ed.). *The Tragedy of Hamlet*. Indianapolis, IN: Bowen Merrill, 1899.

Dutton, Richard. *"Hamlet* and Succession." In *Doubtful and Dangerous: The Question of Succession in Late Elizabethan England*. Edited by Susan Doran and Paulina Kewes. Manchester: Manchester University Press, 2014. pp. 173–191.
Fischer, Sandra K. "Hearing Ophelia: Gender and Tragic Discourse in *Hamlet.*" *Renaissance and Reformation/Renaissance Et Réforme*, New Series/Nouvelle Série, 14.1 (1990): 1–10. http://www.jstor.org/stable/43444750.
Freccero, Carla. "Forget *Hamlet.*" *Shakespeare Quarterly* 62.2 (2011 Summer): 170–173.
Ginsburg, Judith. *Representing Agrippina: Constructions of Female Power in the Early Roman Empire*. Oxford: Oxford University Press, 2005.
Guttmacher Institute. "Requirements for Ultrasound." 1 June 2021. https://www.guttmacher.org/state-policy/explore/requirements-ultrasound.
Hunt, Maurice. "Impregnating Ophelia." *Neophilogus* 89 (2005): 641–663.
Jenkins, Harold (ed.). *Hamlet*. London: Methuen, 1982.
Gregg, Magin Lasov. "Reading *Hamlet* 3.1.121 as Remembrance of *Richard II* 5.1.23." *ANQ* 22.8 (2010 July): 8–13. https://doi.org/10.1080/08957690903227639.
Lind, Vera. "The Suicidal Mind and Body: Examples from Northern Germany." In *From Sin to Insanity*. Edited by Jeffrey Watt. Ithaca, NY: Cornell University Press, 2018. pp. 64–80.
MacDonald, Michael. *Mystical Bedlam: Madness, Anxiety, and Healing in Seventeenth Century England*. Cambridge: Cambridge University Press, 1981.
———. "Ophelia's Maimèd Rites." *Shakespeare Quarterly* 37.3 (1986 Autumn): 309–317.
———. "The Secularization of Suicide in England 1660–1800." *Past and Present* 111 (1986): 50–97.
MacDonald, Michael, and Terence R. Murphy. *Sleepless Souls: Suicide in Early Modern England*. Oxford: Oxford University Press, 1990.
Minois, Georges. *History of Suicide: Voluntary Death in Western Culture*. Translated by Lydia G. Cochrane. Baltimore: Johns Hopkins University Press, 1999.
Montgomery, Abigail. "Enter QUEEN GERTRUDE Stage Center: Re-Viewing Gertrude as Full Participant and Active Interpreter in *Hamlet.*" *South Atlantic Review* 74.3 (2009 Summer): 99–117.
Mountain View Baptist Church. "Ministry Outreach." Mills, WY. http://www.mvbccasper.com/site/ministryteams.asp?sec_id=180014995.
Murray, Alexander. *Suicide in the Middle Ages*. 2 vols. Oxford: Oxford University Press, 1998–2000.
Newman, Lucile F. "Ophelia's Herbal." *Economic Botany* 33.2 (1979 April–June): 227–232.

Painter, Robert, and Brian Parker. "Ophelia's Flowers Again." *Notes and Queries* 41.1 (1994 March): 42ff.
Parker, Patricia. "Black Hamlet: Battening on the Moor." *Shakespeare Studies* 31 (2003): 127–164.
Persoon, James. "Hamlet." *The Explicator* 55.2 (1997 Winter): 70–71.
Pollin, Burton R. "Hamlet: A Successful Suicide." *Shakespeare Studies* 1 (1965): 240–260.
Sanderson, Richard K. "Suicide as Message and Metadrama in English Renaissance Tragedy." *Comparative Drama* 26.3 (1992 Fall): 199–217.
Sato, Makiko. "The Prohibition of Suicide for Affirmation of Human Beings by Augustine." *Scrinium* 11.1 (2015): 135–142. https://doi.org/10.1163/18177565-00111p14.
Sawday, Jonathan. *The Body Emblazoned: Dissection and the Human Body in Renaissance Culture*. Cambridge: Cambridge University Press, 1996.
Seaver, Paul S. "Suicide and the Vicar General in London: A Mystery Solved?" In *From Sin to Insanity* Edited by Jeffrey Watt. Ithaca, NY: Cornell University Press, 2018. pp. 25–47.
Shakespeare, William. *Hamlet*. Edited by Ann Thompson and Neil Taylor. London: Thompson Learning, 2006.
Slater, Michael. "The Ghost in the Machine: Emotion and Mind-Body Union in *Hamlet* and Descartes." *Criticism* 58.4 (2016 Fall): 593–620.
Smith, Barbara. "Neither Accident nor Intent: Contextualizing the Suicide of Ophelia." *South Atlantic Review* 73.2 (Spring 2008): 96–112.
True Care Women's Resource Center, "3 Reasons to Have an Ultrasound before Abortion," https://truecarecasper.org/3-important-reasons-to-have-an-ultrasound-before-an-abortion/.
Upadhyay, U.D., K. Kimport, E.K.O. Belusa, N.E. Johns, D.W. Laube, and S.C.M. Roberts, "Evaluating the Impact of a Mandatory Pre-abortion Ultrasound Viewing Law: A Mixed Methods Study." *PLoS One* 12, no. 7 (2017 July 26): e0178871; https://doi.org/10.1371/journal.pone.0178871.
Watt, Jeffrey R. (ed.). *From Sin to Insanity: Suicide in Early Modern Europe*. Ithaca, NY: Cornell University Press, 2004.
Wiebe, Ellen R., and Lisa Adams, "Women's Perceptions about Seeing the Ultrasound Picture before an Abortion." *European Journal of Contraception and Reproductive Care* 14, no. 2 (2009 April): 97–102. https://doi.org/10.1080/13625180902745130.
Wilder, Lina Perkins. *Shakespeare's Memory Theatre: Recollection, Properties, and Character*. Cambridge: Cambridge University Press, 2010.
Wymer, Rowland. *Suicide and Despair in the Jacobean Drama*. London: Harvester, 1986.

CHAPTER 14

Artless Deaths in *Hamlet*: The Play as *Danse Macabre*

Isabel Karremann

In a play that counts no fewer than nine deaths, and which has supplied the most iconic moment of *memento mori* in Western culture, it is remarkable that there is not a single good or "artful" death in *Hamlet*. None is in keeping with the death arts that aimed at preparing a Christian for dying well, through meditation and prayer, with a clear conscience, at peace with all men, and patience in suffering. The play presents instead a series "Of carnal, bloody, and unnatural acts / Of accidental judgments, casual slaughters, / Of deaths put on by cunning, and for no cause," as Horatio bemoans (5.2.365–67). Ironically, the one death that most closely resembles a good one is withheld when Hamlet refuses to kill a seemingly repentant Claudius at prayer.

This series of "maimed rites" (5.1.218) has given rise to readings of the play as dramatizing the departure from traditional ways of dying brought

---

I. Karremann (✉)
English Department, University of Zurich, Zurich, Switzerland
e-mail: karremann@es.uzh.ch

about by the Reformation. The Reformation constituted the most disruptive experience in the ritual culture of Renaissance England, especially concerning rites of mourning and remembrance. How these rites, and the psycho-social functions they fulfilled, migrated to other cultural sites has received much critical attention in the past twenty years. In particular, their migration to the profane space of the theater has been persuasively explained by the structural affinity of loss, grief, and remembrance with dramatic genres whose plots are driven by violent death and the question of how to deal with its aftermath. Yet, there is a side to the *ars moriendi* that remains comparatively understudied by scholars of early modern drama: how to prepare for a good death. It is this dimension of the medieval death arts which survived into the post-Reformation era, where it thrived—albeit in necessarily changed form—in a Protestant theology that placed special emphasis on the final moment before death.[1] Once notions like Purgatory and intercessory prayer had been abandoned, "the actions of the living could have no effect on the dead"[2]; and therefore, it was "one's state of mind at the final instant of life [that] eternally committed one's soul to salvation or damnation."[3] For Protestants, a good death became a matter of a subjectively apprehended right relation to God, to be forged through prayer and meditation. At the same time, however, the fate of the soul was of course not entirely a matter of *sola fide*: the notions of predestination and election introduced an unresolvable tension into the reformed death arts.[4]

Hamlet registers both the survival of the medieval *ars moriendi* and their changed status in post-Reformation England. When the Ghost of Hamlet's father complains that he went to his death "[u]nhouseled, disappointed, unaneled" (1.5.77) he evokes the Catholic good death that consists in the proper ritual forms of communion, confession, and extreme unction.[5] The counter-image to this unprepared and therefore bad death is staged when we see Claudius at prayer, making "his soul [...] fit and seasoned for his passage" (3.3.85–86). Yet, what looks like a good death at first glance is none: Claudius's repentance is merely a gesture driven by fear, and therefore remains inefficacious. His insincerity registers a wide-spread anxiety about achieving grace through faith. Achsah Guibbory calls this the "trauma of grace" and explains it as the combined result of the abolition of sacraments, through which God could be reliably and reassuringly accessed, and the pressures of predestination: if "salvation was now solely a matter of faith and God's grace," she comments, this "could also produce a sense of loss and anxiety."[6] What if one's faith was not strong enough? What if prayer as the external sign of contrition was not matched with sincere internal repentance? What if in prayer one's "thoughts remain below" (3.3.97)? These two moments in *Hamlet* raise the question of how to prepare properly for death. They evoke the Christian death arts as an important frame of reference in which the string of seemingly gratuitous deaths that *Hamlet* presents could have been understood by Shakespeare's audience as a lesson about both morality and mortality.

This frame is provided more specifically by the tradition of the *danse macabre*, in which human figures "dance" with a figure of death, often without recognizing that their final moment has come, and who therefore die a sudden death, unprepared and unrepentant of their sins: a *mors improvisa* like Old Hamlet's and, more sinister, like Claudius's. The *danse macabre* emerged as a pictorial and literary theme in late-medieval Europe. The earliest extant Dance of Death-poem, the Spanish *Dança general de la muerte*, was composed around 1400; its earliest visual representation (accompanied by verses) was a mural at the Cemetery of the Holy Innocents, Paris, dating from 1425. This was in turn the model for a mural created in 1430 on the walls of the Pardon Court of St. Paul's Cathedral, London. The French verses were translated by the monk John Lydgate, yet "with its fat abbot and well-dressed abbess, its dissolute monk and its worldly parson, could easily be reread for Protestantism" more than a hundred years later.[7] Further depictions in churches and increasingly also in paintings emerged across the divide of the Reformation. The Grossmünster at Basle featured a Dance of Death on the walls of the Dominican cemetery, created in the fifteenth century; it survived the iconoclasm of 1529 and was later restored to reflect reformed sensibilities, with the preacher-figure bearing the features of the Reformer Johannes Oekolampad. It probably inspired the German-born artist Hans Holbein, who in the 1520s created in his workshop at Basle what would become one of the most popular and "most extended elaboration of the Dance-theme" in a series of forty-one printed woodcuts.[8] In post-Reformation England, the theme appeared on popular broadsides such as "The Daunce and Song of Death" by John Awdely in 1569, in which dancing skeletons pull into a circle pairs of antithetical types; an anonymous broadside of c.1580 shows a bishop preaching to a line of figures, first a king, then a woman, a lawyer, and a laborer, pursued by Death; and as late as 1625, the ballad "Death's Dance" features visual elements, including a deathbed scene linking it to the *ars moriendi* tradition.[9] The purpose of these murals, paintings, engravings, or woodcuts was "to teach and impress, but also to change lives in preparation for imminent death," typically through the negative example of figures surprised by Death or violently rejecting his coming, with only few following complacently.[10] No doubt they also attracted attention because of their social critique, which afforded the spectators some measure of triumph at seeing their betters humiliated and all made equal by Death.

The bad or "artless" deaths that Shakespeare's *Hamlet* stages cannot therefore be explained only as a reflection of the dysfunctional rites "maimed" by the Reformation. Rather, the bad death was a familiar motif and a functional didactic device in the death arts. *Hamlet*, I argue, echoes this tradition, which continued to flourish in the fifteenth and sixteenth centuries. By situating the play in this historical context, we can see how it harks back to the medieval *ars moriendi* across the divide of the Reformation.[11] This provides a broader basis for interpretation in which also the *ars memoria*, frequently noted as a dominant device in the play, can be integrated.[12] It complements our understanding of the theater's cultural and socio-psychological function as coming to terms not only with the loss of beloved persons but also with one's own mortality. In particular, the iconography of the Dance and the reception attitudes it invited provide a model for the ways in which *Hamlet* prompts its audience to meditate on their own mortality. I will trace this "mortal dramaturgy" through scenes in which Hamlet appears with figures of death or those in which Hamlet himself becomes a *memento mori* figure, through his soliloquies as meditations on mortality, and through metatheatrical moments that highlight the play's affinities with the *danse macabre*.

Hamlet with Figures of Death

The most iconic moment of the play links it directly to the *memento mori* tradition: Hamlet in the graveyard, contemplating a skull in his hand and reflecting on man's mortality. While the presentation of this scene on the stage was likely a theatrical innovation, Shakespeare's audience would have been familiar with it as a topos that existed in various art forms in England and on the continent.[13] Paintings, engravings, prints, and allegorical carvings on tombs employed the skull as a symbol of death. Introduced to England by Hans Holbein with the famous portrait *The Ambassadors*, young men with skulls became a popular subject.[14]

This visual culture established a reference frame for Shakespeare's audience in which Hamlet's meditation upon a skull could be understood not as "uniquely morbid" but as participating in a rich tradition of the death arts.[15] The scene is also connected to the *danse macabre* in particular: Hamlet holding forth on the vanity of the world doubles as the Preacher-figure from medieval morality plays and as an engaged viewer, providing both didactic instruction and an affective identification point for the spectators.[16] His sermon promises a leveling of the world's hierarchies after death—an appealing message for a dispossessed Prince and a popular audience alike.[17] As Hamlet comments on the various estates leveled by death—the politician, the courtier, the lady, and the lawyer—he evokes familiar protagonists from the Dance and engages in the estates-satire characteristic of this genre where Death is often shown mocking his victims, who typically represent positions of clerical, political or economic power. The Dance thus functioning also as a tool of social criticism: social hierarchies are parodically acknowledged only to be dissolved by Death as the great leveler.[18] Thus while "the graveyard scene's abundant *memento mori* direct thought to the next world," de Grazia comments, it also taps into "a long tradition of radical protest."[19] Likewise, Hamlet's lament for the clown Yorick, whose skull Hamlet believes to be holding, is not merely a moment of individual nostalgia; Yorick becomes Death personified, sent to "my lady's table [to] tell her, let her paint an inch thick, to this favour she must come" (5.1.182–84). This echoes two woodcuts from Holbein's series, "The Countess" assisted in her toilette by a *mors*, embodying the lesson of *vanitas mundi*, and "The Queen" (see Fig. 14.1) torn from her family by a clownesque "capering *transi* in his antic cap and bells."[20]

This motif moreover forges a connection between the figure of Death and the fool, which will later become important for understanding Hamlet's "antic disposition" (1.5.170). Here, however, it is the singing, riddling grave-digger who is identified in the stage directions and speech prefixes as a "clown," a rural figure who "to sophisticated city audiences and readers" would have appeared as a comical figure[21] and whom they could have recognized as the "Sexton Death" from paintings of youths in graveyards.[22]

Scenes where the dead emerge as animated presences among the living provide variations on the theme and deepen *Hamlet*'s connection to the Dance of Death. Thus, the Ghost of Hamlet's father makes several appearances in "the same figure like the King that's dead" (1.1.40) and "in his habit, as he lived!" (3.4.135). Such life-like figures were a familiar

Fig. 14.1 Hans Holbein, death abducts a queen

feature of funeral tombs displaying an effigy of the dead for the mourners to behold and be remembered by. The animation effect is taken a step further with the story of the King's murder: it evokes a scene in which the audience, both onstage and before the stage, are to imagine the King still living and suddenly brought to a bad death by his brother Claudius in the role of Death. Claudius is explicitly likened to the serpent (1.5.39) in the Garden Eden, turning the scene into "a re-enactment of the original sin, in which mankind became a mortal being."[23] We can find the corresponding scene in Holbein's *Dance of Death*, entitled "The Temptation;" from then on, Adam and Eve and their offspring are accompanied by the figure of Death.

Old Hamlet's death is the worst imaginable in medieval culture, a *mors improvisa*. Sleeping in his orchard, he is

> Cut off even in the blossoms of my sin
> Unhouseled, disappointed, unaneled
> No reckoning made but sent to my account
> With all my imperfections on my head. (1.5.76–79)

The suddenness of this death and Claudius's role as *mors* are again highlighted later: "'A took my father grossly, full of bread / With all his crimes broad blown, as flush as May" (3.3.80–81). In Greenblatt's reading, both scenes develop their full force in the context of the *ars moriendi*: that Hamlet senior is "full of bread" marks him as someone living in the midst of his ordinary life and in contrast to someone who, anticipating death, puts his spiritual house in order through fasting, as well as through communion (houseling), deathbed confession (appointment), and anointing (aneling).[24] At the same time, the language of eating evokes the corruption of the mortal body, creating a grotesque double vision that intermingles life and death.[25] Again, Holbein's series provides a visual echo: one woodcut shows "The King," looking strikingly like Henry VIII in Holbein's portrait of 1536–1537, seated at a table laden with dishes, while Death pours him more wine, encouraging his vices only to cut him off in the fullness of his sin.

Hamlet's response to the appearance of the Ghost is to promise "that I with wings as swift / As meditation or the thoughts of love / May sweep to my revenge" (1.5.29–31). That he does not actually proceed to revenge this murder has been read as an expression of a doubtful individuality indicative of a skeptical, secularized modernity, or as an expression of the theological uncertainties brought about by the Reformation. Yet Hamlet does respond to the vision of death, with a swiftness that implies great certainty, by turning to "meditation", that is, thoughts of Christian love, remembrance and prayer—a response entirely in keeping with the practices of Protestant devotion (if not with the conventions of revenge tragedy). In Matsuda's reading, the scenes of death in *Hamlet* present a series of devotional emblems that provide the protagonist with occasions for meditation through which Hamlet's spiritual struggle over the conflicting demands of conscience and revenge is contemplated and finally resolved: "At several pivotal scenes after his initial encounter with the Ghost, he constructs a mental image with the aid of mnemonic objects: the book he holds in his hands as he accuses Ophelia, old Hamlet's picture used to criticise Gertrude, and Yorick's skull are such objects that can function as a visual trigger, so that Hamlet's spiritual struggle can revolve and unfold around past memories."[26] If we read *Hamlet* as the dramatization of an allegorical genre inviting meditation, the Ghost's plea to be remembered poses not just an individual command from one father to his son but "a reminder of every man's death," extending to the audience.[27] Culminating in his contemplation of Yorick's skull in the graveyard, Hamlet has explored these "meditations on the nature of life and the limits of mortality"[28] in his soliloquies throughout the play. But he is not just an observer of human mortality; as the "observed of all observers" (3.1.153), Hamlet also becomes a *memento mori* figure himself.

Hamlet as a *Memento Mori* Figure

Hamlet's first appearance introduces him as a figure insistently reminding the others of the proximity of death. At 1.2., we see the mourning Hamlet clothed in black, set in conspicuous contrast to the gaudy court celebrating a wedding. In the play's dramaturgy of mortality, the visual opposition is important, so important that *Hamlet* is the only play for which Shakespeare tells us exactly how his protagonist is dressed[29]: He wears an "inky cloak," part of the "customary suits of solemn black" (1.2.77–78). This costume sets Hamlet dramatically apart from the court's wedding dresses not only by color but also by volume and shape: the mourning cloak, as contemporary depictions of Elizabethan state funerals instruct us, was a voluminous outer garment with a hood and long train, that left only hand and face free.[30] Because it was so bulky, it would have been worn only for the funeral and then taken off to reveal a sober, black suit. But Hamlet, Roland Frye points out, continues to wear that cloak, which envelops him completely and thereby symbolizes his isolation from the rest of the court.[31] While this important sartorial detail renders Gertrude's and Claudius's remarks on Hamlet's uncommon, obstinate adherence to mourning more plausible, a contemporary audience would not necessarily have followed their verdict that it amounts to "impious stubbornness" showing "a will most incorrect to heaven, / A heart unfortified" by Christian counsel (1.2.94–96). On the contrary, Hamlet would have appeared "as the only decorous and seemly figure."[32] Moreover, his figure would immediately have caught the spectators' attention, rendering even more conspicuous Claudius's efforts to studiously ignore him for the first 65 lines. The visual contrast thus highlights the dramatic irony of Claudius's hypocritical words: it is *his* will to obtain the throne and the hand of his sister-in-law that is "most incorrect to heaven," *his* heart that remains "unfortified" to sin even when he attempts to pray for forgiveness.

Hamlet is a reminder of death here, not its bringer as in the *danse macabre*. The visual structure of this scene nevertheless corresponds to the logic of life-in-death depicted by the *danse macabre*, as does its function of reminding the spectators of their mortality. The next costume Hamlet will put on is the "antic disposition" (1.5.170) of the madman. His madness aligns him even more strongly than his mourning garb does with the *danse macabre* tradition, where Death often appears in the disguise of the Fool. Several woodcuts in Holbein's series show *mors*-figures as grinning, capering fools mocking human pretensions at greatness, glory, piety, or immortality. They engage in odd postures that invite ridicule and mockingly wear attributes of the human type they accompany. Dressed sometimes in proper clothes, sometimes in rags, they always seem disheveled and in disarray, leading humans—oblivious of the danger they stand in—to their graves, while inspiring panic in those that perceive them as messengers from hell. The first glimpse we get of Hamlet as such a figure is in Ophelia's description that identifies him as one who has seen Death and has become its pale messenger:

> Lord Hamlet, with his doublet all unbraced;
> No hat upon his head; his stockings foul'd,
> Ungarter'd, and down-gyved to his ancle;
> Pale as his shirt; his knees knocking each other;
> And with a look so piteous in purport
> As if he had been loosed out of hell
> To speak of horrors [....] (2.1.75–81)

Returned from hell to speak of its horrors, Hamlet resembles here his father's Ghost, as the editors of the Arden 3 edition note.[33] Perhaps taking his visual cues from the apparition he encountered and that the audience saw just in the preceding scene, Hamlet assumes the role of a revenant: a dead person who is thrown among the living, a figure of death in life.

When Hamlet "in his madness hath Polonius slain" (4.1.34), the messenger turns into the bringer of death indeed, a *mors*-figure stepped from the murals on church walls onto the early modern stage. The closet scene, at the beginning of which Polonius gets killed, combines several features of the *memento mori* tradition to gruesome effect. When Hamlet announces his intention to "set you up a glass / Where you may see the inmost part of you" (3.4.18–19), he sets the tone for a didactic lesson about morality and mortality. This lesson is only briefly interrupted by Hamlet's stabbing of Polonius but is, thereby, visually framed as a *danse macabre* scene, as the corpse remains on stage until Hamlet unceremoniously "lug[s] the guts into the neighbor room" (l. 210). The epithet "guts" reduces the dead body proleptically to a *transi*-figure, evoking the image of guts swarming with maggots, of human flesh as food for worms (4.3.19–24). Again, material corruption is connected with eating, which in turn stands metonymically for sinful corporeality. It is important that Polonius's bleeding corpse remains in full view while Hamlet holds forth to his mother about her sinful violation of "innocent love" and "marriage vows" (3.4.41, 42): the corpse serves as a reminder of her own death, a gruesome visual prop that supports Hamlet's sermon. The didactic double view of life and death is continued when Hamlet, attempting to prompt Gertrude's conscience, presents two portraits of Hamlet senior and Claudius. He makes her remember her chaste past as Hamlet's wife and the sinfulness of her present marriage, calling on her to confess and repent. The portraits thus function like emblems to which Hamlet provides an explicatory and exhortatory comment, another moment that might evoke the practice of meditation.[34] Hamlet's admonition "Confess yourself to heaven, / Repent what's past, avoid what is to come" (ll. 147–48) spells out the ways in which Gertrude should prepare for a good death. Shakespeare evokes the Dance of Death tradition visually when the Ghost of Hamlet's murdered father appears among the living. The Ghost functions literally as a *memento mori* ("Do not forget!" 3.4.106) and as a sermon to the like effect: "His form and cause conjoined preaching to stones / Would make them capable" (3.4.122–23). Yet Gertrude, in the typical role of the human sinner oblivious of Death, cannot perceive the figure that is visible and audible to Hamlet as well as the audience,[35] confirming her belief that Hamlet is stark mad. Hamlet's madness, as we have seen, in turn links him to the *danse macabre* tradition in which Death often appears as a grinning, capering, jesting fool. When he abandons the "inky cloak" he has worn earlier for his "antic disposition," Marjorie Garber comments, "he is really only exchanging one *memento mori* for another. Playing the fool—as well as the madman—he brings Gertrude and the court of Claudius to a belated recognition of the meaning of death—and its imminence. Hamlet in his mother's bedchamber, wearing his antic disposition, is in a way a dramatized version of Holbein's woodcut: Death and the Queen."[36]

The closet scene is among the most violent scenes in the play, both physically and emotionally. To call it an enactment of meditation, as Matsuda does, may therefore seem paradoxical. Yet, its violence attests to the horror that a bad death, unprepared and unrepentant, was thought to wreak on the soul: "O horrible, O horrible, most horrible!" (1.5.80). Hamlet's soliloquies likewise present no peaceful meditations, but rather show the fears, doubts and temptations the soul struggles with to comprehend the moment of death.

THE SOLILOQUIES AS MEDITATIONS ON DEATH

In his study *Mortal Thoughts*, Brian Cummings reads Hamlet's soliloquies not as expressions of a modern self-reflexivity but as devotional meditations on the moment of death. The historical usage of the word *soliloquium* and its cognates in early modern dictionaries identify it as a contemplative communication with God or a synonym for a prayer of any kind.[37] A religious meditation in the face of death, the "mortal soliloquy" was part of preparing for a good death.[38] As a dramatic form, the soliloquy also retained its "special relationship with death," Cummings argues: "mortality occasions the most memorable soliloquies" as an "exteriorized mental meditation."[39] While Cummings's analysis focuses on the first and third soliloquy, respectively, all of Hamlet's solo-speeches revolve around matters of death: they express contempt for the gross materiality of earthly existence ("O that this too too solid flesh would melt / Thaw and resolve itself into a dew," 1.2.129–30) and the vanity of the world ("How weary, stale, flat and unprofitable / Seem to me all the uses of this world," 1.2.32–33); consider remembrance and mourning as responses to loss and ponder the cultural techniques available for performing them (1.5.92–112, 2.2.484–540); meditate on the nature of death (3.1.55–89); prepare Hamlet for his task of reminding Gertrude of her mortality and sinfulness (3.2.378–89); acknowledge prayer for forgiveness as a preparation for a good death (3.3.73–96); and deliberate upon the corrupt state of man as consisting in a desire "to sleep and to feed," while they deplore that "godlike reason" in us, the soul, should be left unattended and weigh the value of conscience against worldly honor and courage (4.4.31–65). While they undoubtedly also address a variety of other topics and fulfill diverse functions, the soliloquies thus present a series of meditations on death in the tradition of the *ars moriendi*.

The thematic commonplaces and generic tone of Hamlet's soliloquies have been highlighted by scholars ready to see more in them than original expressions of a modern sensibility characterized by reflexive introspection and secularized individualism. The "to be or not to be"-soliloquy is a striking case in point: its rhetorical form marks it as "generic rather than reflexive," since there are "no deictics fastening the content to [personal] experience"[40] and its content is taken, at times verbatim, from a range of commonplace books, as befits a Humanist scholar.[41] Its orientation toward death, finally, places it in the genre of literature of preparation. Moreover, the earthly sufferings that Hamlet lists—"Th'oppressor's wrong, the proud man's contumely / […] the law's delay, / The insolence of office" (3.1.70–73)—function as an estates-critique like that put forward by the *danse macabre*, which often featured scenes of supplicants together with figures of power and a *mors*-figure about to liberate the suffering by carrying off the "oppressor." The delay and injustice of the law was also a fixed topos, as illustrated by Holbein's "The Judge" or "The Advocate," whose judgments are determined by bribes. Death is depicted by Holbein as being on the side of the suffering, as in the case of "The Ploughman," whom Death helps to finish his arduous task by energetically spurring on and directing his team of meager horses; the sun rising behind a church located beyond the field "suggests that death will come as a relief to the ploughman"—just as Hamlet's speech suggests that suicide might be a viable, indeed even a rational solution, to man's miserable existence.[42]

While self-slaughter was generally condemned as a crime by medieval theology, the early church considered Christ's self-sacrifice, his seeking out death knowingly, as providing a model for martyrs.[43] Moreover, Renaissance humanist discourse—in which Hamlet's speech is steeped here—was more sympathetic toward the Stoic permission of suicide.[44] The play does not answer the vexed question of suicide, which is raised two more times with Ophelia's accidental suicide and Horatio's offer to drain the dregs of the poisoned cup. Is our death a mere accident, beyond the grasp of will and agency, or is it "the most fundamental confirmation of human agency"?[45] *Hamlet*, and early modern drama more generally, is not in the business of providing clear answers. Suicide carries to extremes a problem that death more generally poses: not "to be or not to be" is the question, as we will eventually all die, but how we will prepare for it and whether this will be enough. While the *ars moriendi* reassuringly promises a path to a good death, the lessons of the *danse macabre* are more disturbing, as they highlight the accidentality of life and the limits of our own agency in the face of death.

The Play as *Danse Macabre*

The editors of this volume highlight in their introduction the inherent theatricality of death and dying in the middle ages and the Renaissance. Dying, social historians agree, was a communal event and an instructive spectacle, with family and neighbors attending the deathbed scene.[46] Art historians too have remarked on the dramatic quality of visual representations of death, especially depictions of the final moment as "a form of bedside drama," for instance in the woodcuts of a late fifteenth-century *Ars Moriendi*.[47] The painted Dance of Death was viewed as a "theatrical piece" to the extent that it frequently "prompted performances of it," sometimes involving the artist himself, as was the case with a Dance performed in Bruges in 1449 before the Duke of Burgundy.[48] The theatrical nature of the *danse macabre* developed into the presence of Death as a stage figure in the genre of mystery and morality plays.[49] Art historian Elina Gertsman explains this by pointing to the performative nature of rituals of dying, burial, and mourning as well as of devotional practices that established an "inherent relationship" between visual depictions and dramatic enactments of death.[50] She identifies three crucial aspects that enabled such intermedial transpositions: first, the energized body language and often exaggerated gestures of the protagonists in the Dance, which imply interaction, exchanges, conflicts; second, the figure of the Preacher as a chorus-like commentator, who sometimes featured in paintings, sometimes was heard in the accompanying verses, and sometimes appeared in the role of the Expositor in late-medieval plays, in each case serving "as an intermediary between the audience and the action, guiding, as it were, the appropriate viewer response;"[51] and third, the didactic impact of murals and morality plays, which alike hinged on a mode of viewing that Gertsman terms "engaged spectatorship."[52]

The appropriate response to deathbed scenes, encountered in real life or in representation, was clearly one of awe, pity, and a willingness to learn from the example of a good death. Yet, the exact relationship between spectacle and spectator calls for closer scrutiny, in particular in the case of the horrifying deaths of the *danse macabre*. Early modern textual sources habitually employed the image of the mirror to describe this relationship. Binski[53] cites several examples of this: a fifteenth-century sermon for funerals that begins with "Here is a mirror to us all: a corpse brought to the church;" the *Danse Macabré* (1480) by Guyot Marchant that calls itself a "miroer salutaire;" or John Lydgate's translation of the French verse for the murals created in the cloister of Old St. Paul's that exhort the spectators:

> Ye folk that loken upon this scripture,
> Conceyveth heer that al estatis daunce,
> Seth what ye be and what is your nature:
> Mete unto wormys, nat ellis in substaunce.
> And have this myrrour ay in remembraunce
> Befor your mynde aboven al thing;[54]

The mirror is a conventional emblem of *vanitas* and a frequent object in the *ars moriendi* tradition. It invites the spectators to recognize themselves in what at first sight seems a portrait of other people's sinful transgressions. Yet, the mirror-image does not capture fully the complex perception structure underpinning the genre. For as the accompanying poem by Lydgate implies, the Dance does not only show us who we are in the moment of looking into this allegorical mirror but also what we are about to become, and it exhorts us to keep that vision in remembrance. Thus, to fully apprehend the import of the *danse macabre* involves, alongside the sensual perception of the image, acts of imaginative engagement, of rational or moral deliberation, and of future mindfulness. In terms of early modern faculty psychology, these were the cognitive abilities necessary for true understanding—a process far more complex than the passive acceptance of a didactic lesson.

Moreover, the spectators of the *danse macabre* are encouraged not merely to identify with what they see, but also to distance themselves from it as a threatening future and to deliberately change their ways.

In Gertsman's analysis, the viewers are both affected by the spectacle of suffering, "called upon to identify with the [...] unfortunate sinners who are in dire need of atonement for their transgressions," and at the same time experience themselves as "detached observers of the dancers' drama who have time to contemplate the meaning of the didactic message they have just been given."[55] This perception structure is illustrated by an engraving by Albrecht Dürer, *The Promenade* (c. 1498), in which a couple strolls through an idyllic landscape, stalked by a grinning skeleton holding above his head a fast-emptying hour-glass (see Fig. 14.2). While the lovers have eyes only for each other, remaining oblivious to the threatening presence, for the viewers who notice—perhaps only at a second glance—the figure of death half-hidden behind a tree the message of the painting changes profoundly, from youthful love to the ubiquity of death. The intended effect is a simultaneous identification and distancing as we perceive a "menacing dimension to the situation that is apparently not shared by anyone within the picture frame"—an effect which Marjorie Garber aptly calls "pictorial irony,"[56] drawing on the theatrical model of dramatic irony.

This complex structure of perception and understanding typical of the *danse macabre* can also be discerned in *Hamlet*. The attitude of sympathetic identification and reflective detachment is highlighted especially by the play's metatheatrical moments. One that is particularly relevant for our discussion comes at 3.2., when Hamlet famously instructs the traveling players about their own art: "the purpose of playing [...] is to hold as 'twere the mirror up to Nature to show Virtue her feature, Scorn her own image" (3.2.20–23). While Hamlet is talking about acting styles and theatrical decorum, his comment also directs attention to the audience's cognitive and affective responses: to identify with virtuous behavior and to distance oneself, with loathing, from the sinful. This self-reflexive remark on theater as a moralistic mirror, together with the play's insistence on remembrance, on temporality, and on human flesh as a meal for worms, allow us to recognize in *Hamlet* verbal echoes and thematic traces of Lydgate's poem.[57]

Further into the scene, the dumbshow and Mousetrap provide visual echoes of the *danse macabre*. Repeating the scene of the King's murder, both feature a *mors*-figure taking the life of an unsuspecting and hence unprepared victim. The dumbshow can be understood as a dramatized performance of the "didactic tableau" that is the Dance of Death.[58] Hamlet's comments after it and during the play-within-the-play cast him

Fig. 14.2 Death stalks a couple (Albrecht Dürer, *The Promenade*)

as a chorus-like figure ("You are as good as a chorus, my lord," 3.2.238); that his comments are as much concerned with morality as with theatricality aligns him with the "Preacher" of Dance of Death murals or the "Expositor" of many late-medieval plays, who "remained present during the entire dramatic performance and served as an intermediary between the audience and the action."[59] Like a *danse macabre*, the dumbshow and Mousetrap are aimed at stirring up Claudius's memory and conscience. Thus functioning like a species of emblem, watching them could be understood as a form of meditation, where the visual perception triggers pious thoughts leading to a higher truth and to moral reform.[60] That the word "meditation" first appears when Hamlet encounters his father's Ghost, and that his first response is to withdraw to prayer (1.5.30, 131), seems to establish this reception pattern within the play. It is tempting to argue that it also provides a pattern for the reception *of* the play: watching death being staged should make the spectators realize their own human nature as fallible and mortal, and move them to prayer in preparation of a good death. But as becomes quickly apparent, the spectacles of death at 3.2. fail to conform to the pattern since it is, of course, not at all clear that Claudius's command to stop the play is really an indication of his guilt, except in Hamlet's biased vision.[61] And when we see Claudius next, praying in the chapel for God's forgiveness, his repentance turns out to be superficial. Neither pious meditation nor the self-serving delusions entertained by Hamlet or Claudius necessarily prefigure the spectators' responses to the spectacle of death.

The chapel-scene promises initially to show a good death. However, in keeping with *Hamlet*'s complex relationship with all kinds of traditions, theatrical and religious, this one image of a good death is framed ironically by means of dramaturgy. Hamlet observes Claudius at prayer, and callously decides not to "take him in the purging of his soul / When he is fit and seasoned for his passage" but rather to wait until

> he is drunk, asleep or in his rage,
> Or in th'incestuous pleasure of his bed,
> At game a-swearing, or about some act,
> That has no relish of salvation in't. (3.3.85–86, 89–92)

We as the audience are already aware that image and act, outward show and inner disposition, might be at odds (thus surpassing Hamlet's rather crude mimetic notions of the play as a naturalistic or moralistic mirror).[62]

Claudius's doubts about the efficacy of repentance before engaging in prayer and his admittance afterward that it was in vain, uttered in the absence of Hamlet, place the spectators in a position of discrepant awareness that repeats the pictorial irony of the Dance of Death, albeit with a difference. Where Hamlet sees a good death, we first assume and then know that Claudius's death would have been a bad one. We see Hamlet as *mors* hovering over Claudius, but he does not take his life.

The discrepant awareness generated by the knowledge of previous scenes would have been deepened for those in the audience familiar with disquisitions on futile prayer by Reformation theologians. As Frye points out, Claudius's attempt at praying is already compromised by his "plotting another murder even as he seeks forgiveness for the first," a moral impediment articulated in a sermon by Hugh Latimer: "As long as he is in the purpose of sin, he cannot pray."[63] William Tyndale added detail and drama to his description of "a false kind of praying, where the tongue and his lips labor, and all the body is pained, but the heart talketh not with God, not feeleth any sweetness at all, nor hath any confidence in the promise of God."[64] Primed by Claudius's soliloquy for such a scenario and confirmed by his closing words—"My words fly up, my thoughts remain below. / Words without thoughts never to heaven go" (3.4.97–98)—spectators would have dis-identified with the unrepentant sinner while at the same time been made aware of the importance of true repentance for salvation. They would have been even more repelled, however, by Hamlet's malice which turns him into a devilish stage-villain.[65] The play thus inverts as well the moral structure of the *danse macabre* and thereby the stance of sympathetic identification is withheld, while encouraging instead a dis-identification with both hypocritical Claudius and diabolical Hamlet. Unable to identify with either figure of this bizarre parody of a good death, the spectators are thrown back on their own judgment to reach an understanding of what a good death might indeed entail—and whether it can be achieved at all.

"There's a Divinity that Shapes Our Ends"

From this low-point in the audience's sympathies, it proves difficult to save Hamlet as the protagonist of the play. Pleading his madness as an excuse is pre-empted by having been put on as a deliberate ploy and upstaged by Ophelia's true madness. Shakespeare's solution is to introduce the notion of divine providence, which shapes Hamlet's view of himself and the world in the final act. Whether Hamlet has indeed gained a deeper understanding of life through meditating on the spectacles of death, some of which he is directly or indirectly responsible for, or whether he eagerly embraces a belief that releases him from that responsibility, remains debatable.[66] Questions of character aside, in terms of the play's dramaturgy of mortality, Hamlet's account of how he discovered God's plan once again echoes the *danse macabre*. He explains that his fortuitous escape from a bad death—his discovery of the murder conspiracy set up by Claudius with the help of Rosencrantz and Guildenstern, and his capture by pirates in a "sea-fight" (5.2.54)—have led him to an acceptance of providence. The discovery of God's will in the workings of fortune was often represented by religious emblems using the image of a stormy, dangerous voyage, thus rendering visually Psalms 69:15 where "the sea is likened to the world, and the soul to a ship tossed amidst the waves."[67] Shipwreck was also a standard situation in the Dance of Death: Holbein's "The Seaman" depicts a ship in a storm, about to be entered by a *mors*-figure, like a pirate, who breaks the mast and sinks the ship with its crew. In keeping with these visual traditions, Hamlet's sea voyage prompts him to meditate on God's will, leading him, as he claims, to the realization of divine design beyond man's control. His acceptance of Providence comes with the acceptance of chance or "luck," concepts which in the theological language of the time did not indicate gratuitous events but an acknowledgment of fortuitous patterns in hindsight.[68] Thus, Hamlet interprets the lucky chances that lead him to avert the plot against his life as ordained by heaven (5.2.48). When he says "The readiness is all," this does not express a new-found willingness to take revenge but a commitment to accept the working of providence, which, of course, also allows him to give up agency and the responsibility that comes with it: "There's special providence in the fall of a sparrow. If it be, 'tis not to come. If it be not to come, it will be now. If it be not now, yet it will come" (5.2.197–200). What Hamlet refers to here is a future that is "certain yet unknowable"—just like the moment of one's own death, which therefore one should constantly be ready for although it is beyond our control.[69]

Visual echoes from the *danse macabre* build up as the stage becomes littered with corpses. This time it is Laertes who functions as a chorus-like commentator on the spectacle of death, declaring himself "justly killed" and saying of Claudius's death that "He is justly served" (5.2. 292, 311). In the end, Laertes asks Hamlet's forgiveness (5.2.313), thereby approaching a good death.[70] His role as commentator is taken over by

Horatio who, however, fails to grasp any providential pattern: he can therefore only speak

> Of carnal, bloody and unnatural acts
> Of accidental judgments, casual slaughters,
> Of deaths put on by cunning, and for no cause
> And in this upshot purposes mistook
> Fallen on th' inventors' heads. (5.2.365–69)

Death, for him, is entirely devoid of providence. While Horatio stresses the element of chance and mishap that also the protagonists of a Dance of Death would have experienced at being suddenly pulled out of life, without belief in divine providence these remain void of meaning. It is Hamlet who voices the divine justice at work in seemingly accidental events and who thus embodies the desired reception effect of the *danse macabre*, which is deepened by contrast with the disillusioned Horatio or the worldly minded Fortinbras. What Matsuda calls "the meditative quality of Hamlet"[71] and what Cummings perceptively sees in the soliloquies applies to the play on the whole: "In a series of speeches Hamlet prefigures his own end, so much so that his life seems to become commensurate with the act of imagining his death. In this way, the workings of the theatre become coterminous with living a life. Spectators and actors alike participate in this mimesis of their own mortality."[72] The *danse macabre* enacted by *Hamlet* encourages spectators to ponder these scenes of bad deaths, to meditate on their own mortality, and to step into action to prepare for a good death.

In this sense, the early modern theater can be seen as continuing the didactic-pastoral function of the medieval Dance of Death. It is of course debatable whether that function would have been exactly the same and have had the same effect on Shakespeare's audience as in pre-Reformation times, or indeed when seen in the sacred context of church murals. The continuity of the medieval and early modern world is necessarily refracted by the Reformation; and the stage is not a pulpit. *Hamlet* does not nostalgically revive an idealized, now lost, world of certain faith and pious behavior. An overemphasis on rupture, however, has led critics to see Hamlet as the embodiment of a modern, secularized individualism. Yet, in such a view it would rather be Horatio who embodies the skeptical voice of modernity, explaining death solely in terms of human actions and mere chance, rather than of providence and salvation. By the same token, however, neither can Hamlet be claimed for modernity in a straight-forward fashion: his meditative habits, his dramaturgic function as *mors*-figure, and his avowed faith in providence link him more to the medieval world than the critical narrative of secularization and modernity allows for. If the play is not a mirror in any naturalistic sense, it is one in the very sense that imbued the *danse macabre* tradition: a vehicle for understanding life through death.

Notes

1. I would like to thank Margaret Tudeau-Clayton and Antoinina Bevan Zlatar for urging me to clarify this distinction and its attendant theological and ritual implications.
2. Gitting, "Sacred and Secular: 1558–1660," p. 153.
3. Wunderli and Broce, "The Final Moment Before Death in Early Modern England," p. 260.
4. Predestination became an official article of Anglican theology in 1563, yet it remains debatable to what extent it impacted on the every-day religious practices of the laity. See Collinson, *The Religion of Protestants: The Church in English Society, 1559–1625*, pp. 189–241.
5. Reformed theology accepted only the "houseling," the dispensation of the Eucharist as a sacrament, as part of Protestant rites of dying.
6. Guibbory, "Donne's Religious Poetry and the Trauma of Grace," p. 230.
7. Belsey, *Shakespeare and the Loss of Eden*, p. 145. It was nevertheless destroyed in 1549, despite the provision made by the Edwardian "Act for the abolishing [...] books and images" that the iconoclasm should only be enacted on tombs of saints. Appleford, *Learning to Die in London, 1380–1540*, pp. 83–97, gives a detailed account the material and textual history of the "Daunce of Poulys" as part of a program of civic education commissioned in c.1430 by the influential Clerk of London, John Carpenter.
8. Rublack (ed.), *Hans Holbein: The Dance of Death*.
9. See Belsey.
10. Gertsman, *The Dance of Death in the Middle Ages: Image, Text, Performance*, pp. 87, 89.

11. In spite of its emergence in pre-Reformation culture and its visual nature, the Dance remained an important part of the death arts in Reformed countries and even functioned as a vehicle for anticlerical critique (Rublack, pp. 138–136, 151–155).
12. See Kerrigan, "Hieronimo, Hamlet and Remembrance"; Neill, *Issues of Death: Mortality and Identity in English Renaissance Tragedy*"; and Wilder, *Shakespeare's Memory Theatre: Recollection, Properties, and Character*.
13. Frye, *The Renaissance Hamlet: Issues and Responses in 1600*, pp. 206–207.
14. Ibid., p. 211.
15. Ibid., pp. 219, 213–220.
16. Gertsman, p. 85.
17. de Grazia, Margreta. *"Hamlet" Without Hamlet*.
18. Binski, *Medieval Death: Ritual and Representation*, pp. 156–157.
19. de Grazia, p. 140.
20. Neill, p. 237.
21. de Grazia, p. 132.
22. Frye, pp. 220–225.
23. Willard, "Images of Mortality in Early English Drama," p. 425.
24. Greenblatt, *Hamlet in Purgatory*, p. 237.
25. Ibid., p. 243.
26. Matsuda, "Devotional Emblems and Protestant Meditation in *Hamlet*," p. 566.
27. Garber, "'Remember Me': 'Memento Mori' Figures in Shakespeare's Plays," p. 4.
28. Ibid., p. 4.
29. Frye, p. 94.
30. Examples include the *Funeral Procession of Sir Philip Sidney* (1587) by T. Lant, William Camden's sketch of the cloaked figure of Edward Somerset as principal mourner in the funeral procession of Queen Elizabeth in 1603, or the mourners accompanying the funeral cortege of Henry, Prince of Wales, in 1613, depicted on the title page of George Wither's *Prince Henry's Obsequies*; see Frye, pp. 96–99.
31. Ibid., p. 96.
32. Ibid., p. 84.
33. Shakespeare, n79–81.
34. Matsuda, p. 577.

35. Garber, p. 14.
36. Ibid., p. 24.
37. Cummings, pp. 176–177.
38. Ibid., p. 186.
39. Ibid., pp. 183–184.
40. de Grazia, pp. 69–70.
41. See Lim, "'To Be or Not to Be': Hamlet's Humanistic *Quaestio.*".
42. Rublack, p. 161.
43. Cummings, p. 267.
44. Ibid., p. 243.
45. Ibid., p. 258.
46. Wunderli and Broce.
47. Binski, pp. 40–41.
48. Ibid., p. 156.
49. Willard, p. 413.
50. Gertsman, pp. 79–81.
51. Ibid., pp. 84–85.
52. Ibid., p. 81.
53. Binski, p. 159.
54. Lydgate, *John Lydgate's Dance of Death and Related Works*, B Version, pp. 561–567.
55. Gertsman, pp. 91–92.
56. Garber, p. 5.
57. Lydgate's verses articulated widely known conventions of *danse macabre* poetry and might well have entered the collective imagination at least of the older generation among Shakespeare's audience, who would have been able to see the mural and read the accompanying verse at St. Paul's before its destruction in 1549. Those too young to have seen it in situ could be reminded of its existence by Thomas More's references to it in his meditation of mortality, written in 1522 and published posthumously in 1557 (see Engel, Loughnane, and Williams [eds.], *The Memory Arts in Renaissance England: A Critical Anthology*, pp. 234–235), or by John Stow's description of its history in Stow, *A Survey of London*, pp. 264–265. The St. Paul's Dance of Death was also copied in the nave of the Guild Chapel in Stratford, where it survived the whitewashing of the iconoclastic Royal Injunctions of 1559 (de Grazia 2007, 131 n6).

58. Llewellyn, *The Art of Death: Visual Culture in the English death Ritual, c.1500–c.1800*, p. 19.
59. Gertsman, pp. 84, 85.
60. Matsuda, pp. 273–274.
61. Hobgood, *Passionate Playgoing in Early Modern England*, pp. 15–26. Lewis, *Hamlet and the Vision of Darkness*, pp. 214–219.
62. Ibid., p. 200.
63. Frye, p. 24.
64. Quoted in Frye, p. 136.
65. de Grazia, p. 193.
66. For the two sides of the debate, see Matsuda and Lewis.
67. Matsuda, p. 579.
68. Cummings, pp. 207–235.
69. Cummings, p. 214.
70. Dunne, *Shakespeare, Revenge Tragedy and Early Modern Law*, p. 117.
71. Matsuda, p. 582.
72. Cummings, p. 225.

References

Appleford, Amy. *Learning to Die in London, 1380–1540*. Philadelphia, PA: University of Pennsylvania Press, 2014.
Belsey, Catherine. *Shakespeare and the Loss of Eden*. New Brunswick, NJ: Rutgers University Press, 1999.
Binski, Paul. *Medieval Death: Ritual and Representation*. London: British Museum Press, 1996.
Collinson, Patrick. *The Religion of Protestants: The Church in English Society, 1559–1625*. Oxford: Clarendon Press, 1982.
Cummings, Brian. *Mortal Thoughts: Religion, Secularity & Identity in Shakespeare and Early Modern Culture*. Oxford: Oxford University Press. 2013.
de Grazia, Margreta. *"Hamlet" Without Hamlet*. Cambridge: Cambridge University Press, 2007.
Dunne, Derek. *Shakespeare, Revenge Tragedy and Early Modern Law*. Basingstoke, UK: Palgrave Macmillan, 2016.
Engel, William, Rory Loughnane, Grant Williams (eds.). *The Memory Arts in Renaissance England: A Critical Anthology*. Cambridge: Cambridge University Press, 2016.

Frye, Roland M. *The Renaissance Hamlet: Issues and Responses in 1600*. Princeton, NJ: Princeton University Press, 1984.
Garber, Marjorie. "'Remember Me': 'Memento Mori' Figures in Shakespeare's Plays." *Renaissance Drama* 12 (1981): 3–25.
Gertsman, Elina. *The Dance of Death in the Middle Ages: Image, Text, Performance*. Turnhout: Brepols, 2010.
Gitting, Claire. "Sacred and Secular: 1558–1660." In *Death in England: An Illustrated History*. Edited by Claire Gittings and Peter C. Jupp. New Brunswick, NJ: Rutgers University Press, 2000. pp. 147–173.
Greenblatt, Stephen. *Hamlet in Purgatory*. Cambridge, MA: Harvard University Press, 2001.
Guibbory, Achsah. "Donne's Religious Poetry and the Trauma of Grace." In *Early Modern Poetry: A Critical Companion*. Edited by Patrick Cheney et al. Oxford: Oxford University Press, 2006. pp. 229–239.
Hobgood, Alison. *Passionate Playgoing in Early Modern England*. Cambridge: Cambridge University Press, 2014.
Kerrigan. John. "Hieronimo, Hamlet and Remembrance." *Essays in Criticism* 31 (1981): 105–26.
Lewis, Rhodri. *Hamlet and the Vision of Darkness*. Princeton, NJ: Princeton University Press, 2017.
Lim, Vanessa. "'To Be or Not to Be': Hamlet's Humanistic *Quaestio*." *The Review of English Studies* 70.296 (2019): 640–658.
Llewellyn, Nigel. *The Art of Death: Visual Culture in the English Death Ritual, c.1500–c.1800*. London: Reaktion, 1991.
Lydgate, John. *John Lydgate's Dance of Death and Related Works*. Edited by Megan L. Cook and Elizaveta Strakhov. Middle English Texts Series, 2019. https://d.lib.rochester.edu/teams/text/cook-and-strakhov-lyd gate-dance-of-death-lansdowne. Accessed 23 February 2022.
Matsuda, Misako. "Devotional Emblems and Protestant Meditation in *Hamlet*." *English Studies* 98.6 (2017): 562–584.
Neill, Michael. *Issues of Death: Mortality and Identity in English Renaissance Tragedy*. Oxford: Clarendon Press, 1977.
Rublack, Ulinka (ed.). *Hans Holbein: The Dance of Death*. London: Penguin, 2016.
Shakespeare, William. *Hamlet*. Arden Series 3. Edited by Ann Thompson and Neil Taylor. London: Cengage Learning, 2006.
Stow, John. *A Survey of London*. London, 1598.
Wilder, Lina Perkins. *Shakespeare's Memory Theatre: Recollection, Properties, and Character*. Cambridge: Cambridge University Press, 2010.
Willard, Thomas. "Images of Mortality in Early English Drama." In *Death in the Middle Ages and Early Modern Time*. Edited by Albrecht Classen. Berlin and Boston, MA: de Gruyter, 2016. pp. 411–431.

Wunderli, Richard and Gerald Broce. "The Final Moment Before Death in Early Modern England." *Sixteenth-Century Journal* 20.2 (1989): 259–275.

CHAPTER 15

"A Consummation Devoutly to Be Wished"? Middles and Ends in *Hamlet*

Michael Neill

Men in the middest make considerable investments in coherent patterns which, by the provision of an end, make possible a satisfying consonance with the origins and with the middle.—Frank Kermode[1]

And so the impulse is left incomplete, frustrated and ruined—through fear of its being left incomplete, frustrated and ruined.—Adam Thirlwell[2]

Post mortem nihil est ipsaque mors nihil.—Seneca[3]

A colleague of mine was cursed with a gift reminiscent of Borges's unhappy hero, Funes the Memorious[4]: so capacious was his recall, so unconfined his talent for free association, that he was never able to bring a lecture (let alone a course) to a proper conclusion. On the occasion

M. Neill (✉)
University of Auckland, Auckland, New Zealand
e-mail: m.neill@auckland.ac.nz

© The Author(s), under exclusive license to Springer Nature Switzerland AG 2022
W. E. Engel and G. Williams (eds.), *The Shakespearean Death Arts*, Palgrave Shakespeare Studies,
https://doi.org/10.1007/978-3-030-88490-1_15

of his last class, friends brought champagne to share with his honours students. As the gift-bearers entered, he looked up with a slightly hurt expression, exclaiming in puzzled tones "But I've only just begun!" It was as if his entire career would now be bilked of a proper ending: broken off in this unceremonious fashion, it would leave him suspended forever in the middest. The comic poignancy of that moment had, I think, everything to do with the temptation to read it as a kind of allegory for the human condition with its dread of incompletion.

As our fondness for biographical narrative suggests, we like to imagine our lives as coherent stories: self-consistent tales that move in a prescribed fashion from birth though life towards a conclusion that will make final sense of all that has gone before it. Such indeed is the narrative shape that Aristotle prescribes for tragedy in his foundational *Poetics*: insisting that the plot must imitate "an action that is whole and complete in itself," he explains that to achieve such coherence it must follow a logical sequence from "beginning, [to] middle, [to] end," so connecting "the various incidents [...] that the whole will be disjointed and dislocated if any one of them is transposed or removed."[5] Clearly, however, not all kinds of narrative conform to such decorous regularity, and some deliberately break with it. So, according to Horace, a writer of epic must, like Homer, "ever hurr[y] to the crisis and carr[y] the listener into the midst of the story [*in medias res*] as though it were already known."[6]

Horace's prescription for epic design, Frank Kermode suggests, bears an uncomfortably suggestive relation to lived experience, since human beings themselves "rush 'into the middest,' *in medias res*, when they are born; [but] they also die *in mediis rebus*." Indeed, it is precisely in order to overcome this sense of radical incompleteness that they feel compelled to impose an orderly Aristotelian pattern on their lives: "to make sense of their span they need fictive concords with origins and ends, such as give meaning to lives and to poems. The End they imagine will reflect their irreducibly intermediate preoccupations.... The End is a figure for their own deaths."[7] The Bible, as Kermode suggests,[8] provides the ultimate template for such orderly narratives, with its progress from the moment of creation ("In the beginning" Gen.1:1) to its final vision of apocalypse, after which "time should be no more" (Rev. 10:6).[9] For God himself, however, there is no real middle: "I am Alpha and Omega," he proclaims, "the beginning and the ending [....] the first and the last" (Rev. 1:8, 1:11; 22:13), enfolding all time into himself. We mortals, on the other hand, are consigned to a temporal sequence in which a middle—the span of life itself—is crucial because it will determine the nature of the ending under whose shadow, thanks to the sin of our First Parents, it is necessarily conducted. For that reason life in the middest can also feel like a prison: "In the midst of life we are in death," declares the Book of Common Prayer's Order for the Burial of the Dead, before reminding humankind that only religion offers the possibility of escape from the endlessness of an "everlasting death."[10]

Hamlet is a play noticeably possessed by narrative yearnings, but ones that are repeatedly undone by its conflicted attitudes towards ending. Death—because it offers the prospect of proper completion can seem "a consummation / Devoutly to be wished"—desired because it promises an "end" to "the heartache and the thousand natural shocks / That flesh is heir to" (3.1.61–5).[11] But death is also to be feared: on the one hand, because of the "dread of something after death"—the possibility that it might constitute no true end at all (l. 79); on the other, because its ending might, after all, prove too absolute, offering only the prospect of annihilation represented by the dust and worms of the graveyard.

The first act of the tragedy is dominated by the figure of a Ghost, burdened with the need to tell the suppressed story of its own murderous death. At the end of the play, the protagonist who was charged with revealing that story now longs to tell his own, only for this narrative to be cut off in its turn:

> Had I but time—as this fell sergeant Death
> Is strict in his arrest—oh, I could tell you—
> But let it be. (5.2.289–91)

"I could tell you" uncannily echoes the Ghost's "I could a tale unfold" (1.5.15), while "arrest," in addition to its legal meaning, includes "the act of stopping anything in its course"[12]—an interruption that ties Hamlet's ending to a sequence of abrupted narratives or breakings-off that have punctuated the action of the play from the beginning.

At this point, what matters to the Prince, like his father before him, is proper remembrance: that is why he goes on to insist that Horatio must act as his remembrancer as he himself once acted for the Ghost, undertaking to "report me and my cause aright / To the unsatisfied" (5.2.293–4):

> O God, Horatio, what a wounded name,

> Things standing thus unknown, I leave behind me!
> [...]
> Absent thee from felicity awhile,
> And in this harsh world draw thy breath in pain,
> To tell my story. (ll. 297–302)

We might expect that Horatio, charged with this duty, would then be made to conclude the action with an elaborate narrative summary, like the "story...of Juliet and her Romeo" that is given to the Friar at the end of Shakespeare's earlier tragedy (*Rom.* 5.3.229, 308–9).[13] But in *Hamlet* the progress towards such ending is interrupted by the sound of "*A march afar off, and a shot within,*" marking the arrival of Fortinbras and his soldiers. As a result, Horatio never gets to tell the promised story: he twice promises to "speak to the yet unknowing world" of what sounds like a crude revenge drama of "purposes mistook / Fallen on the inventors' heads" (ll. 332–8); but the actual telling of it will only happen on some offstage "stage" (l. 331), where his voice seems likely to be replaced or silenced by the triumphal sounds of the invading Norwegian army: "Let four captains / Bear Hamlet like a soldier to the stage" ... "and for his passage, / The soldiers' music and the rites of war / *Speak loudly for him.*" ... "Go, bid the soldiers shoot" (ll. 348–56 [emphasis added]).

Fortinbras's concluding speech is suffused with the same rhetorical confidence that characterised Claudius's opening address in 1.2. There, the remembrance of Old Hamlet's history was cannily shuffled away in a subordinate clause: "Though yet of Hamlet our dear brother's death / The memory be green" (1.2.1–2 ff.). Here, while Fortinbras gestures towards a celebration of Hamlet's life, it is not these commemorative "rites of war" (l. 352), but his own political "rights of memory" (5.2.352, 342) that really matter. Of course the repeated metadramatic play on "stage" does invite the audience to think of the performance they have witnessed as a fulfilment of Hamlet's need to have his story told. But this, like so many of the play's narratives, remains in its own way disturbingly incomplete.

The motif of silenced tales and frustratingly deferred endings is introduced at the very beginning of the play with Barnardo's attempt to tell the "story" of the Ghost's previous appearances (1.1.32)—a story that is almost immediately cut short by the sudden reappearance that leaves his tale conspicuously suspended in mid-sentence and on a half-line: "The bell then beating one" (l. 39). The Ghost itself seems about to speak when it suddenly "stalks away" (l. 50), leaving the reason for its visitation unexplained. In an attempt to cast light on a phenomenon that seemingly "bodes some strange eruption [sudden rupture] to our state" (l. 69). Horatio then offers an account of contemporary Danish politics, only to be himself interrupted by the Ghost's return—"But soft, behold, lo where it comes again!" (l. 108). Once again the spirit seems "about to speak" (l. 129), only for it to be summoned away by the crowing of a cock.

It is not until the fifth scene that, in response to Hamlet's insistence, this "questionable shape" (1.4.22) consents to "unfold" its suppressed history; but even then it prefaces that narrative with an apology for another that cannot be uttered:

> But that I am forbid
> To tell the secrets of my prison-house,
> I could a tale unfold whose lightest word
> Would harrow up thy soul [....]
> But this eternal blazon must not be
> To ears of flesh and blood. (1.5.13–22)

It then goes on to reveal the hitherto suppressed facts of its own death—a story designed to supplant the false narrative that has abused "the whole ear of Denmark" (l. 37), but one that is immediately bottled up once more, since Hamlet refuses to reveal it even to his companions, while swearing them (with the support of the Ghost) to remain "secret" about everything they have seen (ll. 126, 149–95).

Secrecy, it soon emerges, is a habit in Denmark: Hamlet's instinctive response on first hearing of the Ghost's visits is to urge "silence" upon Horatio and the others about what might ensue: "And whatsoever else shall hap tonight, / Give it an understanding but no tongue" (1.2.250–2). On one level such injunctions simply reflect the politic evasions of a court where information is systematically repressed—a world where "the candied tongue" serves not to speak the truth but to "lick absurd pomp" (3.2.55), a world whose self-serving caution is exemplified by Laertes's advice to his sister—"best safety lies in fear" (1.3.43)—and Polonius's sage injunctions to his son "Give thy thoughts no tongue [....] Give every man thine ear but few thy voice" (ll. 59, 68). Hamlet, on the other hand, finds himself torn between necessary silence—"But break my heart, for I must hold my tongue" (l. 159)—and commitment to exposing the truth of his father's murder. In this world, as he will remind Horatio, speech can itself become a kind of violence: "I have words to speak in thine ear will make thee dumb; yet are they much too light for the bore of the matter" (4.6.22–4). The immediate consequence of this conflicted state of mind is that it reduces Hamlet to uncanny mimicry of the Ghost's own behaviour, when he confronts Ophelia "with a look so piteous in purport / As if he had been loosed out of hell / To speak of horrors" (2.1.83–5).

Like the Ghost's harrowing story of his "prison-house," however, these "horrors" remain for the moment unspoken. Reproving himself in the following scene as one who remains "unpregnant of my cause, / And can say nothing" (2.2.556–7), Hamlet resolves to make of the Players a "miraculous organ," a surrogate for his own silenced tongue (2.2.582–3). But although he insists that, unlike the denizens of the court, "the Players cannot keep counsel" and will "tell all" (3.2.131–2), his first encounter with them returns to the motif of narrative incompletion: to test the First Player's quality, Hamlet chooses "Aeneas' tale to Dido" with its account of a son's revenge for his father—an account that is temporarily broken off when the avenger's sword seems to "stick in the air," leaving him, Hamlet-like, frozen in inaction just as the verse halts in mid-line: "So, as a painted tyrant, Pyrrhus stood, / And like a neutral to his will and matter / Did nothing" (2.2.471–3). The tale is then resumed only to break off again when the Player moves himself to tears, leaving Hamlet to insist "I'll have thee speak out the rest soon" (ll. 512–13). That, however, is a conclusion that we are never allowed to hear, just as the play with which Hamlet proposes to "unkennel" his uncle's "occulted guilt" (3.2.75–6) is cut short when Claudius makes his angry exit, leaving its action conspicuously unfinished. Hamlet may mock his sometime friends, Rosencrantz and Guildenstern, with their inability to break his silence: "there is much music, excellent voice, in this little organ, yet cannot you make it speak" (l. 351); but the repetition of his punning metaphor only serves to remind us of the sudden silencing of the "miraculous organ" that was supposed to speak for him.

This succession of abrupted narratives draws attention to Shakespeare's own plot as one in which the narrative satisfactions of ending are also repeatedly frustrated—structural procrastination that constantly threatens to leave events much as they began, suspended in the middest.[14] As if consciously remembering Horace's prescription for epic poetry, Shakespeare's tragedy begins *in medias res*, in the wake of the two events that trigger its tragic action—the murder of the protagonist's father by his own brother, and his mother's incestuous marriage to the murderer. Of course revenge tragedies often plunge their audience into the middle of things: Kyd's influential *Spanish Tragedy*, for example, begins with a dramatised prologue in which the Ghost of Andrea ushers in the play's sequence of vindictive killings with an account of his own unavenged death, while in Middleton's *Revenger's Tragedy*, the protagonist, nursing the skull of his dead mistress, pronounces a chorus-like commentary on the courtly procession of those who will die as a consequence of her poisoning. Such beginnings typically emphasise the plot's drive towards a foregone conclusion—one in which the protagonist's own death will complete the fearful symmetries of revenge: "Is there one enemy left alive amongst those?" asks Vindice, surveying the corpses of his enemies, "'Tis time to die when we are ourselves our foes" (5.3.112–13).[15] As Vindice and his brother are led off to execution, however, Antonio's concluding speech admits a nervous hint of doubt about the apparent finality of this ending: "*Pray heaven* their blood *may* wash away all treason" (l. 132; my emphases). Doubt is even more apparent at the end of Kyd's play: there, Revenge's metadramatic insistence that he and Andrea's Ghost are to "serve for chorus in this tragedy" (1.1.91),[16] enhances a sense of the action as a prescribed sequence; but the plot that unfolds turns out to resist proper closure. In Kyd's final Chorus, barely has the Ghost expressed his delight in the seeming conclusiveness of the funeral that ends the main action than Revenge is made to warn of the "endless pain," "endless moan," and "endless flames" that must now ensue: "For here though death hath end their misery. / I'll there begin their endless tragedy" (4.5.34, 40, 43, 47–8). Indeed, as the revenging Hieronimo is made to declare in the play's suggestive Fourth Addition, "there is no end: the end is death and madness" (l. 158).[17] *Hamlet*, in ways that we have begun to see, moves towards its own, more subtle, but equally disturbing inconclusiveness.

The tragedy's resistance to proper conclusion is an aspect of its broader sense of temporal disarticulation. From the opening exchange on the castle battlements, with its dramatised stage directions, Shakespeare's Elsinore is marked by an anxious awareness of time.[18]

> FRANCISCO You come most carefully upon your hour.
> BARNARDO 'Tis now struck twelve. (1.1.6–7)

Later, as the Ghost appears, the clock will beat one (l. 39), and then, in the fourth scene, strike midnight once more to usher in the spirit's reappearance (1.4.3). But, in contrast to these reminders of firm mechanical measurement, there is the suggestion of something temporally amiss: in contrast to the season of Nativity, when spirits dare not walk, "So hallowed and so gracious is the time" (l. 146), this is a time of night "usurped"—improperly possessed, as it were—by the spirit of a dead King (l. 46). By contrast, Hamlet sees himself as time's hapless victim, subject to its "whips and scorns" in a way that "makes calamity of so long life" (3.1.30–1). It is time that continually appears to cheat him of the closure that would result from unburdening himself of the Ghost's story: "the time is out of joint," he declares, following their first encounter, "O cursed spite / That ever I was born to set it right" (1.5.196–7). When he is again confronted by his father's spirit he returns to this sense of temporal dislocation, seeing himself as "lapsed in time and passion" (3.4.100). There is something curiously passive about his language here: he is one who simply "let's go by / Th'important acting of [the Ghost's] dread command" (ll. 100–1)—as though the urgent "acting" were somehow separate from himself, and time moving while he himself remains frozen in a state of moral paralysis. This condition is what is sometimes seen as Hamlet's propensity for "delay" (a word that the play itself never applies to his actions); existentially, however, it merely reflects the feeling of entrapment in a middle state that Hamlet expresses when, lamenting the inaccessibility of a proper "end" or "consummation," he imagines himself "crawling *between* heaven and earth" (3.1.62–4, 128, emphasis added).

The play's own beginning *in medias* is emphasised by the abruptness of its opening line: "Who's there?" Foregoing the expository formalities of Kyd and Middleton, the nocturnal action that follows is itself carefully placed in what Barnardo calls "this dead hour" (1.1.65), the sinister "witching time of night" (3.2.371) of which Hamlet speaks: "When churchyards yawn" (l. 372) and when the Ghost, like other revenants, is "wont to walk" (1.4.6). This is a kind of un-time that not only belongs to the dead, but is itself a dead temporal space—the "dead waste and middle of the night" as Horatio calls it (1.2.199). The unconscious word-play in "dead waste" will be pointed up a few scenes later when Hamlet, as though remembering his friend's phrase, mocks Rosencrantz and Guildenstern for their relation to Fortune: "you live about her waist, or in the middle of her favours" (2.2.230-1)—an obscene nullity with which he will go on to tease Ophelia before the Mousetrap play:

> OPHELIA I think nothing, my lord.
> HAMLET That's a fair thought to lie between a maid's legs.
> OPHELIA What is, my lord?
> HAMLET No-thing. (3.2.109-12)

By the time we hear this piece of seemingly inconsequential bawdy, "nothing" has already acquired a resonance beyond its immediate context: it is one that, as I shall try to show, is bound up with an anxious concern with the "between"—with that sense of imprisonment in the middest that is embodied in the Ghost, whose silenced story is, at this point, about to be given voice by the Players.

Their performance of "The Murder of Gonzago" not only occupies the middle of the tragic action, but is itself cut off in the middle of its narrative, shorn of the vengeful conclusion suggested by its alternative title, *The Mousetrap* (l. 223). Its disruption, moreover, is followed by a sequence that has Hamlet himself once again brooding on revenge as he prepares to visit his mother ("Now could I drink hot blood"), only to repudiate it: "I will speak daggers, but use none; / My tongue and soul in this be hypocrites" (ll. 379-80). In the confrontation that ensues, the Ghost too appears to equivocate on what Hamlet calls "the acting of your dread command" (3.4.101). Its reply "Do not forget" may seem to urge on the "blunted purpose" of revenge (ll. 102-3), but it also harks back to the unexpected conclusion of their first encounter: if vengeance was what the Ghost sought at the beginning of that exchange (1.5.7, 25), its closing injunction—instead of repeating the shrieks of "Revenge!" that had famously characterised its predecessor in the source play—insists only that his interlocutor "Remember me" (l. 91)[19]; and it is to remembrance alone that Hamlet commits himself in the lines that follow:

> Remember thee?
> Ay, thou poor ghost, while memory holds a seat
> In this distracted globe. Remember thee?
> Yea, from the table of my memory
> I'll wipe away all trivial fond records
> [...]
> And thy commandment all alone shall live
> Within the book and volume of my brain

> [...]
> 			Now to my word:
> It is 'Adieu, adieu, remember me.'
> I have sworn't. (ll. 94–113)

Remembrance, however, is an ambiguous commitment. When Polonius speaks of it to Laertes he enjoins silence: "And these few precepts in thy memory, / See thou character. Give thy thoughts no tongue" (1.3.58–9), and when Laertes in turn urges his sister to "remember well / What I have said to you," she too accepts it as a command to say nothing: "'Tis in my memory locked, / And you yourself shall keep the key of it" (ll. 85–6). It is the Players whom Hamlet engages to unlock the secrets which the Ghost has confided: as "the abstracts and brief chronicles of the time" (2.2.515), he asserts, they are uniquely fitted to bridging the gap between remembering and speaking, showing and telling: "Be not you ashamed to show, he'll not shame to tell you what it means" (ll. 134–6). The incomplete nature of their performance, however, will leave their promised revelation unfinished, giving a kind of ironic confirmation to the Player King's warning that "Our thoughts are ours, their *ends* none of our own" (l. 201; emphasis added). "The story is extant [....] You shall see anon," Hamlet promises, in the fashion of a chorus, "how the murderer gets the love of Gonzago's wife" (ll. 46–8), only for Claudius to storm out, while Polonius orders the actors to "'Give o'er the play" (l. 252). In the ensuing dialogue Hamlet maintains to a hesitant Horatio that Claudius's behaviour is enough to confirm the Ghost's word, but the word-play in his subsequent threat to "put [the King] to his *purgation*" (l. 289; emphasis added) serves as a half-conscious reminder of the Ghost's forbidden story.

In its first encounter with Hamlet, the Ghost explains that its restless condition is the consequence of a death that leaves it "Doomed for a certain term to walk the night, / And for the day confined to fast in fires, / Till the foul crimes done in my days of nature / Are burnt and *purged* away" (1.5.10–13; emphasis added)—suspended, that is to say, between damnation and salvation in Purgatory. Here, it seems, lies the explanation for its longing to be remembered. It is not simply the fratricidal murder itself, or the adulterous incest with which it is associated, nor even the official oblivion signalled by Claudius's shameless insistence upon the primacy of "remembrance of ourselves" (1.2.7), but the terrible abruption of a killing that has left him.

> *Cut off* even in the blossoms of my sin,
> Unhouseled, dis-appointed, unaneled,
> No reckoning made, but sent to my account
> With all my imperfections on my head. (1.5.76–8 [emphasis added])

The terminal "reckoning" imagined here is not that of revenge but the formal accounting of life and conduct necessary to make a good death[20]—one that appears to be of a distinctly Catholic character. The suddenness of his end has deprived old Hamlet not just of the eucharist ("Unhouseled") and of confession and absolution ("dis-appointed"), but of the anointed unction ("unaneled") that was peculiar to the last rites in Catholic liturgy. Communion itself, as the repeated injunction to "do this in remembrance of me" insists, is the supreme rite of memory, commemorating and re-enacting a sacrifice that, far from requiring vengeance, promises forgiveness of sins and salvation—hence the peculiarly vindictive cruelty of the mock-communion with which Hamlet ends Claudius's life: "murd'rous damnèd Dane, / Drink off this potion" (5.3.278–9). Cheated of every salvific ritual, the Ghost finds itself consigned to the fearful middle state of Purgatory, that space between Heaven and Hell to which the imperfectly purified had traditionally been condemned pending final expiation of their sins. Viewed from a Catholic perspective, Old Hamlet's need to be remembered is tantamount to an appeal for pious intervention by the living, for those rites of supplication that had once been performed in the old chantry chapels—memorials designed to facilitate the performance of repeated masses for the souls of the dead. In this dispensation, after all, as Hamlet reminds Ophelia before the dumb show, if "a great man's memory" is to survive "he must build churches […] or else he shall suffer not thinking on, with the hobby-horse, whose epitaph is 'For O, for O the hobby-horse is forgot'" (3.2.125–6).

According to reformed doctrine, however, no such intermediate place as Purgatory was supposed to exist,[21] rendering the Ghost a creature of profoundly uncertain status not just for Shakespeare's mainly Protestant audience, but for the play's Danish courtiers, whose religious allegiance is suggested by the fact that their young men study at Luther's famously Protestant university in Wittenberg. To the watchers on the battlements the spectre may seem to resemble "the king that's dead" (1.1.41), but Horatio calls it an "illusion" (l. 109), and throughout the opening scene it remains an indeterminate "it." In the more respectful account that Horatio gives to Hamlet it becomes "him," and even unambiguously

"The King your father" (1.2.189–90), only to revert to the uncertainty of a "figure like your father" (l. 199), an undefined "apparition" (l. 211), while its pronoun now alternates between "it" and "him" (ll. 215–19, 229, 241, 245). For Hamlet, whose use of pronouns is equally unstable, it is either something that may "assume my noble father's person" (l. 246) or actually "My father's spirit in arms" (l. 247), its "questionable shape" either "a spirit of health or goblin damned" (1.4.22, 19)—something that he merely agrees to "*call* [...] Hamlet, / King, father, royal Dane" (ll. 23–4; emphasis added). In the Protestant understanding of things, after all, the Ghost, if not an emissary of the devil, can only be an "illusion," just that empty "coinage of [her son's] brain" that Gertrude supposes (l. 132). Its uncertain nature is emphasised by the fact that for Hamlet's fellow watchers it has no "sound or use of voice" (1.1.110), and when it finally reappears in the Queen's bedchamber to chide Hamlet's tardiness, it will remain for Gertrude herself both invisible and inaudible, a mere "nothing" (3.4.125–8).

As I have argued elsewhere,[22] the uncertain status of the Ghost, its tormented longing for remembrance, and the intense anxiety that these issues arouse in Hamlet all serve as indicators of the traumatic severance of connection with the dead that was occasioned by Reformation theology.[23] The elaborate industry of intercession and indulgences, meant to engineer the release of sinners from the torments of Purgatory, functioned to preserve the dead as another familiar age group in society. Taking the place of such dutiful intervention, there emerged an obsession with the physical evidences of memory—a phenomenon witnessed by the efflorescence of the death arts in the late sixteenth and early seventeenth centuries. Old Hamlet's murder, if the Ghost is to be believed, has subjected him to the abrupt *mors repentina* or *improvisa* so dreaded by the medieval imagination. But, in the Wittenberg-educated world of the play, the ritual consolations that once defined "a good death" can scarcely be available. For Protestants, especially those influenced by the doctrines of Calvin, such an end could only be defined by the unknowable achievement of grace—hence the redefinition of familial piety in terms of proper remembrance of the dead: something that, in the case of the rich and powerful was best demonstrated by the lavish heraldic funerals and increasingly splendid church monuments characteristic of the early modern period.[24]

In *Hamlet* the question of what might constitute a good death is raised repeatedly—most explicitly by Ophelia: in her madness she persuades herself that her father "made a good end" (4.5.186); but Laertes is there to inform us of the truth:

> His means of death, his obscure burial—
> No trophy, sword, nor hatchment o'er his bones,
> No noble rite, nor formal ostentation—
> Cry to be heard. (ll. 213–16)

The "cry" is in a sense a repetition of the Ghost's cries, its need to be heard by "the whole ear of Denmark"—its longing, in other words, for remembrance; but for Laertes it is only the "noble rite" of funeral and the "formal ostentation" of a tomb that could properly speak for Polonius—only these that could proclaim the "good end" of which his sister spoke. Instead the old man is to be given the degraded end that Hamlet describes, one that in effect will make nothing of him: "a certain convocation of politic worms are e'en at him [....] That's the end" (4.3.20–5). This, moreover, is an end that awaits even the mightiest: separated from the body, even a king may be reduced to "a thing [...] of nothing" (4.2.26–8), an annihilation that will embrace Claudius as surely as it has his brother.

Echoing the Prayerbook version of the Psalms, "Man is a thing of nought" (144:40), Hamlet's words also look back to his first encounter with Rosencrantz and Guildenstern, where he teases his sometime friends by musing on the vanity of worldly things and of "man" in particular, the godlike creature whose appearance masks a mere "quintessence of dust" (2.2.306); and it is the graveyard scene, with its mocking parade of skulls, that renders visible the prospect of nullification. The biographical fictions in which the Prince satirically clothes each of its bony relics serve only to draw attention to their utter anonymity, casting doubt even upon the First Clown's identification of the last of them as "Yorick's skull" (5.1.172). For all the sentimental recollections stirred in Hamlet by this supposed vestige of the affectionate jester who "hath borne me on his back a thousand times" (ll. 187–8), the Prince's own rhetoric reminds us that it might just as well be the skull of a beggar or indeed of the greatest emperor in the world: "Dost thou think Alexander looked o' this fashion I'th'earth [....] Alexander died, Alexander was buried, Alexander returneth to dust" (ll. 188–9, 199–200). It is the skull's supposed identity as the old king's fool that fits him to the role of Death the Jester: but the joke is that his "favour" (appearance, look) is one that finally cancels all identity. Like the Players before it, this skull is made to serve as an instrument of memory—but only of that fearful sort known as a *memento mori*.

Carried away by his own satiric wit, Hamlet re-directs the skull's wicked attentions to Ophelia, the sometime mistress whose cosmetic "paintings" he mocked when we first saw them together (3.1.143–5): "Now get you to my lady's chamber and tell her, let her paint an inch thick, to this favour she must come. Make her laugh at that" (ll. 183–6). But the jest is one that turns back on its maker. With especially cruel irony, the procession that interrupts Hamlet's reflections proves to be the stunted funeral of Ophelia, whom we last saw deranged by grief for her own murdered father, her "wits [...] as mortal as an old man's life" (4.5.161–2). Persuading herself that Polonius made "a good end," she offered Laertes the emblem of memory: "There's rosemary, that's for remembrance. Pray love, remember" (ll. 176–7); but the "maimèd rites" of her funeral recall the truth of her father's unceremonious end, while its parade of anonymous skulls consign her to an oblivion from which Claudius's conventional promise of "a living monument" (5.1.287) seems unlikely to rescue her.

Hamlet, for all his graveyard mockery, shares the general concern with making a good end. In the conversation with Horatio that begins the last scene, after another call to "remember," he prefaces his account of Rosencrantz and Guildenstern's sorry fate with a reflection that seems to refer not only to certain "dear plots" that have gone awry but to his own imminent death: "There's a divinity that shapes our ends, / Rough hew them how we will" (5.2.9–11), and this is followed later in the scene by a passive acceptance that brings him close to Calvinist predestinarianism: "There's a special providence in the fall of a sparrow [....] The readiness is all. Since no man know aught of what he leaves, what is't to leave betimes? Let be" (5.2.169–70). Yet for all this talk of self-surrender to providence, the dying Prince, as we saw earlier, remains tormented by the issue of remembrance:

> report me and my cause aright
> To the unsatisfied.
> [...]
> O God, Horatio, what a wounded name,
> Things standing thus unknown, I leave behind me!
> If thou didst ever hold me in thy heart,
> Absent thee from felicity awhile,

And in this harsh world draw thy breath in pain
To tell my story. (ll. 292–3, 297–302)

That half-line might sound like yet another sudden abruption; but Hamlet has more to say, announcing his own death in a last speech that concludes by accepting the end of speech itself: "the rest is silence" (5.2.311).[25] The enigmatic character of this pronouncement results largely from the ambiguity of "rest": if we accept Q2's comma after "solicited"—which many modern editors change to a dash—it might appear to mean simply that the rest of what he had to say is now silenced; while, if we prefer F1's full-stop, then it may seem to refer to an everlasting silence which is all that remains after death. But "rest" in a different sense harks back to Hamlet's last words to the Ghost in first encounter: "Rest, rest, perturbed spirit" (1.5.90), and it is in this sense that Horatio chooses to take it, as he imagines Hamlet's silence filled with angelic music: "Good night, sweet Prince, / And flights of angels sing thee to thy rest" (5.2.312–3). By contrast, for the protagonist himself, whose expressed scorn for "Words, words, words" (2.2.292) arises from his own compulsion "like a whore, [to] unpack my heart with words" (l. 574), silence itself might constitute a welcome form of rest, the sublime "consummation" or "*quietus*" for which he yearned (3.1.64, 76)—the final release from the bondage of "a weary life" that suicide appeared to offer.

At that point, it was no longer the divine "canon 'gainst self-slaughter" (1.2.132) pondered in his first soliloquy that deterred him, but the "dread of something after death" (3.1.79). This fear was presumably aroused by his encounter with the Ghost—though his doubts about the revenant's true nature continued to register in his description of the afterlife as an "undiscovered country, from whose bourn / No traveller returns" (ll. 80–1). However, the alternative to "something" after death is, quite simply, "nothing"—a word that haunts the tragedy like the Ghost itself. From Barnardo's casual-seeming "I have seen nothing" (1.1.21–2), through the vacuous "nothings" of Polonius's ingratiating prattle (2.2.89, 94), Hamlet's self-reproof as one who can "say nothing" (2.2.557), or, like Pyrrhus, do "nothing" (l. 472), through his bafflement at the First Player's extravagant display of grief "for nothing" (l. 545) and his contempt for other actors "capable" (not unlike himself) "of nothing but inexplicable dumb-shows" (3.2.11), through Claudius's impatient "I have nothing with this answer, Hamlet" (l. 89), to the shout of "Nothing neither way" with which Osric fatally interrupts Hamlet's duel with

Laertes (5.2.253), the word appears more often in *Hamlet* than in any play in the canon except (significantly) *King Lear*. Ophelia's studied vacuousness in the Mousetrap scene ("I think nothing, my lord," 3.2.109) is matched by her punning reproof to Hamlet ("You are naught. You are naught," l.137), and ironically by the crazed incoherence of her madness: "Her speech is nothing" declares Horatio, "Yet the unshaped use of it doth move the hearers to collection [....] Though nothing sure, yet much unhappily" (4.5.7–13). For Laertes her ramblings are a "nothing [...] more than matter" (4.5.175). But ironically they will be reduced to the "dust" of mere matter—what Cressida, in Shakespeare's next tragedy, will call "dusty nothing" (*Tro.* 3.2.169)—that her interment in the graveyard leaves her, "As if [she] had never been such" in the words of the First Clown's song (5.1.72). At the end of its final appearance in the play, the Ghost itself is reduced to a mere "nothing," at least in Gertrude's eyes:

> HAMLET Do you see nothing there?
> GERTRUDE Nothing at all; yet all that is I see.
> HAMLET Nor did you nothing heart.
> GERTRUDE No, nothing but ourselves. (3.4.125–8)

It is the decisiveness of her response that partially underlies Hamlet's own viciously playful response when he declares the king to be "a thing [...] Of nothing" (4.2.26–28). Contemplating Polonius's fate as a feast for "politic worms" in the following scene, the Prince amplifies the significance of such nullity in his mockery of Claudius: "Your fat king and your lean beggar is but variable service—two dishes, but to one table. That's the end" (4.3.23–5).

Over this sardonically celebrated ending, however, there still hangs the memory of the Ghost and the "dread of something after death" for which it stands—that fear of entrapment in some middle space from which there is no longer any prospect of rescue; while set against that dread is the fear of an annihilation so absolute that memory itself is given over to the "politic worms" whose impious "convocation" takes the place of those whose prayers for the dead once filled the chantry chapels of Catholic England. There remains the stage on which Hamlet's story will be told and retold; but, because it is a story the finality of whose ending remains profoundly equivocal, those retellings serve only to leave the protagonist dangling in the middest.[26]

In Shakespeare's next tragedy, *Macbeth*, even the meagre consolations of narrative preservation are set aside: life for the doomed protagonist becomes merely "a tale / Told by an idiot, full of sound and fury, / Signifying nothing" (5.5.25–27). Macbeth's soliloquy is cut off on this terrible half-line by the arrival of a messenger, of whom he demands "thy story quickly" (l. 28); but what the messenger has to tell merely confirms his sense of imminent annihilation: "I'gin to be aweary of the sun, / And wish th'estate o'the world were now undone" (ll. 48–49). It is an end that looks forward to the terrible nihilism of *King Lear*—a tragedy triangulated around three great negatives, "nothing," "no cause" and "never,"[27] where another morbid fool will be made to echo Hamlet's satire: "I am a fool, thou art nothing" (*Lr.* 1.4.162). It is that fear of annihilating emptiness which, in *King Lear*, ensures that the longing for coherent pattern is left "incomplete, frustrated, and ruined," undoing the consolations not only of the "brief tale" with which Edgar confers a good death upon his father, but even of the bleak apocalyptic conclusiveness of the "promised end" imagined by Kent (*Lr.* 5.3.259). *Hamlet*, however, hesitates before the prospect, leaving things as they began, suspended "in the dead waste and middle of the night."

Notes

1. Kermode, *The Sense of an Ending*, p. 17.
2. Thirlwell, "It's Still Not Right," p. 38.
3. Seneca, *Troades*, second chorus, l. 397 ("After death there is nothing, and death itself is nothing").
4. See Borges, *Labyrinths*, pp. 87–95.
5. Aristotle, *Poetics*, pp. 15, 17.
6. Horace, *The Art of Poetry*, pp. 132–3.
7. Kermode, p. 7.
8. Ibid., p. 6.
9. Biblical citations follow the *Geneva Bible*, 1599.
10. For an account of how such entrapment in the present moment functions in *King Lear*, see Karremann, "*King Lear* and the Rhetoric of Amnesia" (p. 115): "we are caught with Lear in the hell of the present moment."
11. Citations from *Hamlet* are to the Oxford edition, ed. G. R. Hibbard.
12. OED, "arrest," 5a.

13. All citations from Shakespeare's works, except for *Hamlet*, are to *The New Oxford Shakespeare: Modern Critical Edition*, ed. by Gary Taylor, John Jowett, Terri Bourus, and Gabriel Egan.
14. I have addressed this play's preoccupation with ending in *Issues of Death*. The present essay is in many ways an addendum to that work.
15. Citations from *The Revenger's Tragedy* are to the New Mermaid edition, ed. by Brian Gibbons.
16. Citations from *The Spanish Tragedy* are to the Norton Critical Editions text, ed. by Michael Neill.
17. On ends, endings, and endlessness in Kyd's play, see Dawson, "Madness and Meaning," pp. 53–67.
18. The word "time" recurs no fewer than 40 times in the play—more often than in any other play in the canon, except *Cymbeline*.
19. For further discussion of memory in the play, see Neill, *Issues of Death*, pp. 251–61.
20. Ironically, the Player King, just as he is about to be consigned to such an end—one that in a deep sense is "none of [his own]" (3.2.201)—will insist on the necessity of oblivion in words that echo Claudius: "Most necessary 'tis that we forget / To pay ourselves what to ourselves is debt" (ll. 180–1).
21. The 39 Articles agreed upon by the 1562–3 Convocation of Anglican bishops, in the wake of Queen Elizabeth's accession and her reinstitution of Protestant religion in 1558, expressly declared that "The Romish Doctrine concerning Purgatory […] is a fond thing vainly invented, and grounded upon no warranty of Scripture, but rather repugnant to the Word of God" (Article XXII).
22. See Neill, *Issues of Death*, esp. pp. 38–42, pp. 244–7. Greenblatt's *Hamlet in Purgatory* offers a more detailed account of the controversy and its place in the play, while Karremann discusses its relevance to *King Lear* (110–13).
23. For a critique of the notion that the idea of Purgatory performed an essentially consolatory function, see Belsey, "In Defiance of Death," pp. 9–11, pp. 13–14.
24. See *Issues of Death*, especially Part I, Chapter 1 "'Peremptory Nullification': Tragedy and Macabre Art" and Part III "'Rue with a Difference': Tragedy and the Funereal Arts," pp. 51–101, pp. 265–374.

25. In the Folio text but not in the early quartos, the speech is followed by "O, o, o, o." In such details, F probably reflects performance practice, rather than the dramatist's original intention. Hamlet's silence may, like other details in the play, once more look back to *The Spanish Tragedy* whose protagonist, before exacting revenge and committing suicide, subjects himself to a brutally literal self-silencing: "First take my tongue, and afterwards my heart" (4.5.191); see also McMillin, in "Figure of Silence," pp. 27–48.
26. The conundrum presented by the existence of three very different early texts of the play may suggest that *Hamlet* was a play that Shakespeare himself had difficulty finishing, subjecting it to successive revisions.
27. See Neill, "From Nothing to Never," pp. 43–61.

References

Aristotle. *Poetics*. Translated by John Warrington. London: J.M. Dent, 1963.
Belsey, Catherine. "In Defiance of Death: Shakespeare and Tomb Sculpture." *Memoria di Shakespeare* 6 (2019): 1–20.
Borges, Jorge Luis. *Labyrinths*. Edited by Donald A Yates and James E. Irby. London: Penguin Books, 1970.
Davis, Natalie Zemon. "Ghosts, Kin, and Progeny: Some features of Family Life in Early Modern France." *Daedalus* 106.2 (1977): 87–114.
Dawson, Anthony B. "Madness and Meaning." *Journal of Dramatic Theory and Criticism* 2.1 (1987): 53–67.
Geneva Bible [*The Bible Translated According to the Hebrew and Greek*]. London: 1599.
Greenblatt, Stephen. *Hamlet in Purgatory*. Princeton, NJ: Princeton University Press, 2001.
Horace. *The Art of Poetry*. In *Literary Criticism: Plato to Dryden*. Edited by Allan H. Gilbert. Detroit: Wayne State University Press, 1962.
Karremann, Isabel. "*King Lear* and the Rhetoric of Amnesia." *South Atlantic Review* 83.4 (2018): 103–19.
Kermode, Frank, 1967. *The Sense of an Ending: Studies in the Theory of Fiction*. Oxford: Oxford University Press.
Kyd, Thomas. *The Spanish Tragedy*. Edited by Michael Neill. Norton Critical Editions. New York: W. W. Norton, 2014.

McMillin, Scott. "The Figure of Silence in *The Spanish Tragedy*." *ELH* 39 (1972): 27–48.

Middleton, Thomas. *The Revenger's Tragedy*. Edited by Brian Gibbons. New Mermaid Edition. London: A&C Black, 2008.

Neill, Michael. "From Nothing to Never: Death and *King Lear*." In *Narrating Death: The Limit of Literature*. Edited by Daniel Jernigan, Walter Wadiak, and W. Michelle Wang. London: Routledge, 2019. pp. 43–61.

———. *Issues of Death: Mortality and Identity in English Renaissance Drama*. Oxford: Clarendon Press, 1997.

Shakespeare, William. *The New Oxford Shakespeare: Modern Critical Edition*. General Edited. by Gary Taylor, John Jowett, Terri Bourus, and Gabriel Egan. Oxford: Oxford University Press, 2016.

———. *Hamlet*. Edited by G.R. Hibbard. Oxford: Clarendon Press, 1987.

Seneca, Lucius Annaeus. *Troades: Introduction, Text, and Commentary*. Edited by Atze J. Keulen. Boston, MA: Brill, 2001.

Thirlwell, Adam. "It's Still Not Right." Review of Mario Levrero, *Empty Words*. *London Review of Books* 42.6 (2010): 37–8.

Afterword: Shakespeare and the Duties of the Living

Rory Loughnane

Imagine a play enthusiast among the booksellers in St. Paul's Churchyard in late November 1616. Newly available for purchase at Richard Meighen's shop and elsewhere, for the princely sum of ten shillings, were unbound copies in folio of *The Workes of Beniamin Ionson*. This canon-building, canonizing project of one of England's most famous living poet-dramatists took years to complete, and Jonson himself was involved with revising copy and correcting proofs. The printing house of the collection's printer and publisher, William Stansby, worked intermittently on producing Jonson's *Workes* for over twenty months.[1] Its publication was met with some initial derision, inviting some sniffy complaints about the elevation of a collection of commercial plays, all previously published, to the status of a "Works." Yet Jonson's *Workes* seemed to anticipate such a response, including also some of his court masques and poetry, and eventually it came to be recognized as his lasting achievement. Following Jonson's death in 1637, a group of his friends published a book of elegies in his memory, *Ionsonus Virbius*,[2] where the significance of his *Workes* forms a recurrent theme. One elegist wrote "for none so fit appears / To raise his tomb, as who are left his heirs / Yet for this cause no labour need be spent, / Writing his works, he built his monument,"[3] while another observed that "no Posteritie / Can adde to [Jonson's] Workes; th'had they whole growth then / When first borne, and came aged from thy

---

© The Editor(s) (if applicable) and The Author(s), under exclusive license to Springer Nature Switzerland AG 2022
W. E. Engel and G. Williams (eds.), *The Shakespearean Death Arts*, Palgrave Shakespeare Studies,
https://doi.org/10.1007/978-3-030-88490-1

Pen."[4] Jonson's *Workes*, available to buy in the winter of 1616, set down his marker for posterity.

Ten shillings was a lot of money, however, and perhaps our play enthusiast would choose to first seek out cheaper options. Word of the recent death of William Shakespeare must have reached London by then. Although his passing must have been mourned by some, there was no similar outpouring of grief in print, no volume of elegies. There were also very few of his works newly available for purchase. Over the past several years, during which time Shakespeare had ceased writing for the stage, the only works by him that were re-issued were his old history plays and narrative poems. The fifth quarto of *Richard III* was published in 1612, followed by the sixth quarto of *1 Henry IV* in 1613. An unsavvy buyer, unlike our play enthusiast, may have been attracted to the 1613s quarto of *Thomas Lord Cromwell*, with its title page *bona fides* of "As it hath beene sundry times publikely acted by the Kings Maiesties Seruants" and "Written by W. S.," an attribution repeated from the first quarto.[5] Nothing by Shakespeare found print in 1614, bar some quotations in a reissue of the anthology *England's Helicon*. The fifth quarto of *Richard II* was published in 1615, and, for our would-be buyer in 1616, the only freshly printed work, was the sixth edition of *Lucrece*. What then was available to buy by Shakespeare were mostly very old works, some more than two decades old. His most recent work, if still held in stock several years later, was *Pericles, Prince of Tyre* (1608), last re-issued in 1611 in a corruptly transmitted version. Searching through the booksellers' wares, how underwhelming Shakespeare's presence must have seemed in comparison with Jonson's handsomely produced folio collection. Indeed, for a decade after Shakespeare's retirement from the stage, c. 1613–14, what was available for buyers in his name were largely reprints of very old plays and poems, sometimes misattributed.

In Shakespeare's last will and testament, made on 25 March 1616 a month before his death, he famously makes no mention of any books, scripts, or materials related to his professional life in the theatre. Yet he does include the following provision for his "ffellowes John Hemynges, Richard Burbage & Heny Cundell XXVIs VIIId A peece to buy them Ringes."[6] The rings in question were mourning rings, a material reminder of the departed. Quite how the dead should be remembered and mourned became complicated following the Reformation. With the jettisoning of Purgatory, intercessionary prayer by the living could no longer benefit the dead. They could, of course, still mourn the dead, but to grieve excessively was something to be avoided, a refraction of the sin of despair. Thus, John Donne criticizes "immoderate griefe," while a sermonist in *Thrēnoikos: The House of Mourning* advises "we should mourne, but not as men without hope."[7] In *Twelfth Night*, the Clown gently mocks Olivia "The more fool, madonna, to mourn for your brother's soul, being in heaven" (*TN* 1.5.58–59), while Francis Bacon says that "friends weeping [...] blacks, and obsequies [...] show terrible death."[8] For Heminges, Burbage, and Condell, how could they mark appropriately their fellow's passing? The mourning rings would have kept Shakespeare alive in their memory, as would revivals of his plays for the ongoing operations of the King's Men. But as time passed, a generation removed from the heyday of Shakespeare's professional career, the fellows took it upon themselves to do much more to preserve their friend's memory.

Burbage followed Shakespeare to the grave in 1619, but Heminges and Condell, working with a consortium of stakeholders with interests, both professional and personal, in Shakespeare's works, helped to publish the First Folio collection, which first appeared in November 1623, some seven and a half years after Shakespeare's death. In their prefatory materials, Heminges and Condell describe their project in thanatological terms. In their dedicatory address, they describe how, with this book, they have "done an office to the dead... onely to keep the memory of so worthy a Friend, & Fellow aliue." They are, they say, "a payre so carefull to shew their gratitude both to the liuing [i.e., the dedicatees], and the dead."[9] In their address "To the great variety of Readers," they write they wish Shakespeare had overseen the collection himself, but that "he by death departed from that right."[10] While death is a terminus for the individual, it may not be for those left behind. Here, in and for Shakespeare's memory, Heminges and Condell acted to fight against death's bedfellow, oblivion; they did their duty to the dead.

The idea that the dead could still exert control over the living fascinated Shakespeare. In Shakespeare's plays, from Portia's father's will in *The Merchant of Venice* stipulating that her suitors choose between caskets, to old Hamlet's injunctions about vengeance, the living must often learn to live with what the dead demand. These are very specific examples, of course, but the idea of the posthumous influence over the living was widespread in the period. The severance of the living from the dead in Protestant thought instructed that the living could no longer affect the dead. However, conversely, the dead could still affect those living. While there was no communion between those dead and alive, the living were often restrained by their duties to the dead. In early modern English print culture, books about death and dying proliferated, approached from both the perspective of preparations for death and good remembrance of the dead. The duty to remember the dead—and whatever that entails—brings responsibilities that persist and, in effect, does the work of remembering the dead. Mourning rings, as a blunt example, encourage the wearer to remember to remember death; they are the phrase *memento mori* ("remember to die") made material. But, more significantly, this remembrance of the other's mortality, their cessation of life, forces the wearer to remember their own mortality. The dead exert control over the living because to remember them is to remember shared vulnerability.

The chapters in this collection do their own office to the dead. Identifying a "Shakespearean Death Arts" as an historical category warranting further critical investigation, the editors and contributors reveal some of the various ways in which Shakespeare engaged with the religio-cultural business of preparing to die well. Although (as mentioned in the Introduction) Shakespeare deploys the phrase *memento mori* only once, with Sir John (i.e. Falstaff) mocking Bardolph's red nose as a reminder of "hell-fire" (*1H4* 3.3.23–24), the idea that death is something to be often contemplated and prepared for is pervasive throughout his work. In one of the earliest references to *memento mori* in early modern English print, the preacher John Carpenter, in a sermon about Jesus's invocation to "Remember Lot's Wife,"[11] we find the advice, "know thyself [...] memento mori, remember death."[12] This was not casual advice but a duty of the living. In John More's *A liuely anatomie of death*, we encounter a fuller description of the significance of remembering death:

> *Memento mori*: Remember to dye. *Recordare nouissima*, Remember your latter end: this is your Poesey, and you shall neuer doe amisse, this is the smell, this is the sent of your Nosegay, which if you apply dayly to your sences, it will perfume your soule and body, that all without you, and within you, shall be as a sweete odour, and flagrant incense, to the Lorde of Hostes.[13]

In this striking image, More compares the remembrance of death to the sweet odor of a nosegay or small bouquet of flowers, which must be applied daily to "perfume" the soul and body, making the individual smell sweetly both "without" and "within" to God. But since medieval times, it was thought that disease could enter the body through malodorous vapours and smells, and nosegays were worn to ward off the plague and other maladies, a pre-emptive measure to ward off death. Death cannot be perpetually avoided, but for More its remembrance can ensure the individual "neuer doe[s] amisse" while living. The memory of mortality, thus, helps condition the living towards virtuous living.

Returning to the merry knight who avers virtuous living, Sir John's faking of his own death (his "counterfeit" death) near the end of *1 Henry IV* brings about one of Shakespeare's most arresting discussions of life and death:

> Counterfeit? I lie, I am no counterfeit. To die is to be a counterfeit, for he is but the counterfeit of a man who hath not the life of a man. But to counterfeit dying when a man thereby liveth is to be no counterfeit, but the true and perfect image of life indeed. (*1H4* 5.4.112–116)

In this moment of theatrical magic, where the dead can be resurrected, Sir John's distinction between the vitality of the living and the counterfeit "life" of the dead introduces a simultaneously joyful and solemn note to proceedings. Indeed, it sets in motion one of the most protracted deaths in dramatic history. In the epilogue to the sequel *2 Henry IV*, one of Shakespeare's most death-marked plays, it is noted that "Falstaff shall die of a sweat—unless already a be killed with your hard opinions" (*2H4* Epilogue/19.23–23); that is, that Sir John will die of sweating sickness in the next play, unless he is poorly received in this play and killed off beforehand. Whatever the reception of *2 Henry IV*—and, perhaps significantly, *2 Henry IV* was only printed in quarto once (1600)—Sir John would not appear in the next and final part of the tetralogy, *Henry V*.

Yet Shakespeare gives over much play space to the preparation for, and report of, the death of the unseen character. For early audiences of the play, familiar with the *Henry IV* plays, there must have been a natural expectation that Sir John would soon appear. That appetite was further whetted when his old crew appears in the play's opening scenes, and when the Boy, servant to Sir John, enters to speak of his master. The news about Sir John is not encouraging: he is "very sick, and would to bed" (*H5* 2.1.69). In her inimitable style, Quickly says Sir John's body may be crow-food soon ("he'll yield the crow a pudding one of these days") and claims King Harry has "killed [Sir John's] heart" (*H5* 2.1.72–73). Two scenes later, it is Quickly who recounts Sir John's death. Bardolph wishes he were with Sir John again, "either in heaven or in hell" (*H5* 2.3.6–7). Quickly protests that he cannot be in hell: "A made a finer end, and went away an it been any christom child" (*H5* 2.3.9–10). That is, Sir John, died a good death—as well as any Christian child. Seeming to confirm this, she says Sir John's last words were "God, God, God" as he prepared to die (*H5* 2.3.15). This account of his gracious death is soon undermined, however. Nim says he heard Sir John call out for alcohol, which Quickly confirms; Bardolph claims Sir John called out about women, which Quickly denies, but the Boy insists that he did so only to call them devils. But this altered account pushes the death scene into different territory—the province of hell, once denied, returns to the fore, with a further account of Sir John's death moans about the Whore of Babylon, and then an intriguing intertextual reference to souls burning in hell, harking back to *1 Henry IV*:

> Do you not remember, a saw a flea stick upon Bardolph's now, and a said it was a black soul burning in hell? (*H5* 2.3.30–31)

Sir John earlier made "good use" of Bardolph's ruddy face to remind him of the ceaselessly burning fires of hell and thereby his own mortality (*1H4* 3.3.22). Yet the comparison was nuanced by the sinful activity implied by Bardolph's "burning" redness, caused by venereal disease and/or too much carousing. The further comparison to the biblical figure of Dives a rich man sent to damnation for his maltreatment of Lazarus[14]—"I think upon hell-fire and Dives that lived in purple—for there he is in his robes, burning, burning" (*1H4* 3.3.23–25)—assures us that what Sir John sees in Bardolph is a vision of hell, and eternal punishment specifically. And so, what is recalled here, with this intertextual nod, offers a disquieting note to Quickly's subjective account of Sir John dying well. The audience, it seems, are better prepared for Sir John's death than the character.

I have dwelt on the ends of Sir John—plural—to observe an example where Shakespeare alerts us to the deathbed politics of dying well. The chapters in this collection draw our attention to many more instances where the approach or likelihood of physical death grants pause for characters to meditate upon mortality. While Harry rallies his worried troops in a "pre-battle lesson in the art of dying" in *Henry V* (see McCarthy, Chapter 2), Othello and Desdemona, in their bedchamber, enact a sort of formalized ritual that invokes the death arts (see Vinter, Chapter 8). So, too, several of the chapters describe Shakespeare's interplay with practices of monumentalizing the dead, whether material (see Todd, Chapter 6) or more figurative and rhetorical (see Williams, Chapter 5). The second half of the collection focuses upon Shakespeare's most meditative study about death, *Hamlet*, and reveals the play's extraordinary engagement with the formal rituals of death (see Baldo, Chapter 9), mourning practices (see Karremann, Chapter 14), and burial rites (see Macfie, Chapter 12; and Wilder, Chapter 13). In a fitting and compelling way, the book's final chapter proper, by our leading scholar in Shakespearean death studies, identifies a key point of tension in the contemplation and fear of death: that it "might constitute no true end at all" or that "its ending might [...] prove too absolute, offering the prospect of annihilation represented by the dust and worms of the graveyard" (see Neill, Chapter 15). It is this precise fear, to be engaged with, to be warded off, that holds the key to the generative power of death in Shakespeare's writing.

Rory Loughnane
University of Kent, Canterbury, UK

Notes

1. For the production of the Jonson's *Workes*, see David Gants, "The 1616 Folio (F1): Textual Essay." Gants also provides helpful discussion about the book's early reception.
2. Jonson, Benjamin, *Ionsonus Virbius*.
3. Ibid., sig. B4^v.
4. Ibid., sig. E3^v.
5. *Thomas Lord Cromwell* (London: 1602, STC 21532) and (London 1613, STC 21533).
6. Shakespeare's last will and testament is held at The National Archives, Kew, UK (PROB 1/4). A reliable transcript can be found on the National Archives website: https://www.nationalarchives.gov.uk/museum/item.asp?item_id=21 (accessed July 31 2021).
7. *Thrēnoikos The house of mourning*, sig. D5^v. In Donne's "Elegie on Mistress Boulstred" [Bulstrode], he describes "immoderate griefe" as a "sinne" to "scape." See *Poems, by J.D. With elegies on the authors death* (1633; STC 7045), sig. K4^r.
8. Rory Loughnane, ed. by *Twelfth Night* in *The New Oxford Shakespeare: Modern Critical Edition*. All Shakespeare citations are to individual editions from the *Modern Critical Edition*. For Francis Bacon's essay, "Of Death," see the full entry in William E. Engel, Rory Loughnane, and Grant Williams, *The Death Arts in Renaissance England*, entry III.10.

9. *Mr. William Shakespeares comedies, histories, & tragedies*, sig. A2^{r-v}.
10. Ibid., sig. A3^r.
11. Luke 17:32.
12. Jesus is reassuring ten lepers on his way to Jerusalem, by using the example of Lot's wife who went against God's command to not look back toward Sodom, and was thereby turned to stone. John Carpenter, *Remember Lots wife Two godly and fruitfull sermons verie conuenient for this our time*, sig. A8^v.
13. More, *A liuely anatomie of death*, sig. B2^{r-v}.
14. Luke 16:19–31.

References

Carpenter, John. *Remember Lots wife Two godly and fruitfull sermons verie conuenient for this our time*. London: Thomas Orwin, 1588. STC 4665.
Donne, John. "Elegie on Mistress Boulstred" [Bulstrode]. In *Poems, by J.D. With elegies on the authors death*. London, M[iles]. F[lesher]., 1633. STC 7045.
Engel, William E., Rory Loughnane, and Grant Williams. *The Death Arts in Renaissance England*. Cambridge: Cambridge University Press, 2022.
Gants, David. "The 1616 Folio (F1): Textual Essay." In *The Cambridge Edition of the Works of Ben Jonson Online*. Edited by David Bevington, Martin Butler, and Ian Donaldson. Cambridge: Cambridge University Press, 2012. http://universitypublishingonline.org/cambridge/benjonson/k/essays/F1_textual_essay/.
Geneva Bible [*The Bible Translated According to the Hebrew and Greek*]. London: 1599.
Jonson, Benjamin. *Ionsonus Virbius*. London: E. P[urslowe]., 1638. STC 14784.
———. *The Workes of Beniamin Ionson*. London: William Stansby, 1616. STC 14752.
More, John. *A liuely anatomie of death*. London: G. S[impson]., 1596. STC 18073.
Shakespeare, William. "Last Will and Testament." The National Archives, Kew, UK (PROB 1/4). https://www.nationalarchives.gov.uk/museum/item.asp?item_id=21.
———. *Mr. William Shakespeares comedies, histories, & tragedies*. London: Isaac Iaggard and Ed[ward] Blount, 1623. STC 22273.
———. Shakespeare, William. *The New Oxford Shakespeare, The Complete Works*. General edited by Gary Taylor, John Jowett, Terri Bourus, and Gabriel Egan. Oxford: Oxford University Press, 2017.
Thrēnoikos The house of mourning; furnished with directions for preparations to meditations of consolations at the houre of death. London: John Dawson, 1640. STC 24049.

Index

A
Aaron. *See* Shakespeare, William, *Titus Andronicus*
abject/abjection, 14, 133, 246, 247
Agrippina, 263, 265–268, 276
alchemy/alchemical, 206, 244, 245, 249
Alexander, 188, 189, 251–253, 319
amplification, 225, 231. *See also* rhetoric
anatomy, 2, 5, 269
  as literary genre, 292
  early modern practice of, 2. *See also* Vesalius
angel/angelic, 16, 35, 101, 213, 219, 321. *See also* devil
Aquinas, Thomas, 263, 270
Ariès, Phillippe, 4, 19, 46
Aristotle/Aristotelian, 4, 5, 88, 105, 148, 308, 323
arms/armor, 52, 67, 118, 122, 123, 124, 128, 188, 191, 230, 262, 318. *See also* heraldry/heraldic

ars moriendi, 1, 2, 3, 18, 33–36, 38–43, 45, 46, 67, 69, 70, 75, 79, 91, 147, 158, 263, 282–284, 287, 292–294. *See also* death
  the sin of despair, 329
  the sin of impatience, 43
  ars moriendi, 47
ash/ashes, 18, 114, 115, 116, 126, 128. *See also* dust
atomism, 250, 251, 252. *See also* Lucretius
  democritean, 177
Augustine of Hippo (St. Augustine)/Augustinian, 56, 262

B
Bacon, Francis, 329, 333
bad death. *See* death
Becon, Thomas, 35, 36, 40, 42, 46, 70
  Sicke Man's Salve, 35, 36, 38, 40, 42, 46

© The Editor(s) (if applicable) and The Author(s), under exclusive license to Springer Nature Switzerland AG 2022
W. E. Engel and G. Williams (eds.), *The Shakespearean Death Arts*, Palgrave Shakespeare Studies,
https://doi.org/10.1007/978-3-030-88490-1

Bible, 36, 121, 263, 308
  Geneva, 20, 194, 196, 255, 256, 323
biblical figures. *See also* God
  Adam, 71, 188, 191, 197, 287, 307
  Daniel, 86, 104
  Dives, 332
  Eve, 287
  Jesus Christ, 37, 57, 121, 182, 184, 252, 292, 330, 334. *See also* Eucharist
  Job, 36
  Jonah, 121
  Lazarus, 332
  Lot's wife, 330, 334
  Mary, 60, 182
  Nebuchadnezzar II, 86
  Satan, 37, 71. *See also* devil
blazon, 85, 86, 100, 101, 144, 231
body, 5, 12, 35, 43, 49–63, 67, 69–72, 75–79, 83, 122, 135, 143, 148, 155, 159, 165, 167, 183–185, 188, 191–193, 207, 209, 235, 242, 244–249, 251–254, 264, 269–271, 287, 290, 293, 298, 319, 330, 331. *See also* cadaver; Eucharist; soul
Book of Common Prayer, 115, 252, 256, 264, 309
Book of Martyrs. *See* Foxe, John
burial, 2, 4, 6, 18, 49, 50, 60, 61, 62, 86, 97, 115, 117, 118, 181, 188, 189, 191–193, 241, 252, 264, 265, 293, 333. *See also* Catholicism; funeral; Protestantism; sepulchre; tomb
  at sea, 6, 119, 125
  of Elizabeth I, 60, 61
  of Mary Queen of Scots, 60

C
cadaver, 5, 6, 117, 122, 247, 269. *See also* body
Caesar. *See* Shakespeare, William, *Julius Caesar*
Caligula, 91, 266, 267
Calvin, John, 69, 318, 320. *See also* election; predestination
Camillo, Giulio, 206, 207, 209, 216, 218, 220
Catholicism
  burial rites, 264
  Counter-Reformation (Catholic Reformation), 158
  funereal practices, 53
  protestant break with, 174
Caxton, William, 19, 36, 47
  The Arte and Crafte to Know Well to Dye, 34, 43
  To Know Well To Die, 2
Christ. *See* biblical figures
chronicle, 49, 95, 104, 126, 316. *See also* history
Church of England, 35, 69
Cicero, 5, 87, 88, 90, 97, 225
  De Officiis, 89, 102
Claudius. *See* Shakespeare, William, *Hamlet*
closet scene, 217, 262, 290, 291. *See also* Shakespeare, William, *Hamlet*
closure, 313, 314
  instrument of, 193. *See also* narrative
commemoration, 6, 92, 97, 102, 103, 128, 181, 182, 184
  minne, 182, 183, 195
  month's mind, 181, 192, 193
  rituals of, 182. *See also* remembrance
commonplace books, 3, 89, 96, 292. *See also* humanism/humanist

commonplaces, 2, 9, 10, 17, 71, 75, 89, 96, 118, 235, 237, 292. *See also* rhetoric
verbal, 235
visual, 235, 237. *See also* emblem books
confess/confession, 36, 37, 39, 45, 94, 134, 147, 166, 183, 191, 217, 282, 287, 290, 317. *See also* repent/repentance
conquest of England, 180, 185–187
contemptus-mundi, 95
corpse, 4, 12, 53, 55–61, 69, 76, 97, 115, 117, 118, 124, 125, 154–156, 159, 165–168, 182, 184, 191, 192, 247, 248, 254, 290, 294, 299, 313
as unstable signifier, 50
speaking, 18, 154, 155, 167, 168
Cranmer, Thomas, 57, 63
Cressy, David, 7, 46, 118, 129, 181, 192, 194, 195, 198

D

damnation, 35, 70, 185, 214, 282, 316, 332. *See also* grace; salvation
Dance of Death/*Danse Macabre*, 62, 154, 156, 158, 164, 168, 169, 283–285, 287, 289, 290, 292–295, 297–301, 303
as estates satire, 285
performative nature of, 293
visual tradition of, 299
Dante, 212
Day, John, 97, 98, 107
death. *See also ars moriendi*; Dance of Death/*Danse Macabre*; suicide
and *moriens*, 1, 147
and sleep, 6, 14, 76, 77, 166, 167
annihilation, 154, 309, 333
as fool/jester, 17, 44, 285, 289, 291, 319, 329
as leveler, 72, 154, 285
as *mors*, 285, 287, 298
attributes of, 17, 241
bad death, 16, 282, 284, 286, 299, 300
good death, 2, 7, 8, 38, 40, 46, 69, 147, 261, 262, 282, 290–294, 297–300, 317, 318, 323, 332
memento mori, 2, 4, 8, 11, 16–18, 21, 52, 62, 68, 70, 71, 79, 81, 102, 154, 156, 158, 159, 162, 164, 166, 168, 281, 284, 285, 288, 290, 291, 293, 330. *See also* skull
mors improvisa, 283
personification of, 285
staging/performance of, 4, 6, 7, 11–13, 16–18, 52, 53, 57, 75, 86, 114, 115, 124, 128, 135, 140, 153–157, 159, 160, 165–167, 184, 282, 284, 286, 293, 295, 297
symbol of, 11, 17, 124, 125, 185, 284. *See also* death's head
death arts, 1–4, 6, 7, 9, 11–19, 22, 68, 70, 75, 76, 79, 81, 102, 114–118, 122–125, 127, 128, 133, 135, 147, 155, 168, 204, 219, 233, 237, 263, 281–285, 302, 318, 332
and memorial practices, 127
and theatre's relationship to, 114
explanation of, 102
deathbed, 34–37, 42, 44, 47, 67, 68, 70, 72, 75, 76, 78–80, 82, 154, 158, 283, 287, 293, 294, 332. *See also ars moriendi*
death's head, 11, 21. *See also* death, symbol of; skull
decay, 6, 8, 49, 59, 70, 80, 113, 114, 117, 122–124, 126, 156, 247

338 INDEX

and decomposition, 114. *See also* cadaver
descriptio/description, 11, 51, 57, 88, 99, 100, 123, 144, 160, 161, 183, 211, 223–239, 241, 246, 253, 254, 265, 266, 289, 298, 303, 321, 330. *See also energeia*; rhetoric
Desdemona. *See* Shakespeare, Wiliam, Othello
devil, 35, 37, 158, 203, 213, 214, 219, 264, 270, 275, 298, 318, 332. *See also* angel/angelic; hell; Satan
Donne, John, 6, 8, 20, 264, 301, 329, 333
dramatic irony, 44, 87, 91–93, 102, 103, 289, 295
dream/dreaming, 9, 85, 86, 101, 185, 203, 235
dust, 115, 188, 242, 247, 249–254, 256, 309, 319, 322, 333. *See also* ash/ashes; death, symbol of
dynastic line, 78. *See also* heraldry/heraldic

E
earth/earthy, 9, 34, 37, 49, 85, 113, 179, 180, 183, 187, 194, 204, 205, 207–211, 216, 218, 241, 247–249, 251–254, 291, 292, 314, 319
earworm, 161–163
Eddas, 189
Edward the Confessor, King of England, 186, 187, 197
effigy, 116, 117, 118, 165, 286. *See also* tomb
ekphrasis, 100, 230, 235, 232, 238. *See also* rhetoric
election, 69, 282. *See also* Calvin, John; predestination

elegy, 43, 127, 224, 226, 227, 229, 253
Elizabeth I, Queen of England, 60, 61
Elizabeth II, Queen of England, 62
emblem/emblematic, 2, 71, 73, 95, 166, 185, 191, 271, 288, 290, 294, 297, 299, 320
emblematic associations, 245, 246. *See also* death, symbol of
emblem books, 2, 89. *See also* commonplaces, visual
empathy, 133–140, 142, 143, 145, 147, 148, 161, 164
enargeia, 223, 225–227, 229, 231, 232, 236, 238. *See also descriptio/description*; rhetoric
England, 18, 50, 60, 69, 70, 117, 122, 180–182, 184–187, 192, 193, 195–197, 225, 238, 264, 282–284, 322, 327
  Danish conquest of, 180, 185
  Norman conquest of, 180, 185–187
  Wars of the Roses, 50
Enlightenment, 4, 7, 263, 272
Erasmus, Desiderius, 9, 20, 35, 46, 50, 51, 88, 89, 96, 103, 105, 107, 158, 225–229, 233, 237–239, 267
  De Copia, 88, 96, 105, 107, 227
et in arcadia ego, 226. *See also* death, symbol of
Eucharist, 184, 185, 301, 317. *See also* Christ; remembrance
eulogy/eulogize, 86. *See also* funeral
exemplum/exempla, 86–92, 93–97, 99–103, 105, 106. *See also* rhetoric

F
faith, 37, 57, 87, 148, 180, 185, 192, 194, 251, 282, 300, 301

Christian, 62
  loss of, 34, 41
Falstaff. *See* Shakespeare, William, *1 Henry IV, 2 Henry IV, Henry V*
  figura, 56. *See also* Protestantism
figural/figurative, 3, 63, 114, 119, 121, 203, 205, 245, 256, 270, 333
forgetting, 60, 90, 95, 96, 102, 119, 120, 124, 125, 182, 188, 290, 315, 324. *See also* remembering
Fortinbras. *See* Shakespeare, William, *Hamlet*
Foxe, John, 97, 98. *See also* martyr
Book of Martyrs, 97
Frye, Roland, 9, 11, 20, 288, 298, 302, 304
funeral, 2. *See also* burial; sepulcher; tomb
  military, 54, 56
  royal, 50, 60
  state, 288
futurity. *See also* time
  anticipation of, 155
  desire for, 28

G
Galen, 245. *See also* humoral theory
gender/gendering, 18, 21, 94, 154, 155, 159, 160, 163, 164, 168, 245, 247, 253, 262, 263, 265, 270, 274
Gertrude. *See* Shakespeare, Wiliam, *Hamlet*
Ghost, 53, 184–186, 204, 210–215, 224, 227, 229–232, 247, 250, 266, 271, 282, 285, 287–290, 297, 309–319, 321, 322
  uncertain status of, 317, 318. *See also* phantasms; Shakespeare, William, *Hamlet*; specters; spirits

Girard, René, 139, 149
Globe Theatre. *See* Shakespeare, William
God, 37, 40, 43, 44, 53, 57, 70, 72, 79, 85, 90, 91, 101, 182, 189, 203, 204, 206, 208, 212, 217, 235, 252, 262–264, 282, 291, 297–299, 308, 330, 332, 334. *See also* angel; biblical figures; devil; heaven; purgatory
good death. *See* death
Gower, John. *See* Shakespeare, William, *Pericles*
  tomb of, 114–117, 119, 120, 125, 128
grace, 37, 56, 249, 264, 282, 318. *See also* redemption; salvation
grave, 3, 11, 17, 49, 50, 62, 113, 116, 119, 120, 123, 125, 126, 128, 154–156, 159, 163, 165, 166, 188, 192, 197, 204, 248, 249, 254, 271, 289, 329
  mass graves, 117. *See also* burial; monument; sepulcher; tomb
Gravedigger. *See* Shakespeare, William, *Hamlet*
graveyard, 9, 17, 113, 117, 159, 188, 190–193, 250, 251, 253, 284, 285, 288, 309, 319, 320, 322, 333
Graveyard Scene, 180, 184. *See also* Shakespeare, William, *Hamlet*; Yorick
Greenblatt, Stephen, 20, 63, 82, 129, 136, 137, 148, 149, 158, 180, 183, 195, 196, 220, 287
  Hamlet in Purgatory, 20, 63, 169, 194, 220, 302, 324
grief/grieving, 15, 43, 44, 45, 127, 209, 224, 225, 227, 229–231, 233, 237, 238, 255, 282, 320, 321, 328. *See also* mourning

H

Guildenstern. *See* Shakespeare, William, *Hamlet*

Hamlet. *See* Shakespeare, William, *Hamlet*
heaven, 37, 39, 43, 85, 179, 187, 188, 194, 203–205, 207, 208–219, 236, 289, 290, 298, 299, 314, 317, 329, 332. *See also* hell; purgatory
hell, 37, 166, 168, 203, 207, 208, 210, 211, 212–218, 236, 289, 312, 317, 323, 332. *See also* heaven; purgatory
Henry VII, King of England, 60, 61
Henry VIII, King of England, 11, 287
heraldry/heraldic, 86, 97, 118, 123, 318. *See also* arms/armor; dynastic line
Herbert, George, 6, 20
Hercules, 90, 106
Hippocrates, 245
history, 7, 8, 21, 50, 51, 61, 78, 88, 93, 97, 104, 116, 117, 168, 181, 185, 187, 189, 213, 237, 247, 301, 303, 310, 311, 328, 331. *See also* chronicle
and historical writing, 253, 273, 328
English, 181, 185
Roman, 267, 268
Holbein, Hans (the Younger), 62, 283–287, 289, 291, 292, 299
Homer, 228, 308
Horace, 308, 312
Art of Poetry, 323
Hotspur. *See* Shakespeare, William, *1 Henry IV*

humanism/humanist, 2, 87–93, 96, 97, 99, 102, 103, 206, 223–225, 292
educational program, 97
project of, 96, 97. *See also* rhetoric
humiliation, 49, 95. *See also* shame
humoral theory, 255. *See also* body; medicine

I

Iago. *See* Shakespeare, William, *Othello*
identification, 70, 71, 139, 156, 159, 161, 237, 243, 245, 246, 253, 285, 295, 298, 319
image. *See also* memory, art of
deathbed, 70, 71, 73–75
graven, 86
posthumous, 87, 88, 92, 93, 95, 97, 99, 101, 102, 158
visual, 100, 156, 158
imagination
and empathy, 71, 135, 136
bereaved, 224
faculty of, 93, 94, 99
opinions, 98
phenomenology of, 253
pictorial, 234
popular, 21
in medias res, 308, 312
in mediis rebus, 308
irony, 7, 45, 101, 158, 217, 295, 298, 320

J

James I, King of England, 60
Jonson, Ben, 38, 43, 113, 114, 128, 237, 239, 327, 328
Workes, 327, 328, 333

K

Kantorowicz, Ernst, 75, 82. *See also* sovereign's two bodies
Kyd, Thomas, 234, 237, 313, 314, 324
Spanish Tragedy, 13, 21, 233, 239, 270, 313, 325

L

Laertes. *See* Shakespeare, William, *Hamlet*
Lamord, 181, 183–186, 195. *See also* Shakespeare, William, *Hamlet*
life, 4–9, 13, 16–18, 35, 37, 38, 40–42, 44, 45, 51, 53–55, 57–59, 62, 71, 77, 80, 85, 86, 88, 90, 104, 114–119, 121, 123–125, 127, 128, 133, 135, 137, 140, 144, 147, 154, 156, 158, 167, 181, 185, 186, 188, 190, 192, 204, 238, 247, 248, 252, 261–263, 267, 271, 273, 285, 287–290, 293–295, 298–301, 308–310, 314, 317, 320, 321, 323, 328, 330, 331
eternal, 121, 125, 252, 282
transitoriness of, 8, 42, 71, 192. *See also contemptus mundi*
lineage, 69, 74, 78, 97, 115, 119, 123. *See also* dynastic line
literary form, 69
locus amoenus, 241–244, 255
loss, 6, 18, 37, 55, 58, 95, 125–127, 129, 134, 140, 146, 154, 180, 182, 224–229, 231, 233, 234, 236, 237, 253, 270, 282, 284, 291. *See also* mourning
Lucretius, 243, 250, 251, 252, 256
clinamen, 251
primordia, 251. *See also* atomism
Luther, Martin, 56, 317

Lydgate, John, 156–158, 165, 169, 283, 294, 295, 303

M

Macbeth. *See* Shakespeare, William, *Macbeth*
maimed rites, 281. *See also* Protestantism, Reformation
Marlowe, Christopher
Dido, Queen of Carthage, 266
Doctor Faustus, 46
The Jew of Malta, 39
2 Tamburlaine, 39
martyr/martyrdom, 2, 165, 262, 292. *See also* Foxe, John
Mary I, Queen of England, 60
Mary, Queen of Scots, 60
material, 4, 37–40, 71, 88, 96, 97, 116, 122, 137, 147, 188, 198, 228, 247–250, 252, 274, 290, 301, 328–330, 333. *See also* physical; spiritual
medicine, 4, 41, 138. *See also* humoral theory
memento mori, 2, 4, 8, 9, 11, 16–18, 21, 52, 62, 68, 70, 71, 79, 81, 91, 102, 154–156, 158, 159, 162, 164, 166, 168, 281, 284, 285, 288, 290, 291, 320, 330. *See also* death's head; vanitas
memorial, 11, 86, 87, 92, 93, 95, 97, 103, 104, 115–124, 127, 128, 147, 155, 159, 164, 227, 237, 248, 317. *See also* effigy; memory; monument; remembering
memory
art of (*ars memoria*), 205, 206, 208, 215, 284
as storehouse, 89, 206
as treasure house, 87
faculty of, 93, 180, 188

of the deceased, 114, 124
metatheatre. *See* theater
Middleton, Thomas, 21, 313, 314
　The Old Law, 21
　The Revenger's Tragedy, 159, 270, 313
minne. *See* commemoration
mirror, 71, 89, 206, 294, 295, 297, 301
　as *vanitas* symbol, 294
mnemonic. *See* memory, art of (*ars memoria*)
Montaigne, Michel de, 38, 103, 250
month's mind. *See* commemoration
monument, 2, 6, 11, 18, 85–87, 92, 93, 97–99, 101–104, 114, 116–120, 122–125, 128, 245, 318, 320, 327, 333
More, Thomas, 263, 303
　Utopia, 264
mortality, 2, 4, 7–9, 11, 16, 17, 42, 69–71, 73, 74, 77–81, 90, 133, 154–156, 158, 162–168, 204, 233, 283, 284, 288–292, 299, 300, 303, 330–332. *See also* death's head; *memento mori*; *vanitas*
mourning. *See also* grief/grieving; loss; remembrance
　garb, 289
　period of, 183
　rings, 328–330
Mousetrap Scene, 184, 214, 215, 268, 295, 297, 315, 322. *See* Shakespeare, William, *Hamlet*
mud/muddy, 126, 127, 242, 244, 245, 247, 248, 249, 253, 254
　compared with clay, 249. *See also* ooze

N
narrative

closure, 176
epic, 233, 236, 237
false, 311
progression, 225
strategies, 155, 161
trajectory, 225, 234
Neill, Michael, 108, 146, 246, 255, 302, 325, 333
　Issues of Death, 104, 150, 324
Neoplatonism, 244
　Plotinus, 244
Nero, 91, 263, 265–269, 273
nothing/nothingness, 9, 37, 54, 55, 73, 95, 137, 147, 148, 162, 167, 189, 225, 231, 251, 262, 271, 312, 315, 316, 318, 319, 321–323, 328

O
ooze, 18, 114, 125–128, 244, 248. *See also* mud/muddy; slime
Ophelia. *See* Shakespeare, William, *Hamlet*
Osric. *See* Shakespeare, William, *Hamlet*
Othello. *See* Shakespeare, William, *Othello*
Ovid, 242, 254, 266
Ovidianism, 3

P
paradox, 68, 71, 74, 75, 78, 80, 154, 161, 219, 263, 291. *See also* riddles
performativity, 13, 16, 128, 133, 135, 155
　language of, wounding words, 135. *See also* theater
Petrarchanism, 3
phantasms, 94, 100, 101, 224, 235

physical, 40, 50, 56, 57, 59, 61, 63, 74, 82, 86, 93, 100, 101, 117, 122, 140, 185, 227, 238, 250, 264, 266, 269, 291, 318, 332. *See also* body; material; spiritual
Plutarch, 86, 88–93, 99, 100, 104–107
　The Lives, 107
Polonius, 53, 186, 189, 232, 269, 270, 290, 316, 319, 320. *See also* maimed rites; Shakespeare, William, *Hamlet*
posterity, 87, 88, 90, 92–94, 97, 99, 101–104, 328. *See also* lineage
prayer, 2, 34, 35, 37, 38, 42, 53, 70, 181, 182, 215–217, 281–283, 287, 291, 292, 297, 298, 322, 328. *See also* Book of Common Prayer
predestination, 282, 301. *See also* election
primal, 244, 247, 252
print/printing, 2, 34, 70, 78, 89, 95–97, 102, 105, 248, 327, 328, 330
Protestantism, 283
　doctrine, 317, 318
　Reformation, 117, 184
　university (Wittenberg), 317. *See also* Catholicism; faith
providence, 194, 298, 299, 300, 301, 320. *See also* Protestantism, doctrine
pun/punning, 97, 146, 244, 312, 322
punishment
　divine, 86
　eternal, 332
　public, 140
　self, 270. *See also* damnation; purgatory

purgatory, 53, 117, 182, 194, 211–213, 216, 282, 316–318, 324, 328. *See also* Greenblatt; heaven; hell
purge/purgation, 121, 140, 147, 211, 212. *See also* purgatory
puritan, 2, 182
　as a religious tendency, 175

Q
Quintilian, 225–228, 231, 235, 236, 238, 239
　The Orator's Education, 238

R
race, 21, 136, 154, 155, 159, 160, 163, 164, 168, 274
　performance of, 158
　racial difference, 158
redemption, 62. *See also* grace; salvation; sin
Reformation, 302
remembering, 2, 8, 11, 53, 61, 85, 90–93, 95–97, 102–104, 115, 119, 120, 123–125, 128, 162, 179, 180, 181, 182, 187–189, 193, 203, 205, 207, 208, 210, 226, 286, 288, 290, 312, 314, 316, 317, 320, 328, 330. *See also* commemoration
remembrance, 50, 53, 71, 72, 88, 97, 104, 117, 181–185, 188, 194, 282, 287, 291, 294, 295, 309, 310, 315–320, 330, 331. *See also* forgetting; memory
remorse, 39. *See also* shame
repent/repentance, 2, 165, 264, 282, 283, 290, 297, 298. *See also* confess/confession
reproductive rights, 271

revivification, 114–116, 124, 125, 128
rhetoric, 3, 5, 18, 51, 58, 72, 86, 88, 90, 92, 96, 98, 102, 105, 116, 133, 135, 137, 139, 146, 147, 203, 204, 206, 208, 223–229, 231–233, 235–238, 242, 265, 273, 292, 310, 319, 333
  copia, 96
  humanist, 87, 97, 223–225
  inventio, 98. *See also* Erasmus, Desiderius
Richard III, King of England, 49, 62
  corpse of, 49
riddles, 9, 18, 119, 189–193, 197, 198
  integral to burial customs, 191
Rome/Roman, 3, 12, 55, 56, 87–89, 92, 95, 104, 196, 263, 264, 267, 268
rosemary, 271, 320. *See also* rue
Rosencrantz. *See* Shakespeare, William, *Hamlet*
rue, 271. *See also* rosemary

S

sacrament/sacramental, 56, 57, 185, 282, 301. *See also* Eucharist
saints, 115, 165, 168, 182, 301
salvation, 185, 282, 298, 300, 316, 317. *See also* damnation; grace; redemption; sin
Satan, 37, 71. *See also* devil
satire/satiric, 157, 285, 323
secrecy, 311
Seneca (the Younger), 3, 19, 231, 232, 239, 307, 323. *See also* stoicism
sepulcher, 86, 248. *See also* grave; monument; tomb
Shakespeare, William
  and The Globe Theatre, 9

Antony and Cleopatra, 3, 18, 85–88, 90–93, 95–97, 99, 101–103, 126, 248
Cymbeline, 126, 127, 324
First Folio, 329
Hamlet, 9, 11, 13, 16–18, 21, 50, 52, 57, 63, 103, 144, 159, 180, 181, 186, 189, 191, 193–196, 204, 207, 212, 224, 225, 229, 232, 233, 238, 262, 264, 265, 267, 268, 275, 281–284, 285, 287, 288, 293, 295, 297, 300, 309, 310, 313, 318, 322, 323, 325, 333. *See also* soliloquy/soliloquies
Henry V, 39, 41, 42, 51, 58, 60, 126, 223, 238, 331, 332
1 Henry IV, 328, 331, 332
2 Henry IV, 69, 74, 75, 78, 79, 82, 169, 331
1 Henry VI, 58, 60
2 Henry VI, 122
Julius Caesar, 50, 54, 57, 85, 99, 103
King Lear, 42, 43, 250, 322–324
last will and testament, 328, 333
Love's Labour's Lost, 27
Locrine (attr.), 50, 61
Macbeth, 21, 45, 323
Measure for Measure, 37, 41, 42
Merchant of Venice, 329
Midsummer Night's Dream, 13–15
Much Ado About Nothing, 118
Othello, 18, 133–138, 140, 143, 144, 147, 148, 153–155, 158–160, 162, 164, 168, 169, 244
Pericles, 10, 11, 18, 113–115, 119, 124, 126–129, 190, 328
Richard II, 75, 328
Richard III, 265, 328
Romeo and Juliet, 11, 14, 120

INDEX 345

Sonnets, 9, 86, 104
Tempest, 127, 167
Third Folio, 31
The Rape of Lucrece, 3
Titus Andronicus, 39
Twelfth Night, 329, 333
Venus and Adonis, 3
shame, 91, 95, 133, 134, 138, 139, 140, 142–144, 146, 147, 270, 316. *See also* remorse
Sidney, Philip, 226, 238
  Defence of Poesy, 238
  funeral of, 226
sin, 35, 36, 40, 43, 45, 53, 127, 135, 158, 166, 210, 230, 263, 264, 283, 287, 289, 298, 309, 317, 329. *See also* punishment; redemption
skeletons, 5, 72, 82, 97, 156, 157, 164, 166, 283, 295. *See also* Dance of Death/*Danse Macabre*
skepticism, 103, 250
skull, 5, 10, 11, 17, 71, 81, 188, 249, 284, 285, 313, 319, 320. *See also* death's head
  Yorick's, 7, 9, 16, 17, 181, 188, 197, 285, 288, 319
slime, 126, 248. *See also* mud/muddy; ooze
Socrates, 3, 96
soliloquy/soliloquies, 204, 208, 210, 211, 214–216, 218, 219, 291, 292, 298, 321, 323
  in *Hamlet*, 42, 179, 183, 192, 204, 210, 211, 213–219, 244, 284, 288, 291, 292, 300
  in *Romeo and Juliet*, 15
sorrow, 95, 183, 226, 228, 229, 246. *See also* grief/grieving
soul, 11, 35, 53, 56, 71, 80, 99, 160, 192–194, 212, 215–218, 231, 244, 252, 262, 265, 282, 291, 292, 297, 299, 315, 317, 329, 330, 332. *See also* body
  belief in thirty-day lingering of, 193
  immortality of, 75
sovereign's two bodies, 69, 75, 77
specters, 119, 138, 227. *See also* ghosts; phantasms; spirits
Spenser, Edmund, 106, 196
spirits, 42, 55, 56, 183, 188, 192, 194, 195, 207, 208, 211, 213, 270, 311, 314, 318, 321. *See also* ghosts; phantasms; specters
spiritual, 33, 34, 40, 53, 56, 57, 69, 116, 180, 186, 189, 203, 244, 250, 287, 288. *See also* material; physical
stoicism, 3. *See also* Cicero; Seneca (the Younger)
Suetonius, 86
  The History of Twelve Cæsars, 104
suicide, 3, 19, 44, 61, 85, 95, 140, 147, 153, 248, 261–265, 270, 271, 273–275, 292, 293, 321, 325
Sutton, Christopher, 69–75, 78–80
  Disce Mori, 67–72, 78–80, 82, 83, 156

T
thanatological plenitude, 6, 7
theater. *See also* Shakespeare, William, The Globe
  early modern, 300
  medieval, 156, 211, 213
  metatheater, 12, 15, 295
  of God's Judgment, 204, 211
  of memory, 188, 204–206, 211, 212, 216. *See also* memory, art of
  stage directions in, 35, 55, 59, 63, 82, 313
  theatrum mundi, 204, 205, 217, 219
Theocritus, 242, 243, 254
time, 3, 4, 8, 9, 11, 13, 17, 19–22, 40, 45, 55–57, 60–62, 69,

72–74, 78–81, 86, 93, 96, 102, 115, 116, 118–120, 124, 125, 127, 128, 155, 162, 167, 184–186, 191, 192, 197, 205, 209, 210, 212–217, 223, 226, 228–230, 232, 233, 235–237, 245, 248, 264, 267, 282, 287, 292, 293, 295, 298–300, 308, 313–316, 319, 324, 328–330

fleeting nature of, 50

iconography of, 217. *See also* mortality; untimely

tomb, 2, 5, 11, 14, 17, 18, 60, 61, 86, 97, 102, 113–125, 128, 254, 284, 286, 301, 319, 327. *See also* effigy; grave; monument; sepulcher

sea as, 125, 127

self-fashioning of, 118, 119

transi, 117, 119, 122, 156

Tottel's Miscellany, 3

translate/translation, 2, 20, 105, 107, 205, 208, 220, 228, 283, 294

into symbolic images, 208

of bodies, 249, 253

of texts, 34

tribute, 19, 52, 181, 186, 187, 196, 197, 243. *See also* conquest of England

"*tu fui, ego eris*", 68–71, 73–76, 78–81, 155, 156, 158, 159, 165, 166, 168

dialectic of, 78

paradox of, 72, 78, 155, 156

U

untimely, 154. *See also* time

V

vanitas, 156, 294. *See also* death's head; *memento mori*; mirror

Vesalius, Andrea, 5, 269

De Humani Corporis Fabrica, 5, 20, 269

Virgil, 226, 228, 230, 232, 233, 237, 242, 243, 254

visionary literature, 204, 211, 212, 220

W

water/watery, 21, 57, 89, 92, 100, 119–121, 125, 127, 128, 182, 224, 241–250, 253, 254, 265

Webster, John, 6

Duchess of Malfi, 6, 159

weeping, 246, 248, 329. *See also* grief/grieving; mourning

Willow Song, 154, 159–162, 164, 165, 167, 168. *See also* Shakespeare, William, *Hamlet*

will writing, 2. *See also* Shakespeare, William, last will and testament

worm, 11, 290, 295, 309, 319, 322, 333. *See also* death, symbol of

Y

Yorick, 7, 9, 16, 17, 180, 188, 197, 285, 288, 319. *See also* Graveyard Scene; Shakespeare, William, *Hamlet*

Printed by Printforce, United Kingdom